ALMOST PRESIDENT

THE MEN WHO LOST THE RACE
BUT CHANGED THE NATION

SCOTT FARRIS

LYONS PRESS
GUILFORD, CONNECTICUT
An imprint of Globe Pequot Press

For my marvelous and loving family: Patti, William, and Grace

To buy books in quantity for corporate use
or incentives, call **(800) 962-0973**
or e-mail **premiums@GlobePequot.com**.

Lyons Press is an imprint of Globe Pequot Press.

Ross Perot photo (p. 232) courtesy U.S. Dept. of Veteran Affairs; Al Gore official VP photo
(p. 260); John Kerry (p. 261) and John McCain (p. 263) photos courtesy U.S. Congress;
all other photos courtesy the U.S. Library of Congress.

Text design: Sheryl Kober
Layout artist: Justin Marciano
Project editor: Ellen Urban

Library of Congress Cataloging-in-Publication Data
Farris, Scott.
 Almost president : the men who lost the race but changed the nation / Scott Farris.
     p. cm.
 Includes bibliographical references and index.
 ISBN 978-0-7627-6378-8
 1. Presidential candidates—United States—Biography. 2. Presidents—United
States—Election—History. 3. United States—Politics and government. 4. United
States—Biography. I. Title.
 E176.F23 2012
 324.973—dc23

                                                        2011033001

Printed in the United States of America

10 9 8 7 6 5 4 3 2 1

CONTENTS

INTRODUCTION

In very rural northwest Kansas, midway between Kansas City and Denver, there is a shrine of sorts dedicated to losing presidential candidates. On a wall of the First State Bank in the wind-swept prairie town of Norton hang the portraits of fifty-nine men who have run for president as the nominee of a major political party and lost. The line of photos and short biographies begins with Thomas Jefferson, who became our nation's first losing presidential candidate in 1796, and ends—as of this writing—with John McCain, the 2008 "also-ran" with his loss to Barack Obama. The display began in the 1960s, after the then-president of the bank learned that Horace Greeley, the losing presidential candidate of 1872, had once stopped in Norton on his way by stagecoach to Denver and was likely the most prominent person ever to visit the small farming and ranching community.

How appropriate that the only place in America dedicated to honoring losing presidential candidates was established in such an out-of-the-way location and for such an obscure reason, for historical obscurity is generally the lot of those who run for president and lose. Names like Lewis Cass, Horatio Seymour, Winfield Scott Hancock, James G. Blaine, Alton B. Parker, or John W. Davis are unknown to all but the most obsessed political junkies. Even the better-known unsuccessful aspirants to the White House, such as Henry Clay, William Jennings Bryan, Thomas Dewey, or Adlai Stevenson, are not fully appreciated for how they changed American politics and how their candidacies continue to shape our political discourse.

These men actually have had a far greater impact on American history than many of those who became president. They created, transformed, and realigned our political parties. They broke barriers and taboos around religion and gender, ushered in new political movements, introduced sweeping policy changes that would, in time, become the law of the land, and changed our expectations of political candidates.

Journalist Theodore White, chronicler of five presidential campaigns, agreed: "Again and again in American history it has happened that the losers of the presidency contributed almost as much to the permanent tone and dialogue of politics as did the winners."

They were able to accomplish these things, in part, because they lost. How can losing have more impact than winning? As American political scientist William Riker noted in 1983, "Winners have won and do not immediately need to change things. But losers have nothing and gain nothing unless they continue to try to bring about new political situations."

In the immediate aftermath of an election, it may appear there is nothing left of the losing campaign but scattered debris. Reshaping our political structure can be like remodeling a house—salvaged from the demolition is the framework on which to hang new construction. Those who lose, especially those who lose by a wide margin, are often accused of discrediting conservatism or liberalism, as was the case with Barry Goldwater and George McGovern, when years or decades later it is clear that their campaigns were not the end of something old and stale, but the beginning of something fresh and different.

Still, despite the enormous contributions made by some losing presidential candidates, it is the winning candidates who are lavished with attention by historians. Abraham Lincoln, our most revered president, has had more than sixteen thousand books and scholarly articles written about him. Even nonconsequential presidents such as William Henry Harrison, James Garfield, and Chester Arthur are the subjects of multiple biographies, while a historical giant like Henry Clay has, in times past, gone fifty years without a scholarly reappraisal. And poor Judge Parker, who lost to Theodore Roosevelt in a landslide in 1904, has never been the subject of a single biography.

History is written by and for the victors, true, but to ignore the contributions made by losing presidential candidates is to not merely ignore half the result of every presidential election, but also to warp our understanding of American history. No election is a referendum on a single person or party. In each election, voters make a *choice* between competing personalities, programs, and ideologies. In understanding our history, and in using history as a guide to understanding the present and forecasting the future, it is as illuminating to know who and what voters did *not* choose as to know who and what they *did* choose.

It seems understandable not to dwell on perceived failure. Even though losing is a universally shared experience (most of us lose far more often than we win), we are a nation and a culture that simply worships winning and recent success. We are guided by maxims, such as that (falsely) ascribed to Green Bay Packers football coach Vince Lombardi, "Winning isn't everything, it's the only thing." But winning is a narrow definition of success. A presidential campaign is a single battle in a much longer "war" over the policies and direction of the nation.

Like the scientific process, political struggles test hypotheses. Policies rejected by the public today often become the laws and regulations of tomorrow. New voter coalitions that seem to doom a political party to minority status evolve, sometimes quickly, sometimes slowly, into new governing majorities. It is often the losing candidate who is prophetic, while time proves it was the winning candidate who was stuck in the policies of the past.

Yet, in America a single lost election can seemingly wipe out a lifetime of achievement overnight and transform the image of an otherwise successful politician from gallant champion to pathetic goat. As we do with great athletes whose otherwise exemplary careers are overshadowed by a single, crucial error in a championship game, we often define losing presidential candidates not by their substantive accomplishments before, during, and after their campaigns, but by their failure on this one great stage of a presidential election.

Television exacerbates this tendency because, in politics as in sports, one recorded moment can become an enduring representation of failure. Michael Dukakis, who lost to George H. W. Bush in 1988, will always be pictured in the public mind looking terribly out of place while riding in an Army tank, even though Dukakis was an Army veteran. John Kerry's voice will always summon memories of the tape played endlessly during his 2004 campaign in which he articulates senatorial procedural gibberish about how "I voted for the bill before I voted against it." When all eyes are watching and all ears are listening, an error can become a moment that encapsulates a career.

There was a time when America was more forgiving of failure and when a single loss did not define a person's legacy. In a study of changing American attitudes toward failure in business, Scott A. Sandage notes that before the nineteenth century, the whole concept of failure applied only to the world of commerce and even then "failure was an incident, not an identity." In the early days of our republic, industriousness was admired, but ambition was not. Ambition would lead to corruption, extravagance, debt, and dependency. As Ben Franklin's Poor Richard admonished, in advice that would be scorned today, "In success be moderate."

This republican ideal of industriousness without ambition was applied to politics as well. While we know that in truth Jefferson and John Adams jockeyed behind the scenes to succeed George Washington as president in 1796, the ruse was that no gentleman actively sought public office; rather, the public sought out the gentleman. If an individual did not strive for office, then not receiving the office meant no personal failure.

Our attitude toward ambition and failure evolved with the market revolution. Subsistence farming provided little opportunity for advancement, while crop failures, due to drought or war, were clearly understood to be beyond an individual's control. Commerce, however, rewarded ambition and provided opportunity for advancement, but if initiative bred success, then failure could be ascribed to a personal defect. By 1842, Ralph Waldo Emerson noted a proverb popular among men of business that said, "Nobody fails who ought not to fail," and then added his own thought, "There is always a reason, in the man, for his good or bad fortune."

Unsurprisingly, these changing attitudes were applied to politics. Political ambition was no longer a disqualifier for office, but political failure was now ascribed to a defect of the candidate. Contemporaries who sought to explain why Henry Clay, one of the greatest Americans never to become president, failed in his three bids for the White House usually cited his character, noting that Clay was loved, but not trusted.

In the twentieth- and twenty-first-century world of mass communication and advertising, and with Dale Carnegie replacing Horatio Alger as provider of the roadmap for success, the fault of the individual was expanded to include personality as well as character. Style and assertiveness were valued and those who failed were assumed to lack both. Losing candidates internalize the idea that failure is the result of an active defect within the person. They eschew the likely fact that most election results are foreordained by factors such as peace, prosperity, or demographics, and instead take to heart Cassius's admonition in *Julius Caesar*, "The fault, dear Brutus, lies not in our stars but in ourselves." Or as Dukakis put it more bluntly, "[I] ran a crappy campaign."

Perhaps, but it is also true that America in 1988 was in a period of conservative ascendancy and Dukakis's best efforts might not have changed the final result. Because the fault is always ascribed to the candidate's shortcomings, losing candidates can come to resent the honor of being a nominee for president. What should bring status instead becomes a stigma. As John W. Davis, the brilliant Wall Street attorney who lost the 1924 presidential election to Calvin Coolidge, noted defensively, "I believe I have been a fair success in life except as a candidate for president." They also resent the voters who made such a disappointing choice. Losing candidates everywhere no doubt smiled at Arizona congressman Mo Udall's wry comment upon ending his 1976 presidential primary bid: "The people have spoken—the bastards."

Arthur Miller, whose 1949 play, *Death of a Salesman*, eloquently captured the American fear of failure, said we like to keep our distance from losers because they remind us of our fear of death. That may be extreme, but losers certainly remind us of defeat.

There was a time when a losing candidate might aspire to lead his party once more. Clay and Bryan were each rewarded with presidential nominations three times, and even in the mid-twentieth century, partisans saw fit to nominate Dewey and Stevenson twice each. But not since 1968 has a losing candidate been successful in securing another presidential nomination. Today, if you lose, it is one and done.

Losing candidates also once maintained the role of titular head of their party, their party's leading spokesperson. No losing candidate has remained his party's acknowledged leader or spokesperson since

Stevenson, though, as will be discussed in a later chapter, John McCain tried to re-establish the role. Losing candidates are now often given some of the worst time slots to speak at subsequent political conventions, if they are allowed to speak at all, as parties fear their very appearance on television will attach the stench of past failure to the present campaign.

Nor are losing candidates anymore rewarded for their service with important appointments in other administrations. Charles Evans Hughes, loser to Woodrow Wilson in 1916, was later reappointed to the U.S. Supreme Court as chief justice, and Hughes was one of five losing presidential candidates, along with Clay, Cass, Blaine, and Bryan, who later served as secretary of state. But since the 1960s, the only losing presidential nominees to have been given any posts in a future administration were Stevenson, McGovern, and Walter Mondale, and they each received relatively minor ambassadorial posts.

Capturing the sense of abandonment losing candidates feel, Al Smith, the first Catholic nominee for president, who lost to Herbert Hoover in 1928, suggested that those who have lost the presidential general election be named a U.S. senator at-large. Those who lost the presidency served the nation well, and it is the nation's loss that we do not fully utilize their experience to the nation's advantage.

Small wonder, then, that Arthur Miller identified one other consequence of failure; losers worry that they have lost the capacity to be loved. And yet, many losing candidates retain their admirers generations after their defeat. Conservatives involved in Goldwater's uncompromising 1964 campaign against Lyndon Johnson still fondly recall Goldwater's candor, masculinity, and the self-deprecating humor that led him to conclude after his defeat: "[America's] a great country where anybody can grow up to become president—except me."

Liberals of a certain age have similar reminiscences of Adlai Stevenson. His two campaigns against Dwight Eisenhower ignited a passion that drew segments of the population into politics and public service for the first time. Stevenson's enduring image as the rare public figure who raised politics to a new and higher level of discourse was reflected in a panel of the Garry Trudeau comic strip, "Doonesbury," published in 1984, nearly twenty years after Stevenson's death. In the strip, a character bemoans the current state of politics and pleads with his wife that if anything should happen to him, "You must tell our son about Adlai Stevenson!"

For all our love of winning, we still admire the underdog who competes nobly, and shared failure can create a powerful bond among those who experience it. Sportswriter Roger Kahn wrote in his marvelous book, *The Boys of Summer*, "My years with the Dodgers were 1952 and 1953, two seasons in which they lost the World Series to the Yankees. You may glory in a team triumphant but you fall in love with a team in defeat. Losing after great striving is the story of man, who was born to sorrow, whose sweetest songs tell of saddest thought."

Those who supported Goldwater, or Stevenson, or any of the partisan champions who never reached the White House cannot help but wonder what might have been, and the few previous books that have focused on presidential losers as a group are preoccupied with the question of whether those who lost would have made good presidents—or at least better presidents than the men who defeated them. Those are questions that cannot be answered. It is better to focus on what we do know and on what losing candidates did accomplish—and they have accomplished a great deal.

This book covers those men (and so far, they have all been men) who won the presidential nomination of a major political party but lost the general election. It does not cover those men who lost and later won the presidency or those who served as president but lost their re-election bid. They receive enough attention from other writers. Also included is the most successful third-party candidate of modern times, Ross Perot, whose candidacy has had a great impact on modern politics. Many third-party candidates have run, and some did well, but Perot and former president Theodore Roosevelt in 1912 are the only third-party candidates who were "almost president."

Chapters two through ten feature nine men whose candidacies have had the greatest impact on our political system, and where that impact can still be felt today. Those nine are Henry Clay, who resurrected the two-party system; Stephen Douglas, who ensured the Democratic Party survived the Civil War; William Jennings Bryan, who transformed the Democratic Party from a conservative to a progressive party in a single election; Al Smith, whose campaign changed how Americans thought about Catholics and how Catholics thought about America; Thomas E. Dewey, who brought the Republican Party into accommodation with the welfare state; Adlai Stevenson, who raised the question whether someone can be too intellectual to be president; Barry Goldwater, whose campaign changed the allegiance of the Deep South to the Republican Party; George McGovern, who built a new Democratic coalition that paved the way for our first African-American president; and Ross Perot, who changed the way candidates use television and who inspired other wealthy businessmen and women to enter politics. There is also a special chapter on three recent "also rans"—Al Gore, John Kerry, and John McCain—the only three presidential nominees to have served in the Vietnam War. Their legacies cannot yet be fully assessed, but, as of this writing, they seem to be redefining the role of the presidential loser. This book also offers a series of short essays on the other men who won a presidential nomination and lost, but whose lasting impacts on our political system were, in this author's judgment, less consequential than those featured in the chapter-length treatments.

And there is also the first chapter, which discusses the great and vital service every losing candidate has provided to the nation, which is the simple act of accepting his defeat. In many nations, losing candidates reject the electoral result and lead their nations into chaos, rioting, and even civil war. That our losing presidential candidates, often graciously, accept their defeat and make way for the winner has been essential to the success of American democracy. As William Riker noted, "The dynamics of politics is in the hands of the losers. It is they who decide when and how and whether to fight on."

The importance of a gracious concession deserves special attention in today's unusually polarized political environment when so many Americans seem reluctant to accept the verdict of majority rule. During the past two decades, Americans have been put on edge by the trauma of the terrorist attacks of September 11, 2001, the two wars the United

States fought in response to those attacks, and the 2008 collapse of the financial markets. Politically, these tensions were exacerbated by the prior attempted impeachment of President Clinton and a series of extraordinarily close presidential elections. The closest was in 2000 when, for only the fourth time in our history, the candidate who received the largest number of popular votes did not become president. To win the most votes and still lose is an especially bitter pill; to accept this result for the good of the nation is an especially heroic act.

In each of these recent elections, and in several elections past, there were attempts by some to delegitimize the results *and* the presidency of the winning candidate. But every time, we have been fortunate that the losing candidate took his defeat graciously, and in so doing reinforced the legitimacy of our electoral system and of the administration elected to govern us. To do otherwise could lead to a level of rancor and chaos that could debilitate the country. It is not overstatement to say that without this essential contribution of concession from the losing candidate, the stable, resilient democracy, which is so often taken for granted in the United States, would be impossible.

CHAPTER ONE

THE CONCESSION

An election does not end when the winner declares victory; it ends only when the loser concedes defeat. This may seem a minor distinction, but it is what makes American democracy work.

Election night, November 4, 2008, Republican presidential nominee John McCain had one final opportunity to be the focus of the nation's undivided attention before his presidential campaign concluded. And even though the election returns indicated he would be the loser, McCain wielded a power whose potency even he may not have fully appreciated.

Before Barack Obama could give his televised victory address before 125,000 ecstatic supporters in Chicago's Grant Park, McCain first had to admit defeat. Until he did, the election wasn't over. By tradition, McCain would get to speak first, while Obama remained out of view, his supporters still stewing with anticipation, for he was not yet the president-elect.

There was a sense of real drama when McCain finally appeared at 11:18 p.m. EST, before the television cameras and seven thousand dejected supporters who had gathered at a Phoenix, Arizona, resort. Tensions had been high during the campaign, and the nation watched to see if McCain would say anything that might lead his supporters to question the results of the day.

Obama was the first African American ever nominated for president by a major political party. As the son of a Muslim father from Kenya, his background was exotic to many. His opponents had repeatedly labeled him a radical. The world economy was in a tailspin. American troops were fighting two wars, in Iraq and Afghanistan. The two previous presidential elections had been remarkably close, and America seemed evenly divided by party loyalty and widely separated by ideology.

At campaign rallies for McCain and his polarizing running mate, then Alaska governor Sarah Palin, there had been shouts of "traitor!", "terrorist!", and even "kill him!" at the very mention of Obama's name. Throughout the campaign and through Election Day, there were allegations of voter fraud and voter intimidation from both sides.

But that Election Day evening, McCain, after first hushing the boos that erupted at every mention of Obama's name, graciously conceded his defeat and pointedly referred to Obama as "my president." Moved by McCain's words, the crowd stopped jeering the man now conceded to be the president-elect and instead cheered the historic nature of Obama's election as our first African-American president.

McCain, at least for the moment, had set a tone of reconciliation that helped legitimize Obama's election in the eyes of millions who had voted against him. This period of civility gave Obama time to reach out to those who had not supported him. Within a week of the election, nearly three-quarters of Americans professed to view Obama favorably. Certainly, Obama's own inspirational words, which followed McCain's that evening, had helped persuade Americans to rally to his side at that moment, but the power and importance of McCain's address, by conveying to his supporters that it was his and their patriotic duty to be good losers, were an essential tonic to soothe the nation.

Had McCain expressed anger or bitterness at his loss, had he alleged that fraud had swayed the election, had he questioned Obama's fitness to lead, or continued his campaign assertions that Obama's policies would bring the nation to ruin, McCain would have widened the division caused by the passion of a presidential election. Such a response would have created political chaos and even invited violence.

Yet, McCain had done nothing extraordinary beyond performing his role exceptionally well, for our losing presidential candidates have repeatedly chosen to be good losers, and, as counter-intuitive as it may sound, they have played a crucial part in making politics in America a source of unity, not division.

We may think election-related violence is inconceivable in the United States, even in today's highly polarized political environment. But there is always a thin line between a peaceful election and armed conflict. We acknowledge this close relationship in the way we use martial jargon to discuss our politics. Candidates *battle* for states, *campaigns* are run from *war* rooms, commercials are part of a media *blitz*, and campaign volunteers are *foot soldiers*. "Politics," the Prussian military theorist Carl Von Clausewitz said, "is the womb in which war develops."

Violent conflict is born out in other nations where the martial language of politics is not metaphorical. In the same year that McCain and Obama held their heated but ultimately peaceful contest, post-election violence in Kenya left some fifteen hundred people dead and a quarter-million homeless. Also in 2008, post-election rioting killed eighteen in India, the world's largest democracy, and five in Mongolia. Historic elections in Bangladesh led to rioting that injured one hundred. In 2010, there was post-election violence in Guinea, Belarus, Iran, and the Ivory Coast, and additional examples can be found in virtually any year to remind us, in the words of political scientist Paul Corcoran, "the transition of power is often a matter of life and death on a grand scale." And lest we think post-election violence is confined only to supposedly immature "Third World" democracies, riots in France protesting the election of President Nicolas Sarkozy in 2007 injured seventy-eight policemen, caused more than seven hundred cases of arson, and led to the arrests of nearly six hundred people.

With the hubris that is part of being an American, we may assume our lack of protest is because, unlike other nations, *our* elections are fair and honest. Yet, American elections are rife with fraud, abuse, and incompetence, which are forgotten and ignored until a close election requires a recount and we realize how imprecise our balloting is.

We devote remarkably few resources to that cornerstone of American democracy: a free, fair, and accurate election process. Election standards vary widely by location, top election officials are elected partisans, and poll workers receive minimal training and compensation. There are multiple examples in every election cycle of outright corruption and concerted efforts to disenfranchise one set of voters or another (particularly minority voters), but violations of election law are seldom prosecuted, and the penalties are minimal for those that are. The result of virtually any close election could be in dispute because running efficient, professional elections is not a national priority. We have minimal interest in probing the question of the fairness of our elections. Few states even have a mechanism for challenging an election result.

Nor is the tradition of relatively peaceful elections in the United States due to any special American aversion to violence. Rioting is a time-honored tradition in America. We have had riots associated with race and religion. We have had riots related to political disputes, dating back to the Whiskey Rebellion. We have had riots against war and the military draft. We have had riots against police brutality, and riots that involved police brutality, such as occurred during the 1968 Democratic National Convention. We have had labor riots, prison riots, riots by anarchists, and even riots after sporting events—an average of ten to fifteen per year, in fact—and by fans of both losing *and* winning teams. And yet, while we riot after football games, we do not have violence related to our greatest electoral prize, the presidency.

The notable exception, the election of 1860, proves the rule. The refusal of the South to accept Lincoln's election led to our Civil War and six hundred thousand war dead. But the behavior of the losing candidates in that election in no way contributed to the dissolution of the Union, as we will see in the subsequent chapter on Stephen Douglas. Further, that catastrophe has perhaps been a lesson for subsequent generations of the dangers in rejecting the democratic process and the rule of law. In his Gettysburg Address, Lincoln said men had fought and died in the war so that the "nation might live." In less dramatic fashion, each presidential election tests Lincoln's concern that "government of the people, by the people, for the people, shall not perish from the earth."

The losing candidate, then, must set the tone of acceptance, or at least resignation, that tamps down the possibility of violence in the wake of electoral disappointment. A group of five political scientists from five countries, including the United States, who have studied the role electoral losers play in the democratic process concluded in their 2005 book, *Losers' Consent*, that "what makes democracy work . . . is not so much the success of the winners, but the restraint of the losers."

Many losing candidates have certainly had to exercise great restraint. Four times since 1824, when the popular vote was first used to help determine the presidential winner, the man who won the largest number of popular votes did not become president because he did not receive a majority in the Electoral College. This occurred in 1824, 1876, 1888, and 2000, and there have been other elections, such as 1880 or 1960, where the margin of victory was so close as to be in dispute.

Presidential elections are almost always close, at least in terms of the popular vote. Only four times—1920, 1936, 1964, and 1972—has the winning candidate won more than 60 percent of the vote, a true landslide. In roughly half of all presidential elections, the winning candidate has received 51 percent or less of the popular vote; 40 percent of the time, because of third parties, the person elected president has not even received a majority of the popular vote.

The narrowness of these victories is masked because of our Electoral College system, which often makes the result seem more definitive than it is. In 1980, for example, Ronald Reagan received less than 51 percent of the popular vote in his victory over President Jimmy Carter and independent candidate John Anderson, but he received 90 percent of the Electoral College vote. Because of the Electoral College, we do not have a single, national election for president, but rather fifty-one separate elections conducted by the states plus the District of Columbia.

After 1860, the closest our nation has come to blows over a presidential result was in 1876, when Governor Samuel J. Tilden of New York won the popular vote by a comfortable 51 to 48 percent margin but lost the presidency to Rutherford B. Hayes in the Electoral College by a single elector. To obtain that result, Republicans had engaged in outright voter fraud in three Southern states, including Florida, though Democrats had also engaged in intimidation to prevent African Americans from voting in those states.

In the uproar that followed, Democratic mobs cried, "Tilden or blood!" and fear of a renewed civil war was so real that President Ulysses S. Grant fortified Washington, D.C., with troops and gunboats to repel an expected army of Tilden supporters. But Tilden was a successful attorney who believed in the rule of law, and he declined to sanction any such offensive by those on his side. At Tilden's urging, tempers cooled and, ultimately, the U.S. Supreme Court established a method by which the election was resolved in favor of Hayes; though, in truth, behind the scenes a deal had been made—Hayes was given the presidency in return for a promise to withdraw federal troops from the South and end Reconstruction. When Tilden, an eccentric character, finally spoke publicly in June 1877, he offered comfort to his supporters, urging them to "be of good cheer. The Republic will live. The institutions of our fathers are not to expire in shame. The sovereignty of the people shall be rescued from this peril and re-established."

In 2000, Vice President Al Gore faced a remarkably similar situation and was criticized as Tilden had been for not making a more forceful claim to the presidency. Having won the popular vote by a margin of 500,000, Gore lost the election to George W. Bush when he failed to win the state of Florida by 537 votes. Gore had said that on election night he felt considerable pressure "to be gracious about this," which led him to concede perhaps too quickly when his own interests would have been served by waiting a while longer. Gore had called Bush to concede at about 2:30 a.m. EST the morning following Election Day, and that call was widely reported in the media. It was while Gore was en route to give his formal public concession speech that aides intercepted him and urged him to retract his concession because of tightening vote totals in Florida. Gore again called Bush who, incredulous, asked, "Let me make sure that I understand: You're calling back to retract that concession?" Gore replied, "You don't have to be snippy about it."

A partial recount was halted by a 5-4 U.S. Supreme Court decision that the court itself said set no precedent. The month-long dispute had resulted in some minor scuffles—a few Gore partisans protesting in Washington, D.C., even tried to rouse a cheer of "Gore or blood" to evoke the Tilden crisis—but the tradition of a good loser is now deeply rooted in American politics. Tensions rapidly dissipated when Gore gave a remarkably cheerful concession speech and there was no violence, even though surveys later showed that 97 percent of those who voted for Gore believed he was the "rightful" president. But once Gore had conceded, even in a private phone call, the perception was that he had lost and then was trying to overturn the results; had he never conceded, the public perception might have been that both candidates had an equal claim to the election.

Gore is not the only cautionary tale of a loser willing to concede too soon. President Jimmy Carter conceded to Ronald Reagan on Election Day in 1980 with a telephone call at 9:01 p.m. Eastern time, followed by a speech an hour later at the Sheraton Washington Hotel ballroom. Carter had been urged to delay his concession until 11 p.m. Eastern time, after the polls were closed on the West Coast. But Carter was worried the public, knowing that Reagan was projected to win by a wide margin, would think he was sulking in the White House and he did not want to appear to be a "bad loser."

"It's ridiculous," Carter said. "Let's go and get it over with." That decision infuriated Democrats, who thought Carter's early concession led some voters in the West to skip casting their ballots. House Speaker Thomas P. "Tip" O'Neill raged that Carter had cost a half-dozen Democrats seats in Congress and perhaps two Senate seats. He yelled at a Carter aide, "You guys came in like a bunch of jerks, and I see you're going out the same way!"

Despite what appeared to be a mistake in retrospect, Gore was not unwise in trying to avoid being labeled a sore loser, for complaints about the fairness of a result seldom receive much sympathy beyond the losing candidate's most rabid followers. Americans simply do not want to consider that an election has been unjust or worse.

Gore and Carter were not alone in fearing what the label of "sore loser" might do to their reputation. Ohio governor James M. Cox said of his 1920 defeat to Warren Harding, "A wrong reaction then could have ruined my life." James G. Blaine demonstrated the danger of complaining about a perceived injustice when he attributed his 1884 loss to disenfranchisement of African-American voters in the South. He had fallen to Grover Cleveland by barely fifty thousand votes. The *New York Times* accused Blaine of sour grapes because he was "smarting from defeat."

Richard Nixon weighed both the danger to the nation and to his own political future in deciding against challenging the results of his narrow loss to John Kennedy in 1960—even when there were credible allegations of Democrats stealing votes in Illinois and Texas (though Democrats also alleged Republican vote stealing in Ohio). Nixon discovered that few states even had a mechanism to challenge election results, and worried about the damage to the nation that a months-long process might cause, especially its "devastating" impact on national foreign policy. On a personal level, he also knew that "charges of 'sore loser' would follow me through history and remove any possibility of a further political career."

Two years later, Nixon forgot his own advice when he lost the governorship of California and famously announced he was through with politics, telling newsmen, "Just think how much you're going to be missing. You won't have Nixon to kick around anymore." It was the testiest concession since the frontiersman Davy Crockett, defeated in his 1834 bid for re-election to Congress, told his Tennessee constituents they could "go to hell; I'm going to Texas." Crockett did, only to die at the Alamo in 1836, but Nixon came back to win the presidency in 1968.

The man Nixon beat that year, Hubert Humphrey, lost a race nearly as close as the 1960 Nixon loss to Kennedy, and he also considered the personal stake in making a graceful concession. "I told myself," Humphrey said, "'This has to be done right because it is the opening speech of your next campaign!' I was already looking ahead."

There was historical precedent for Humphrey's hope that losing graciously would place him in good stead for a future election. After the 1824 election of John Quincy Adams, which had been decided in the U.S. House of Representatives, Andrew Jackson was privately seething at the supposed "corrupt bargain" whereby Adams named Henry Clay secretary of state in return for Clay's support in the House. Yet, when Jackson bumped into Adams at a social event on the very day the U.S. House decided for Adams, Jackson was expansive and gracious while Adams, the nation's most experienced diplomat, seemed rigid and ill at ease. Jackson's grace during the encounter was the talk of the capital, with one friend writing him: "You have, by your dignity and forbearance under all these outrages, won the people to your love." His demeanor in defeat enhanced his reputation and helped Jackson claim the presidency when he ran again in 1828.

Disappointed supporters of losing candidates, too, seem to immediately begin looking ahead to the next election and hoped-for retribution

—with ballots, not bullets. The authors of the aforementioned *Losers'
Consent* found that voters who supported the losing candidate in an election certainly do have a higher distrust of our electoral system than those
who supported the winner. But that level of distrust is lessened if the
person is an active partisan member of one of our two major parties.
Given that the two major parties in America routinely win some and
lose some, those who strongly identify with one of the major parties
know that while their candidate may have lost this time, their time will
come again. Our oft-maligned two-party system may limit voter choices,
in the opinion of some, but having two, large, relatively evenly matched
parties is a key reason America does not suffer from election-related violence. It is not surprising, then, that the highest level of mistrust in our
political system is felt by those who consider themselves independent or
who are prone to supporting third parties. Based on the past history of
third parties, these folks will likely never be on the winning side.

Interestingly, studies have also found that distrust of the electoral
system is higher after a landslide loss rather than after a close election.
According to data from U.S. presidential elections from 1964 to 2000,
the highest level of distrust among voters who supported a losing candidate came in the lopsided 1964 and 1972 elections, which were landslide
defeats suffered by Barry Goldwater and George McGovern. The lowest
levels of distrust occurred after the very close 1968 and 1976 elections,
the 1980 election, when Ronald Reagan won with less than 51 percent
of the popular vote, and the 2000 election, despite all the controversy
surrounding it.

There are three possible explanations for this. First, when the ideological gap is wide, as was the case in the Goldwater and McGovern losses,
those who support the losing candidates are likely discouraged and disbe-
lieving that more of their fellow citizens did not see what was so obvious
to them. Second, in the close elections cited, there may have been some
ambivalence among the supporters of the losers; close elections occurred
when the losing candidate was associated with a previous administration marked by controversy. In other words, even an intense partisan may
grudgingly have to agree that it was time for a change, after all.

Third, it is not a coincidence that Goldwater and McGovern themselves did little to hide their disappointment. Each did what is expected of a losing candidate, but no more. In his concession, McGovern said that while he congratulated Nixon on his victory, he and his supporters would "not rally to the support of policies we deplore." Despite his obvious defeat, Goldwater declined to concede on election night because, well, he was Barry Goldwater and Goldwater, his friend, Lee Edwards, said, "ended his campaign as he began it—doing things his way, regardless of what others thought." Goldwater sent Lyndon Johnson a congratulatory telegram the next morning, but it struck a defiant pose, pointedly telling LBJ that the Republican Party would remain "the party of opposition when opposition is called for."

If even such a relatively mild negative reaction can influence voter trust in the system, this simply reinforces the key role the actions of a losing candidate play in maintaining a functioning democracy. In a nation where private citizens own 270 million guns, we can only speculate about what type of crisis might erupt if a candidate ever refused to concede, or conceded in a way that created deep antagonism toward the incoming president.

If defeated candidates want to avoid looking like sore losers, winning candidates also do not want to appear presumptuous (or worse) by declaring victory too soon. Winning candidates have waited hours—even days—for the loser to concede before declaring victory. Only when the losing candidate clearly intends to delay the concession for an extraordinarily long time, either because he believes he still has a chance to win the election, as Charles Evans Hughes did in 1916, or because of an ornery streak, as Goldwater exhibited in 1964, will the winner issue a victory statement before hearing the loser concede.

Advances in communications technology have shaped the evolution of the concession. Through most of the nineteenth century, losing candidates either said nothing publicly or issued statements reprinted in partisan and general circulation newspapers. The lack of instant communication meant there was no shared peak moment of emotion that might trigger a violent reaction to an election result. But as communications improved, the possibility for a mass reaction increased. The telegraph was invented in 1844 and changes in printing technology and newsprint led to an explosion in the number of newspapers—from three hundred nationwide in 1814 to more than twenty-five hundred by 1850. This boom in timely communications certainly helped stir passions and form opinions in the lead-up to the Civil War. Fortunately, these instant communications could also help contain passions by allowing losing candidates to calm their supporters.

William Jennings Bryan takes credit for issuing the first congratulatory telegram, to William McKinley in 1896. Bryan said he did so to underscore that he had no personal animosity toward McKinley, that their contest had been over different political ideas, not personalities, and that "a courteous observance of the proprieties of such an occasion tends to eliminate the individual and enables opponents to contend sharply over the matters of principle, without disturbance of social relations."

With one exception (Thomas Dewey in 1944), losing candidates continued to send telegrams to the winners through the 1980 campaign. After that, a congratulatory phone call was deemed sufficient. Al Smith gave the first concession speech over the radio in 1928; Adlai Stevenson's concession was the first made on television in 1952.

Dewey's failure to send a congratulatory note in 1944 irritated Franklin Roosevelt a great deal. Dewey did make a statement on the radio in the wee hours of the morning after Election Day to state that he would "wholeheartedly accept the will of the people." Roosevelt, still angry at the snub, sent a terse telegram to Dewey stating, "I thank you for your statement, which I have heard over the air a few minutes ago." Heading off to bed, Roosevelt said of Dewey, "I still think he's a son of a bitch."

While Dewey was the only candidate since 1896 to decline to contact his victorious opponent, others besides Goldwater have procrastinated. Hughes, who had resigned from the U.S. Supreme Court to run for president, needed time to absorb a stunning turn of events. Early returns from the East put Hughes so far ahead that, thirty-two years before the *Chicago Tribune* infamously printed the headline "Dewey

Defeats Truman," the *New York Times* declared Hughes the winner over Woodrow Wilson. But Wilson ran stronger than expected in the West and when he carried California by a very narrow margin, he had won re-election. Hughes waited two weeks before sending a congratulatory telegram to Wilson, who joked that Hughes's note was "a little moth-eaten when it got here but quite legible."

Even though the winning candidates and the public wait to hear it, the concession speech is commonly dismissed by commentators as a series of meaningless bromides. If concession speeches, for all their importance, seem formulaic, it is because they have assumed the character of a liturgy—even to the point of now ending with an obligatory blessing.

Each concession speech now contains three basic sections: the validation of the result by conceding the outcome, the explanation of what the losing campaign had been about, and a final benediction with the now ubiquitous "God bless America!"

In the first section, we hear kind words for the victor that help unite the country. The key moment is usually a simple statement, accepting the outcome as fact. McCain began his concession speech by saying, "The American people have spoken, and they have spoken clearly." Similarly direct prose was found in Wendell Willkie's concession to Roosevelt in 1940: "People of America, I accept the results of the election with complete good will." Adlai Stevenson seemed to virtually copy Willkie when he conceded to Dwight Eisenhower in 1952 with the words, "The people have rendered their verdict and I gladly accept it." Bryan in his first concession telegram to McKinley said, "We have submitted the issue to the American people and their will is law."

The words are carefully chosen, and any alteration in such a set piece offers a small window into how a candidate really feels. Following the controversial 2000 election, for example, Gore congratulated George W. Bush on "becoming" the forty-third president of the United States, rather than on being "elected" president.

By cheerily (or at least with a minimum of complaint) accepting the result, the losing candidate has essentially vouched that the process was fair, or fair enough that the result cannot—or at least should not—be disputed. By conceding, the loser has effectively announced that he will not challenge the result. He also precludes those who might want to challenge the results on his behalf. If the person with the most standing to make the challenge, the losing candidate, declines to formally question the result, then no one else has a prayer of forcing an examination. The concession, then, more effectively concludes the election than any state canvassing board.

Often, the losing candidate goes out of his way to describe the victor as "*my* president" or "*our* president," with a pledge to support the new president or to at least "work with him." Often added is a testament to the electoral system that has, after all, served these men well in previous electoral efforts. In conceding to Bill Clinton, President George H. W. Bush spoke of respecting "the majesty of the democratic system." Walter Mondale, too, spoke of a system that had both "dignity and majesty."

It may speak to our growing worry that our nation is being pulled apart by its diversity that the word "unity" or a variation thereof now is also always included in a concession speech. Willkie was the first to use the term in 1940, as the nation prepared to enter the struggle against fascism, but it is now virtually obligatory, with John Kerry declaring in 2004 that the United States was in "desperate need for unity."

The call for unity is not pabulum. America is still a comparatively young nation. The American experiment still seems fragile, which is why our entire political system is designed to marginalize radicalism, forge consensus, and prevent sudden shifts in public policy that might threaten our unity. "That which unites us as American citizens is far greater than that which divides us as political parties," Stevenson said in his 1952 concession speech. Perhaps campaigns and media coverage seem to focus on trivial issues or personalities because we subconsciously worry that larger issues featuring sharp ideological division, such as slavery in 1860, may stir passions that could become too strong to absorb the disappointment of defeat.

Having only two major, relatively equal, ideologically centrist political parties also helps maintain national unity, but this may be changing. Where forty years ago, both parties had liberal and conservative wings, there has been a realignment in which the Republican Party is now essentially conservative and the Democratic Party essentially liberal. Whether this increased ideological divide will alter the concession ritual remains to be seen, but polling shows many Americans base whom they vote for as president on who they believe can bring America together.

After validating the result, the second element of the concession speech is the loser's explanation of what his campaign was all about. As Paul Corcoran, a scholar who has studied concession speeches, put it, "The rhetorical challenge is to pronounce one's own defeat as a chapter of honor in the nation's history, to put a brave face on failure, transforming defeat into a semblance of victory."

Sometimes, a losing candidate has been so closely identified with a single issue that he declares that while his campaign did not win, the campaign advanced the cause. In 1972, McGovern, whose campaign was based on promising a speedy end to the Vietnam War, told his supporters that the campaign had "pushed this country in the direction of peace," adding, "If we pushed the day of peace just one day closer, then every minute and every hour and every bone-crushing effort in this campaign was worth the entire effort."

When there is no overriding issue on which a campaign was based, the losing candidates have often offered a laundry list of causes for which they promise to keep fighting. This particular rhetorical device has been especially prevalent in more recent campaigns where modern telecommunications demands instant analysis under circumstances not conducive to introspection. Prior to the age of television and radio, candidates had at least a few days to assess the meaning of their candidacy.

In a slower age, having issued the customary congratulatory telegram, candidates would develop a major post-election address, often around the theme that voters would soon realize the error of their choice and make amends at the next election. In a post-election speech in 1904, Alton Parker said of the Republican victory, "Before long the people will realize that the tariff-fed trusts and illegal combinations are absorbing the wealth of the Nation. . . . When that time comes, and come it will, the people will return to the Democratic Party for relief." Al Smith offered a similar sentiment in

1928, while referring to the Democratic Party as "the democracy." If "the cause of Democracy was right before the election, it is still right, and it is our duty to carry on and vindicate the principles for which we fought." And William Jennings Bryan philosophically noted that the burden of proof after an election is then on the ruling administration. Of McKinley's victory, he said, "If his policies bring real prosperity to the American people, those who opposed him will share in that prosperity. If, on the other hand, his policies prove an injury to the people generally, those of his supporters who do not belong to the office-holding class, or to the privileged classes, will suffer in common with those who opposed him."

Concern about a campaign's legacy is probably why modern losing candidates focus on how their campaigns involved the young. Until the ascendance of the "youth culture" concept in the second half of the twentieth century, losing candidates rarely mentioned their youthful supporters in their concession remarks. Then, in 1972, McGovern, not coincidentally a college professor, said, "If we have brought into the political process those who never before have experienced either the joy or its sorrow, then that, too, is an enduring blessing."

Before McGovern, except for a brief mention by Smith in 1928 (during another decade that catered to the young), no losing candidate singled out his youthful supporters for recognition. Since then, concession speeches have had a trace of the high school commencement address. In 1984, Walter Mondale offered a "special word to my young supporters this evening ... in every defeat is to be found the seeds of victory," while Michael Dukakis, who became a college professor after his defeat, advised his young supporters in 1988 to consider a career in the "noble profession" of public service because "there is nothing you can do in this world more fulfilling and more satisfying than giving yourself to others and making a contribution to your community and your state and your nation and your fellow citizens."

In 2004, John Kerry borrowed a rhetorical device first used by Ronald Reagan during the latter's "State of the Union" addresses, singling out individuals for recognition to illustrate a broader point. In Kerry's case, his concession speech cited young supporters—very young supporters—he had met during the campaign. To demonstrate his influence upon those who would govern America in future generations, Kerry singled out a six-year-old boy who had raised $680, "a quarter and a dollar at a time," selling campaign paraphernalia, and an eleven-year-old girl who formed a group called "Kids for Kerry." This led humorist Jon Stewart to observe, "I know why [Kerry] lost . . . you have to be eighteen to vote! Why are you going after the six-year-olds and the eleven-year-olds?"

Recent losing presidential candidates have also paid homage to Reagan's acknowledged mastery of political communication in the third distinct portion of the concession speech. Virtually all have adopted Reagan's trademark conclusion to most major addresses: "God bless America." Since 1984, from Mondale to McCain, every losing presidential candidate, except Dukakis, has ended his concession speech with "God bless America," and only George H. W. Bush provided even a modest variation on the phrase, ending his address with "May God bless the United States of America." Before Mondale, no losing candidate had ever concluded his concession speech with "God bless America."

Two scholars who analyzed major presidential addresses from 1933 to 1981—a total of 229 presidential speeches—found that the phrase "God bless America" was used only in a speech Nixon gave on the Watergate scandal in 1973. Since Reagan took office in 1981 through 2007, these scholars analyzed another 129 major presidential speeches, 49 of which concluded with "God bless America." So routine is its usage that the scholars who analyzed the phrase concluded it was just a form of "religious . . . branding" with no more depth of meaning than an advertising slogan like Nike's "Just Do It" or Coca-Cola's "The Real Thing." A speechwriter for President Carter, who seldom invoked God despite being one of the most religiously observant of modern presidents, agreed that "God bless America" has become so shorn of meaning that it is just shorthand for "the speech is over now," and is "the political equivalent of 'Have a nice day.'"

Before "God bless America" took hold, the norm was not to mention God in a concession speech, though there were exceptions. Stevenson, in his 1952 concession, said, "We vote as many, but pray as one . . . we shall move forward with God's guidance toward the time when His children shall grow in freedom and dignity in a world at peace." Compared with Stevenson's eloquence, simply ending a speech with "God bless America" sounds trite and theologically lazy.

While a higher percentage of Americans regularly attend church today than at any time in our history—62 percent today compared to 45 percent one hundred years ago and just 20 percent at the time of the American Revolution—we have lost the ability to have a serious discussion about religious faith in the public square. The use of "God bless America" now seems to serve the different purpose of reinforcing the concept of American "exceptionalism"—the widely held belief throughout American history and today that America has a divine mission in the world—without making any real effort to explain why we are an exceptional people.

While every nation likely believes that it has a special destiny, as the Pulitzer Prize–winning historian Russel Nye noted, "No nation in modern history has been quite so consistently dominated as the United States by the belief that it has a particular mission in the world, and a unique contribution to make to it." The simple expression of "God bless America" becomes a very safe way for the politician to tap into our national yearning for a sense of purpose.

Admittedly superficial, the invocation of "God bless America" or any reference to the divine in a concession speech, when considered alongside the "deeply embedded" national belief in a divine destiny, allows the losing candidate to subtly suggest that the election was an expression of divine will, not just the popular will. The candidate and his supporters are consoled by the belief that victory was denied, not because of any fault of the candidate or error in the cause, but because defeat at that moment serves some inscrutable higher purpose.

Given the stakes involved and the martial language used in our presidential elections, it is not surprising that some, such as the historian John R. Vile, suggest we consider the concession as a form of military surrender or even a funeral oration.

Just as after a war, the public wants peace after a presidential campaign. They hope that politicians will emulate that most famous surrender in American history, when Robert E. Lee and the Army of Northern

Virginia yielded to Ulysses S. Grant and the Army of the Potomac. Despite the bitterness accumulated during four years of civil war, chivalry reigned. Lee acknowledged his defeat, Grant offered generous terms, and Lee told his soldiers to fight no more, but to go home and be "good citizens." Voters expect no less at the conclusion of a political squabble: The loser's dignity is left intact, both sides are praised for their valiant behavior, generous terms and words are offered, and the losers foreswear future conflict so that they may work together for the good of the nation.

Generosity and magnanimity is easier for the winner. The loser, after all, has suffered a devastating disappointment. The exhausted losing candidate is aware of what his candidacy has meant to millions of supporters, and that he has let them down. For many losing candidates, defeat means not only the end of what may have been a lifelong quest, but also the end of a career in public service. Hubert Humphrey called losing to Nixon "the worst moment of my life," adding that he felt "so empty . . . I could cry." George McGovern said, "There are some things that are worse than losing an election. It's hard to think what they are on Election Day."

Psychologists tell us that it is important for those who experience loss to be able to articulate their emotions in order to place the loss in perspective. Yet, this is the opposite of what we expect our losing candidates to do. So the emotions are masked, sometimes by nothing more than civility, other times with humor. Adlai Stevenson, after losing to Dwight Eisenhower in 1952, used an anecdote so well received that McGovern repeated it twenty years later. Losing a presidential election, Stevenson explained, reminded him of a story told by his fellow Illinoisan, Abraham Lincoln, about "the little boy who had stubbed his toe in the dark. He said he was too old to cry, but it hurt too much to laugh."

Humor is for public consumption; privately, candidates are more likely to be hurt and angry. When Henry Clay lost to his archenemy Andrew Jackson in 1832, he confided to a friend, "Whether we shall ever see light, and law and liberty again, is very questionable." Walter Mondale, who lost to Ronald Reagan in 1984, reportedly asked McGovern, who had lost a dozen years before, when losing stops hurting. "I'll tell you when it does," McGovern replied.

Losing candidates do not brace themselves for the possibility of defeat. "I never conceded to myself . . . or anybody else that that election couldn't be won," said McGovern, even though he was crushed in his landslide loss to Richard Nixon. "At two o'clock in the morning on election day, I was still campaigning." No matter what the polls have said, the candidates maintain the hope that they will surprise the pundits and pull off an upset, as President Harry Truman did in 1948. In 1992, President George H. W. Bush received only 38 percent of the popular vote, but "when you are in the bubble," one of his aides said, "you feel the momentum and the crowds are lively and you know in the outside world you're behind, but in the inside world you're thinking, 'This is going to be 1948 all over again.'"

It is not surprising then that the concession speech can resemble the five-step process psychologists have identified for those coping with grief: denial, anger, bargaining, depression, and acceptance. Some have even feigned relief that they have avoided the burden of the presidency. They are, of course, lying. Bryan insisted to reporters, who marveled at his equanimity, that, despite his loss to William McKinley in 1896, he "went to bed happy" on election night. But a friend who observed him that evening instead saw a man summoning all his strength to conceal his emotions, and later wrote, "It is a terrible thing to look upon a strong man in the pride of youth and see him gather up in his hands the ashes of a great ambition."

This sense of finality (which Bryan avoided by running for president twice more) can make the end of an unsuccessful campaign seem a type of death. In a traditional funeral, it is usually obligatory to display the body, although in the case of a concession speech it is the corpse who gives the eulogy (and who, like Bryan, prays for a possible political resurrection).

Dewey noted the similarity between the end of a campaign and a funeral, with his own role as that of the corpse, in 1948, shortly after losing to Truman. In a speech to the Gridiron Club a few days after the election, Dewey, who had also lost the presidency in 1944, said he felt like the drunk who had passed out during a wake. "If I am alive," he said to himself, "what am I doing in this coffin? If I am dead, why do I have to go to the bathroom?"

CHAPTER TWO

HENRY CLAY

1824, 1832, 1844

Sir, I had rather be right than be president.

One irony of contemporary politics is that the annual celebration of the Democratic Party is still known as "Jefferson-Jackson Day" when it is Andrew Jackson's arch-nemesis, Henry Clay, who helped lay the foundation of modern liberalism. If alive today, small government advocate Jackson (and probably Thomas Jefferson, too) would more likely be considered a conservative Republican, while Clay and his political disciple, Abraham Lincoln, would be Democrats in their shared belief in the necessity of an assertive national government to act positively for the economic, social, and moral well-being of the nation.

But Clay, the greatest legislator in American history, has no national political dinners named for him, nor is his face chiseled on Mount Rushmore. His is the greatest example of how failing to become president obscures a candidate's place in history. At his death, Clay was eulogized by the *New York Times* as "too great to be president," and given the several mediocrities who have occupied the White House, this may be a fair comment. Clay himself despised our national fixation with the presidency to the exclusion of the other branches of government, though, Lord knows, he sought the office often enough himself.

Three times Clay was nominated for the presidency and came within a whisker of election. On two other occasions he actively sought nomination.

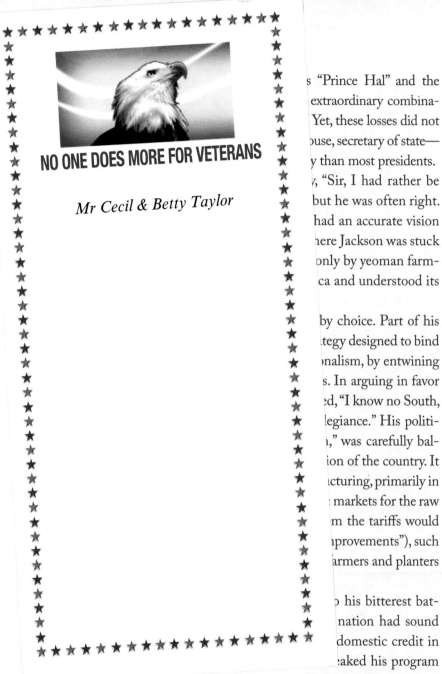
s "Prince Hal" and the
extraordinary combina-
Yet, these losses did not
ouse, secretary of state—
y than most presidents.
, "Sir, I had rather be
but he was often right.
had an accurate vision
here Jackson was stuck
only by yeoman farm-
ca and understood its

by choice. Part of his
tegy designed to bind
onalism, by entwining
s. In arguing in favor
d, "I know no South,
legiance." His politi-
," was carefully bal-
ion of the country. It
cturing, primarily in
markets for the raw
m the tariffs would
provements"), such
armers and planters

o his bitterest bat-
nation had sound
domestic credit in
aked his program
to add such far-sighted ideas as using the sale of public lands to finance
public universities and establishing an international copyright law to
protect American writers and artists. Much of the American System
would become law when Lincoln, who called Clay his "beau ideal of a

statesman," became president. Lincoln, according to his relatives, idolized Clay, and a study of Lincoln's writings and speeches clearly shows that much of his political philosophy was directly inherited from Clay.

If Clay was the quintessential American in his ardent nationalism, the services he rendered to the nation were also essential to its survival. Three times our greatest legislator forged compromises that reduced the likelihood of civil war: in 1820, 1832, and 1850. Had war come in any of those years, it goes without saying that American history would be very different. In those years, the North did not enjoy the advantages in population and industry that virtually assured victory when the war did come. Furthermore, while Jackson, a determined foe of secession, was president in 1832, the presidents in 1820 and 1850, James Monroe and Zachary Taylor respectively, would not have provided the caliber of leadership and the determination to save the Union that Lincoln would demonstrate.

But Clay did more than prevent war through legislative compromise and sterling oratory. He helped create our enduring two-party system that features two broad-based, "big tent" national parties. Particularly embittered by his 1832 loss to the hated Jackson, Clay was the leader in then creating the Whig Party, which for a generation was the alternative to Jackson's Democratic Party and which became the foundation of the new Republican Party. Clay's American System concept created a national party, when an alternative history might have led to the creation of multiple narrowly focused or sectional opposition parties and a less stable American democracy.

The split between Clay and Jackson and their dueling Democratic and Whig Parties was a continuation of the historical debate that began between Jefferson and Alexander Hamilton, and reminds us anew that personalities as much as policies create political unions. Jackson favored Jefferson's view that the best government is the least government, especially for a rural and agricultural nation of yeoman farmers. Clay adopted Hamilton's more prophetic vision of America developing into a powerful industrial and commercial state.

The Founding Fathers had hoped the United States might avoid having political parties, which they called "factions," but those rallying to Hamilton soon became known as Federalists, while Jefferson's

This exceptional man known to his admirers as "Prince Hal" and the "Western Star" failed again and again through an extraordinary combination of poor judgment, rotten timing, and bad luck. Yet, these losses did not prevent Clay—Kentucky senator, Speaker of the House, secretary of state— from shaping American history far more profoundly than most presidents.

Clay once said, perhaps a bit disingenuously, "Sir, I had rather be right than be president." He was never president, but he was often right. To a degree far beyond his contemporaries, Clay had an accurate vision of the nation the United States was to become. Where Jackson was stuck in the Jeffersonian fantasy of a country populated only by yeoman farmers, Clay foresaw the industrial potential of America and understood its destiny as a great world power.

A Southerner by birth, Clay was a Westerner by choice. Part of his genius was in developing a political program and strategy designed to bind the nation together and reduce the concept of sectionalism, by entwining the interests of each section with those of the others. In arguing in favor of his Compromise of 1850, Clay famously proclaimed, "I know no South, no North, no East, no West, to which I owe my allegiance." His political program, which he called the "American System," was carefully balanced to meet the needs and aspirations of every section of the country. It included protective tariffs to bolster American manufacturing, primarily in the North, which would in turn create stable, domestic markets for the raw goods produced in the South and West. Revenue from the tariffs would then be used for public works (then called "internal improvements"), such as roads, canals, and later, railways, which would help farmers and planters in the West and South move their goods to market.

Key to Clay's program, and the plank that led to his bitterest battle with Jackson, was a national bank to ensure the nation had sound currency, a safe place to deposit funds, and access to domestic credit in order to facilitate trade and commerce. Clay later tweaked his program to add such far-sighted ideas as using the sale of public lands to finance public universities and establishing an international copyright law to protect American writers and artists. Much of the American System would become law when Lincoln, who called Clay his "beau ideal of a statesman," became president. Lincoln, according to his relatives, idolized Clay, and a study of Lincoln's writings and speeches clearly shows that much of his political philosophy was directly inherited from Clay.

If Clay was the quintessential American in his ardent nationalism, the services he rendered to the nation were also essential to its survival. Three times our greatest legislator forged compromises that reduced the likelihood of civil war: in 1820, 1832, and 1850. Had war come in any of those years, it goes without saying that American history would be very different. In those years, the North did not enjoy the advantages in population and industry that virtually assured victory when the war did come. Furthermore, while Jackson, a determined foe of secession, was president in 1832, the presidents in 1820 and 1850, James Monroe and Zachary Taylor respectively, would not have provided the caliber of leadership and the determination to save the Union that Lincoln would demonstrate.

But Clay did more than prevent war through legislative compromise and sterling oratory. He helped create our enduring two-party system that features two broad-based, "big tent" national parties. Particularly embittered by his 1832 loss to the hated Jackson, Clay was the leader in then creating the Whig Party, which for a generation was the alternative to Jackson's Democratic Party and which became the foundation of the new Republican Party. Clay's American System concept created a national party, when an alternative history might have led to the creation of multiple narrowly focused or sectional opposition parties and a less stable American democracy.

The split between Clay and Jackson and their dueling Democratic and Whig Parties was a continuation of the historical debate that began between Jefferson and Alexander Hamilton, and reminds us anew that personalities as much as policies create political unions. Jackson favored Jefferson's view that the best government is the least government, especially for a rural and agricultural nation of yeoman farmers. Clay adopted Hamilton's more prophetic vision of America developing into a powerful industrial and commercial state.

The Founding Fathers had hoped the United States might avoid having political parties, which they called "factions," but those rallying to Hamilton soon became known as Federalists, while Jefferson's disciples were known as Republicans. Scholars differ as to whether the Federalists and Republicans were true political parties as we understand the term today, for there were no party organizations as such, no nominating conventions, or other similar partisan paraphernalia. In any event, this partisan division did not last. The Federalists disappeared as a viable political faction from a combination of factors, including John Adams's disastrous presidency, the death of George Washington, and the murder of Hamilton in a duel with Vice President Aaron Burr.

The last remnants of the Federalists were discredited when some New England Federalists openly discussed secession during the unpopular War of 1812. For nearly a generation after that, there was only one political faction in the United States and the vast majority of Americans considered themselves part of it: Jeffersonian Republicans. When James Monroe was re-elected president in 1820 without opposition, a distinction shared only with Washington, a newspaper mislabeled this period of nonpartisanship the "Era of Good Feelings." It was hardly that.

Because they were the only game in town, the Jeffersonian Republicans had to accommodate a wide range of views, not to mention competing personal ambitions. The election of 1824, therefore, was a watershed event in American political history. It reflected a generational change in leadership, as Monroe was the last of his Revolutionary War peers to serve as president.

Five men stepped forward to offer themselves as Monroe's successor, though John C. Calhoun withdrew to run for vice president when the two executive offices were still elected separately. That left William Crawford of Georgia, who had served in the Senate and as both secretary of war and treasury, but who was now debilitated by a stroke; John Quincy Adams, son of the second president and America's foremost diplomat; Andrew Jackson; and Henry Clay.

Clay had begun his political career believing himself a Jeffersonian, but when the War of 1812 exposed America's many weaknesses, he became a fierce and tenacious advocate of an active, vital national government. He called his love of the Union "the key to my heart." Jackson was devoted to the Union, too, but was Jeffersonian in his belief that the national government should be remote from the daily lives of Americans (except, it must

be said, when federal power was needed to clear away aboriginal populations to open up new settlement areas for white Americans).

Given that Clay and Jackson were the first two statesmen of national
renown to emerge from the frontier West, their rivalry seems inevitable—though Clay, particularly, did his best to exacerbate their mutual
animosity. Their early lives had many parallels. Both were born in the
Southeast: Clay in Virginia in 1777 and Jackson in South Carolina in
1767. Both lost their fathers at a young age, had childhood memories of
abuse at the hands of British soldiers during the Revolutionary War, and
later moved west—Clay to Kentucky and Jackson to Tennessee—to seek
their fortunes as young attorneys.

Neither man had much formal schooling, but Clay enjoyed two
advantages over Jackson in education. First, as a boy in Virginia, he had
the opportunity to observe some of the nation's finest orators, including the great Patrick Henry. Second, when his genius was recognized at
a young age, his stepfather secured a position for him as a clerk in the
Virginia High Court of Chancery. There, at age sixteen, he became secretary to the chancellor himself, George Wythe, who had been the law
professor of Jefferson, Monroe, and John Marshall, among others.

Armed with this extraordinary legal education, Clay earned his license
to practice law at age twenty-one. He concluded that his ambitions could be
more readily realized on the frontier, so he moved to Lexington, Kentucky,
and dove into public affairs. Upon arrival, he was part of an effort to revise
and liberalize Kentucky's state constitution. Even though he was already
a slaveholder, Clay urged in public letters that the constitution include a
provision for gradual emancipation. The effort failed, but Clay's obvious
political talents and prominence in the legal profession (he was Aaron
Burr's defense attorney against charges of sedition) were rewarded with
election to the Kentucky Legislature at the age of twenty-six, temporary
appointment to the U.S. Senate at age twenty-nine (a year younger than
allowed by the Constitution, though no one complained), and election to
the U.S. House in 1810 at age thirty-three.

Remarkably, he was elected Speaker of the House as a freshman congressman—on the first ballot. Before Clay, the duties of the Speaker were

largely ceremonial, but Clay transformed the position into what is considered by many the second most powerful office in the country. Generally acknowledged the most effective Speaker in history, Clay asserted wide powers, including determining which congressmen sat on which committees and to which committees bills would be assigned for study and recommendation to the full House. Like other legislative savants, Clay had a near-telepathic ability to understand and motivate his members, and he was already exuding the charm for which he became famous. Said Missouri congressman Edward Bates, "There is an intuitive perception about him, that seems to see and understand at a glance, and a winning fascination in his manners that will suffer none to be his enemies who cooperate with him. When I look upon his manly and bold countenance, and meet his frank and eloquent eye, I feel an emotion little short of enthusiasm in his cause.... He is a great man—one of Nature's nobles!"

As Speaker, Clay led a group of young congressmen known as the "War Hawks" who were outraged by Britain's treatment of America as a minor power and its variety of abuses, including pressing American seamen into service in the British navy. President James Madison, who was a mentor to Clay, was not a strong leader, so Clay filled the power vacuum and was, according to Congressman (and later Harvard president) Josiah Quincy, "the man whose influence and power more than that of any other produced the War of 1812 between the United States and Great Britain." Clay's bellicosity was remarkable. The man had two duels during his lifetime (in which no one was killed), but generally so abhorred violence that he never went hunting.

The war did not go well for the United States. A series of military disasters on sea and on land, punctuated by the British razing of Washington, led to strong anti-war feelings. Prosecuting the war proved difficult due to the United States' reliance on foreign manufactured goods and foreign credit, a problem that altered Clay's philosophy of government into what would become the American System. Anxious to end the war, Madison made Clay part of the American delegation that negotiated the Treaty of Ghent, an agreement more or less along the status quo. The British had also grown tired of the conflict, as they were simultaneously battling Napoleon's armies. But the greater glory went to Jackson, who led the stunning American victory at the Battle of New Orleans in January 1815—weeks after the war had formally ended because word of the treaty had not yet reached America.

Clay joined his fellow citizens in praising Jackson's triumph but was soon unhappy that newly elected President Monroe did not reward his diplomatic service by naming him secretary of state. He became a constant critic of the Monroe administration, even foolishly trying to dress down Monroe by attacking Jackson for his behavior in Florida during the Seminole War.

At the conclusion of the Creek War, which was waged concurrently with the war against the British, Jackson had imposed an especially harsh and heartless treaty that forced the Creek Indians to surrender twenty-three million acres of ancestral tribal land in Alabama and Georgia. Many hostile Creeks fled to Spanish-owned Florida where they joined the Seminoles in border attacks on American settlements. In 1818, Monroe ordered Jackson to invade Florida to halt the attacks. In addition to burning Indian villages and slaughtering its inhabitants, Jackson exceeded his authority and seized Florida from the Spanish, while also hanging two British subjects accused and convicted in a military court of aiding the Seminoles.

Many Americans, especially in the South, praised Jackson's work. But Clay, who never comprehended Jackson's popularity with the public, was both legitimately outraged by Jackson's behavior and also excited about the opportunity to score points against Monroe's administration. Clay, a fellow congressman observed, was "the most imprudent man in the world." Clay criticized the "dictatorial spirit" with which Jackson treated the Indians, and claimed the fault of the war with the Creek and Seminoles "was on our side." He then excoriated Jackson for risking a new war with Britain by hanging two British subjects. While Clay, with the faux politeness exhibited on such occasions in Congress, insisted he had no malice toward Jackson, he nonetheless demanded that Jackson be reprimanded for his "insubordinate" behavior as a way to assert civilian authority over the military. "Remember that Greece had her Alexander, Rome her Caesar, England her Cromwell, France her Bonaparte, and, that if we would escape the rock on which they split, we must avoid their errors," Clay said.

Clay considered the speech mere politics and did not expect Jackson to take his words personally, but Jackson took great umbrage at being compared to some of history's more infamous tyrants. When Clay later tried to call on Jackson to make amends, only to find him not at home, Jackson was all the more outraged by the "hypocracy [sic] and baseness of Clay in pretending friendship to me." Clay might have tried to reach out to Jackson again, but did not, perhaps in the belief that Jackson, whom he always disparaged as a simple "military chieftain," would never be a real threat to his political ambitions. And so Clay began the feud that, more than anything else, prevented him from becoming president.

Shortly after this incident with Jackson, Clay's reputation as America's most skilled legislator received a boost when he forged the first of what would be three great legislative compromises during his career, all of which averted the real possibility of civil war for a time. The crisis began when Missouri applied for admittance to the Union as a slave state, upsetting the balance of power between free and slave states. Clay worked out a deal whereby Maine would also be admitted as a free state, and henceforth slavery would be prohibited in any territory north of Missouri's southern border. Clay used a tactic that he would repeat later. Recognizing that each element of this compromise had enough opponents that collectively they could defeat the entire package, Clay broke the compromise into three separate pieces of legislation, each of which had enough supporters for passage. What could not be swallowed whole "was instead consumed in three smaller bites." For these efforts, Clay earned the sobriquets "the Great Compromiser" and "the Great Pacificator."

With slavery still not the nation's dominant political issue, Clay campaigned for president in 1824 on his American System—and was mystified that it did not catch fire with voters. He was even more mystified that Jackson was turning into his most formidable opponent. "I cannot believe that killing twenty-five hundred Englishmen at New Orleans qualifies for the various, difficult, and complicated duties of the Chief Magistracy," Clay complained.

But when the balloting was completed, Jackson had won the most popular votes and the most electoral votes. He had not, however, received a majority in the Electoral College and so the Constitution provided that the election would be decided in the U.S. House of Representatives, as it had been once before in the presidential election of 1800. Clay finished a dismal fourth in both popular and electoral voting, while John Quincy Adams finished second and William Crawford third.

Clay might have finished third and been among the three candidates whose names would be submitted to the House for consideration, but for two misfortunes, one of his own doing and one just bad luck. Had Clay agreed to a suggestion by Adams supporters to run a split ticket and share electors in New York, or had two Louisiana state legislators who supported Clay not been injured in a carriage accident and missed voting on that state's electors, then Clay would have won enough electors to put him among the top three finishers. Given his enormous prestige in the House, many historians believe Clay would have been elected president. It was his first close call with the office.

With Clay out of the running, the question was: Who would he support? His influence in the House was such that it was assumed that whoever Clay backed would become president. Supporters of all three candidates made overtures to Clay, but he felt he could not support the stroke-debilitated Crawford. He simply would not support Jackson, even though the Kentucky Legislature instructed him to do so. This process of elimination led him to Adams. When Martin Van Buren heard that Clay was going against the wishes of his home state, he said Clay had signed his own "political death warrant" and predicted he "will never become president be your motives as pure as you claim them to be."

Jackson and his supporters did not impute pure motives, but instead charged that Clay had entered into a "corrupt bargain" with Adams because a few days after the House vote made Adams president, he appointed Clay secretary of state. There is no evidence that Clay and Adams ever had an explicit quid pro quo, but Clay would later acknowledge that accepting the appointment as secretary of state was the greatest mistake of his life.

Why did Clay do it? Besides not being able to support Jackson, he still thought secretary of state was the logical final step to the presidency.

No Westerner had ever held an important Cabinet post, so Clay was making history, and he wanted to make more history by influencing Adams's policies. He was also getting bored in the House, while he found foreign affairs fascinating.

Clay had grand designs, especially in developing a new American policy in the Western Hemisphere by recognizing and supporting the independence of the new Latin American republics that had broken away from Spanish rule. Anticipating by one hundred years Franklin Roosevelt's Good Neighbor Policy toward Latin America, Clay gave passionate speeches in which he envisioned an alliance of democracies in the Western Hemisphere that would "constitute the rallying point of human freedom against all the despotism of the Old World." Clay was also the first American official to propose a canal across Panama, a canal that would be operated for the benefit of all nations, not just the United States. For such enlightened views, Clay is still one of the few American statesmen held in high regard in Latin America.

Jackson and his allies, however, thwarted most of Clay's plans, making the Great Compromiser's tenure as secretary of state generally unsuccessful. And even though Adams was president, Jacksonians directed their most bitter attacks against Clay. For those who think politics and elections in our own time are uncivil and negative, it is worth remembering that in the presidential campaign of 1828, Clay was accused of being a regular patron of brothels and embezzling large sums of money from Kentucky's Transylvania University. Adams was accused of having been a pimp for the czar while he had been minister to Russia. Newspapers friendly to Clay and Adams charged that Jackson's mother was "a COMMON PROSTITUTE" (showing that using all caps for emphasis predates e-mail by one-and-a-half centuries), and they asked of the Jacksons: "Ought a convicted adulteress and her paramour husband to be placed in the highest office of this free and Christian land?"

The latter slur referred to the fact that Jackson had married his wife, Rachel, before she was officially divorced from her first husband at a time when legalities on the frontier were still ambiguous. Rachel Jackson died shortly after the 1828 election. Jackson blamed the slanders flung against her during the campaign for her death, and he blamed Clay for those slurs. There is "nothing too mean or low for him to condescend to," Jackson said. Clay denied spreading rumors about either Jackson's mother or his wife, but otherwise felt justified in encouraging personal attacks against Jackson. "The course adopted by the Opposition . . . against the Administration and supporting presses leaves to its friends no alternative than that of following their example."

While Clay seldom held a grudge, he and Jackson hated each other with a biblical fury. Following the 1824 election, Jackson called Clay the "Judas of the West" and prophesied, "His end will be the same." Given that he blamed Clay for the death of his beloved wife, it is not surprising that Jackson thought Clay "the basest, meanest scoundrel that ever disgraced the image of his god." So great was his hatred of Clay, that Jackson later privately exulted in the sudden death of President William Henry Harrison because Clay would have far less influence on the presidency of Harrison's successor, John Tyler. While Jackson did give a deathbed absolution to his enemies, near the end of his life he was asked if he had any regrets and replied, "Yes. I didn't shoot Henry Clay."*

In turn, Clay was convinced that Jackson was a hotheaded ruffian who intended to implement a military dictatorship in the United States. After Jackson defeated Adams in the 1828 election, Clay publicly characterized Jackson's administration as a "compound of imbecility, tyranny, and hypocrisy," and said Jackson's rule was similar to a cholera epidemic—only worse. "Cholera performs its terrible office and its victims are consigned to the grave, leaving their survivors uncontaminated. But Jacksonism has poisoned the whole Community, the living as well as the dead."

The feud between Clay and Jackson had split the Jeffersonian Republicans into two factions. The faction led by Clay, and to a lesser degree by Adams, was initially called the "National Republicans," while Jackson and his followers assumed the label "Democratic Republicans," which was soon shortened to the "Democratic Party," the name it still bears. An exceptionally strong personality, Jackson had many opponents,

---

* For good measure, Jackson added he also wished he had hanged John C. Calhoun.

but only Clay had the genius to coalesce that opposition into a single national entity.

A political master, Clay initiated a number of innovations to help Adams's cause in 1828. He urged adoption of a set of principles under which not only Adams, but sympathetic candidates for other offices would run—the forerunner of a party platform. He urged the formation of "committees of vigilance" in each community to distribute newspapers, pamphlets, tracts, and other communications to advance the cause, with these local committees reporting to a state central committee—the framework on which our modern political parties are still organized. Clay and Massachusetts senator Daniel Webster also developed a plan to secure a considerable amount of funds from wealthy Northern businessmen to finance the publication of friendly partisan newspapers.

But these political innovations, matched in turn by Jackson's campaign, could not stem the popular tide for Jackson, who captured 56 percent of the popular vote and, to Clay's embarrassment, even won Kentucky by a large margin. Jackson's supporters saw the victory as a triumph of the common people over the elites. To Clay's mind, "The military principle has triumphed, and triumphed in the person of one devoid of all the graces, elegancies, and magnanimity of the accomplished men of the profession." Jackson had been in office all of two months when Clay began preparing for his own second run at the presidency by attacking Jackson on the issue of federal appointments. Alleging corruption and complacency in the executive branch, Jackson had entered office promising to clean house. Clay understood, correctly, that Jackson primarily intended to remove officials sympathetic to his National Republicans. He claimed the removals echoed Napoleon's policy of shooting disloyal soldiers and suggested Jackson was trying to establish a political "monopoly." While Jackson set the unfortunate precedent of the "spoils system" in American government until civil service reform during the Progressive era, the number of federal officeholders turned out was actually quite small—less than 10 percent of the federal workforce—so his policy had little practical effect.

Reversing some of his own earlier positions, Clay next attacked Jackson's Indian removal policy. Having returned to the Senate in 1831,

Clay delivered a number of speeches that passionately condemned the cruelty of forcing Native Americans to leave their ancestral lands and resettle in the territory that is now Oklahoma, a journey that became known as the "Trail of Tears." Jackson's policy, Clay said, "threatens to bring a foul and lasting stain upon the good faith, humanity, and character of the Nation."

But the key issue upon which Clay decided to base his planned 1832 campaign against Jackson was the re-charter of the Second Bank of the United States. Jackson claimed to hate all banks, even though he used banks, borrowed money from banks, and even held stock in one Tennessee bank. Jackson even hated paper money and would later push through legislation requiring all public lands be purchased with gold or silver. Yet, on the advice of some members of his Cabinet, he had already considered supporting a limited re-charter of the bank—until Clay threw down the gauntlet and made it clear this would be the issue upon which he would stake his presidential campaign.

Some historians have portrayed the battle over the bank as a struggle between Jackson and bank president Nicholas Biddle. It makes a nice contrast; "Old Hickory," the simple tribune of the people, versus the sophisticated Philadelphian. But Biddle took his political cues from Clay, who earned a large portion of his income performing legal work collecting debts owed the bank. The bank's current charter was not set to expire until 1836, and Clay initially counseled Biddle not to push for an early re-charter. But once Clay was officially nominated by the National Republicans to be their presidential nominee, he decided the bank re-charter would make an outstanding campaign issue and so he now directed Biddle to apply for the re-charter. Told that Jackson would certainly veto the re-charter, Clay bragged, "I will veto him."

Astonishing both Clay and Biddle, Jackson's veto message proved quite popular with the public, who were told by Jackson that the bank benefited only a few hundred wealthy and well-connected shareholders and borrowers. "It is to be regretted that the rich and powerful too often bend the acts of government to their selfish purposes," Jackson said. Biddle and Clay might have considered the bank essential to facilitating the nation's commerce and promoting prosperity for all classes and sectors, but Jackson had cleverly framed the argument as being about favoritism. Jackson, historian Henry L. Watson observed, was arguing for the principle of equality, not by providing government support to the weak but by removing government support from the strong.

Assessing Clay's electoral chances, Philadelphia mayor B. W. Richards noted, "Attachment to a large moneyed corporation is not a popular attribute." Even though Clay and Webster had articulated why a sound currency and a thriving economy benefited ordinary people most of all, voters did not understand the subtle economic arguments for central banking. What they certainly did oppose were alleged special privileges for a few. Jackson won nearly 55 percent of the popular vote, and Clay won only 49 of 274 electoral votes.

Clay promised to return to the Senate and work "to check the mad career of the tyrant," but first was called upon to save the nation from civil war a second time. Tariff policy may seem esoteric today, but it was the primary method of generating federal revenue in the 1820s and 1830s, and as great a wedge between the North and South as slavery. Clay's American System relied on protective tariffs to help America's fledgling industries grow on a scale that would be competitive with Europe and also to raise revenue that he hoped would fund his program of internal improvements. Clay saw this program as strengthening the entire Union, but the South deeply resented protectionism that benefited Northern manufacturers, which in turn increased the cost of manufactured goods purchased by Southern planters while also reducing the prices planters could receive for their export of raw materials, most especially cotton.

Oddly enough, Jackson supporters led by Van Buren had pushed even higher tariffs on some goods in 1828. The strategy was to improve Jackson's electoral support in the North in the belief that the South would never desert him for Adams. This so-called Tariff of Abominations had pushed South Carolina's John C. Calhoun—then serving as Jackson's vice president!—to refine a theory first articulated by Jefferson a generation earlier. Because the Constitution was no more than a voluntary compact among the states, Calhoun concluded, states could nullify federal laws they did not like, and if the federal government attempted to force states to observe laws they did not support, then a state was justified in seceding from the Union. In late November 1832, a South Carolina legislative convention adopted an Ordinance of Nullification that declared the tariff laws null and void in South Carolina with the attendant promise of secession if the federal government attempted to coerce South Carolina into obeying the law.

Jackson was livid. Instead of focusing on tariff reduction as a conciliatory gesture to defuse the crisis, he gave his primary attention to a bill asking Congress to authorize him to use federal troops and ships, if necessary, to force South Carolina's compliance with federal law. He ordered his secretary of war Lewis Cass to prepare three artillery divisions for dispatch to South Carolina along with one hundred thousand soldiers. Clay supported this so-called force bill, but given his already low opinion of Jackson, he had no confidence that Jackson would use force judiciously. He was certain the president's "vengeful passions" would plunge the nation into civil war.

Clay had a special horror of civil war. "God alone knows where such a war would end," he told the Senate. "In what state will our institutions be left? In what state our liberties?" To defuse the crisis, Clay hit upon an ingenious idea whereby all protectionist tariffs would be abolished—but not for nearly another decade. He thought this would appease the North because another ten years of protective tariffs would buy Northern industries time to grow and strengthen their position against foreign competition. He thought this would appease the South because it acknowledged the justness of their grievances and made the end of protectionist policies by a specific date certain. It took an enormous amount of work to lobby the two sides, including Clay's dramatic offer (not accepted) to resign permanently from public life if only Congress would adopt his compromise, but Clay's proposal was adopted and the crisis averted.

Jackson then instigated another crisis. His successful veto of the re-charter of the Second Bank of the United States still left four more years to go on its existing charter. The president wanted its death to come quickly. He directed his secretary of the treasury William Duane to remove United States government deposits from the bank and to put them in state banks operated by men who supported Jackson. Duane refused, so Jackson sacked him and replaced him with longtime aide

Roger Taney, who had helped author the re-charter veto and who now began the process of deposit removal. In retaliation, Biddle tightened credit and called in loans in hopes of creating an economic crisis that would force Jackson to back off. Business conditions were awful in much of the country, but Jackson would not relent. "The bank, Mr. Van Buren, is trying to kill me. But I will kill it!" he told his new vice president.

Clay and his allies were apoplectic. "We are in the midst of a revolution," Clay told the Senate, "hitherto bloodless, but rapidly tending towards a total change of the pure republican character of the Government, and to the concentration of all power in the hands of one man." Jackson countered with his belief that the president should have more authority than Congress because only the president was "the direct representative of the American people" and because only the president was voted on by all voters.

Clay and his allies in the Senate were unable to stop Jackson's deposit removal plan, but they were successful in approving a censure motion of Jackson's conduct by a vote of 26-20. Clay pursued censure because impeachment must originate in the House, where Jackson's supporters held a majority. No president had ever been censured by the Senate before and none have been since. Jackson was furious and said of Clay, "Oh, if I live to get these robes of office off me, I will bring that rascal to a dear account!" Two years later, Jackson's supporters were successful in expunging the censure from the Senate record. Clay and Jackson never did fight a duel.

It was during debate on deposit removal that Clay borrowed a phrase he had heard used in local elections in the South and in New York to describe all those opposed to the concentration of power in the hands of the president: "patriotic whigs." In Britain, "Whig" had described those opposed to the Restoration of the monarchy by Charles II, so it seemed an especially appropriate label for those who expressed concern that Jackson intended to become "King Andrew the First." Such was Clay's influence that within weeks Whig replaced National Republican as the common term nationally for those allied in opposition to Jackson.

Democrats immediately sought to label the Whigs as elite, unreconstructed Federalists. The *Richmond Whig* newspaper complained that Democrats "have classified the rich and intelligent and denounced them as aristocrats," when in reality Whigs came from all classes of society and all areas of the country. Reflecting Clay's call for a new definition of freedom that included freedom of opportunity, Whigs challenged the branding of their party by Democrats as the party of the rich by asserting that the rich could be anyone of intelligence who worked hard. "Who are the rich men of our country?" the *New York American* editorialized. "They are the enterprising mechanic, who raises himself by his ingenious labours from the dust and turmoil of his workshop, to an abode of ease and elegance; the industrious tradesman, whose patient frugality enables him at last to accumulate enough to forego duties of the counter and indulge a well-earned leisure."

The Whigs, then, became the name of the national party of opposition to the Democrats and would remain so until supplanted in 1856 by the Republicans. The scope of the Whigs' appeal is demonstrated by the fact that in the five presidential elections held from 1836 through 1852, Whigs averaged 48.3 percent of the popular vote while Democrats averaged 48.2 percent. Without Clay's nationalist vision, the variety of sectional and special interest parties that rose and fell in America during the antebellum period in opposition to Jackson—the Anti-Masons, Free Soil, Native American (Know-Nothings), or Liberty Parties, to name a few—might have set a very different precedent for the American political system.

The Whig Party, while short lived, was important because it was a truly national party that drew support from every section of the Union. It helped hold the Union together at a time when the republic was young enough that a sectional split might have been irrevocable. Having Whig support in the North, South, and West helped postpone the dissolution of the Union until 1860, when a divided nation was no longer acceptable to the North and West. As long as a Whig in Alabama felt he had more in common with a Whig in Connecticut than he did a Democrat in Mississippi, then that provided a little more glue to hold the nation together. When the Whig Party imploded before the war, largely over the issue of slavery, one of the most important checks on fervent sectionalism failed.

Clay's Whigs were also largely the foundation upon which the Republican Party was built. Most of those who formed the Republican Party had been Whigs, particularly Northern "Conscience Whigs" who embraced Clay's economic program, but who were also aggressively anti-slavery. Lincoln described himself as "an old-line Henry Clay Whig," and to prove the point Lincoln quoted Clay more than forty times during his debates with Stephen Douglas. Lincoln's views on slavery (at least until well into the Civil War) and his economic program were nearly identical to Clay's. Various observers have compared Clay's influence on Lincoln with Jefferson's on Madison or Franklin Roosevelt's on Lyndon Johnson. It might even be said that when Lincoln and the Republicans who followed him implemented a good deal of Clay's American System, they created a true Whig regime at last.

Finally, in considering the Whigs' legacy, more and more historians are concluding that the Whigs, not Jackson's Democrats, are the real ideological forerunner of modern American liberalism. Some still argue that Jackson spurred modern liberalism by broadening the suffrage to include all adult white males, by antipathy toward elites, and by the Democratic Party's embrace of immigrants. But broadening democratic participation is only one measure of liberalism. Historian Arthur Schlesinger Jr., whose epic study, *The Age of Jackson*, set the tone for much modern Jackson scholarship, has since acknowledged that he gave Clay and the Whigs "a good deal less than justice" in using Jackson's precedent as the rationale for Roosevelt's New Deal. Whig policies that were designed to broaden economic prosperity "had a sounder conception of the role of government and a more constructive policy of economic development than the anti-statist Jacksonians," Schlesinger wrote in his memoirs.

But Clay, the very "embodiment and polar star of Whig principles," did more than outline a new conception of the purpose of government; he expanded the definition of freedom in America. From Revolutionary times, liberty had been defined simply as freedom from an oppressive government; Clay, who coined the phrase "the self-made man," expanded the definition to include freedom of opportunity. Clay argued that the federal government had a *duty* to supply what was necessary for the "safety, convenience and prosperity" of the American people. This was a sharp break with Jeffersonian orthodoxy, yet it captures one of the most appealing aspects of America, which is the opportunity to make a better life than you or your parents enjoyed before—often with the help of the government.

It is easy to imagine Clay championing such twentieth-century innovations as the GI Bill, student loans, or the creation of the Internet. Clay, for example, proposed government regulation of the telegraph so information could not be monopolized. For Clay, the American experiment was about more than just political equality, it was also the equality of opportunity to do well and prosper. It was Clay's great intellectual achievement, said renowned historian Richard Hofstadter, to broaden the appeal of what was essentially a Hamiltonian economic program by infusing it with a "Jeffersonian spirit."

Clay's extraordinary influence was due in large part to his immensely appealing personality. He was a witty conversationalist who loved parties, brandy, and cards. Once, he reportedly lost and won eight thousand dollars in a single night, and many who knew him said the most important thing to understand about Clay was that he was by nature a gambler—a trait that did not always serve him well in politics. Hearing contemporaries describe Clay brings to mind President Bill Clinton, another brilliant politician capable of forging imaginative political compromises. Like Clinton, Clay was known to be able to win over enemies with his charm if given a chance. When a new congressman from Georgia, General Thomas Glascock, was offered the opportunity to meet Clay, he refused, saying, "No, sir! I am his adversary, and choose not to subject myself to his fascination."

Also like Clinton, Clay was repeatedly accused of having lax morals. When Clay and John Quincy Adams were in Europe to negotiate the treaty to end the War of 1812, the dour and proper Adams would complain that Clay was usually just going to bed when Adams was rising. While cards and brandy were the main staples of his amusements, Clay also liked to flirt and make playful and, for the time, risqué remarks. During a speaking tour in New England, for example, he shocked some in the audience by insisting on calling Virginia "the dominion of the virgin queen."

Perhaps it was this reputation for being a bit of a bad boy that made Clay especially attractive to women. Even in his old age female admirers mobbed him, sometimes snipping a lock of his hair as a souvenir. Clay joyfully returned their affection with kisses, joking that kissing was like the presidency, "it was not to be sought and not to be declined." Despite such behavior, there is no evidence that he was ever unfaithful to his wife, Lucretia, a plain, kindly woman who abhorred Washington society and preferred to remain in Kentucky to manage Ashland, the family estate near Lexington.

Clay was tall, at six feet in height, and bony, with long arms and legs. He had a narrow face with a high forehead, small blue eyes, and a mouth so wide and so thin it was said he could not whistle and had trouble spitting tobacco. No portrait ever did him justice, those who knew him said, because he was at his most attractive when in motion. "There was not a look of his eye, not a movement of his long, graceful right arm, not a swaying of his body, that was not full of grace and effect," one admirer gushed.

And then there was his voice, a "majestic" bass that "filled the room as the organ fills a great cathedral." It was "music itself," one enraptured observer recalled, "and yet penetrating and far-reaching, enchanting the listener; his words flowed rapidly, without sing-song or mannerism, in a clear and steady stream." Another said of Clay's voice, "Whoever heard one more melodious? There was a depth of tone to it, a volume, a compass, a rich and tender harmony, which invested all he said with majesty."

Clay possessed the soul of a thespian. In this golden age of American political oratory, when entertainment options were limited, a short Clay speech might last two hours while an important speech might be continued over several days. To hold his audience, Clay would speak as an orchestra performs a symphony, with a wide range of tones, gestures, and movements. During one emotional assault on Jackson's Indian removal policy, the British author Harriet Martineau said, "I saw tears, of which I am sure he [Clay] was wholly unconscious, falling on his papers as he vividly described the woes and injuries of the aborigines."

Despite these performances, Clay often lamented that in popular politics emotion trumped reason, and he had trouble connecting with the common voter. Clay's speeches were generally sophisticated in content, and those lucky enough to be present when Clay was at his best claimed that hearing him speak was "a noble intellectual treat." Clay seldom used humorous anecdotes to make a point, as Lincoln did, but he was quick with a quip. When one long-winded congressman insisted that he spoke for posterity, Clay sighed, "Yes, and you seem resolved to speak until the arrival of your audience." Another time, while campaigning back in Kentucky, Clay asked the audience where an old friend and rival attorney was. Told the man was out stumping for President Van Buren's election, Clay replied, "Ah! At his old occupation, defending criminals."

But like any live performance, Clay's speeches were best experienced in the moment. Clay was considered by many contemporaries to be the greatest orator of his time, yet his popular reputation has been surpassed by that of his colleague and rival, Daniel Webster, primarily because Webster's logical and powerful prose reads so well even today. Clay's words do not jump off the page because, as his best biographer, Robert V. Remini, says, "Even his surviving speeches do not adequately carry the power and brilliance of his performances." Clay's performances were so enthralling that many of his speeches are lost to posterity because enraptured reporters forgot to take notes.

The House and Senate galleries were almost always full to overflowing any day it was known that Clay would speak. On his several national speaking tours, Clay routinely drew crowds in the tens of thousands, including one memorable Whig barbecue in Dayton, Ohio, in 1842 that drew more than one hundred thousand people. During his astonishing forty-plus years as a major national political figure, it is likely that Clay spoke before more Americans than any person of his time. It was his misfortune to run for president at a time when convention required that candidates not actively campaign for themselves. Had Clay been able to actively campaign during elections, the results of those elections would likely have been different.

Still, he left an extraordinary legacy. No American legislator had a more distinguished congressional career, and none has achieved such distinction in both houses of Congress. While Clay, like politicians of any period, tended to exaggerate the humbleness of his origins, his was an extraordinary rise to power and influence for one not born to wealth or privilege. Margaret Bayard Smith, author, diarist, and grande dame of Washington society from 1800 to 1841, suggested that in some respects Clay was a superior man to Jefferson and Madison because he did not enjoy their aristocratic upbringing. Clay's "own, inherent power, [was] bestowed by nature and not derivative from cultivation or fortune," Smith wrote. "He has an elasticity and buoyancy of spirit, that no pressure of external circumstances can confine or keep down. He is a very great man."

The pity of Clay is that such a great man could not see a way to resolve the issue of slavery in the United States. Clay was himself a slave owner from childhood, when he inherited two slaves from his father's estate at the age of four. Later in life, he owned as many as fifty slaves at one time. He freed several of his slaves during his lifetime, and his will made provisions for the gradual emancipation of all his slaves after his death.

Clay maintained all his life that slavery was "a great evil." Ruminating on the condition of slaves in Kentucky, Clay wrote empathetically:

> *Can any humane man be happy and contented when he sees near thirty thousand of his fellow beings around him, deprived of all the rights which make life desirable, transferred like cattle from the possession of one to another; when he sees the trembling slave, under the hammer, surrounded by a number of eager purchasers, and feeling all the emotions which arise when one is uncertain into whose tyrannic hands he must next fall; when he beholds the anguish and hears the piercing cries of husbands separated from wives and children from parents; when, in a word, all the tender and endearing ties of human nature are broken asunder and disregarded . . .*

To abolitionists, it was the worst sort of hypocrisy to expound on the evil of slavery while not only owning slaves but forging legislative compromises that protected its existence in the South. Because they thought he should know better, abolitionists held a special antipathy toward Clay, and their enmity was key in depriving Clay of the presidency in 1844.

Clay felt constrained by the fact that while slavery might run counter to the basic tenet of the Declaration of Independence that "all men are created equal," slavery was nonetheless legal under the Constitution. Further, while Clay acknowledged that blacks could, with proper education, reach great intellectual potential, he was equally convinced that blacks could never be the social equals of whites. Immediate emancipation would only bring misery, Clay thought, for uneducated slaves would be unprepared to survive as free men, and the natural tensions between the white and black races would lead to bloody conflict. Clay insisted the only practical "solution" to ending slavery was gradual emancipation coupled with colonization of willing blacks back to Africa. Clay helped form and served a long tenure as president of the American Colonization Society, which was dedicated to resettling free blacks in Africa. The effort, of course, made hardly a dent; the society's efforts resulted in the settlement of only about thirteen thousand African Americans in the American colony that became the nation of Liberia.

Late in life, when his presidential ambitions finally cooled, Clay became more outspoken on the need for the nation to adopt a plan of emancipation, but still cautioned, "Public opinion alone can bring about the abolition of slavery, and public opinion is on the march. We should wait in patience for its operation without attempting measures which might throw it back. It is, I admit, a slow remedy, but it is to be remembered that slavery is a chronic disease, and I believe that in such maladies speedy recovery is not expected . . . it will not happen in our time."

Recognizing that the Whigs had a superb chance to win the 1840 presidential election following the financial "Panic of 1837," Clay had expected to be the Whig nominee, but he was rejected because of abolitionist hostility. "I am the most unfortunate man in the history of parties," Clay moaned, "always run by my friends when sure to be defeated, and now betrayed for a nomination when I, or any one, would be sure of an election." Clay's misfortune (or poor judgment) continued when he declined to run as the vice presidential nominee—not knowing, of course, that the first Whig president, William Henry Harrison, would die less than a month into office, which would have made Clay president.

Harrison's death also thwarted Clay's more general plans for a Whig government. The only Whig principle held by Harrison's vice president, John Tyler, was his personal dislike of Jackson. When Tyler refused to establish a new national bank, Clay excommunicated Tyler from the Whig Party and set up a shadow government in Congress. Clay was able to ram a few Whig proposals into law, including bankruptcy protection and using some tariff revenue for internal improvements, but it was an unsatisfying outcome given the hopes that Harrison's election had aroused.

A national speaking tour through the Midwest and the North in 1842 drew such extraordinary crowds that it greatly reinvigorated Clay's presidential ambitions. But he had missed a major change in public opinion. Despite the recent recession, voters cared little about Whig economic polices; instead voters in 1844 wanted to talk about territorial expansion, slavery, and how the two meshed.

Clay opposed annexation of slave-holding Texas because it would upset the political balance between free and slave states, and because he was certain annexation would lead to war with Mexico unless Mexico agreed to voluntarily sell its claims to Texas. Clay also gambled on what he thought was a sure bet; he was convinced Martin Van Buren would again be the Democratic nominee, and Van Buren also opposed annexation, making it a non-issue. But Van Buren had also misread public opinion, and his opposition to annexation cost him the Democratic nomination. Democrats instead turned to Jackson protégé and Tennessee senator James K. Polk, who turned out to be a gifted politician.

Clay won the Whig nomination by acclamation but soon learned his stand on Texas was destroying his campaign in the South. When he tried to subtly backtrack from his position, saying he would not object to annexing Texas if it did not jeopardize the Union, he only inflamed abolitionists in the North, who again poured out their venom on Clay for his perceived hypocrisy on slavery. Clay lamented, "I believe I have been charged with every crime enumerated in the Decalogue."

More damaging was the decision of the abolitionists to run James G. Birney for president on the Liberty Party ticket, primarily with the intention of denying Clay the presidency. While Polk and Clay were both slaveholders, Birney said abolitionists should "deprecate" Clay more because he was more intelligent than Polk and therefore could do more harm as president.

The election was extraordinarily close, with Polk winning the popular vote by a margin of about thirty-eight thousand out of 2.7 million ballots cast. More importantly, Clay lost New York by just 5,106 votes when Birney had won 15,812 votes in the state. Had a relatively small fraction of those abolitionist voters supported Clay, he would have won New York, and thereby won the presidency by receiving a majority in the Electoral College. It was Clay's third and final close call with the presidency.

A dispirited Clay supporter concluded, "The result of this election has satisfied me that no such man as Henry Clay can ever be president of the United States. The party leaders, the men who make a president, will never consent to elevate one greatly their superior." Jackson, who would die the following year, praised God for letting him live long enough to see Clay humiliated one more time. "I thank my god that the Republic is safe and that he had permitted me to live to see it and rejoice," he said.

An aged and increasingly sympathetic figure, given his many services to the nation, Clay was, following Jackson's death, easily the most popular political figure in the nation. Remarkably, he still thought of running for president again. "Is the fire of ambition never to be extinguished?" Tyler exclaimed. The seventy-one-year-old Clay advised the Whigs he was available if wanted in 1848, but in another slap at one of Clay's core beliefs, the Whigs instead nominated a military hero in the mode of Jackson, Zachary Taylor, who added insult to injury by proclaiming he did not feel bound by any Whig principles. Coincidentally, like the only other Whig to win the presidency, Taylor died in office, elevating a true Whig, Millard Fillmore, to the White House. But it was of little consequence. The Whig Party was slowly dissolving, and the nation was splitting in two.

Clay, with the vital assistance of Stephen Douglas, had the opportunity to postpone that split one more time via the misnamed Compromise of 1850—misnamed because it involved no real compromise, no finding of middle ground. Rather, it was a complicated series of resolutions designed to cool tempers. California was admitted to the Union as a free state but with slavery unmentioned as a condition of admittance; the residents of Utah and New Mexico were left to decide whether their states would be slave or free (Clay was sure the climate in both meant they would be free states); the slave trade was theoretically abolished in the District of Columbia (it continued underground); and the fugitive slave laws were toughened. Since, as with the Missouri Compromise, each resolution was voted on separately, members voted their convictions on each, did not meet their opponents halfway, and ended up hating half of what was passed. The day of reckoning had only been postponed.

Holding the nation together with string and gum, the Compromise of 1850 was nonetheless crucial to the eventual outcome of the Civil War, for it gave the North another decade to develop the industrial resources that would ultimately overwhelm the South when the conflict came. It also gave the North another ten years to become increasingly hostile to the existence of slavery, and therefore committed to the cause. And it ensured that the war came when a man equal to the task of keeping the Union together—Lincoln being a Clay man at that!—was in the White House.

Many understood at the time what Clay had accomplished. Van Buren wrote a friend, "Tell Clay for me that he added a crowning grace to his public life . . . more honorable and durable than his election to the Presidency could possibly have been." There were many who believed that if Clay had lived another decade, he might have been able to postpone the Civil War once more. He was not there to try, of course, but the conflict was likely inevitable given that, as Lincoln would ultimately conclude, no nation could survive forever half slave and half free.

After his death in 1852, Clay was the first American accorded the honor of having his body lay in state in the Capitol Rotunda. Presaging Lincoln's death thirteen years later, tens of thousands of mourners lined the route of Clay's funeral train back to Lexington.

A few months after Clay died, the Whigs ran their last candidate for president, General Winfield Scott. After that, the Whigs were no more. There were many factors contributing to the party's dissolution, of course, but the party essentially died when Clay died. He had wanted a party rooted in principles, but his own personality dominated the party, perhaps to an extent that ultimately suffocated it.

Ten years after Clay's death, with the Civil War raging in full fury, his great admirer Lincoln wrote a note to one of Clay's surviving sons to thank him for the memento of a snuff box once owned by Clay. Thinking of the great statesman for the Union, Lincoln wrote, "I recognize his voice, speaking as it ever spoke, for the Union, the Constitution, and the freedom of mankind."

CHAPTER THREE

STEPHEN DOUGLAS

1860

There can be no neutrals in this war, only patriots—or traitors.

Having lost the 1860 presidential election to his lifelong rival, Abraham Lincoln, Illinois senator Stephen A. Douglas astonished observers by becoming one of Lincoln's staunchest defenders and his apparent confidant in devising a strategy to crush the Southern rebellion. Douglas's Democratic followers were confused. Why had Douglas, who had worked so hard to conciliate the South and avoid war, now become a strident advocate of military coercion to maintain the Union? Why should they now support Republican policies and a president whose candidacy they and Douglas had so vigorously opposed?

Even following the Confederate attack on Fort Sumter, Democrats were uncertain what path to follow. Lesser Democratic leaders in the North, such as outgoing president James Buchanan, had been ready to throw up their hands and let the South secede in peace. Now that war had come, Democrats debated whether the Union cause was only a Republican cause. But Douglas, as the only politician of his day with a truly national following, insisted, "There can be no neutrals in this war, *only patriots—or traitors.*"

He traveled home to Illinois to rally Democratic opinion. "Do not allow the mortification growing out of defeat in a partisan struggle . . . convert you from patriots to traitors against your native land," Douglas said. Defense of the Union did not require fusion with the Republican

Party in a national unity party (as some Republicans demanded), or even deference to Republican policies. It did require repudiation of secessionists. The nation, Douglas explained, needed the Democratic Party to chart an independent course and would be best served by—and strong enough to handle—a loyal opposition party, providing vigorous debate even in the midst of civil war.

"Unite as a band of brothers and rescue your government," Douglas entreated his followers. It was not only the right thing to do, it was good politics. Already mindful of the Republican taunt, "Every Democrat may not be a traitor but every traitor is a Democrat," Douglas admonished his followers, "If we hope to regain and perpetuate the ascendancy of our party, we should never forget that a man cannot be a true Democrat unless he is a patriot."

Protesting that he was exhausted in "strength, and voice, and life" from two years of exertions to prevent civil war, Douglas could happily report that the "ablest and bravest" opponents of secession were now Northern Democrats, who were "firm and unanimous" in their loyalty to the Union. In those few months following his presidential defeat, Douglas had assured the Democratic Party would survive the war as a viable independent political party. Less than a month later, on June 3, 1861, he died at the age of forty-eight.

Douglas's exhortations had an enormous and lasting impact upon his party. Northern Democrats—and some Southern Democrats, too— did fight for the Union, as Douglas urged. The *North American Review,* in its July 1886 edition, investigated the question of the partisan makeup of the Union Army and concluded Democrats willingly enlisted and fought for the Union in the same numbers and percentages as Republicans—and with an equal fervor. Many key Union commanders were Democrats, including Secretary of War Edwin Stanton and Generals George McClellan, George Thomas, Benjamin Butler, and Winfield Scott Hancock. Even Ulysses S. Grant was a nominal Democrat before and during the war, quoting Douglas's remark about their being only "traitors and patriots" in a letter to his father that explained why he was accepting a Union officer's commission.

The value of a loyal opposition party, however, was not limited to the battlefield. Douglas's insistence that Democrats remain independent from Republicans even as they remained loyal to the Union had enormous ramifications during and after the war. While unity may seem critical in a time of civil war, scholars have concluded that continued partisan bickering was to the Union's benefit.

A 1967 essay written by historian Eric L. McKitrick outlines the several ways that a vigorous Democratic opposition strengthened the Union war effort. First, Democratic opposition unified Republicans and greatly reduced intraparty squabbling that might have undermined Lincoln's administration. Second, Democratic critiques sometimes helped correct flawed administration policies. Third, an independent Democratic Party provided those opposed to Lincoln's policies with a peaceful means to express their grievances. Those who criticized the administration could be treated simply as ambitious politicians seeking partisan advantage within the established political system, rather than as traitors.

In contrast, the absence of political parties in the South greatly weakened the Confederacy. Political parties are designed to weave together various and differing constituencies for a larger national purpose. Lacking a national perspective, many Southern political leaders acted parochially. Further, without the system of discipline and rewards that political parties provide their members, Southern politicians suffered little consequence for acting out in petty ways that undermined the Confederate cause. Georgia governor Joseph Brown, for example, expressed his displeasure with Confederate president Jefferson Davis by arbitrarily furloughing ten thousand Georgia troops for thirty days—the week after the fall of Atlanta! In contrast, states with Democratic governors in the North, including New York and New Jersey, always met their Union conscription quotas.

As the war dragged on, and as emancipation of the slaves (an idea unpopular with Democrats) became a key war aim, an element known as the "Peace Democrats" grew in strength, demanding a negotiated peace with the Confederacy. But they remained a minority within the party. While their political activities annoyed the Lincoln administration, there was no "fifth column" of disaffected Northern Democrats undermining the Union war effort. The course Douglas set for the party at the beginning of the war ensured that, in 1864, Democrats nominated "War Democrat" General George McClellan, who, during a heated but peaceful campaign, said only the unconditional reunion of North and South could lead to peace.

Douglas had had to fight on several fronts to ensure the Democratic Party would survive the war. In addition to the Republican proposal to meld the two parties into one, Southern Democrats, known as "Fire-Eaters" for their aggressive pro-slavery and pro-secession views, had tried to destroy the party before the war began. Former Democratic Alabama congressman William Lowndes Yancey, one of the South's great orators and leading proponents of secession, actively promoted "the disorganization of the Democratic Party." Yancey and his cohorts believed that all institutions that continued to bind North and South together must be dissolved for secession to succeed. With even religious denominations, such as the Methodists and Baptists, having split North and South, the Democratic Party was one of the few remaining institutions in which Southerners and Northerners might find common cause.

Even election of another pliant Democratic president like James Buchanan was anathema to the Fire-Eaters, for that would only postpone by a few years what secessionists believed was inevitable. Better to ensure Lincoln's election by sabotaging the Democrats and Douglas in order to drive other Southerners to embrace secession.

Yancey's belief in the power of the Democratic Party to unite the nation was proven correct after the war. Then, the Democratic Party played a vital, if controversial, role in the reconstruction of the nation. It had survived the war intact, one of the few national institutions ready to welcome white Southerners back with open arms, and one of the few that Southerners would willingly join. As such, the Democratic Party was an important tool in bringing white Southerners back into national affairs and providing them with lawful means to express their political passions—though this did not prevent appalling post-war violence against newly freed blacks.

While Republicans continued to "wave the bloody shirt" during every national election for a generation after the war ended, because of Douglas's leadership in establishing the Democrats as *loyal* opposition, the label "party of treason" fell short of its intended effect. The Democratic Party was competitive in national elections during and after the war. Indeed, it emerged from the war with its political fortunes improved. Republicans had been united by the war effort, but with the war over, fissions developed within the party. Meanwhile, Southern states, which would overwhelmingly vote Democratic for the next one hundred years, perversely saw their political strength increase: Slaves had counted as three-fifths of a person for purposes of congressional apportionment, but post-slavery African Americans now counted as full human beings.

That the end of slavery could increase the political influence of slave-holding states is another illustration of Douglas's complicated legacy. Compared with his fellow Illinoisan, the sainted Lincoln, the man known as "The Little Giant" may seem a small man indeed. Black abolitionist Frederick Douglass charged that no man in antebellum America had "done more to intensify hatred of the negro" than Douglas. No Northern politician had tried harder to appease the slave-holding South, and no individual, because of his introduction of the Kansas-Nebraska Act, was more directly responsible for the chain of events that led to the Civil War.

Yet . . . no man had worked harder to prevent that war or to rally public opinion behind Lincoln and the Union. Douglas's premature death was brought on by a lifetime of heavy drinking but even more by exhaustion from his yearlong exertions on behalf of the Union. Months before the 1860 election, realizing that he could not defeat Lincoln, Douglas devoted the remainder of his campaign not to soliciting votes, but to convincing Southerners that Lincoln's election could not justify secession. Despite death threats, including one from future Confederate president Jefferson Davis, Douglas traveled into the heart of Dixie to make his case. After the election, Douglas worked feverishly with Kentucky senator John Crittenden to try to forge a last-minute compromise to end the secession crisis.

While Douglas's and Crittenden's proposals were unacceptable to Lincoln (and some were genuinely outrageous, such as prohibiting even free blacks from voting), their work provided a valuable service to the Union. Faith in Douglas's ability to forge an acceptable compromise led four Southern states to delay their secession until after Lincoln's inaugural. This delay, particularly in the secession of Virginia, gave Lincoln crucial time to form a government, preventing the Confederacy from becoming a *fait accompli* before he could take office and plan his response to the secession crisis.

The slave-holding border states of Missouri, Kentucky, Delaware, and Maryland declined to secede at all, which led an admirer to write to Douglas that without his efforts by March 1, 1861, "Mason and Dixon's line would now be the boundary of the Southern Confederacy"—and the Mason-Dixon line was north of Washington, D.C. Douglas did not merely preserve the Democratic Party; he also played an important role in creating a set of facts on the ground that proved to be essential to the preservation of the Union.

Despite his final attempt at appeasement, once the war began, Douglas left no doubt where his loyalties lay. Embittered that his efforts at conciliation were so poorly received by the South, when secession came Douglas proposed to fight it with a greater ferocity than Lincoln. When Lincoln told Douglas he initially planned to call up seventy-five thousand militia, Douglas urged him to call up nearly three times that number, telling Lincoln that he would have to deal sharply with the South. "You do not know the dishonest purposes of these men as well as I do," Douglas told Lincoln of the secessionists. "If I were president, I'd convert or hang them *all* within forty-eight hours."

In a private meeting, which he later reported to the press with Lincoln's permission, Douglas assured Lincoln that Northern Democrats would seek no partisan advantage from the conflict. "Our Union must be preserved," he said. "Partisan feeling must yield to patriotism. I am with you, Mr. President, and God bless you." After Douglas left their meeting, Lincoln exclaimed, "What a noble man Douglas is!"

Lincoln had not always thought so. For most of their adult lives, their rivalry was one-sided in favor of Douglas, which made Lincoln uncharacteristically jealous. Lincoln was four years older than Douglas, and while

Lincoln achieved considerable political success at a young age (he was a state legislator at age twenty-five), it paled next to Douglas's extraordinary rise to prominence. Douglas was an Illinois Supreme Court justice at age twenty-seven, a U.S. senator at thirty-three, and a serious presidential contender in 1852 at age thirty-nine, by which time he was the most famous, respected, and controversial statesman in America. Lincoln, meanwhile, remained unknown outside Illinois, until he ran a gallant but losing race against Douglas for the U.S. Senate in 1858.

Lincoln spent his adult years measuring himself against Douglas and, at least until he won the presidency, found himself lacking. Shortly after returning to politics in 1856, Lincoln wrote:

> *Twenty-two years ago, Judge Douglas and I became acquainted. We were both young then; he a trifle younger than I. Even then we were both ambitious; I perhaps quite as much as he. With me the race of ambition has been—a flat failure; with him it has been one of splendid success. His name fills the nation, and is not unknown even in foreign lands. I would rather stand on that eminence than wear the richest crown that ever pressed a monarch's brow.*

Lincoln, of course, would far exceed that eminence by becoming what most consider our greatest president. Douglas, meanwhile, is forever linked to and overshadowed by Lincoln. Worse for Douglas, with Lincoln being America's foremost secular saint, popular perception has been that his great opponent, Douglas, must have been a great sinner. Yet, as Douglas repeatedly pointed out in their famed 1858 Senate debates, he and Lincoln held many similar political views—so similar that, to Lincoln's great chagrin, several prominent Republicans tried to recruit Douglas to become a Republican and the party nominee in 1860. But in the monumental disagreement between Lincoln and Douglas—the morality of slavery—there was a chasm between them as great as their disparity in height.

The names "Lincoln and Douglas" are as comfortably paired in the popular imagination as Abbott and Costello or Laurel and Hardy, and standing side-by-side, as they so often did, they must have appeared a perfectly mismatched vaudevillian duo. Lincoln was six-feet-four-inches tall, thin, gaunt, and homely, with a reedy tenor voice that spoke in a soft Kentucky drawl. Douglas was a full foot shorter at five-feet-four-inches tall with legs so short that Senator Thomas Hart Benton complained, "That part of his body, sir, which men wish to kick, is too near the ground." But above these stumpy legs was a pair of broad shoulders topped by a massive head with a pompadour of thick, brown hair that gave Douglas a leonine appearance. He also had a deep, melodious bass voice that loved to roar.

Where Lincoln favored reason in his speeches, Douglas believed emotion carried the day and he could work himself into a fit when aroused, which was often. John Quincy Adams, who served with Douglas in the House of Representatives, gave a memorable description of the young Illinoisan's debating technique: "His face was convulsed, his gesticulation frantic, and he lashed himself into such a heat that if his body had been made of combustible matter, it would have burned out. In the midst of his roaring, to save himself from choking, he stripped off and cast away his cravat, and unbuttoned his waist coat, and had the air and aspect of a half-naked pugilist."

Douglas's fury, sincere or feigned, was perhaps one means by which he overcompensated for his small stature. As Lincoln no doubt found that droll humor helped put people at ease when his height might have otherwise been intimidating, Douglas conversely compensated for his short stature and boyish looks with a forceful and vivacious personality that made him appear larger than he was. He also self-consciously adopted the vices of a "man's man."

Douglas drank to excess (and may have died from cirrhosis of the liver), greatly enjoyed the company of women, and was always seen with a Cuban cigar clenched between his teeth. Despite his size, he would brawl when necessary, once nearly biting off a man's thumb to release the man's grip on his throat. Douglas worked hard to ensure his constituents thought of him as one of them, boasting, "I . . . eat with my constituents, drink with them, lodge with them, pray with them, laugh, hunt, dance, and work with them; I eat their corn dodgers and fried bacon and sleep two in bed with them."

Lincoln had no need to pretend to be one of the common folk, for he had been born to a poor farmer on the Kentucky frontier in 1809. Douglas, however, was born April 23, 1813, into a prosperous family in Brandon, Vermont, his ancestors tracing their New England lineage to 1640. Douglas's father was a physician who died when Douglas was only two months old. The death of his father postponed his formal schooling for a while, but Douglas eventually was able to study English, mathematics, and classical languages at a local college preparatory academy.

While he had been briefly apprenticed to a cabinet-maker, Douglas concluded early in life, as did Lincoln, that he was not made for manual labor. Like Lincoln, Douglas decided to pursue the practice of law, which is why he moved west to Illinois where all that was needed to pass the bar was a simple oral examination by a judge and a character reference. Asked by his mother when she would see him again as he departed for Illinois at age twenty-one, Douglas supposedly replied, "On my way to Congress."

Though not as brilliant at law as Lincoln, Douglas gained the reputation of being "the best lawyer for a bad case" in all of Illinois, usually by misrepresenting opposing counsel's position and twisting the logic of his opponent's case. It was a trait he brought to politics, which led Lincoln to once exclaim that while Douglas seldom told an outright lie, "I think he cares as little for the truth . . . as any man I ever saw."

Despite Lincoln's feeling of inferiority in comparison to Douglas's achievements, Douglas thought highly of Lincoln. When Lincoln became the Republican presidential nominee in 1860, Douglas surprised his Democratic colleagues with his praise, saying Lincoln was the toughest debater he had ever faced and the strongest nomination the Republicans could have made. This echoed what he said of Lincoln during their 1858 Senate contest: "He is the strong man of his party, full of wit, facts, dates—and the best stump speaker, with his droll ways and dry jokes, in the West. He is as honest as he is shrewd, and if I beat him, my victory will be hardly won."

Lincoln, who had a petty streak, seldom reciprocated this praise. He sarcastically referred to Douglas's reputation as a "great" man—although Lincoln thought enough of Douglas's influence to ask his help in getting his son, Robert, admitted to Harvard, which Douglas did. Despite this kindness and Douglas's admiration, Lincoln indulged in insults based on Douglas's diminutive stature. He called Douglas "the least man I ever saw," and on another occasion suggested to his fellow Whigs that the best method of handling Douglas was to never mention his name, since this was "the best mode of treating so small a matter."

The jibes were brought on by competing ambitions. Lincoln's ambition was memorably described as "the little engine that knew no rest"; Douglas was similarly labeled a "steam engine in breeches." Nor was their rivalry exclusively political. Douglas briefly courted Mary Todd, and many thought the little dynamo was a better match for the vivacious Mary than her future husband, who was prone to melancholia. But Mary had vowed to marry a president, and her intuition served her well—though until 1860 it seemed she had made the wrong choice.

Douglas lost his first race for Congress by thirty-five votes out of thirty-six thousand cast. But he was rewarded for his service to the Democratic Party by his appointment to the Illinois Supreme Court, which is why Lincoln always referred to him as "Judge Douglas." By 1844, Douglas was elected to Congress, and in 1846 to the Senate.

Douglas earned national renown when, as chair of the Senate Committee on Territories, he provided critical assistance to Henry Clay in passing the Compromise of 1850. This success, short-lived as it proved to be, made him a serious candidate for the 1852 Democratic nomination for president, even though he was but thirty-nine years old. The Democrats eventually turned to dark horse Franklin Pierce, but Douglas was not disappointed. He thought his better chance for the nomination would come in 1856. In the meantime, he could achieve his long-standing goal of organizing the Nebraska Territory.

As the leader of a group of congressmen known as the "Young Americans," Douglas advocated national expansion and settlement. He believed that America's future was in the West, and the West needed homesteaders and railroads to bring them there. It was his support of a transcontinental railroad that led Douglas to push legislation to organize the Nebraska Territory, which included the present-day states of Kansas,

Nebraska, and the Dakotas. Territorial organization would encourage lawful settlement and create the legal and regulatory system that would guide railway construction across the country. "No man can keep up with the spirit of this age who travels on anything slower than the locomotive, and fails to receive intelligence by lightning," Douglas said. "We must therefore have Rail Roads and Telegraphs from the Atlantic to the Pacific, through our own territory."

Because he had been born in New England, lived in the West, and ended up marrying two different Southern women (his first wife died in childbirth), Douglas fancied that he possessed a unique national perspective. He therefore advocated multiple transcontinental rail routes, including a Southern one. He especially favored two routes that not only were good public policy, but also promised to be personally profitable. Douglas, a great early booster of Chicago, had large real estate holdings in that city and strongly supported a central route from that emerging Midwest metropolis to San Francisco. Douglas also purchased large amounts of real estate near Duluth, Minnesota, where he expected the eastern terminus of a Northern rail route would be located.

Unfortunately for Douglas, others did not share his national vision (or own as much real estate). Southern legislators continued to block organization of the Nebraska Territory in part to give the proposed Southern transcontinental route that would originate in New Orleans a head start over the competing Central and Northern routes. Railroads were supposed to unite the country, East and West, but instead created division between North and South. If Douglas wanted to organize the territory and move forward on a transcontinental railroad, he would need to find some means to win over Southern support.

Douglas had already tried several possible compromises regarding slavery in the territories, but North and South were becoming increasingly radicalized on the issue. Southern writers no longer simply defended slavery as a necessary evil; Southern radicals now advocated slavery as a positive good and the basis of a better society than that supposedly suffered by the "wage slaves" of the North. Feeling besieged and isolated, the Southern elite wanted more and more guarantees of their minority rights as slaveholders, including the guarantee to take their slaves into any new territory—and perhaps any state.

Northerners, meanwhile, chafed at the South's demands for new concessions, and the initially small abolition movement had grown, fueled in part by the publication in 1851 of *Uncle Tom's Cabin,* Harriet Beecher Stowe's relatively sanitized but spectacularly best-selling depiction of the horrors of slavery. Where compromise had been possible in 1850, Douglas found conciliation less appreciated in a time of much greater political polarization.

Douglas believed he could circumvent this impasse by taking the slavery debate out of Congress, where the issue was paralyzing action on a host of issues important to the nation's development, and giving it to the people to decide. This was the doctrine of "popular sovereignty," which simply meant that the residents of each territory would vote and determine for themselves whether the territory should be free or slave. Douglas had not originated the concept (it had been first advocated by Lewis Cass in his 1848 presidential campaign), but Douglas became its most passionate exponent and he had the hubris to think it would solve the slavery question once and for all.

As Douglas saw it, popular sovereignty not only rested on the bedrock American principle of democratic self-rule, but it also met each region's needs. He thought it would appeal to what was then called the West (what we would now call the Midwest) because most of the emigrants to the Nebraska Territory would come from that region and desire as much local autonomy as possible. Douglas thought (incorrectly) that popular sovereignty met the South's needs because it treated those favoring slavery as moral equals with the same rights as those who opposed it and because it removed the issue from Congress, where the South's political power was diminishing in relation to free states. Finally, the North should see wisdom in popular sovereignty because it was a practical means of limiting slavery expansion. It was clear to Douglas that the arid lands of the West would not be conducive to growing cotton or the other agricultural staples that were grown and harvested by slaves. So, while the "theoretical right" to extend slavery into the territories would exist, in practice most of the territories would most certainly be free.

When he introduced it in January 1854, Douglas predicted his legislation, which essentially repealed both the Missouri Compromise of 1820 and the Northwest Ordinance of 1787, would "raise a hell of a storm," but he still underestimated the fury it caused. Ignoring his arguments that slavery would be impractical in the West, Northerners believed Douglas had now opened territories previously expected to be free to the possibility of slavery. So numerous were the protests against the measure in the North that Douglas lamented, "I could travel from Boston to Chicago by the light of my own effigy."

The South provided tepid support initially, with a few applauding Douglas for removing "an unjust and odious discrimination against her domestic institutions," but the South soon understood that popular sovereignty would not truly protect the right to own slaves in the territories. The more rapidly increasing population of the North would provide more emigrants to the territories than the South, and they would vote to make the territories free and those territories would later become free states. The slave states would soon be an overwhelmed minority, inviting congressional action to eliminate slavery even in the Southern states. So while many in the North believed Douglas was a pawn of the "slave power," many Southerners concluded that he was a closet abolitionist.

Despite the outcry, the Kansas-Nebraska Act actually passed the Senate, 37-14, and the House by a much smaller 113-100 margin. Southern Whigs had supported the legislation, while Northern Whigs had not. The political effect of it all was an irrevocable split in the Whig Party on the greatest issue of the day. Disaffected Whigs would now join with members of the Free Soil Party and anti-Nebraska Democrats to create the new Republican Party. The Whigs were no longer a viable national political party.

An "old-line Henry Clay Whig" in Illinois named Lincoln said he was "thunderstruck and stunned" when he heard the Senate had approved the Kansas-Nebraska Act. Having served only one undistinguished term in Congress, Lincoln himself said had it not been for the ruckus caused by Douglas's Kansas-Nebraska Act he would likely have been through with politics and would have remained, in the words of one chronicler, "merely a good trial lawyer in Springfield, Illinois, known locally for his droll sense of humor, bad jokes, and slightly nutty wife." Lincoln now ended his four-year absence from politics and began following Douglas around Illinois, trying unsuccessfully to provoke a debate on the merits of Kansas-Nebraska, and also plotting a run for the U.S. Senate against Douglas four years hence, in 1858, when the two would engage in their famous debates.

The period leading up to 1858 was unkind to Douglas and his principles. Democrats who supported Kansas-Nebraska suffered tremendous defeats in the 1854 elections. The situation worsened in 1855 when pro- and anti-slavery emigrants flooded into Kansas. If Douglas had envisioned popular sovereignty entailing peaceful debate and elections, he badly misread the times. Kansas exploded into such an orgy of violence that it became known as "Bleeding Kansas," each side seeking to intimidate the other into forming either a free territory or a slave territory.

Despite these debacles, Douglas remained the dominant figure in the Democratic Party and was a leading candidate for the Democratic presidential nomination in 1856. But the party decided its nominee should be someone untainted by Kansas-Nebraska and so gave its nomination to James Buchanan, whose main qualification was that he had been out of the country as ambassador to Great Britain during the entire controversy. Douglas graciously withdrew in favor of Buchanan, again thinking he was young enough that his time would yet come. In 1857, however, Douglas broke with both Buchanan and the South, which effectively ended his chance to become president.

Kansas caused the rupture. Free-soil settlers outnumbered pro-slavery settlers by a margin of at least two-to-one, but the territory had produced two competing legislatures, one in Topeka advocating free status and another in Lecompton advocating slavery. The pro-slavery legislature in Lecompton organized a constitutional convention that developed a pro-slavery constitution, which they decided to send to Congress and President Buchanan for approval *without* a citizens' referendum.

Buchanan, a self-described "Northern man with Southern principles," was willing to accept the Lecompton constitution for fear that the South would secede if he did not, but Douglas furiously objected to the Lecompton charade. It was, he insisted, a blatant transgression of the principle of popular sovereignty that had been at the heart of the Kansas-Nebraska Act. In a showdown at the White House, Buchanan warned Douglas that he would politically destroy him for his disloyalty to the administration, reminding him of how Jackson had dealt with disloyal senators. Much as vice presidential candidate Lloyd Bentsen advised Dan Quayle during the 1988 campaign that he was "no Jack Kennedy," Douglas testily advised Buchanan, "Mr. President, I wish to remind you that General Jackson is dead, sir." When Kansas settlers were finally allowed to vote on the Lecompton pro-slavery constitution in a fair election in 1858, they defeated it by a five-to-one margin.

For his apostasy, Douglas lost his chairmanship of the Senate Committee on Territories. For good measure, Buchanan also vetoed a Douglas-sponsored bill to provide free homesteads for settlers in the Western territories, legislation that would eventually be approved during the Lincoln administration. Douglas's break with Buchanan shocked North and South alike, and fueled the Republicans' fantasy that Douglas might bolt the Democratic Party.

But Douglas, who began in politics while a lad of fifteen, campaigning for Andrew Jackson in 1828, would never leave the Democratic Party. Northern Democrats praised Douglas for saving their party, for had he backed Lecompton, the Democrats would have been decimated in the North. The South, meanwhile, felt further betrayed by a statesman they had thought of as a sympathetic friend. "Douglas was with us until the time of trial came, then he deceived and betrayed us," said a Georgian in one of the milder rebukes. Others fretted over his "treachery," his "detestable heresies," and (in contrast to the intellectually feeble political invective of today) the "filth of his defiant recreancy."

The furor over Kansas, however, was only the second most important development of 1857 that shoved the nation toward dissolution. In March of that year, the U.S. Supreme Court issued its decision in the Dred Scott case with its infamous dictum, authored by former Jackson crony Chief Justice Roger Taney, that African Americans have "no rights which a white man was bound to respect." Nominally, the case was about whether a slave who lived two years in free territory was no longer a slave, but the court's majority opinion went far beyond answering that question. The court concluded that no black person, slave or free, was a citizen of the United States, and that neither Congress nor any entity designated by Congress, such as a territorial legislature, had the power to keep slaves out of the territories.

The decision seemed to make the whole doctrine of popular sovereignty moot. A discomfited Douglas scrambled to reconcile the Dred Scott decision with the principle on which he had staked his political career. The court decision was the law of the land and must be obeyed, Douglas reasoned, but citizens could still keep slavery out of the territories in which they lived because the right of property in slaves was "worthless . . . unless sustained, protected, and enforced by appropriate police regulations and local legislation." This interpretation, intended to hold Northern and Southern Democrats together, seemed ingenious, but Douglas only further alienated Southerners and convinced them that what was really needed was a federal slave code that would supersede local regulation.

Meanwhile, Republicans, including Lincoln, argued that the Supreme Court seemed but one more decision away from decreeing that no *state* had the power to ban slavery within its borders. In accepting the Republican nomination to run against Douglas for the U.S. Senate in Illinois, Lincoln, quoting the Gospel of St. Matthew, warned that "a house divided against itself cannot stand" and predicted America was reaching a point where it would need to become either all slave or all free to survive as one nation.

Douglas found Lincoln's stance absurd. The founders had designed the federal system to allow different states to adopt different policies that best suited their unique situations, histories, and traditions, and the Court would never interfere with this basic precept. Diversity was a strength not a weakness, Douglas said, and if only the extremists on both sides would shut up, the issue could be resolved amicably.

When Lincoln and Douglas met for their storied series of seven debates in the late summer and fall of 1858, each man insisted the other was the extremist. Lincoln firmly insisted he was no abolitionist and emphasized he did not advocate equality for African Americans (as few Americans of the time, North or South, would have). "I am not nor ever have been in favor of making voters or jurors of negroes, nor of qualifying them to hold office, nor to intermarry with white people," Lincoln said, adding, "I believe there is a physical difference between the white and black races which I believe will forever forbid the two races living together on terms of social and political equality." Conversely, Douglas insisted he was no apologist for slavery, despite Lincoln's summation of popular sovereignty as the belief that "if one man chooses to enslave another, no third man has a right to object."

Posterity has judged that Lincoln won the debates, which is why they are famous. Even though he lost the election, by performing so well against the nation's leading Democrat, Lincoln was now mentioned as a potential presidential candidate. More importantly, Lincoln was on the right side of history in condemning slavery in moral terms. Even though he did not favor full civil equality for blacks, Lincoln believed every human being had the right to be free and reap the benefits of his own labor. His debates with Douglas, Lincoln said, were over "the eternal struggle between these two principles. . . . The one is the common right of humanity and the other the divine right of kings."

Where Lincoln was articulating the rights of the minority in a free society, Douglas focused on democracy's faith in majority rule. "I care more for the great principle of self-government, the right of the people to rule, than I do for all the negroes in Christendom," he said, summarizing why the other great impact of the debates was to cement a very negative image of Douglas in the modern mind.

Douglas so frequently used the word "nigger" that William Seward once taunted, "Douglas, no man will ever be president of the United States who spells 'negro' with two 'g's." Lincoln complained that Douglas was "the most dangerous enemy of liberty, because the most insidious one," and agreed with the runaway slave turned abolitionist Frederick Douglass (whom he would one day host at the White House) that Stephen Douglas's insistence that the Declaration of Independence's creed that "all men are created equal" did not apply to African Americans was "debauching" public opinion and causing people to consider blacks "brutes."

Douglas's race baiting was unseemly and disturbing, but his views on race and slavery were more complicated than he let on publicly. During the furor over the Kansas-Nebraska Act, in a private conversation recorded by the son of a friend, Douglas insisted, "I am not pro-slavery. I think it a curse beyond computation to both white and black." He added that he both believed and hoped that "sometime, without a doubt, slavery will be destroyed." In a Senate speech, Douglas noted, "The cause of freedom has steadily and firmly advanced, while slavery has receded in the same ratio." There could no longer be, contrary to Southern demands, a perfect balance between free and slave states. Further, Douglas said he hoped the states of the Upper South—Virginia, North Carolina, Tennessee—and border states where slavery was not essential to the economy would soon adopt a policy of gradual emancipation.

Douglas professed to have no special animus toward African Americans. In a statement he issued in response to the Dred Scott decision, he said the supposed inferior racial status of African Americans did not require that they should be enslaved. While blacks might not be entitled to rights, Douglas said, they could be granted "privileges." "Humanity [and] . . . Christianity requires that we should extend those privileges to them"—provided, Douglas said, that these privileges were granted by the approval of a majority of the voting population and were "consistent with the safety of society."

Douglas's squeamishness regarding slavery, or perhaps only his concern for political appearances, was demonstrated by his refusal of a twenty-five-hundred-acre Mississippi plantation with more than one hundred slaves as a wedding gift in 1847, offered by the father of his first wife, a North Carolina woman named Martha Martin. When Martha's father died a year later, he left the plantation to his daughter in his will, naming Douglas as the plantation's administrator, earning a 20 percent commission per year. Douglas retained ownership of the plantation after Martha died during childbirth in 1853.

Like Henry Clay, Douglas believed nothing could be done to outlaw slavery legislatively because the Constitution explicitly protected slavery where it already existed. "I am not willing to violate the Constitution to put an end to slavery . . . to violate it for one purpose will lead to violating it for other purposes," Douglas said, sounding an early note of constitutional originalism. Douglas felt self-pity that others could not see the wisdom of his practical approach to the issue, confiding to the son of a friend:

> *Never go into politics! If you do, no matter how sincere and earnest you may be, . . . no matter how clear it may be to you that the present is an inheritance from the past, that your hands are tied, and that you are bound to do only what you can do with loyalty to institutions fixed for you by the past, rather than what you might prefer to do if free to choose; no matter for all this or more you will be misinterpreted, vilified, traduced, and finally sacrificed to some local interest or unreasoning passion!*

For Lincoln, Douglas's position was more easily explained by the fact that he "has no very vivid impression that the Negro is human; and consequently has no idea that there can be any moral question in legislating about him." Douglas acknowledged this was true. "I do not know of any tribunal on earth that can decide the question of the morality of slavery or any other institution. I deal with slavery as a political question involving questions of public policy."

Douglas was a pragmatist to the core who, like Clay, always favored compromise and understood that once an issue was defined in moral terms, compromise was nearly impossible. He hated to mix religion with politics. "No man loves his country better than I do. I know she is not faultless. I see as clearly as they that she is afflicted with a dangerous tumor. But I believe she will slough it off in time, and I am not willing to risk the life of the patient by the illegal and unscientific surgery they demand." Douglas despaired at what civil war would mean to American democracy and what a loss a debilitated American democracy would be to the world.

Lincoln's election as the first Republican president in 1860 is often seen as the final event that triggered secession, but secession was likely inevitable from the time Douglas won the Democratic nomination for president in 1860. With the Fire-Eaters' determination to destroy the Democratic Party, several Southern delegations, including Alabama, Mississippi, and Texas, had instructions to walk out of the Democratic National Convention if Douglas's nomination could not be stopped, which it nearly was, for the event was held in Charleston, South Carolina, the center of secessionist sentiment.

Douglas had delusions that the party might unite around his popular sovereignty platform, but a platform fight broke out over whether to accede to the South's demand for a federal slave code. Egged on by the Fire-Eaters, eight Southern state delegations walked out. Convention rules required that Douglas secure support from two-thirds of all credentialed delegates to win the nomination, but with so many delegates now absent Douglas could not reach the required threshold. His supporters moved the convention be adjourned and reconvened in Baltimore six weeks later.

Things were such a mess that Douglas offered to withdraw in favor of a compromise candidate, but his supporters refused even to let the offer be made public. It was "Douglas or nobody," one supporter said. "Unless he is nominated, our party is gone for all time to come." Secessionists bolted the Baltimore convention, too, but this time Douglas had arranged for enough alternate delegations that he had the votes to be nominated.

Douglas's nomination paved the way for Lincoln's by the Republicans, who concluded that the election would be won or lost in the West and that Lincoln, as a fellow Westerner, could counter Douglas's extraordinary popularity in the region. Once again, Lincoln's success depended upon being matched against Douglas. Had the Democrats nominated a Southerner, the Republicans might have been free to nominate a Northerner with more radical views, such as William H. Seward or Salmon Chase.

To complicate the electoral equation, there were two other significant presidential candidates in the race. The secessionists had met at a rump convention and nominated Buchanan's vice president, John Breckenridge, under the banner of the National Democratic Party, which existed solely in the South. Meanwhile, Tennessee senator John Bell was nominated to lead the Constitutional Union Party, which primarily consisted of the few remaining members of the conservative wing of the defunct Whig Party. Breckenridge's hope was to get enough votes to throw the election into the House of Representatives where a Southern compromise candidate might arise, but such was Douglas's anger at the secessionists that he was quoted as saying he would throw the election to Lincoln before he would let it be decided in the House.

Douglas had no need to throw the election because it was soon evident that Lincoln would be the next president. Douglas's first goal was to save the Democratic Party by driving from the party those advocating disunion and denying the Breckenridge organization any claim to legitimacy. "Secession from the Democratic Party means secession from the federal Union," Douglas said. "He may not be elected," one supporter said of Douglas, "but he will defeat the Vandals."

Douglas hoped that if pro-Union Southerners rallied to his cause, he could keep the Democratic Party together as a viable national institution and play an invaluable role in holding the Union together. Douglas's running mate, former Georgia governor Herschel Johnson, said the goal was to preserve at least a fragment of the Democratic Party, using a word that would soon have a different meaning in the South, "for reconstruction, at a future day."

Breaking precedent—and criticized for doing so—Douglas decided to campaign personally for the presidency. Douglas mystified observers by traveling even to states he had no hope of winning, such as Rhode Island, though a reporter there surmised his real purpose was not to win votes but "to crush out utterly and forever [Breckenridge's] Disunion Party, if it is in his power to do so." After his tour of New England, Douglas went south where he astonished the Northern press and angered Southerners with his bold pronouncements in opposition to secession. This, historian Allen Nevins proclaimed, was Douglas's "finest hour."

In Norfolk, Virginia, Douglas said, "I desire no man to vote for me, unless he hopes and desires to see the Union maintained and preserved intact." He insisted Lincoln's election alone would not justify secession, and said if the South proceeded to break up the Union, he would endorse the use of force that Jackson had threatened against the nullifiers in 1832. In Petersburg, which would soon be the site of some of the most horrendous fighting of the Civil War, Douglas said, "There is no evil, and can be none, for which disunion is a legitimate remedy. . . . The last hope of freedom in the old world is now centered in the success of the American Republic." In Raleigh, North Carolina, he added, "The only mistake we Democrats made was in tolerating disunionist sentiments in our bosom so long." Southern papers warned he might be hanged if he spoke such sentiments farther south, and Jefferson Davis, soon to be president of the Confederacy, suggested that two gallows be built, one for Lincoln and one for Douglas, so that they could take into account the difference in the two men's heights.

Republicans, meanwhile, scoffed at Southern threats to secede, believing it was another bluff. Douglas knew better, and even though the intensity of his campaigning was destroying his health, he persevered. In three-and-a-half months, he campaigned in twenty-three states, a frantic pace even by today's standards, let alone using mid-nineteenth-century modes of transportation. His voice had been reduced to a "spasmodic bark," which he kept up by ferociously sucking on lemons all day, and he could now walk only with the aid of a crutch. Still, he pressed on, saying, "Mr. Lincoln is the next president. We must try to save the Union. I will go South."

Defying death threats and rotted fruit and eggs occasionally hurled in his direction, Douglas went deep into Dixie, to Georgia and Alabama, reiterating that the Constitution did not allow secession and calling on all loyal Southerners to thwart the plan of radical leaders for disunion. He drew huge crowds that gave him hope his tour was not in vain. "Well, if Lincoln is elected *perhaps* we can stand it for four years," a planter remarked after hearing Douglas's plea. Alexander Stephens, who would serve as vice president in the Confederacy, stated that Douglas was the only hope to save the Union, and an Augusta newspaper proclaimed, "He is certainly the greatest intellect of the western world."

But it turned out to be an illusion. Sectional pride and secession fever swept the South. Douglas was disappointed by his poor showing in the South, mystified at how his standing had tumbled in just four short years, not understanding how Dred Scott, Uncle Tom, and John Brown's foiled attempt to arm a slave insurrection had so altered public opinion in all sections. Eighty-eight percent of the popular vote he received came from the North; just 12 percent came from slave states, and most of those came from border states. Missouri was the only state he carried outright. "With your defeat," a friendly newspaper editor in Mobile told Douglas the day after the election, "the cause of the Union was lost."

But Douglas refused to accept that maintaining the Union was a lost cause. Believing his campaign might have opened a crack in the door, Douglas immediately began to search for some compromise that might yet avert civil war. Douglas begged Southern members of Congress to return to Washington, and all but South Carolina complied. "The whole country is looking to you," wrote a North Carolinian. But Douglas found few allies. Buchanan agreed the South had no right to secede, but argued that the federal government had no power to prevent it. President-elect Lincoln, meanwhile, had decided the time for compromise was past. "The tug has to come and better now than later," he said.

Douglas himself was ambivalent about compromise. He denied the South had legitimate grievances, noting the 1850 fugitive slave act, for example, was enforced as well as any other law. At one point he exclaimed, "Better a million men should fall on the battle field than that this government should lose one single state!" Yet, he understood the horrors of a civil war, so after South Carolina officially seceded on December 20, 1860, Douglas worked with Senator Crittenden to draft a set of constitutional amendments that might appease the South, including a particularly odious pair from Douglas himself that prohibited even free blacks from voting and another that would fund a freed-slave colonization scheme. The efforts at compromise came to nothing, even though Congress debated the issues until just hours before Lincoln's inaugural on March 4.

During Lincoln's inauguration, Douglas positioned himself on the platform as close to Lincoln as possible to visually demonstrate his support of the new administration. Contemporary news accounts claimed Douglas even held Lincoln's hat as the new president delivered his inaugural address. While Lincoln succinctly articulated the basic source of division—"One section of our country believes slavery is right, and ought to be extended, while the other believes it is wrong, and ought not to be extended"—he sought to reassure the South that Republicans had no intention of interfering with slavery in states where it existed and that the administration would faithfully enforce the fugitive slave law. Lincoln promised to seek peaceful means to break the impasse, including a possible constitutional convention that had been pushed by Douglas and Seward. He also foreswore the use of force for any reason beyond the enforcement of existing federal laws, such as the collection of tariffs and import duties, even as he dismissed the idea that any state had a lawful right to secede from the Union.

During the speech, Douglas audibly murmured his approval of the tone and specifics of the address, saying "good," "that's so," "good again," and "no coercion." When Lincoln was finished, Douglas was one of the first to warmly congratulate him and told a reporter standing nearby that Lincoln was "all right." Later that night, Douglas danced with Mrs. Lincoln at the inaugural ball. It all led the *New York Times* to ask the next day, "What means this evident weakness of Mr. Douglas for Mr. Lincoln?"

The answer to that question was that Douglas wanted to reinforce Lincoln's inclination toward peaceful resolution of the conflict, and he hoped to have influence with his old acquaintance in order to assure the South that his assessment of Lincoln's peaceful intentions was correct. When Democratic congressmen attacked Lincoln's address as provocative, the first to defend the new president in the Senate was not a Republican, but Douglas, who proclaimed Lincoln's speech "a peace offering rather than a war message." When asked if he was speaking for Lincoln, Douglas avowed that he wanted it understood he was not an apologist for the administration, "but on this one question, that of preserving the Union by a peaceful solution of our present difficulties . . . if I understand his true intent and meaning, I am with him."

The South, however, had interpreted Lincoln's remarks differently and was certain the president intended to use coercion to keep the Union together. Douglas received no help from the Republicans, who preferred to remain mute on the administration's intentions, despite Douglas's provocations. "Silence is criminal when we are on the eve of events like these!" Douglas exclaimed on the floor of the Senate a week after Lincoln's inaugural.

Meanwhile, Douglas was trying to hold the Democratic Party together and to provide direction on how Democrats should behave during the growing crisis. Prominent Democrats were wary of supporting Lincoln for fear of appearing Republican sympathizers. Democrats convening in Illinois reported considerable sympathy for secession among its members. Some thought Douglas should lead an effort to fuse with conservative Republicans and John Bell supporters to form a new party, even scrapping the Democratic name. Others simply believed the North should let the South go in peace. Douglas ally and Illinois congressman John A. McClernand spoke for his friend when he said, "If we become entangled with disunionism we will be lost as a party."

Douglas refused to consider party fusion or any action that might end the Democratic Party as he knew it. When a supporter asked Douglas what Democrats should do, Douglas replied simply, "We must fight for our country and forget all differences." On April 12, 1861, Confederates began bombarding Fort Sumter outside Charleston, the first shots of the war, and on April 14 the beleaguered garrison there surrendered. Douglas was entreated by his wife, Adele, and others to visit Lincoln to see how he could be of assistance. For two hours, the friendly adversaries went over strategy. Douglas described the meeting to the press as "a cordial feeling of a united, friendly and patriotic purpose." In a later statement, Douglas said he was "prepared to sustain the president in the exercise of all his constitutional functions to preserve the Union." To a friend, Douglas said, "I've known Mr. Lincoln a longer time than you have, or than the country has; he'll come out right, and we will stand by him."

There was now considerable public demand, especially given Lincoln's inexperience in government and as an administrator, that he rely heavily on Douglas's counsel. Douglas, however, decided it was time to leave Washington, unless Lincoln urged him to stay (which he did not), and travel to Illinois to stem secession sympathy there. Douglas believed that if he was to build the Democratic Party into a strong but loyal opposition party, the key would be party elements in the Northwest. Traveling through Harper's Ferry, Douglas's train was stopped and searched by Virginia militia, who recognized him and spoke of detaining him. Douglas warned that if they did, a large force would be sent to rescue him, and he was let pass.

Having missed a train connection in Wheeling because of the delay, Douglas stopped in the Ohio town of Bellaire, where he expressed pleasure at addressing a large crowd consisting of Americans from both sides of the Ohio River, Ohioans and Virginians, each cheering the American flag, "the emblem of peace and union, and of constitutional liberty."

Reminding those assembled that free and open commerce throughout the Ohio River Valley and into the Mississippi was essential to the life-blood of the region, Douglas denounced this "new system of resistance by the sword and bayonet to the results of the ballot box." The issue was no longer slavery, but the survival of the nation.

Arriving in Springfield on April 25, Douglas conferred with Democratic and Republican leaders alike, urging that they work in concert and harmony for the benefit of the nation. In an emotional address to the Illinois Legislature that brought many men to tears, Douglas said, "For the first time since the adoption of the Federal Constitution, a wide-spread conspiracy exists to destroy the best government the sun of heaven ever shed its rays upon."

He had a special message for Democrats: Their party would one day rise again and govern, but in the meantime, "Give me a country first, that my children may live in peace, then we will have a theatre for our party organizations to operate upon." The quickest way to peace, Douglas said, was "the most stupendous and unanimous preparation for war. The greater the unanimity, the less blood will be shed."

After his speech, Douglas reported back to Lincoln that he had made progress in tamping down sentiment favorable to secession: "There will be no outbreak, however, and in a few days I hope for entire unanimity in the support of the government and the Union." Now, Douglas wanted rest and recuperation. He was ill from his marathon of campaigning and all the activity since. Depressed by the breakup of the Union, he had other burdens, too. An infant daughter had recently died, and the cost of his campaigns, for the Senate in 1858 and for the presidency in 1860, had left him heavily in debt.

On May 1, while addressing a large crowd in Chicago, Douglas complained of not feeling well. By May 10, he could not use his arms because of a severe attack of what was diagnosed as inflammatory rheumatism. He also had an ulcerated sore throat and "torpor of the liver." He became delirious as his condition worsened. When Adele asked if he had any last words for his sons, Douglas allegedly replied, "Tell them to obey the laws and support the Constitution of the United States." He died on June 3 at age forty-eight, shocking the nation.

When Lincoln learned of Douglas's death, he ordered the White House and other government buildings draped in black crepe. Secretary of War Simon Cameron, as ardent a Republican as there was in the administration, ordered all military units to observe a period of mourning, and issued a circular that praised Douglas as "a great statesman . . . who nobly discarded party for his country." His second wife, Adele, wanted Douglas buried in Washington near their infant daughter, but the leading citizens of Illinois persuaded her to let him stay in Illinois. He was interred on a rise overlooking Lake Michigan, on a spot where he had hoped to build his and Adele's final home.

Shortly after Douglas's death, plans were made to construct a memorial over his gravesite. The sculptor Leonard Volk, one of several young artists to whom Douglas had been a patron, created a forty-six-foot column of white marble from Douglas's native Vermont topped by a lifelike statue of "The Little Giant." But Douglas's real monument is the living, breathing Democratic Party. It survived the war when it might have gone the way of the Whigs.

As Douglas had hoped and predicted, the Democrats emerged from the Civil War a competitive national party. In 1868, even as Republicans ran for president the most popular military hero from the war, General Ulysses S. Grant, the Democratic candidate, Horatio Seymour, was still able to poll 47 percent of the popular vote and carry eight states located in the North, South, and West—even as large numbers of Southern whites remained disenfranchised. Six years later, in 1874, the Democrats regained control of Congress for the first time in twenty years.

Douglas never became president, but saving the Democratic Party, which remains the longest, continually functioning political party in the world, was, a friend wrote, "glory enough for one man." Once the party of white supremacy, it is the party that elected America's first African-American president. Such an occurrence would have shocked Douglas's sensibilities, had he been alive to see it, but he would have been pleased that it was at least a Democrat who broke such a long-standing taboo.

Chapter Four

WILLIAM JENNINGS BRYAN

1896, 1900, 1908

The poor man is called a socialist if he believes that the wealth of the rich should be divided among the poor, but the rich man is called a financier if he devises a plan by which the pittance of the poor can be converted to his use.

William Jennings Bryan believed that the evangelical Christian concept of a person's being "born again" could and should apply as readily to politics as to religion. If one person could have a radical conversion experience, Bryan said, then "it can be true of any number. Thus, a nation can be born in a day if the ideals of the people can be changed." Under Bryan's influence, the Democratic Party was born again in a single presidential election—the 1896 election he lost to William McKinley—and became a progressive party after a century of conservatism. Fittingly for a man who doubted evolution, it was a sudden act of creation.

Bryan took a weary and discredited party that favored the laissez-faire policies of limited government and immersed it in a font of populist reform principles. He convinced millions of voters that their Christian duty required them to vote for a candidate who would expand the power of government and use that power to aggressively help those in need. Democrats emerged from this baptism of 1896 energized and reborn, clothed anew in the liberal and progressive ideals that the party continued to wear into the twenty-first century. Woodrow Wilson, Al Smith, and Franklin Roosevelt would each build upon this tradition, but the transformation began with Bryan.

Even though the sum of his experience in elected office was two terms as a junior congressman from Nebraska in the early 1890s, Bryan was the Democratic Party nominee for president three times. He lost each election by an increasingly larger margin. But it was that first campaign in 1896, when he came so close to winning despite having the entire power structure of the country against him, which still has the ability to thrill. His campaign was "an excitement that was almost too intense for life," said a reporter who covered it. It was so vital a contest that it inspired poetry, such as this verse by Vachel Lindsay:

> I brag and chant of Bryan, Bryan, Bryan
> Candidate for president who sketched a silver Zion,
> The only American Poet who could sing outdoors,
> He brought in tides of wonder, of unprecedented splendor,
> Wild roses from the plains, that made hearts tender . . .

"You are a prophet sent by God," one admirer from Kentucky wrote Bryan during the campaign.

The great issue that inspired such idolatry was the otherwise stolid campaign topic of currency reform, yet the 1896 Bryan presidential run so took on the character of a revival that it seemed impossible to discuss it in anything other than religious language and imagery. Josephus Daniels, the North Carolina editor who would later serve with Bryan in Woodrow Wilson's Cabinet, said Bryan had "rolled away the stone from the golden sepulcher in which democracy was buried." Bryan was described as a new Moses, a St. Paul, or a young David out to battle the Goliaths of big business, Wall Street, and the Republican Party.

This time, Goliath won. So committed were these powerful interests to Bryan's defeat that they expended campaign funds in amounts that would not be equaled for a century—well in excess of one hundred million in today's dollars.

Before Bryan, the Democrats had been the party of small government conservatism, which the party's patron saints, Thomas Jefferson and Andrew Jackson, argued was necessary to protect the people. For Jefferson and Jackson, a powerful government would only serve the interests of the well connected. Better to limit what government can do then risk having government side with the powerful. This was the philosophy embraced by the only Democrat to serve as president between 1860 and 1912, Grover Cleveland, who while in the White House in 1896, was still presiding over the lingering effects of the "Panic of 1893," with one in six workers still unemployed. "Though the people support the government, the government should not support the people," said Cleveland.

Rejecting the policies of his party's sitting president, Bryan had a much different creed: "The power of the government to protect the people is as complete in a time of peace as in time of war." Government was not a weapon, but a tool. More than eighty years before Ronald Reagan would be accused of advocating "trickle down economics," Bryan criticized "those who believe that, if you will only legislate to make the well-to-do prosperous, their prosperity will leak through on those below. The Democratic idea, however, has been that if you legislate to make the masses prosperous, their prosperity will find its way up through every class which rests upon them."

During his more than thirty years in public life, Bryan was instrumental in the passage of a host of progressive reforms. The breadth of the list is extraordinary. Four major reforms—a progressive federal income tax, women's suffrage, Prohibition, and the direct election of senators—required constitutional amendment. Bryan's support and advocacy was critical to the adoption of each, causing one biographer to suggest that Bryan is personally responsible for more constitutional amendments than any person but James Madison. Bryan's influence is particularly extraordinary given that, except for his four years in Congress, the only other public office he held in his life was two years as Wilson's secretary of state. His influence came not from any office but from the roughly fifteen years he spent as titular head of the Democratic Party and the large popular following he enjoyed until his death in 1925.

Despite this lack of official portfolio, other reforms advocated by Bryan—utility and financial regulation, pure food and drug laws, the eight-hour workday, disclosure of campaign contributions, and the citizens' initiative and referendum process—became law during his lifetime. Even more, such as bank deposit insurance, subsidized crop prices, federal protection for the right of labor to organize and strike, and old age pensions would be implemented later under the New Deal, which Herbert Hoover called, "Bryanism under new words and methods." A few Bryan initiatives are still on the progressive agenda, including publicly financed elections and a guaranteed living wage.

Bryan did not justify the need for these reforms based on social science, but on a religious imperative. For Bryan, all "great political questions are in their final analyses great moral questions." The law, Bryan said, "is but the crystallization of conscience; moral sentiment must be created before it can express itself in the form of a statute." Religion was the basis of moral sentiment, Bryan believed, therefore religion is "not only the most practical thing in the world, but the first essential."

Because religion had practical value in restructuring society, Bryan deplored ministers who thought the only function of the church was personal salvation. In his Bible classes, Chautauqua sermons, and religious articles, Bryan liked to point out that only one-fifth of the Gospel is devoted to the discussion of salvation and the afterlife; the other four-fifths provide instruction in how human beings are to interact with and treat one another. "Christ went about doing good," said Bryan, and he believed it was the duty of every Christian to do the same.

Individual charity was not enough. A Christian's duty, Bryan believed, was also to work politically for a more just and compassionate society with the goal of creating, as near as practicable, a heaven on earth. "I have no patience with those who feel they are too good to take part in politics," Bryan said. "When I find a person who thinks he is too good to take part in politics, I find one who is not quite good enough to deserve the blessings of a free government."

Bryan did not concern himself with the morality of citizens in their private lives. There is no record of him criticizing anyone's personal foibles or infidelities, even those of his political enemies. He cared about *public* morality. The wealthy individuals who believed a few charitable contributions could make up for the unjust methods they used to earn their fortunes disgusted him. A special target of his ire was the founder of Standard Oil, John D. Rockefeller, who had become the richest man in America through ruthless business practices. Rockefeller was a great philanthropist, and he, too, liked to teach Bible school, which only caused Bryan to snort, "Many people will wonder how Rockefeller summons the courage to preach so much religion while he practices so much sin."

Such sentiments made Bryan as much preacher as politician, although despite his many speeches and writings on religion, he was never ordained. And while he was a Presbyterian, he transcended denominations. He was a broad ecumenical spiritual leader for Protestant Middle America in his time, much as the Reverend Billy Graham would be a half-century later. Bryan admitted that even though he enjoyed making political speeches, "I would rather speak on religion than on politics." With Bryan, however, the line between the two was indistinguishable. "When you hear a good democratic speech it is so much like a sermon that you can hardly tell the difference between them," he said.

Despite the caricature he became in popular culture following his death, Bryan was not, in the strictest sense, a Fundamentalist, the conservative vein of Protestantism that arose in the late nineteenth century in response to historical criticism of the Bible. Bryan shared some of the Fundamentalists' concerns, toward evolution and how other forms of modernity seemed to challenge and undermine the Christian faith, but he did not share their belief in the Bible as a literal historical record. During the Scopes Trial, for example, he acknowledged that the creation story in Genesis could refer to six eons of time, not six twenty-four-hour days. He also did not believe, as many of the Fundamentalists of the time did, that Christians should separate themselves from society; rather, he wanted to bring more of society under "the Christian spirit." Also unlike the Fundamentalists, Bryan was not pessimistic about humanity's ability to change society. Many leading Fundamentalists were pessimistic about Bryan, admitting to never voting for him.

Though he might have blanched at the adjective, Bryan was a liberal Christian. He would have preferred being tied to the Social Gospel movement, which he called "applied Christianity" and which sought to apply Christian ethics and values to the worst problems of society. The literal truth of the Bible concerned him less than his belief in the fundamental truth that "'Thou shalt love thy neighbor as thyself,' if fully lived up to, would solve every problem; economic, social, political and religious." His enemies could rightly accuse him of self-righteousness, but all acknowledged his sincerity. Even President William Howard Taft, who foiled Bryan's third try for the presidency in 1908, acknowledged that he was "the least of a liar I know in public life."

Bryan's total devotion to the truth (as he understood it) would sorely damage his progressive legacy. His final crusade would be a widely misunderstood (and mischaracterized) campaign against the teaching of evolution as fact in the public schools. His performance during the Scopes Trial led critics to portray him as naïve, simple-minded, and, most cruelly of all, bigoted. In truth, he was broadly ecumenical, speaking before all denominations (although the Unitarians' denial of Christ's divinity bothered him a great deal). Neither anti-Catholic nor anti-Semitic, Bryan actively courted Catholics and regularly spoke in synagogues. He studied the other religions of the world outside Christianity but found Islam appalling in its treatment of women and concluded during a world tour he made in 1905 and 1906 that Hinduism was guilty of idolatry. Bryan, as will be discussed shortly, saw his crusade against evolution as not only fully compatible with, but crucial to the cause of progressive reform.

Bryan had first demonstrated an independence of thought on religion and a willingness to buck convention when he was a youth. Born in Salem, Illinois, on March 19, 1860, to a Baptist father who had been a Democratic judge and state senator and a Methodist mother, Bryan the boy became a Presbyterian after having a personal "born again" experience at a revival at age thirteen. He later attended little Illinois College, where courses in biology and geology led him to question whether certain stories in the Bible, such as the creation story, should be taken literally or allegorically. He wrote the famed agnostic lecturer Robert Ingersoll for advice but only got a form letter in return. This seems to have been his only serious crisis of faith.

Bryan was a straight arrow even then, but not suffering from sanctimony. "For some reason Bryan's goodness was not the kind that rubbed against you and turned the fur the wrong way," a classmate recalled. Bryan studied at the Union Law College in Chicago, but he did not like the big city and so missed some opportunities to better acquaint himself with the problems of urban workers and families. Worried that rural Illinois was too Republican to elect many Democrats, Bryan concluded that the opportunity for a political career was in Nebraska, and so he moved there in 1887, immediately diving into local Democratic politics.

He served two terms representing Nebraska in Congress and lost a bid for the U.S. Senate. This was the sum of his political experience, and although he was only thirty-six years old in 1896, he was as certain that he would be nominated for president at the Democratic National Convention in Chicago as he was of the divinity of Christ. Despite his short tenure in Congress, he had become known in much of the country as an exceptional orator. He was also a brilliant tactician and blessed with keen political instincts. But more than anything, he had empathy. He could feel the pain and the near frantic desire for relief that existed in the many parts of the nation that had been in economic crisis for most of the previous twenty years.

Beginning in 1873, the year the United States officially went on the gold standard, farmers in the South and Midwest suffered from a seemingly never-ending period of deflation. Year after year, American farmers saw prices continue to go down. Corn that had sold for 83 cents a bushel in 1881 sold for 28 cents a bushel in 1890. A farmer who could have paid a debt with one thousand bushels of wheat in 1865 needed three thousand bushels to repay the same sized debt thirty years later. Tens of thousands of farmers went broke and lost their farms.

Credit that might have helped some farmers weather the hard times was almost impossible to find, and when it was available, the interest rates were exorbitant. Rates of 18 to 24 percent were typical, and in the

South interest rates in excess of 40 percent were not uncommon. There was simply no money available that could circulate and stimulate the economy. All the currency in circulation in the state of Arkansas, for example, came out to just thirteen cents per resident! By 1893, the nation was facing the greatest economic depression in its 117-year history.

Out of this anguish, the People's Party, better known as the "Populists," was born. While some Populist leaders were colorful characters, urging farmers to raise more hell than corn, they were not unsophisticated rubes. They understood that there were causes for their problems beyond whatever constraints the gold standard placed on the money supply, and they proposed a wide range of reforms to deal with the crisis, including state regulation of railroads, utilities, and grain elevators. Farmers even engaged in collective action, similar to their urban brethren who formed labor unions, by creating the Grange movement, which allowed them to try to coordinate and control production, storage, transportation, and ultimately prices.

But central to the Populist platform was expanding the money supply. The Populists proposed that silver be coined as well as gold at a ratio of sixteen-to-one. The coinage of silver would increase the supply of money, but by coining it rather than using it to back the issuance of more paper money, the Populists hoped to avoid creating the inflation experienced during the Civil War. Scholars then and since have derided the free coinage of silver issue as a simplistic response to a complicated financial crisis, but the renowned economist John Maynard Keynes later wrote that the Populists were not wrong to believe currency reform was part of the answer to the nation's problems and that the United States' stubbornness in remaining on the gold standard until 1933 severely limited the government's ability to deal with the Great Depression.

Bryan, then and now, was also ridiculed for adopting the free silver issue as his own. When first asked about free silver as a young congressman in 1891, he famously admitted that he was not entirely certain why the minting of silver made sense. All he really needed to know, Bryan said, was that his Nebraska constituents favored free silver: "I will look up the arguments later." He did and two years later gave a three-hour speech, without notes, before the House in which he offered a sophisticated explanation of monetary policy, full of facts and details, and which included, in addition to free silver, such ideas as the creation of a federal reserve system for banking, a managed currency, and federal insurance for bank deposits. Despite this and other displays of intellect, Bryan was repeatedly tagged as someone who just gave pretty speeches, and histories of the election of 1896 almost always focus solely on the silver issue.

Seldom explained is that Bryan's strategy was to use the silver issue to advance a broader agenda. Silver was the issue that resonated with the crowds who came to hear him speak and Bryan was a politician who needed votes; if advocating silver monetization provided an audience to educate on other reforms, so be it. Bryan had toured the country throughout 1895 and early 1896, speaking before groups large and small, and meeting party leaders and potential national convention delegates. By the time the Democrats gathered for their national convention in Chicago in July 1896, Bryan reckoned he had personally met with more convention delegates than any other potential candidate, which enhanced his confidence that, if given the right opportunity, he would win over the convention and his party's nomination.

The opportunity came when Bryan cleverly arranged to be the final speaker in the debate over a free silver plank at the convention. A supporter scribbled a note of encouragement to Bryan, saying, "This is a great opportunity." Bryan, fully aware of his gifts as an orator, wrote a short note back. "You will not be disappointed."

The young Bryan, slender but broad-shouldered, moved with the grace of an athlete, bounding up the stairs, two at a time, to reach the rostrum. His physical energy further galvanized the crowd's attention. He began quietly but was still easy to hear even in the farthest reaches of the massive Chicago Coliseum. Bryan had a mesmerizing baritone voice that could be heard clearly without amplification from a distance of three city blocks. In the days before microphones and loudspeakers, it gave him an extraordinary advantage over other speakers.

Bryan had another advantage; he was a talented writer who wrote all of his own speeches, every word. He had tried and refined large portions of the speech in other places, and he knew the reaction each line would generate. Knowing that the audience was with him from his opening words, Bryan would later write that he could actually see the crowd react "like a trained choir," responding "instantaneously and in unison . . . to each point made."

The address featured many memorable points. Scoffing at those who insisted protecting business meant protecting the rich, Bryan said, "The man who is employed for wages is as much a business man as his employer," and deserved the same considerations. He ridiculed those who seemed to believe the problems of the farmer were less important than those of the industrialist. You could burn down the cities, but as long as people had something to eat, the cities would rise again "as if by magic; but destroy our farms and the grass will grow in the streets of every city in the country."

The crowd roared its approval again and again as Bryan built up to his peroration and the most electrifying moment in the history of American presidential conventions.

"You shall not press down upon the brow of labor this crown of thorns," Bryan thundered in conclusion, first bringing his hands to his temples, "you shall not crucify mankind upon a cross of gold!" He then extended his arms wide in the near sacrilegious pose of a man crucified upon a cross—a pose he held for a full five seconds—while the convention sat in stunned silence before erupting into pandemonium with delegates deliriously shouting, crying, and stomping their feet for a full forty minutes, twice as long as Bryan had spoken.

The reaction was akin to religious ecstasy. "Everyone seemed to go mad at once," the *New York World* reported. A delegate who had come into the convention an avowed opponent of Bryan and the free silver movement pulled a still unconvinced companion out of his seat and screamed, "Yell, for God's sake, yell!" The next day, on the fifth ballot, the convention nominated Bryan as its presidential candidate, the youngest person, at age thirty-six, ever nominated by a major party. Later, the People's Party decided to make Bryan their nominee as well. Adopting the Democratic nominee as their own ended the Populists as a serious third party challenge to the established order, but they had found a worthy champion in Bryan.

Thus began one of the most class-conscious and overtly religious campaigns in American history. "The poor man is called a socialist if he believes that the wealth of the rich should be divided among the poor," Bryan said, "but the rich man is called a financier if he devises a plan by which the pittance of the poor can be converted to his use." The journalist William Allen White, writing from the heartland of Kansas, said, "It was the first time in my life and in the life of a generation in which any man large enough to lead a national party had boldly and unashamedly made his cause that of the poor and the oppressed."

Religious imagery abounded. Bryan supporters proclaimed his campaign led the nation to witness "a new Pentecost" and a "new baptism of fire." Others were scandalized. Bryan was accused of sacrilege, with one cartoon proclaiming, "No man who drags into the dust the most sacred symbols of the Christian world is fit to be president of the United States." Others stood amazed, either appalled or inspired, that anyone would try to apply the Golden Rule to practical politics. Even the influential twentieth-century historian Richard Hofstadter, who was no fan of Bryan or the Populist movement, acknowledged that Bryan "swept away much of the cynicism and apathy that had been characteristic of American politics" for the previous thirty years.

There was no apathy on Wall Street. Big business interests were terrified of the possibility of a Bryan victory. The Republican National Committee alone raised and spent the equivalent of fifty million in today's dollars campaigning against Bryan. Other sources spent one and a half times as much. Republicans mailed out 120 million pieces of campaign literature printed in ten languages to a nation of fourteen million voters, and hired fourteen hundred professional speakers to stump for the Republican McKinley, who stayed in Ohio and campaigned from his front porch. There were allegations of employers threatening employees with dismissal if Bryan won and other charges that workers who supported Bryan were transferred to new plants in the days before the election so they would be disqualified from voting by residency requirements.

Against this array of Republican political might, the Democrats countered with Bryan—"one man, but such a man!" as described by Anna Lodge, the wife of Republican stalwart Henry Cabot Lodge. Writing to an English friend, Mrs. Lodge noted that Bryan had been able to raise but a half-million dollars, perhaps no more than 5 percent of what the Republicans had gathered. Bryan was unable to tap the resources of the Democratic establishment as many conservative Democrats, including Grover Cleveland, aghast at being swept aside by the populist Bryan, not only refused to campaign for Bryan, they announced they intended to vote for McKinley. And most urban newspapers, even those that had been reliably Democratic in the past, abandoned him and endorsed the Republican.

So Bryan did what had not been done since Stephen Douglas; he campaigned for himself at a pace that would be difficult to match even with today's means of travel. He traveled eighteen thousand miles through twenty-six states and spoke an average of eighty thousand words a day. He drew crowds as large as seventy thousand. In West Virginia, it was estimated fully half the voters in the state attended a Bryan speech at least once, and his total audience during the campaign was estimated at five million people. Further, his speeches "spoke to the heart and intelligence of the people, with a capital 'P,'" Mrs. Lodge said. After Bryan, the tradition of the "front porch" campaign, in which the voters went to the candidate instead of the other way around, was dead. Given all Bryan's disadvantages, he ought to have been buried in a landslide; instead, he carried twenty-two Western and Southern states and won more than 47 percent of the popular vote.

As shrewd as he was pious, Bryan had a simple explanation for his defeat. "I have borne the sins of Grover Cleveland," he said, noting that he ran as a Democrat when a Democratic president was presiding over an economic depression. Tellingly, in regard to his future plans, Bryan titled his campaign memoirs *The First Battle*. Nominated unanimously at the next Democratic convention, he lost in his rematch against McKinley in 1900. With the economy having improved modestly (in part due to the discovery of gold in Alaska and the Yukon Territory, which loosened the money supply), Bryan focused the new campaign on criticizing McKinley's "imperialist" designs in the Philippines following the Spanish-American War. The United States, having freed the archipelago from Spanish rule, declined to grant its independence, which led to an ugly and now largely forgotten four-year guerilla war with Filipino insurgents. More than four thousand American soldiers were killed, as well as twenty thousand Filipino combatants; another two hundred thousand Filipino civilians succumbed to famine and disease caused by the war. The American public in 1900 cared more that the economy was improving and followed the cry of McKinley's campaign to "let well enough alone."

In 1904, Bryan stepped aside to let conservative Democrats try their luck once more. They nominated New York appellate court judge Alton B. Parker, who lost in a landslide to Theodore Roosevelt, the White House resident since McKinley's assassination in 1901. In the past, Roosevelt had accused Bryan of "communistic and socialistic" ideas; Bryan in turn now tweaked TR for earning the title of a progressive by passing watered-down versions of Democratic reform measures.

In 1908, the Democrats turned once more to Bryan to run against Roosevelt's handpicked successor, his secretary of war William Howard Taft. It was a lackluster campaign that Bryan had thought he could win. In the end, he actually received fewer votes than he had in 1896. His lasting accomplishment that year was winning the endorsement of the previously nonpartisan American Federation of Labor, and organized labor has remained a bedrock constituency of the Democratic Party ever since.

Now a three-time loser, Bryan, only forty-eight years old, was already a has-been as a presidential candidate. He was still idolized by millions, but it was the magic of the 1896 campaign that had bonded his followers to him in a way almost unprecedented in American history. His image hung like an icon in a million American homes next to portraits of Jesus. Overseas, the only image that hung in Leo Tolstoy's bedroom was a picture of Bryan, who had become friends with the great Russian novelist and pacifist during one of Bryan's world tours. Unlike later critics who disparaged Bryan's intellect and his politics, Tolstoy declared he found Bryan "remarkably intelligent and progressive."

Bryan corresponded widely with the famous and the unknown. Hundreds of thousands of admirers wrote to him, to ask a favor, to tell him their troubles and ask for his prayers, and to talk about how his words and example had profoundly changed their lives. A young Presbyterian cleric wrote, "I want you to know that I am one of the thousands of young men in this country that you have helped into lofty conceptions of life and its meaning." Still a politician, Bryan used the correspondence to his political advantage by creating a database of a half-million names that aided him in his campaigns.

Bryan radiated goodwill. His essential kindness and decency, which some mocked as yet another sign that he was a simpleton, caused admirers to open up and reveal their most intimate secrets. A woman named Amy Howley, who had attended one of Bryan's massive outdoor Bible classes when he lived in Miami, confided to Bryan in a letter that she had a husband who committed suicide and had recently watched a daughter die during childbirth. "God only knows why I am telling you all this. But somehow I thought you'd pray for me," Mrs. Howley wrote, adding that while she never expected to see Bryan again, she hoped that they might meet in Heaven.

Such maudlin sentiments drove cynics to distraction. Historian Richard Hofstadter accused Bryan of possessing "a childish conception of religion." The radical journalist John Reed joined Bryan on a tour of rural Florida and wrote a condescending profile of Bryan floating down the Ocklawaha River "on a gasoline yacht, in black statesmanlike cutaway, white clerical tie, light grey fedora hat, his hands clasped across his stomach, benevolently bringing love and order into his simple world." The acerbic journalist H. L. Mencken, who had once thought Bryan's speeches as sublime as a Beethoven symphony, forgot that he had been a youthful admirer of Bryan and later wrote one of the most hateful obituaries ever published about a beloved public figure, calling Bryan "a vulgar and common man . . . a peasant come home to the dung pile."

"What his enemies could not understand," said University of Chicago political scientist Charles Edward Merriam, a strong supporter of Bryan's progressive policies, "was that the people are as much interested in knowing about their leader's heart as in knowing about his head, and that sympathy no less than intelligence plays its part in the great process of popular control."

Bryan was especially sympathetic toward women, though there was never a hint of sexual scandal surrounding him. He adored his wife, Mary, who was his full partner in politics. One of his daughters, Ruth, became a congresswoman from Florida and the U.S. minister to Denmark, the highest rank a woman had achieved in the U.S. Foreign Service at that time. He paid his female employees at his magazine, the *Commoner*, the same union wages received by men. Bryan not only advocated women's suffrage years earlier than most Democratic leaders, he argued for other measures of sexual equality. He said that the age of sexual consent should be the same for women as for men and that men who solicited prostitutes deserved punishment just as much as the prostitutes themselves.

Bryan was not particularly sympathetic, however, to African Americans. While he never used racial epithets and took no steps to make the lot of African Americans worse, he held the racial prejudices common to his day, and his reform agenda never included anything to correct racial injustices. He accepted the "Jim Crow" segregation laws of the South as a fact of life, no doubt in part because the South was a large portion of his political base. This moral blind spot is a shame because Bryan did, from time to time, exhibit some cognizance of the plight of African Americans. He occasionally entertained blacks in his home, and he criticized the Republican Party for rewarding the loyalty of African-American voters with nothing more than a few "janitorships." He also chastised Southern Democrats for failing to support expanded government power over railroads because he knew what they really feared was federal interference in segregation. "As if your personal objections to riding with negroes should interfere with a great national reform!" he said. A few black leaders, including W. E. B. Du Bois, endorsed Bryan in the 1908 election, but Bryan knew 1908 was his last chance to be president and that could not happen if he alienated the South. So he stepped back from even the very modest outreach he had made to African-American voters in past campaigns and never really applied his Christian ethics to addressing their unique problems. The same could be said of virtually all the major progressive leaders of the day and indeed most Americans.

In 1912, the Republican Party split in two, and Bryan might finally have won the presidency. He worked for an unprecedented fourth nomination but was rebuffed. Eventually persuaded of Woodrow Wilson's progressive credentials, Bryan then used his still considerable influence to make Wilson president. He led a switch of delegates at the Democratic National Convention that eventually gave Wilson the nomination on the forty-sixth ballot.* More as a reward for his party service than out of gratitude or friendship, Wilson named Bryan his secretary of state.

When World War I broke out, Bryan and Wilson agreed to a policy of strict neutrality, but Bryan was soon alarmed by Wilson's growing support for the Allied cause and his increasing inclination to have the United States enter the war. Bryan was not a true pacifist, but he did abhor violence and was appalled by the slaughter going on in the European trenches. Wilson was angered by Germany's use of submarines; Bryan thought the U-boat attacks were no less despicable than Britain's blockade of Germany, which was causing widespread hunger and the threat of starvation. When Wilson declined to couple condemnation of Britain's blockade with his protest of the German sinking of the *Lusitania*, which killed more than one hundred Americans, Bryan resigned.

During his short tenure as secretary of state, Bryan had proposed treaties that promoted arbitration over war in international disputes. "The killing of human beings," Bryan said, "shall not be commenced by any nation until the world knows what crime has been committed that requires so high a penalty." He had negotiated twenty-nine "cooling off" treaties, as they were known, and Bryan had sincerely thought, given all the advancements in science, travel, and understanding, that humanity might be on the verge of making war a thing of the past. Now, with military and civilian deaths estimated at sixteen million in the most catastrophic event in modern history, he tried to grasp how the world had gone so wrong.

---

* Bryan would also play an essential role in securing Wilson's re-election by barnstorming in critical states that went to Wilson in an extremely close win over Charles Evans Hughes, this even after he resigned from Wilson's Cabinet.

Despite his earlier avowal of neutrality in the conflict, Bryan came to believe that a German culture increasingly hostile to traditional religion was the cause of the war. Before the war, Germany had been the center of the new "higher criticism" of the Bible, which was scholarship that challenged traditional beliefs about the authorship of the books of the Bible and which challenged the literal truths of its accounts. Germany had also produced the philosopher Friedrich Nietzsche, who provocatively referred to himself as "the Antichrist," and whose work disparaged Christianity as a religion for the weak and unhealthy. His book *Thus Spoke Zarathustra*, with its concept of "will to power," was distributed as inspirational reading to thousands of German troops during World War I. Particularly influential on Bryan was a book by Vernon Kellogg, an American biologist who spent part of the war years with members of the German high command. Kellogg reported that the Germans had applied to international relations the theories of Charles Darwin, which Herbert Spencer had boiled down to "survival of the fittest," thereby provoking the bloodiest war in human history.

This "Social Darwinism," as it is known, had been used by some in America, including E. L. Youmans, founder of *Popular Science Monthly*, to discredit the type of reforms advocated by Bryan. Social Darwinists argued, essentially, that biology was destiny; therefore, the government had no power to redress social inequalities. The theory clashed with everything Bryan believed about the duty and the power of a Christian to change the world. Still, the Social Darwinism movement before the war was so small that it did not particularly disturb Bryan. In 1909, he said that while he was not convinced of the truth of evolutionary theory, "I do not mean to find fault" with those who accept evolution as fact.

But the war and his perception of its root causes changed Bryan's attitude. Bryan, as we have seen, linked the impulse for progressive reform to religious faith. If the teaching of evolutionary theory was undermining the faith of students, then it was undermining progressive reform as well. To prove his point about the impact of evolutionary instruction upon religious belief, he cited a survey conducted by a Bryn Mawr College psychologist, which found that while only 15 percent of college freshmen said they did not believe in God, more than 40 percent of graduating seniors said they did not. Coming to grips with the first wave of the American youth culture in the Jazz Age of the 1920s, Bryan was also appalled by surveys that found only 10 percent of college students were seriously interested in religion, while 50 percent gambled and 62 percent drank alcohol (then illegal under Prohibition).

Bryan believed Darwin's theories were being improperly applied to a host of human endeavors—even though, as far as he was concerned, it had not been proven as fact, even as it applied to biological evolution. In commentary printed in the *New York Times* in 1922, Bryan addressed the question, "Did God use evolution as His Plan? If it could be shown that man, instead of being made in the image of God, is a development of beasts we would have to accept it, regardless of its effect, for truth is truth and will prevail. But when there is no proof we have a right to consider the effect of the acceptance of an unsupported hypothesis."

Bryan said he had no issue with the teaching of evolution as *theory* but insisted it should not be taught as *fact*. He further argued that while private schools could teach whatever they wished, public schools had an obligation to respect the wishes of those who paid the taxes to support the schools. As Walter Lippmann later observed, Bryan had flipped Jefferson's dictum regarding the "separation of church and state" on its head. If, Bryan argued, the state could not compel someone to practice a certain religion, then the state also could not compel someone to challenge his or her religious faith, either. He therefore went on a national campaign to persuade state legislatures to pass laws that would prohibit the teaching of evolution as fact in the public schools (although Bryan insisted that such laws should not carry a fine or any other form of punishment). Five states passed such laws. One was Tennessee.

The American Civil Liberties Union, only six years old in 1925, decided to challenge one of the anti-evolution laws not on the basis of adjudicating the correctness of evolutionary theory, but on the issue of freedom of speech. Dayton, Tennessee, meanwhile, had once been a prosperous iron and coal-mining town that had fallen on hard times. As industrial as it was agricultural, Dayton was known as a tolerant community with only a few members of the resurgent Ku Klux Klan. But city leaders grasped that such a trial would bring visitors and national attention. Therefore, in order to boost the local economy, city leaders thought it would be grand if Dayton, with its lovely three-story courthouse built during better times, was the site of the trial sought by the ACLU. The local high school football coach, John T. Scopes, acknowledged that he had unintentionally violated the law while substituting for the regular biology teacher and, after meeting with town leaders, agreed to be charged with unlawfully teaching evolution—if it could help the town economy.

Bryan agreed to assist in Scopes's prosecution while the most famous criminal defense attorney in the nation, Clarence Darrow, agreed to assist with Scopes's defense. Darrow had been a progressive ally and supporter of Bryan, but he was also an agnostic who found Bryan's attack on evolution silly, dangerous, and obnoxious. Immediately dubbed "The Monkey Trial" and the focus of worldwide attention, it would be inadequate to label it a spectacle. It remains *sui generis* in American history.

It was hardly a trial at all because both sides acknowledged Scopes was guilty of breaking the law. When the judge threw out the testimony of a host of scientific and religious experts as irrelevant to Scopes's guilt or innocence, Bryan and Darrow agreed to the highly unusual idea that each would take the stand and be cross-examined by the other. Bryan took the stand first and, while he knew most of the Bible by heart, he was no theologian. He sputtered in a rare display of inarticulateness as Darrow peppered him for two hours with questions designed to show that a literal interpretation of the Bible was nonsensical. Did Bryan think God created the world in just six, twenty-four-hour days? Did he believe Jonah was really swallowed by a whale? Did Joshua literally make the sun stand still? When Darrow pressed Bryan to name the exact date of the great flood, Bryan replied, "I don't think about things I don't think about." Darrow thrust a knife into the opening, "Do you think about things you do think about?"

The *New York Times* called Bryan's time on the witness stand "an absurdly pathetic performance." Bryan at first did not seem aware of how badly he had done, but he looked forward to getting Darrow on the stand. Darrow, however, outfoxed Bryan again. The next day, he moved that the judge direct the jury to find Scopes guilty, ending the trial and beginning the appeals process. Bryan did not get to cross-examine Darrow, nor did he get to give his closing summation. Scopes was quickly found guilty and fined one hundred dollars.

Bryan, meanwhile, had failed to make the central point of his whole crusade. During the trial, he wasted time and effort trying to disprove evolution, rather than bringing attention to the nefarious ways in which evolutionary theory was being applied outside the realm of biology. Had Bryan taken the time to read the textbook, *A Civic Biology,* which Scopes had used in class, he would have discovered the author providing evidence to support Bryan's point by arguing that human beings should be bred more like horses to improve "future generations," and lamenting that the feeble-minded, whom the author called "true parasites," were only placed in asylums to prevent their breeding when lower order animals with comparative deficiencies would simply be destroyed.

Had Bryan focused on how evolutionary theory was being abused, which is what drew him to the issue in the first place, he might have seemed the prophet he appeared to be in 1896. Soon, eugenics would take hold in much of the world, most notably in Nazi Germany, and the consequences would be as brutal and frightening as Bryan had imagined.

Bryan stayed in Dayton a few days to polish the closing argument he had intended to give and which he now intended to turn into an article for publication in newspapers around the country. In his text, Bryan argued again that his quarrel was not with science, but how science was applied to human endeavors. (To prove he was not against scientific inquiry, Bryan had earlier joined the American Association for the Advancement of Science.) In language that foreshadowed an argument that would later be made in favor of nuclear disarmament, Bryan said, "Science is a magnificent material force, but it is not a teacher of morals. It can perfect machinery, but it adds no moral restraints to protect society from the misuse of the machine."

Having finished work on the article on a Sunday afternoon, July 26, 1925, five days after the Scopes Trial had ended, Bryan took a nap and did not wake up.

Despite Mencken's snide obituary, Bryan's reputation had not been immediately shredded in Dayton. Most eulogies praised his many accomplishments and his role in progressive reform. Later, both Franklin Roosevelt and Harry Truman acknowledged the debt liberalism and the Democratic Party owed Bryan. "He kept the faith," Roosevelt said, using one of Bryan's favorite verses from the letters of St. Paul.

Roosevelt made a key point. Many who admired Bryan the young progressive concluded from the Scopes Trial that he had transformed into a reactionary, "a bitter and malignant old man," in Hofstadter's words. In fact, his crusade against evolution was consistent with his belief in progressive politics. He believed that it was a Christian's duty to help the weakest members of society. This was God's will, and Bryan would cede nothing to those who might counter that it was biology's will that there are the poor and hungry, or that society has no ability or obligation to improve their condition.

Bryan's reputation was badly damaged later by the cruel parody of him that appeared in the 1955 play and 1960 film *Inherit the Wind*, which was not, according to its authors, a play about Bryan or evolution at all, but an allegory on McCarthyism and the danger of mass movements. Unlike many mid-twentieth-century intellectuals, Bryan did not fear popular movements. He believed, "When reform comes to this country, it starts with the masses. Reforms do not come from the brains of scholars."

Many fail to understand Bryan because he occupies what is now a rare space in society. Much like Pope John Paul II in more recent times, Bryan saw no contradiction between traditional religious values and the need for radical social change. He saw them being in perfect harmony. Bryan did not see religion as making people small and mean, but as motivating them to be expansive and good. He believed people would be motivated to reform society, not because scientific experts told them it made sense, but because their religious faith informed them that it was the right thing to do.

The language of Bryan is still heard today. When Al Gore claimed that his 2000 presidential slogan was "The People vs. the Powerful," he was channeling Bryan, but so, too, was 2008 Republican vice presidential nominee Sarah Palin when she professed to cater to the "real America." Still, Bryan's spirit is missing. Too liberal for today's religious, he is too religious for today's liberals. With the significant exception of certain civil rights leaders of the 1960s, Bryan was the last great reformer to speak in religious terms.

There are some progressive Democrats today who are making tentative efforts to reclaim Bryan's legacy. As Barack Obama did in his 2004 Democratic National Convention keynote address, they want the party to focus on a "politics of hope" that inspires people to want their government to do good. They fret about what journalist Amy Sullivan has labeled a "God gap" where the religiously observant favor conservative Republican candidates over liberal Democratic candidates. They worry that liberalism has framed the questions of the day on the rights and entitlements of individuals rather than the obligations and potential of society. Books such as *What's the Matter with Kansas?* profess bafflement that the grandchildren of Bryan's core constituencies in places like Kansas seem to place a higher priority on moral issues than policies that could improve their economic well-being. As these progressives consider how more religiously observant voters can be lured back into the fold, they might especially consider the example of Bryan.

"The people do not act through gratitude, but from expectation," Bryan said. In 1896 and in his subsequent campaigns, Bryan greatly raised the expectations of the people. He did so by appealing to something beyond their self-interest. Bryan believed "love of one's neighbor is the only visible proof that can be given of love of God." That he believed such a sentiment could be a catalyst for political change says much about who he was and his power to inspire; that we ridicule such a notion today as being simple and naïve may explain why modern liberalism, aiming more at the mind and the pocketbook, no longer captures the hearts and the souls of the people as it once did.

CHAPTER FIVE

AL SMITH
1928

The world knows no greater mockery than the use of the blazing cross, the cross upon which Christ died, as a symbol to install into the hearts of men a hatred of their brethren.

Al Smith, the first Roman Catholic nominated for president by a major political party, did more than pave the way for John Kennedy to become the first Catholic president thirty-two years later. His 1928 campaign changed the way America viewed Catholics (and how Catholics viewed America) to such a degree that when Kennedy did run in 1960 his religion was at least as much an asset as a liability.

Catholicism became so widely accepted in the wake of the Smith campaign that it seemed to be the preferred religion in popular culture, reaching its apex in 1944 when Bing Crosby won the Academy Award for Best Actor by portraying an extraordinarily sympathetic Catholic priest. Anti-Catholicism, which historian Arthur M. Schlesinger Jr. has called "the deepest bias" in American life, so receded in American life that by 2012, six of nine U.S. Supreme Court justices would be Catholic—with nary a peep of protest from Protestant America.

The burning crosses of the Ku Klux Klan that had greeted Smith all along the campaign trail—and not just in the Deep South, but also in Indiana, Montana, and Oklahoma—had illuminated a dark and ugly recess of American history that shamed many Protestants, and also lit a fire under American Catholics.

Disturbed by the bigotry directed at Smith and the magnitude of his loss to Herbert Hoover, American Catholics began to much more aggressively assert themselves in the public square. They particularly used the new and wildly popular entertainment mediums of film and radio to redefine themselves to Protestant America. Movies featuring positive portrayals of Catholic figures, such as Crosby's Father Charles Francis Patrick ("Father Chuck") O'Malley in the 1944 Best Picture winner *Going My Way*, became so ubiquitous that movie studios received complaints that Protestants were now getting short shrift in Hollywood.

A variety of factors contributed to this transformation in public attitudes toward Catholicism—the severity of the Great Depression made religious differences seem trifling, changes in American immigration law reduced the influx of Catholic immigrants that nativists found so threatening, and the Catholic Church took a leading role in the struggle against communism, winning many admirers. But as religious historian Martin E. Marty notes, overt anti-Catholicism demonstrably diminished after the Smith campaign, signifying its pivotal role as a catalyst in this American reassessment of Catholicism.

Many Americans, including Smith himself, had naïvely hoped that his religion would not be an issue in the campaign and that anti-Catholicism·was a relic of the previous century. They had hoped that Smith's personal integrity and his progressive record in public service during four terms as governor of New York, particularly the reforms that revolutionized safety in the workplace, would trump any remnants of religious bigotry. But anti-Catholicism still flourished in 1928, and it is clear that Smith's Catholicism was the defining issue of the 1928 election, prompting Raymond Fosdick, then a Rockefeller Foundation trustee and a Protestant, to lament, "Do we learn nothing from experience? Here is an issue that after three hundred years of bloody warfare was finally given a decent burial by our forefathers. And now like ghouls we drag it from the grave."

Some historians, including the ubiquitous Richard Hofstadter, stubbornly assert that Smith's religion had little to do with his defeat in 1928 and that "not a Democrat alive" could have won that year. The nation was prosperous under Republican rule and Republicans had nominated for president one of the chief architects of that prosperity, Secretary of Commerce Hoover, whose work to relieve famine during World War I had made him an international hero. Others believed that Smith, a "Manhattanite," was from too alien an environment to be embraced by Middle America—even though half of all Americans were living in cities by the 1920s. Smith had also alienated many "dry" Democrats, Hofstadter argued, especially in the South and Midwest, because of his belief that Prohibition had failed and should be at least partially repealed.*

Yet none of these factors explain the size of Smith's loss—he carried only eight states and won barely 40 percent of the popular vote—and they cannot mask the breadth and brazenness of the opposition to Smith because of his religion. If we follow Smith's famous advice and the catchphrase most associated with him—"Let's look at the record"—we see that these objections to Smith, reasonable as they may sound, were often convenient excuses for those who wished to deny they were bigots and wanted to explain their opposition to Smith in polite terms that did not raise the religion issue.

The impact of Prohibition on Smith's campaign is particularly misunderstood. Scientific polling did not yet exist in the 1920s, but historians generally agree, based upon analysis of local returns in elections where Prohibition was a central issue, that by 1926 a majority of American voters had become disenchanted with Prohibition. When repeal finally received a vote in 1933, it received the support of 73 percent of voters, although Prohibition still enjoyed strong support in parts of the South

---

* Smith was known to enjoy a highball—though not the eight per day Republicans alleged during the campaign—but he tried to stake out a moderate position by favoring "temperance" over Prohibition. He argued that only the ban on the sale of beer and wine should be lifted and praised Prohibition for eliminating the saloon and reducing the per capita consumption of alcohol in the United States.

and Midwest.* Even leading Prohibition activists acknowledged their problem with Smith was more his religion than his stand on Prohibition. Evangelist Bob Jones, who later founded the South Carolina university that bears his name, told crowds throughout the South, "I'll tell you, brother, that the big issue we've got to face ain't the liquor question. I'd rather see a saloon on every corner of the South than see the foreigners elect Al Smith president."

The truth of Jones's candor is reflected by the radically different voting patterns that occurred in 1928, alterations that can only be ascribed to Smith's Catholicism, according to historian Allan J. Lichtman. Reliably Democratic Southern states that had not voted Republican since Reconstruction—Texas, Florida, North Carolina, and Virginia—supported Hoover. Conversely, the overwhelming support of Catholic voters allowed Smith to carry two New England states (Massachusetts and Rhode Island) that had only gone Democratic once before, in 1912, when the Republican Party split between Taft and Roosevelt.

Excepting Prohibition, there were few major issue differences between Smith and Hoover, yet the 1928 election drew intense interest. Voter turnout hit 57 percent after having dropped below 50 percent in the presidential elections of 1920 and 1924, while total campaign spending by both parties probably exceeded twenty million dollars—or four times what had been spent in a 1924 election that had involved three major candidates. The primary difference between 1928 and those earlier elections was the religious affiliation of one of the candidates.

In the 1932 election, Democrats again nominated a "wet" New Yorker, the patrician Franklin Roosevelt, yet FDR brought all the prodigal Southern states back into the Democratic fold. Where Smith had lost Texas, Roosevelt carried the state with 88 percent of the popular vote. Where Smith had barely carried Alabama with 51 percent of the vote, Roosevelt won the state with 85 percent of the popular vote. Even taking into account the dramatic change in political fortunes brought on by the Great Depression, if we take Smith's opponents at their word that it was Smith's stand on Prohibition and his status as an out-of-touch

---

* In the late 1940s, it was estimated that 38 percent of the American population lived in areas where the sale of alcohol was still prohibited by local regulation.

New Yorker that generated so much of their opposition, it would seem the same qualms would have remained regarding Roosevelt's candidacy. Except, of course, that Roosevelt was a Protestant, not a Catholic.

Roosevelt himself polled hundreds of Democratic leaders nationwide after the 1928 election and found that fully 55 percent attributed Smith's defeat to his religion while just a third argued it was Smith's stand on Prohibition and less than 3 percent stated it was the prosperous economy that benefited Republicans. "They wiped us off the face of the earth down here because of religion; do not let anybody tell you different [sic]," an Oklahoma official wrote FDR.

American Protestants did not consider their anti-Catholicism irrational, and American Catholics did not find it unusual. America had been settled by Europeans in the mid-seventeenth century while Europe was engulfed in a series of religious wars between Catholics and Protestants. Early English colonists, almost all Protestant, brought their mistrust of Catholicism over on the boats along with the rest of the baggage. It was a given among Protestants that the pope wanted political as well as ecclesiastical power over the Christian world. Lacking knowledge of the many nuances of Catholic dogma, Protestants misunderstood such concepts as papal infallibility, and believed all Catholics, lay or religious, owed absolute fealty to the pope. Nor did American Protestants fully understand how the American Catholic church had developed with a remarkable level of autonomy from Rome and possessed a uniquely American character that respected the Jeffersonian tradition of separation of church and state.

The few early Catholic colonists were prohibited from voting, holding office, holding worship services, owning property, or even settling in many communities. There is no record, for example, of any Catholic settling in New Hampshire until 1822! Even the government of Maryland, the colony given to Lord Baltimore as a haven for Catholic immigrants, was taken over by Protestants in 1690 and anti-Catholic laws imposed.

The Revolutionary War softened some anti-Catholic attitudes with the Declaration of Independence's assertion that "all men are created equal" and with Catholic France a crucial American ally. The Constitution forbade a religious test as a condition for public office. But increased Catholic immigration, modest at first but rapidly increased with the onset of the great potato famine in Ireland, stirred strong anti-Catholic feeling in the 1830s and 1840s. Spurious exposés of Catholic debauchery forged by Protestant ministers helped instigate dozens of anti-Catholic riots in those decades that left scores dead and many Catholic churches and convents in ashes. Politically, anti-Catholic and anti-immigrant sentiment coalesced around the American Party, labelled the "Know-Nothings" because members refused to acknowledge any such organization existed, though at one time it held the allegiance of more than a hundred congressmen.

Anti-Catholic sentiment took on a farcical air when construction of the Washington Monument was halted in 1854 after Pope Pius IX sent a stone from an ancient Roman temple as a gift to be included in the structure. Rumors spread that completion of the monument incorporating the pope's gift would be a signal for a Catholic uprising that would install papal rule in America. Construction did not resume until the 1870s, which is why the lower quarter of the giant obelisk is a different shade of color than the rest—a visible reminder on our National Mall of religious intolerance in American history.

The debate over slavery and the onset of the Civil War overtook immigration as the great national issue. Meanwhile, Catholics, like many minorities seeking to assimilate in an adopted culture, became ultra-patriots. More than a fifth of the Union Army was foreign-born and primarily Irish or German Catholics, but it was in World War I that Catholics believed they had offered irrefutable proof of their patriotism. More than eight hundred thousand Catholics served in the American Expeditionary Force and twenty-two thousand lost their lives in battle—a fifth of all U.S. military deaths in the war. Smith's campaign, Catholic commentators said, would now demonstrate whether Catholics would continue to be "debarred from any share in the government they support with their blood and money," or whether they would finally be accepted as equals.

The campaign proved that many Protestants believed they should remain debarred. A general in the Army was widely quoted as stating that Catholics were fine as "cannon fodder" but one should never become commander-in-chief. Prominent Protestant minister and author Charles Hillman Fountain went further and wrote that not only was a Catholic unfit to be president, but "no Catholic should be elected to any political office."

Remarkably, Fountain insisted he was not prejudiced against Catholics because it was Catholics who had declined to embrace America, not the other way around. A leading publication of the Presbyterian Church offered the same rationale: "If the Protestants hesitate to vote for Catholics, because Catholics hold and teach their children a political creed which is un-American . . . it is neither just nor honest to accuse Protestants of religious intolerance." *Christian Century* magazine labelled Catholicism "an alien culture, of a medieval Latin mentality," and insisted a reasonable voter could oppose Smith "not because he is a religious bigot" but because there is "a real issue between Catholicism and American institutions."

Smith, perhaps insulated by the polyglot nature of New York, understood that there was anti-Catholic bias in America but seemed genuinely taken aback by those who believed Catholicism was fundamentally incompatible with American democracy. His background had convinced him that America could successfully assimilate people from all faiths and backgrounds.

Smith was born on December 30, 1873, in the Fourth Ward of the Lower East Side of Manhattan to a father who was a Teamster (and most likely of Italian heritage) and an Irish mother. Smith was delighted that "my father, my mother, my sister, my wife, all five of my children and I, were all born within five blocks of one another." Proud of his heritage, he declared he was not the type who cooked his corned beef and cabbage in the basement to hide the smell from the neighbors. The close-knit Fourth Ward boasted residents of many different ethnic origins and religions, which gave Smith the belief that people of good will from all backgrounds and faiths could peacefully co-exist.

At St. James Catholic School, Smith was taught American history through a series of fables, such as George Washington fessing up to chopping down a cherry tree, designed to demonstrate civic and personal virtues. These stories resonated with Smith, whom the humorist Will Rogers called "the most sentimental prominent man I ever met."

Smith's father died when he was eleven, and before Smith could complete the eighth grade, he quit school to work and support his mother and siblings. Always insecure about his lack of formal education, Smith liked to tell the story of when he was in the New York Legislature and debate was interrupted to announce the results of an Ivy League boat race. As legislators rose to exclaim their own alma mater, one from Harvard, another from Yale, yet another claiming to be a "U. of M." man, Smith rose and announced that he was an "F.F.M. man." Asked what school those initials stood for, Smith replied, "Fulton Fish Market. Let's proceed with the debate."

Smith began work at the Fulton Fish Market at the age of twelve. An all-purpose helper who cleaned, wrapped, and sold fish, he was paid twelve dollars a week and worked twelve-hour days. The easily spoiled wares were hawked in the market with the intensity of brokers buying and selling at the New York Stock Exchange, which often led to confrontations among rival fishmongers. Smith was known as someone who could settle disputes with words rather than fists. A friend told him, "If you don't have the biggest mouth in the market, you've sure got the loudest."

Smith's vocal abilities were also put to good use performing in amateur theatricals put on by the St. James Players. "For innocent pastime, for recreation, for knowledge, for training the memory, and for giving a person a certain degree of confidence, there is not better amusement," Smith said. He even considered the stage as a career before he met his future wife, Catherine "Katie" Dunn. Dunn came from a respectable family and marrying an actor would not have been tolerated.

But politics are another form of show business—show business for homely people, goes the joke. Smith was not homely, but neither was he handsome. He stood five-feet-eight-inches tall and had the broad chest of a swimmer. His oval-shaped face with pink skin, blue eyes, and bad teeth was framed by blond hair, which he parted in the middle. His most distinctive feature after his large nose was his voice. It was gravelly like "the gruff bark of an Irish setter," according to one description. With his Lower East Side accent, work was pronounced "woik," and Smith loved to talk on the new device called the "raddio" about making things "betta" for "poisuns" through public "soivice." Despite his accent, he was an effective speaker. H. V. Kaltenborn, one of the great voices in early radio, considered Smith a superb public speaker because "he knew just how to win and hold . . . [an] audience. Instinctively, he said just the right things in the right way."

That ability caught the attention of Tammany Hall, the political machine that ruled New York City except for brief intervals when the better elements of society rallied to impose flurries of reforms that would melt away as quickly as a spring snow. To secure its power, Tammany embraced New York's burgeoning immigrant population. Because New York lacked a public welfare system and its private charities were Dickensian in their indifferent brutality, Tammany stepped in to provide the services—food, a job, help with the police—the new immigrants needed to integrate into American society, thereby winning their loyal political support at the polls.

Smith, who regularly attended Tammany meetings and events, was brought under-wing by Boss Tom Foley, who provided him with his first political job in 1895 as a process server. Eight years later, Foley and Tammany tapped Smith to be the Fourth Ward's candidate for the State Assembly, an election Smith won with 75 percent of the vote.

In sending Smith to Albany, Foley offered the advice, "Don't speak until you have something to say. Men who talk just for the pleasure of it do not get very far." Smith kept quiet as advised but still did not get very far. Frustrated and disheartened, Smith asked Foley if he could quit the legislature. Foley insisted he give it another try. So Smith resolved that if he were stuck in the post, he would learn everything he could to be a first-rate legislator.

Unlike most of his colleagues, Smith read every bill before the Assembly and mastered the arcane legislative procedures. He also hosted regular dinners at his home, inviting every legislator in turn to share some beer, corned beef, and cabbage, so that he might get to know them, learn from them, understand them, and learn how to influence their votes. By 1909, Smith was an Assembly leader, and among his early legislative accomplishments was creation of the nation's first Workmen's Compensation Law.

But his greatest legislative achievement came in the wake of one of the worst workplace disasters in American history. On March 25, 1911, a fire swept through the Asch Building at Green Street and Washington Place in New York City. The top three floors of the ten-story building were occupied by the Triangle Shirtwaist Company. The firm's workers, mostly immigrant women but including children, tried to put out the blaze only to find that the fire hose was rotted and cracked and there was no water pressure. Panicked, the several hundred workers desperately sought to escape the growing inferno only to discover that the back entrance had been chained shut by their employer to prevent employee theft. The fire escape, ungoverned by any building code, collapsed under the weight of the first few people to use it. Workers who rushed to the front door found that the door opened inward, meaning it could not be budged as the mass of workers pushed forward to get out. A fire drill had never been conducted in the building.

The building's single, small elevator ferried a few lucky survivors to the ground floor. On the final descent, those inside the elevator heard bodies crash onto the roof of the elevator, as workers decided to jump to their death rather than be burned alive. Other workers who made their way to the building's roof, usually with hair in flames, made the same choice. A firemen's safety net collapsed when the first woman to jump hit with a force equal to sixteen tons of pressure. Horrified onlookers now watched as others jumped to certain death and impaled themselves on a wrought iron fence below or hit the ground with such force that the pavement cracked. The fire killed 146 workers, 126 of whom were women.

Smith and future U.S. senator Robert Wagner led the Factory Investigating Commission formed in the wake of the tragedy. In its work, the commission learned that workers, including children, earned as little as one-and-a-half cents an hour in sweatshops like the Triangle Shirtwaist Company. They found that many factories lacked toilets; one mill owner provided workers with only a barrel in the basement—and he, shockingly, was a member of the local board of health. They found children as young as three "employed" at jobs such as sorting fruits and vegetables. For these unfortunates, workdays began at 4:00 a.m. and lasted until ten at night. When one child was asked how long he had been working at his job of rolling cigarettes, he blankly replied, "Ever since I was."

The commission produced thirty-two state bills and New York City another thirty ordinances, and these reforms initiated by Smith and his commission changed the way each of us live and work even today. Because of Smith, every office in America has regular fire drills, sprinklers, and exit doors with panic bars that open outward, and all exit doors are clearly marked with red signs. Other workplace reforms included mandatory clean toilets and washrooms, limited shift hours, restrictions on child labor, and many other initiatives to limit the danger and drudgery of industrial work—plus the inspectors necessary to enforce these new rules.

Given such results, it was not surprising that Smith moved up the political ladder. In 1918, he was elected governor of New York and was already discussed as a potential presidential candidate. He lost his first re-election bid in 1920, when Republicans swept the nation, but won again in 1922 and was re-elected twice more—the first person ever elected governor of New York four times. With his brown derby and ever-present cigar, he was a distinctive figure, but what most distinguished him from so many politicians was his extraordinary record of accomplishments. Smith had completely reorganized New York state government, consolidating New York's 189 different agencies and commissions into a handful accountable to the governor. He increased New York's spending on education ten-fold in eight years, from seven million dollars in 1918–19 to seventy million in 1926–27, doubling teachers' salaries during that same period. He had the state invest heavily in new infrastructure, and, remembering that his own playground as a child had been the pavement, enjoyed promoting a dynamic parks program. When some local millionaires protested plans for a new state park in Long Island on the grounds that it would attract "rabble from the city," Smith bellowed, "Rabble? That's *me* you're talking about!"

For all his reforms and state investments, Smith still considered himself fundamentally a conservative. "It is a mistake to think that the people approve of reduced appropriations when in the process of reducing them the state or any of its activities are to suffer," he said. "What the people want is an honest accounting of every dollar appropriated. They want every dollar of public money to bring a dollar's worth of services to the state." Even with his fiscal prudence, Smith had many progressive admirers. Both Frances Perkins, who later served as FDR's secretary of labor, and the socialist reformer and presidential candidate Norman Thomas concluded that Smith was a "much better [governor] than Roosevelt."

With such accolades, it is not surprising that Smith was again a strong contender for the Democratic presidential nomination in 1924, but 1924 was also the year membership crested in the resurrected Ku Klux Klan, and what to say and do about the Klan split the Democratic Party in two.

The Klan is primarily remembered in its first and third iterations for its persecution of African Americans during Reconstruction and again during the civil rights movement of the 1950s and 1960s. But the second iteration of the Klan that rose during and immediately after the First World War was focused primarily on resentment by white, middle class Protestants of immigrants, Catholics, and Jews. It also represented, in the words of one scholar, "the most powerful movement of the far right that America has yet produced."

By 1924, Klan membership peaked, with some estimates placing it as high as five million. It was stronger in some parts of the country than others, but its reach went far beyond the South. Between one-quarter and one-third of all adult white males in Indiana belonged to the Klan, and the Klan openly controlled the state government of Colorado and wielded considerable clout in other states. In Oregon, the Legislature passed a Klan-sponsored law (later ruled unconstitutional) that banned parochial schools.

A resolution was offered at the 1924 Democratic National Convention held in New York City to specifically denounce the KKK by name, but it failed by a single vote (with the shameful help of William Jennings Bryan). William Gibbs McAdoo, the other leading contender for the Democratic presidential nomination besides Smith, had the Klan's backing; Smith had the Klan's contempt. So neither man could gain the two-thirds vote of delegates needed for nomination in this badly split convention, and on a record 103rd ballot the party finally turned to former West Virginia congressman, diplomat, and Wall Street attorney John W. Davis, who was trounced by Calvin Coolidge in the general election.

Smith gave one of the more memorable speeches during the 1924 campaign in Buffalo when he attacked the Klan for the sacrilege of christening infants in a Klan ceremony whereby a supposed "disciple of the Christ of Love and Peace, [breathed] into the heart and soul of an infant the spirit of hate and war." Smith said of the Klan's bigotry, "The Catholics of the country can stand it; the Jews can stand it; our citizens born under foreign skies can stand it; the Negro can stand it; but the United States of America cannot stand it."

Despite the experience of 1924, Smith believed he could win the presidency, and it is remarkable that he seemed the inevitable choice to lead the Democratic Party in 1928. Harking back to his life in the Fourth Ward, Smith was convinced that, if given the chance, he could unite Catholics, Protestants, and Jews nationally just as he had in New York. Smith told the *New York Times* in February 1928 that "there was no essential difference between the average man of a Middle Western mining town and the man he might meet anywhere in the Bowery."

That was decidedly not the view of many Americans to whom Smith was a New Yorker in the narrowest sense of the word. Smith was, in the words of one hostile Tennessee editor, "a Manhattanite; of that kith and kin and caste which, complacent in its egotistic self-sufficiency, regards Ninth Avenue as the Far West and the Jersey meadows as beyond the frontier." Smith was also a "wet," meaning he believed that the Eighteenth Amendment to the Constitution, which prohibited the manufacture and sale of alcohol, either needed to be repealed or seriously modified. Smith considered Prohibition unenforceable, and in 1923 approved the repeal of

New York's enforcement mechanism of Prohibition (alcohol remained illegal, but the state now considered it a matter for federal enforcement only).

Smith was also acutely aware that Prohibition was targeted especially at urban immigrants, like himself and his neighbors, for whom beer, wine, and whiskey were components of their traditions and customs. Many "drys" expressed that prejudice openly. American Methodist bishop James Cannon, a leading dry cleric, said, "Governor Smith wants the Italians, the Sicilians, the Poles, and the Russian Jews. . . . We shut the door to them. But Smith says, 'Give me that kind of people.' He wants the kind of dirty people that you find today on the sidewalks of New York." For his part, Smith observed that it was "curious" that reformers who pushed Prohibition as an important cure for the country's social ills "never took much interest in social legislation such as the Factory Code, workmen's compensation, pensions for widowed mothers, public health or parks."

The unintended consequence of Smith's opposition to Prohibition was that it gave cover to many who opposed Smith on religious grounds but who could not bring themselves to say so publicly. Josephus Daniels, the North Carolina newspaper editor who had served as Woodrow Wilson's secretary of the Navy, said Southerners were weary of being accused of religious bigotry because they opposed Smith's candidacy when "nearly all of it is based upon . . . his attitude against Prohibition." Some insisted Smith's anti-Prohibition stance was political suicide. Virginia senator Carter Glass said, "Any one is a fool who thinks the Eighteenth Amendment will be repealed in the next hundred years." Prohibition was repealed five years later.

But others stated with great clarity that the nature of their opposition to Smith was due to religion, not policy. The most rabid anti-Catholic in Congress, Alabama senator Tom Heflin, said that God himself had "raised up this great patriotic organization [the Klan] to unmask popery." A Klan leader who identified himself only as "The Human Dynamo" told a Presbyterian Church congregation in New York City itself that "there are six million people in the United States who have pledged their lives that no son of the pope in Rome will ever sit in the presidential chair."

In the early stages of the 1928 campaign, this seemed all bluster. Primary elections to decide a party nominee were still relatively new, but Smith won the handful of Democratic primaries in place in 1928 with ease, including the critical California primary that clinched his nomination. Smith even charmed audiences in the South, trying to meld his Lower East Side accent with a Southern drawl by telling a group in Asheville, North Carolina, that he hoped to "meet yez-all personally."

Smith also hoped he had put the religious issue behind him the year before when the *Atlantic Monthly* mischievously asked a prominent Episcopalian attorney named Charles Marshall to address the issue of whether Smith, were he president, could be both a loyal Catholic and a loyal American. In a dry scholarly article filled with quotes from an array of papal bulls, encyclicals, and other church documents, Marshall made the case that "there is conflict between authoritative Roman Catholic claims on one side and our constitutional law and principles on the other." The *Atlantic* then invited Smith to reply.

Smith was reluctant at first. While a regular Mass attendee, he was hardly a theologian. He had once been photographed kissing the ring of a papal legate visiting the country while he was governor, but he was not a church insider interested in Catholic apologetics. As Frances Perkins noted, "He knew religion, and that was all that he needed. And he took it . . . simply and naturally." After reading Marshall's turgid article, Smith admitted he did not understand most of it and reportedly asked his staff, "What the hell is an encyclical, anyhow?" But Marshall's article was front-page news all over the country, and upon reflection, and with the help both of Father Francis Duffy, the famed World War I chaplain, and one of Smith's Jewish aides, Judge Joseph Proskauer, Smith penned a response.

Smith noted that he had been in public life for twenty-five years, had taken an oath to uphold the Constitution nineteen times, and had never found an occasion where his religion interfered with his public duties. Nor could such a thing ever happen, Smith said, noting, in language that would likely appall modern secularists, that "the essence of my faith is built upon the Commandments of God. The law of the land is built upon the Commandments of God. There can be no conflict between them."

He concluded with the hopeful plea that "never again in this land will any public servant be challenged because of the faith in which he has tried to walk humbly with his God."

Smith's strong and laudable response simply pushed the issue underground for a while. The *New York World* observed, "The opposition to Smith has identified him so thoroughly with the principles of religious tolerance, personal liberty and social equality that a refusal to nominate him would be . . . a rejection of these principles." But there were ominous signs in Houston where the Democrats held their convention and nominated Smith on the first ballot. Delegations from eight Southern states declined to take the traditional step and switch their allegiance to Smith to make his nomination symbolically unanimous. When the convention demonstration for Smith began, most Southern delegates stayed in their seats in disgust. A Texas delegate complained that when he watched the procession for Smith pass by "the faces I saw . . . were not American faces. I wondered, where were the Americans?"

The face of America was changing. The 1920 census was the first in which America counted more citizens living in cities than on farms and in rural areas. Many found this shift unsettling, and the Catholic journal *Commonweal* at first guessed that Smith's biggest hurdle was that he was an unabashed urban dweller when every previous president had some connection to the country. Even Theodore Roosevelt liked to emphasize his rather brief experience as a rancher in the North Dakota Badlands despite being, like Smith, a Manhattanite. Having country roots seemed key to fulfilling the American myth of what a president should be.

Because Southern delegates did not actually bolt the convention, some observers, including *Commonweal's* chief political reporter, Charles Willis Thompson, mistakenly thought the religious issue, at least within the Democratic Party, had been resolved. Thompson even opined that with two high quality candidates in Smith and Hoover, 1928 would prove to be "a campaign conducted honestly and without humbug." It took a very short time to prove that assessment wrong.

While one Catholic historian called the "campaign of vilification" against Smith "even more ridiculous than it was malicious," Smith biographer Robert A. Slayton is closer to the mark when he called the 1928 presidential campaign "arguably the strangest and sickest in American history."

There were certainly elements of the ridiculous. A photograph of Smith dedicating the opening of the Lincoln Tunnel was described in many publications as the opening of a direct tunnel to the Vatican. The school board in Daytona Beach, Florida, sent a postcard home with every student, warning that if Smith were elected, no one would be allowed to own or read a Bible. There were other charges that a Catholic president would end the public school system, annul all Protestant marriages, and sterilize Protestant women.

It speaks to the credulousness of the American public that American Catholics felt the need to respond to such nonsense. At one point, Catholics asked prominent members of the Masons, a primarily Protestant service club, to investigate and refute rumors that members of the Catholic service club the Knights of Columbus took secret oaths to cheat, spy on, or even kill Protestants if ever given the order to do so by the pope. The Masons concluded in a public letter that such charges were "scurrilous, wicked, and libellous."

But mixed with the ridiculous was the dangerous. In its publications, the Klan described Smith as "the AntiChrist" and Klan membership, which had been declining since 1924 due to a series of scandals involving Klan leaders, was increasing once again. In a campaign stop in Billings, Montana, Smith was greeted not only with burning crosses on a ridge overlooking the city, but also several explosions of dynamite in the city. There were burning crosses and threats of violence in Oklahoma, where a crowd of ten thousand filled an Oklahoma City auditorium to hear the pastor of the state's largest Baptist congregation warn that Smith was leading "the forces of Hell" and that anyone who voted for Smith would be "voting against Christ and ... be damned."

More disturbing than the ridiculous and the dangerous was the respectable anti-Catholicism. One of the nation's most renowned journalists, William Allen White, editor of the *Emporia* (Kansas) *Gazette,* charged that Smith was the candidate of "the saloon, prostitution, and gambling," and seriously fretted that "the whole Puritan civilization which has built a sturdy, orderly nation is threatened by Smith." A Methodist newspaper in Georgia called Catholicism "a degenerate type of Christianity," while a Baptist newspaper warned that Smith, if elected, would close down all Protestant churches and end not only freedom of worship but freedom of the press as well.

Mabel Walker Willebrandt, who had been an assistant attorney general in the Harding administration charged with overseeing Prohibition enforcement, addressed a gathering of twenty-five hundred Methodist ministers in Ohio and urged them to denounce Smith from their pulpits in order to swing the election to Hoover. Many obliged. A high-ranking Methodist bishop was quoted as calling Smith "utterly un-American," while a survey of eighty-five hundred Southern Methodist ministers found exactly four who intended to vote for Smith.

Several Republicans, most notably Robert Taft, urged Willebrandt to keep quiet before she cost Hoover the election, and Hoover, himself a Quaker, avoided any comment on Smith's religion. His campaign issued pro forma denunciations of the slanders against Smith's religion as "vicious and beyond the pale of decent political campaigning." However, a reporter working undercover discovered that the Republican National Committee routinely referred inquiries for information about Smith to the Ku Klux Klan, and the Klan co-hosted a number of events with state and local Republican parties. And while Hoover himself avoided the ugliness, his wife, Lou, defended Protestants who chose to vote against Smith because he was a Catholic. "There are many people of intense Protestant faith to whom Catholicism is a grievous sin," Mrs. Hoover wrote a friend. "And they have as much right to vote against a man for public office because of that belief" as any other, adding, "That is not persecution."

Silent on religion since his 1927 *Atlantic* article, Smith could not let such open bigotry go unanswered, and he decided to address the issue in the Klan stronghold of Oklahoma City. Smith had drafted his remarks on the train, which had been greeted with burning crosses, and he had jotted down some notes for his speech in the margins of a letter he had been sent from the Klan's Grand Dragon in Arkansas. He brought some in the crowd to tears when, his voice low and solemn, Smith declared, "The world knows no greater mockery than the use of the blazing cross, the cross upon which Christ died, as a symbol to install into the hearts of men a hatred of their brethren, while Christ preached and died for the love and brotherhood of man."

Smith concluded that he hoped no one would vote for him because he was Catholic and no one should vote against him because he was Catholic. Rather, the election should be judged on who the voters believed would make the best president. "Let us debate it on the level . . . bring it out in the open, have the record consulted, and the platforms scrutinized," and if the voters made their choice based on those criteria, then Smith would be satisfied with the result.

That is not how the election was prosecuted, and the results on November 6, 1928, satisfied neither Smith nor his fellow Catholics. He had drawn enormous and emotional crowds—two hundred thousand in St. Louis, four hundred thousand in Boston—that gave him false hope that his campaign would succeed. While he did earn fifteen million votes—more than any Democratic candidate had ever received—it still represented barely 40 percent of the popular vote.

He had lost in a landslide, the size of which was devastating to Smith personally, but perhaps even more so to Catholics in general. It was not that Smith had simply been defeated—Hoover was a formidable candidate running in ideal conditions—but that he had been humiliated, and Catholics attributed this level of humiliation to American antipathy toward Smith's (and their) religion.

"What shall the Catholic do?" *Commonweal* asked in an editorial a few months after the election. Smith's campaign had increased interest in the Catholic faith, and priests nationwide were reporting conversions in record numbers, even including one of Hoover's campaign chairmen. But generally, Catholic leaders had been dismayed during 1928 to find that many Catholics were unable to defend their faith from attack because, like Smith, they had no idea what a papal encyclical was or even the basic tenets of their religion. Catholics and non-Catholics needed to be educated about the reality of the faith.

As a direct result of the Smith campaign, the National Conference of Catholic Men began in March 1930 to broadcast the *Catholic Hour* radio program Sunday evenings on the NBC radio network. NCCM executive director Edward J. Heffron said the goal of the show was to "set before the radio audience, in their true light, the teachings and practices of the Catholic Church, hoping only that this will create better understanding and overcome prejudice." Originally broadcast on twenty-two stations in seventeen states, by 1940 the *Catholic Hour* was heard on ninety-four stations in forty-one states. One of the hosts of the *Catholic Hour* was Bishop Fulton J. Sheen, who later made an effective transition into television, where his program on ABC, *Life Is Worth Living*, was the highest-rated regular religious program in television history with an estimated thirty million weekly viewers during its five-year run in the 1950s.

The most popular figure on radio during the 1930s was a Catholic priest, Father Charles Coughlin, whose weekly audience was estimated at forty million at its peak. Coughlin began broadcasting in 1926 when a local radio station invited him to solicit funds on air after the Klan had burned down his Detroit-area church. Coughlin's early sermons were simple homilies on religious themes, but as the Depression worsened, he turned to more political fare. Initially a New Deal supporter, Coughlin became more radical, more anti-Semitic and more aggressive in attacking Roosevelt, and his popularity waned.

Despite the broad-based popularity of Catholic personalities like Coughlin and Sheen, Catholics were under no illusion that Protestant America was ready to fully embrace them into their institutions, so another response to the Smith debacle was to create vigorous parallel Catholic institutions. Every diocese began to print its own Catholic newspaper, and the general-interest *Catholic Digest* was begun as an alternative to the Protestant-oriented *Reader's Digest*. The Catholic Youth Organization gave Catholic children a place to play other than the Protestant YMCA. There were now bar associations for Catholic lawyers and medical associations for Catholic physicians, not to mention an American Catholic Sociological Society, a Catholic Poetry Society of America, a Catholic Economic Association, a Catholic Anthropological Society, a National

Council of Catholic Nurses, and an Association of Catholic Trade Unionists that would soon be a force in the rise of the CIO.

But many Catholics argued that establishing parallel institutions outside the dominant Protestant culture was not the answer. "How then can one transform America into a Catholic country (or at least relatively, by the infiltration of principles and ideals) by declining all invitations to take root in the American mind?" a *Commonweal* editorial asked. Instead, they intended to "Catholicize" American culture.

The most important invitation accepted by Catholics was to help "clean up" Hollywood and the motion picture industry. Prior to World War II, no better mechanism than motion pictures existed to change American attitudes. During the 1930s, eighty million Americans—65 percent of the entire population—attended movies weekly. Films became infused with Catholic ideals, which took root in the public consciousness through the most popular entertainment medium in the nation, and which changed Catholicism from the strange to the familiar—even to the ideal.

The impact of motion pictures upon the nation's morals had been a concern for many Americans from the first filmed kiss in 1896, but the scandal surrounding the popular comedian Fatty Arbuckle in 1922 (even though Arbuckle was cleared of responsibility in the death of a young woman at an Arbuckle party) led studio executives to ask President Harding's postmaster general Will Hays to head up the Motion Picture Association of America (MPAA) to develop standards on and off set. As film content became even more prurient, however, the MPAA invited two Catholics, Father Daniel Lord, a Jesuit priest, and Martin Quigley, who edited the influential distributors' journal *Motion Picture Herald*, to develop a new Production Code, which was adopted by the MPAA in 1930.

The Production Code, as one scholar of this era in Hollywood, Thomas Doherty, has noted, was "deeply Catholic in tone and outlook," especially reflecting "the intellectual lineage of Ignatius Loyola." The code demanded that filmmakers show deference to civil and religious authority, insist that characters accept personal responsibility for their actions, demonstrate a belief that suffering has value as a step toward salvation, resist the glorification of sin, and never depict the ultimate triumph of evil over good. The code was written with a confidence that non-Catholics would agree with the Catholic view of what was right and what was wrong, what was proper and what was improper. In essence, Catholic philosophy would now guide the production of the most popular entertainment form in the United States, and this was at least partially the result of the penance the country had decided to accept for the way Smith was treated.

But Hollywood did not immediately and fully conform to the Production Code. For several more years, Hollywood continued to churn out a slew of provocative films that ignored the code, including *Blonde Crazy, Divorcee, Night Nurse, Baby Face, Bombshell,* and *Other Men's Women.* A few filmmakers, most notably Cecil B. DeMille, were clever enough to insert nudity, orgies, and other licentious fare into biblical epics in order to make it difficult for clergy to condemn the films. The Catholic hierarchy, however, had had enough of Hollywood ignoring the code, especially a code written by Catholics. "We believed we were dealing with moral gentlemen. We were mistaken," said George Cardinal Mundelein of Chicago.

In 1933, the church hierarchy organized the Legion of Decency, which has been described as "the most successful endeavor undertaken by the church to influence American culture." Catholics at Sunday Masses were directed by their clergy to join the legion and take oaths that they would refuse to attend movies that violated the Production Code. The legion claimed that twenty million Catholics, or virtually every adult Catholic in the United States, signed the pledge. In 1934, Dennis Cardinal Dougherty of Philadelphia upped the ante by ordering good Catholics to "avoid *all* motion pictures" until all movies conformed to the code, putting Hollywood in jeopardy of losing fully one-quarter of its audience. Other religious denominations followed suit by suggesting boycotts, and there were threats of federal intervention as well. The film industry had no choice but to promise self-regulation.

The studios formed the Production Code Administration and hired a Catholic journalist named Joseph Breen, whose responsibility was to ensure every film released by the studios carried the PCA code of approval. Any studio that released a film without PCA approval faced a hefty twenty-five thousand dollar fine.

It is probably not surprising that Hollywood, working with a Catholic-written production code that embodied Catholic values and which was enforced by a Catholic censor, began making more films that placed Catholics, especially parish priests, in a positive light. *Commonweal* had predicted as much in a 1929 editorial. If Catholic apologetics were to be "an integral part of the American experience" then the church needed to find the means to make people listen. *Commonweal* volunteered that the most positive Catholic image that could be put forward was "the parish priest—the 'padre' or the 'father'—[who] wears the aura of virtuous romance." And it was the parish priest to whom Hollywood turned as the center of some of its finest films during what is generally considered the "golden age" of motion pictures.

The archetype began with Spencer Tracy in *San Francisco* (1936) as the priest determined to clean up the Barbary Coast, virtuous but still masculine enough to win a fistfight with Clark Gable. Two years later, Tracy played a priest again, this time as Father Flanagan in *Boys Town* (1938), creating a home for orphaned and wayward boys. The film emphasized that Flanagan welcomed all boys in need, regardless of race or faith, and that no boy was required to become Catholic. Yet, in a scene that must have been mildly startling for Protestant audiences, particularly because it evoked Al Smith's greeting to the papal legate a decade before, Tracy is seen bowing before his bishop, a kindly man in full regalia, and then kissing his ring. What had seemed so alien a decade before was now part of mainstream entertainment.

Led by Crosby's Oscar-winning turn as the "hip," masculine, yet sympathetic "Father Chuck" in *Going My Way* (1944), there were so many glowing portrayals of Catholic priests, from Pat O'Brien in *Angels with Dirty Faces* (1938) to Karl Malden in *On the Waterfront* (1954) and even Catholic saints, *The Song of Bernadette* (1943), that a Michigan woman was moved to complain by letter to the MPAA: "How much longer do we have to tolerate Catholic pictures? As much as we like Bing Crosby, I, and many others have resolved not to see any more of his pictures—until he adopts a different theme," she said. "After all America is still a Protestant country, and the majority prefer non-sectarian stories."

Yet, Crosby was Hollywood's top box office draw in both 1944 and 1945, so his films were being seen by millions of Protestants and Jews as well as Catholics. Why? First, these and many more like them were fine films, well written and well acted, deserving of their accolades. But more important, Catholicism seemed familiar and compatible with American culture. It was as Smith had argued; a Catholic from the Bowery was really no different from a Baptist from Iowa. The films might feature characters who were Catholic, even focus on their Catholicity, but the themes were universal. And Catholicism, so rich in the imagery and visual symbolism that filmgoers crave, could easily convey those universal themes. Americans had learned, through films, through radio, through the experience of 1928 and since, that Catholics were not a separate people, but just another part of America.

By the 1950s, the Catholic Church was at the forefront of the crusade against communism. Joe McCarthy and many of his followers were proud Catholics who now played the role of the Klan in deciding who was and was not a good American, and the Knights of Columbus successfully petitioned Congress to add the phrase "under God" to our Pledge of Allegiance. The ugliness of widespread and overt religious prejudice (at least against Catholics) had seemingly dissipated. It had at least receded enough that a young Catholic senator from Massachusetts named John Kennedy, with great encouragement from his family, believed that he might succeed where Smith had failed in becoming the nation's first Catholic president.

Ironically, Kennedy, to advance his own cause, helped cement the myth that Smith's religion was not the reason he had lost so severely in 1928. A 1956 memorandum, written by Kennedy aide Ted Sorensen for the purpose of persuading Adlai Stevenson to select Kennedy as his vice presidential running mate, argued that Smith had fallen victim to general prosperity, his stand on Prohibition, and his ties to Tammany Hall. Sorensen further argued that being Catholic was now an advantage for Kennedy because millions of Catholics who had voted for Eisenhower would return to the Democratic Party in order to vote for a Catholic on the national ticket. A Gallup survey taken earlier in the year found three-quarters of Americans claimed they would vote for a well-qualified Catholic candidate for president.

Kennedy was not the Democrats' vice presidential nominee in 1956, but he was the party's presidential nominee in 1960. His opponent that year, Richard Nixon, was certain Kennedy's religion was now an advantage, not a liability, for all the reasons Sorensen had laid out in his memorandum, most particularly that Catholics would turn out in droves to vote for a Catholic nominee. A Gallup survey found more than half of all Catholics said they would vote for a Catholic candidate even if nominated by the other party. Nixon would receive only 22 percent of the Catholic vote—the lowest any GOP nominee had received since polling began in the 1930s.

But Kennedy, who was personally not very religious, was never certain that his Catholicism was not a liability. Late in the campaign, he took the precaution of addressing a gathering of Protestant ministers in Houston where he so forcefully argued for the total separation of church and state that the joke was that Kennedy became America's first Catholic president by promising to be the nation's first Baptist president.

Kennedy's 1960 candidacy evoked some faint echoes of 1928; an estimated twenty-five million copies of anti-Catholic literature were distributed during the campaign. But Kennedy faced nothing like the onslaught endured by Smith. Still, based on polling and other information, Kennedy had expected that he would win the presidency with 53 percent to 57 percent of the popular vote. When he won with just 49.7 percent of the vote, he privately blamed anti-Catholic bigotry for the narrow margin over Nixon.

And so it is assumed the ghost of Al Smith has been put to rest and Catholics are now full participants in American civic life. This is true to a point. As noted earlier, as of 2012, six of the nine justices on the U.S. Supreme Court were Catholic, including Chief Justice John Roberts, and with the other three justices being Jewish there was not a single Protestant on the nation's highest court. While it is remarked upon, it is not seen as particularly threatening to American Protestants. The United States has also had its first Catholic vice president in Joe Biden, which is hardly remarked upon.

But surveys indicate a majority of Americans still worry that Catholics are trying to force their moral values on the country at large. Further, no Republican Catholic has yet been nominated by that party for either of the two highest offices in the land, and only once since Kennedy have the Democrats nominated another Catholic for president. When John Kerry was nominated in 2004, the issue again arose, as it had in 1928, of whether a Catholic politician must heed the commands of Catholic prelates—but this time the question was asked by some of the Catholic prelates themselves in questioning whether Kerry would abide by the church's teaching on abortion.

Smith, whom Roosevelt tagged "The Happy Warrior" of American politics, might have found the irony amusing, but in truth he found little amusing after 1928. After his defeat, he was hired to run the Empire State Building, then the world's tallest office building. But the Wall Street Crash of 1929 came in October, the very month construction had begun on the Empire State. Smith, who thought his job would provide a lifetime of security, instead found he could not even secure enough tenants to fill a third of the building, even with reduced rents. When the king of Thailand came to visit the imposing but nearly empty skyscraper, he told Smith they had the same things in Thailand. Smith asked what in the world the king could mean? "White elephants," his highness replied.

Smith had hoped the Democrats might turn to him once more in 1932. He even defeated Roosevelt in the Massachusetts primary and arrived at the convention with two hundred pledged delegates. But it was Roosevelt's turn and it was Smith himself who had put FDR on the road to the White House by insisting Roosevelt run for governor of New York in 1928. That Roosevelt, whom Smith considered a light-weight despite their friendship, could succeed where Smith failed, and that this was due at least in part to religious bigotry, embittered Smith, and he became a leading critic of Roosevelt and the New Deal, damaging Smith's own reputation among liberals.

At the annual Washington, D.C., dinner of the Liberty League, before the group of industrialists and financiers who were solidly opposed to Roosevelt and who also were Smith's new friends and business partners, Smith gave an angry speech over nationwide radio, accusing Roosevelt and his New Deal of fomenting class warfare. "There can be only one capital, Washington or Moscow," he said. When Roosevelt won an enormous landslide victory later that year, Smith could only remark, "You can't lick Santa Claus."

In time, Smith's bitterness ebbed, and when war seemed imminent, he judged it his patriotic duty to support the president and his policies. Roosevelt had always been more baffled than angry by Smith's enmity, and during the war he invited Smith to the White House for a chat that led to reconciliation. In May 1944, Smith's beloved wife, Katie, died, and he followed her in death five months later. *Commonweal* said in Smith's obituary that his defeat in 1928 "was a blow from which he never fully recovered." But the country recovered from the bigotry infecting that election, and that is the great legacy of Al Smith.

CHAPTER SIX

THOMAS E. DEWEY
1944, 1948

It is our solemn duty . . . to show that government can have both a head and a heart; that it can be both progressive and solvent; that it can serve the people without becoming their master.

Thomas E. Dewey, despite having lost not one, but two presidential elections, can stake a claim to being the most influential Republican of the twentieth century. Dewey, along with his protégés Dwight Eisenhower and Richard Nixon, moved the Republican Party away from an agenda of repealing the New Deal to a grudging acceptance of the permanent welfare state. The philosophy of "Modern Republicanism" inspired by Dewey's pragmatic politics continued to define the limits of Republican conservatism into the early twenty-first century, when the "Tea Party," dedicated to shrinking the federal government, still shied away from even relatively modest reforms of federal entitlements, including not only the New Deal's Social Security program, but also the Great Society's Medicare program.

Yet, to the degree Dewey is remembered today, it is as a supposedly tepid and bumbling campaigner who allowed Harry Truman to defy the odds in 1948 and win re-election in the greatest upset in presidential election history. The shock of that upset is forever enshrined by the infamous *Chicago Tribune* headline DEWEY DEFEATS TRUMAN. But as much as any presidential loser in history, Dewey reminds us that a lost election is only the loss of one political battle in a much larger struggle to set the political direction of the nation. Under Dewey's leadership—and both Eisenhower and Nixon owe a considerable debt for their presidencies to Dewey's favors and efforts—the so-called Eastern establishment wing of the Republican Party dominated the GOP for more than three decades and altered the central thinking of even the party's conservative wing. In the more than half century since Dewey outmaneuvered the right wing for control of the Republican Party, only one Republican presidential nominee, Barry Goldwater in 1964, seriously challenged the idea that the welfare state is here to stay, and he suffered the most overwhelming defeat of any Republican candidate since Alf Landon in 1936.

Dewey's image as "the little man on a wedding cake," an epithet hung on him by a sharp-tongued socialite (which one is in some dispute), is in need of revision. In truth, Dewey was a charismatic crime fighter, as feared by the underworld as "The Untouchable" Eliot Ness. Dewey made his name and his political career as a fearless New York prosecuting attorney whose exploits inspired dozens of Hollywood films, with Dewey portrayed on screen by tough guys like Humphrey Bogart. His fame made him a presidential contender at age thirty-seven—while he was still just a district attorney. In his career, Dewey put behind bars the man advertised as head of Murder Inc., as well as the former president of the New York Stock Exchange, a leading boss of Tammany Hall, and most famously, the racketeer Charles "Lucky" Luciano. So effective was Dewey in his crime busting that the gangster Dutch Schultz was plotting Dewey's assassination when Schultz himself was murdered in a gangland killing.

There were plenty among the right wing of the Republican Party who later wished Schultz had been able to finish the job. Dewey was a heretic to conservatives because he had concluded in the early 1940s, after he had already sought the Republican nomination once, that the GOP should embrace rather than repeal the New Deal and such liberal reforms as Social Security. To do otherwise, Dewey insisted, would be political suicide, for if Republicans yielded to the forces of reaction, they would be doomed to permanent minority status. Rather, Dewey argued, Republicans needed to pursue progressive ends by conservative means. It was fine for the federal government to initiate social reforms, Dewey believed, but those reforms should be implemented at the state or local level and they should be funded in a fiscally responsible manner that did not increase the national debt. Dewey's fine biographer, Richard Norton Smith, called Dewey's philosophy "pay-as-you-go liberalism."

To true blue conservatives, such as Dewey's arch-nemesis Ohio senator Robert Taft and later Goldwater, Dewey was not offering a conservative alternative to liberalism, only more "me-too-ism." They questioned why the Grand Old Party should follow the lead of a man who had been defeated not once but twice. But as of this writing, Dewey's warning that the GOP cannot repeal popular social programs without facing electoral disaster has been heeded by Republicans.

While espousing conservative rhetoric may have helped elect Nixon, Ronald Reagan, and George W. Bush, each also presided over (and often initiated) expansions of federal spending, federal power, and domestic programs. None dismantled a major New Deal or Great Society program. Echoing Dewey, Eisenhower conceded that the most accurate label for his own two-term presidency was "responsible progressive." As Nixon prepared to assume the presidency, his attorney general–designate, John Mitchell, told Southern civil rights leaders, "Watch what we do, not what we say." The 2008 Republican presidential nominee, John McCain, said his model president was the Republican progressive Theodore Roosevelt—who had also been Dewey's boyhood political idol.

Even Goldwater had to concede that the election of an avowedly conservative president like Reagan had not led to a dismantling of federal power. During the Reagan presidency, Goldwater complained to conservative journalist William F. Buckley, "We used to say about the Democrats, 'They spend and spend and elect and elect.' Now the Republicans—'They borrow and borrow and elect and elect.' So there's basically no difference."

Goldwater has been the only Republican presidential nominee since 1948 to ignore Dewey's advice and instead offer what Dewey scorned as "a platform of back to Methuselah." Goldwater fulfilled Dewey's prediction of the fate of such a platform when Lyndon Johnson trounced him in 1964 by winning the largest popular vote percentage in presidential election history. Dewey could only shake his head in wonder at those who insisted on ideological purity and who wanted to purge the party of moderates and liberals. If the Republican Party were only a party of conservatives, Dewey warned, and truly became the party of reaction that yearned to return the nation to "the miscalled 'good old days' of the nineteenth century . . . you can bury the Republican Party as the deadest pigeon in the country." Democrats would win every election, Dewey said. The United States would end up being ruled by one party, which would be a prelude to totalitarianism and the end of liberty.

Dewey had no desire to see the parties sharply divided along ideological lines and thought a large part of the strength of American democracy was the general similarities between the two parties. Having struck up an unlikely friendship with Hubert Humphrey, whom he called "about the best liberal around," Dewey argued that when Nixon and Humphrey ran against each other in 1968 there weren't "five degrees" separating them on the political spectrum and that was just "swell" because in America "all the votes are still to be found in the middle of the road."

"This similarity is highly objectionable to a vociferous few," Dewey said during a series of lectures he gave at Princeton University in 1950 (which were republished, not coincidentally in 1966, two years after the Goldwater debacle):

> *They rail at both parties, saying they represent nothing but a choice between Tweedledee and Tweedledum. I must say that I have most often heard this view expressed by people who have no experience in government and are either extreme reactionaries or radicals who want a neat little party to carry out their special prejudices, or these people are pseudo-intellectuals, or just plain obstructionists. None of them contributes much to the sober, tough business of modern government.*

To Dewey, Americans are all one family who share the same basic values and objectives. The argument between the two parties is over which methods best achieve those objectives. "The disparaging epithets of those who want everything clear-cut and simple cannot erase the stubborn fact that our objectives and interests as Americans are not neatly opposed but are, I hope always will be, mutual."

Dewey had referred to himself as "a New Deal Republican" and vigorously defended Social Security, unemployment insurance, farm supports, and securities legislation as ideas that cost relatively little "when compared with the gain in human happiness." In determining a governmental course of action, Dewey had two questions he needed answered: Is it right? Will it work? Dewey did share the general belief of American conservatives that programs work best when they are initiated and operated locally as opposed to centrally in the federal government, and he often proved that to be true while serving as governor of New York for a dozen years.

Dewey was often far ahead of the Democratic administrations of Roosevelt and Truman in tackling such domestic issues as racial discrimination. Anti-discrimination legislation in New York signed into law by Dewey in 1945 ended segregated public transportation, prevented unions from using race as a qualification for entering a trade, and greatly expanded the hiring of minorities in a wide range of professions. Congressman Adam Clayton Powell heralded the law as the most important legislation benefiting African Americans since the Fourteenth and Fifteenth Amendments to the Constitution. Dewey later pushed and approved similar laws to end discrimination in education and housing.*

Dewey scoffed at those who said he was enabling the "welfare state." "Of course they are running a welfare state," he said. "There has never been a responsible government which did not have the welfare of its people at heart." The question, Dewey believed, was how to provide for the people's welfare without sacrificing personal freedom. That was where he believed

---

* A Dewey-appointed commission charged with implementing the 1945 anti-discrimination laws urged New York's three baseball teams, the Yankees, Giants, and Dodgers, to sign a fair employment pledge. The clubs declined, but the request reassured Dodgers general manager Branch Rickey that his plan to integrate baseball had at least local political support. Dewey, therefore, liked to take partial credit for Jackie Robinson breaking the color line in baseball.

the Republicans held an advantage over the Democrats. Republicans would first consider whether the private sector could address the needs of the people, or whether it would be better handled at the local or state government level, before turning to the federal government. But if the federal government were the right place to address a public need, then Republicans would be more fiscally responsible, more efficient, and less corrupt in the administration of the program.

At least this was Dewey's faith based on his own remarkable record as governor of New York. One of the more impressive achievements of his years as governor was completely revamping New York's mental health care system after discovering the appalling condition of state hospitals. He bitterly noted that the squalid conditions of these facilities were "left to me by those who claimed to be liberals."

In addressing public welfare, Dewey echoed the words of Henry Stimson, who had served in the presidential Cabinets of Taft, Hoover, and Franklin Roosevelt. "To me it seems vitally important that the Republican Party, which contains, generally speaking, the richer and more intelligent citizens of the country, should take the lead in reform and not drift into a reactionary position," Stimson said.

Stimson's statement reeks of class-consciousness and a condescending noblesse oblige, but Dewey would not have objected to the basic sentiment; he had been taught from birth that "all good people" were Republicans.

Dewey was born on March 24, 1902, in Owosso, Michigan, the son of the local newspaper editor, who was also a local Republican official and activist. His birth announcement stated: "A ten-pound Republican voter was born last evening to Mr. and Mrs. George M. Dewey." Dewey's mother later told the story of how young Tom, overhearing a political argument between his father and a neighbor, complained to his parents that he had been falsely told the neighbor was a nice man. "Why, he is, Tom," his mother replied. "But he's a Democrat!" Tom countered.

Dewey was raised to work hard. At age nine, he was not merely a paperboy; he was the local distributor for the *Detroit News* and managed nine other boys who actually delivered the papers. At age ten, in 1912, when Theodore Roosevelt bolted the Republican Party because it would not turn out the conservative incumbent, William Howard Taft, Dewey was an avid Roosevelt supporter, distributing literature door-to-door and even earning the nickname "Ted," partly because of his devotion to TR and partly because *t*, *e*, and *d* were his initials.

The cool perfectionism that would prevent Dewey from becoming a beloved political figure, rather than just an admired one, was present at an early age. Dewey was, his high school principal said, "by all odds the smartest kid in school," but so arrogant he had trouble getting along with classmates. Dewey was aware that he was considered obviously straight-arrow. Not only did he never miss a single day of school in twelve years, he was never even tardy. When this came to light in his later political campaigns, Dewey begged his mother to joke that she had purposely scheduled his bout with chicken pox during summer vacation, and in high school, he deliberately earned a few Bs so that he would not receive straight As.

Yet, throughout his life, Dewey was abnormally conscious of image and duty. He smoked but refused to be photographed smoking. He insisted a magazine profile change a reference to him playing poker to him playing bridge. One of his great loves was the farm he purchased in rural New York and he had a genuine passion for raising livestock, but thought being photographed in his overalls seemed gimmicky, so "candid" photos of the Deweys on the farm showed Dewey and his sons incongruously lounging about in three-piece suits. Extraordinarily disciplined, while district attorney and governor, Dewey would routinely work from 9:00 a.m. until midnight. When tired, he had the uncanny ability to lie on his office couch, fall asleep immediately, and awake precisely fifteen minutes later, refreshed. He was also a creature of habit. He had the same lunch every day—a chicken sandwich, an apple, and a glass of milk—and he drank three quarts of water every day. On those occasions when he dined out, he always sat with his back to the wall—but that was perhaps a habit he picked up while a prosecutor when the mob had supposedly placed a twenty-five-thousand-dollar bounty on his head.

Yet, while wags said you had to know Dewey to really dislike him, his friends testified that in private Dewey could be warm, funny, caring—even sentimental. Once, concerned he had hurt a friend's feelings with an intemperate joke the week before, he suddenly showed up at the friend's house late at night, put his arm around the fellow, and said, "Whenever you feel you have hurt a friend of a lifetime, heal that hurt at once. I love you." Then he turned and left, leaving his friend comforted if befuddled. A Dewey intimate said, "It was almost tragic how he put on a pose that alienated people. Behind a pretty thin veneer was a wonderful guy."

Dewey would eventually revolutionize the methods of a criminal prosecutor, but his first calling was as an opera singer. Possessor of a marvelous, deep, rich baritone voice that would also make him the second most effective radio speaker in politics after FDR, Dewey placed third in a national singing contest in 1923. Eager to continue his training in New York City, Dewey left the University of Michigan to study law at Columbia University and to be near another singing student he had met—Frances Hutt, a five-foot-three-inch brown-haired beauty from Texas, who would later become his wife. In 1924, Dewey gave a recital attended by the renowned music critic Deems Taylor, who later narrated the Disney film *Fantasia*. Unfortunately, Dewey was suffering from laryngitis the night of the performance, and Taylor's review was sufficiently negative that Dewey decided to stick to law.

Shortly after graduating from law school, Dewey had the good luck in 1931 to be selected chief assistant to the U.S. attorney for southern New York, George Medalie. In his post, Dewey tackled cases involving securities fraud, stock manipulation, and the field with which he would be most identified: racket busting. In New York City, rackets were thought to raise the cost of living for New Yorkers by a whopping 20 percent. Racketeering drained an estimated eleven billion dollars out of the national economy each year, an amount ten times greater than what the federal government spent on national defense.

The young Dewey earned his boss's admiration and affection. To boost Dewey's career, Medalie timed his resignation in 1933 so that Dewey had to be temporarily appointed U.S. attorney in order to complete a major racketeering trial and so that he could become, at age thirty-one, the youngest U.S. attorney in history. Two years later, Dewey received another career boost from his mentor. When the State of New York decided to name a special prosecutor to bust the rackets, Medalie and other prominent Republicans declined the post and insisted Dewey be appointed instead. "This was just the chance to do the biggest job that any lawyer could do," Dewey said. And he did it well.

Just like in the movies (and many movies were based on Dewey's exploits), Dewey was given broad autonomy and nearly unprecedented authority to bypass the civil service system and handpick a team of dedicated and incorruptible aides and experts in various specialties to take down the leaders of the underworld. The use of teams of lawyers and investigators to crack complex cases was a Dewey innovation. He also "revitalized" the grand jury system, using the panels to gather evidence that he could not have obtained otherwise. To be sure, he engaged in questionable activities in his zeal for convictions. He arrested hundreds of potential witnesses and held them in secret (sometimes for their protection, sometimes just because he could), until they agreed to testify. And not only was he able to select jurors he believed would vote for convictions, using methods that would not be allowed today, he even had the latitude to choose the judges who would hear the cases.

Not surprisingly, he had a remarkably high conviction rate (94 percent, to be exact), though not always for the crimes of racketeering. Just as Al Capone was convicted not for murder but for income tax evasion, so Dewey's most famous conviction of a racketeer was for an offense not directly related to racketeering: prostitution.

There remains debate about how important a mobster Salvatore Lucania, better known as "Lucky" Luciano, really was. The one-time bootlegger and sometime associate of Meyer Lansky and Bugsy Siegel was certainly a major criminal force, and his lavish lifestyle attracted public attention. Dewey, however, was successful in portraying Luciano as America's arch gangster, and the legend grew that Luciano created the modern Mafia and was the chieftain of the underworld. Yet, Dewey had difficulty building a case against Luciano for racketeering, including his alleged control of various labor unions, such as the longshoremen. "Sometimes I feel the entire town is against me," Dewey said.

"You'd be surprised at the places where people like these defendants have friends."

It was Dewey's lone African-American and only female assistant, Eunice Hunton Carter, a "street smart" lawyer who had once worked as a social worker, who persuaded him to investigate Luciano's control of prostitution in New York City.* Dewey discovered, according to one madam working for Lucky, that Luciano had grand plans to syndicate prostitution "the same as the A&P." A massive raid on eighty houses of prostitution led to witnesses and evidence that identified Luciano as the prime operator of prostitution in New York City. Luciano was found guilty on an astounding 538 counts and was sentenced to thirty to fifty years in prison.†

Luciano's conviction made Dewey a national hero. Warner Brothers quickly churned out a film based on the case called *Marked Woman*, with Bogart and Bette Davis, and many other films with titles like *Racket Buster* and *Smashing the Rackets* soon followed. Dewey declined offers to portray himself in movies, but it was reported that whenever he appeared in newsreels, theater audiences would wildly applaud and cheer.

Despite his diminutive five-foot-eight-inch stature, Dewey cut a dashing figure. He had high cheekbones, a jutting jaw, dark brown hair, and, in the words of an associate, "the only piercing brown eyes I've ever seen. Those eyes tell you this guy doesn't crap around." Then there was the mustache. Dewey had grown it after graduating from law school while on a trip to Europe with a Columbia classmate (and future Supreme Court justice) William O. Douglas. He intended to cut it off when he returned, but Frances liked it and so, to the gratitude of editorial cartoonists, it stayed. He later trimmed it short when a campaign advisor said it would be easier to raise contributions if he looked more like Clark Gable.

---

* Later as district attorney and then governor, Dewey had an excellent record, for the period, in appointing African Americans, Jewish Americans, and members of other minority groups to positions of authority. He was also the first major party candidate to endorse the Equal Rights Amendment for women.

† Remarkably, given the profile of the case, Dewey commuted Luciano's sentence in 1946 and had him deported to Italy, reportedly as a reward for Luciano using his gangland contacts in Sicily, Italy, and even New York to help the Allied cause during World War II.

Dewey was eager to cash in on his newfound fame and weighed an offer to earn $150,000 per year at John Foster Dulles's law firm, but the New York Republican Party had other ideas. To avoid being thought a "skunk," Dewey agreed to run as the party's nominee for New York district attorney with its $20,000 annual salary instead.

Dewey's reputation as a crusader for decency and good government (he began the first public defender program) received additional boosts when he secured convictions against the purported "head" of Murder Inc., Louis "Lepke" Buchalter (though Dewey's conception of a corporation of professional killers was fanciful); against Tammany Hall boss Jimmy Hines for selling protection to the city's numbers racket for thirty thousand dollars a year; and against former New York Stock Exchange president Richard Whitney for embezzlement. "No! Not Dickie Whitney!" Franklin Roosevelt exclaimed when told of his fellow aristocrat's indictment.

Dewey lost a bid for governor of New York in 1938, but his vote totals were the highest of any Republican in twenty years. William Allen White compared Dewey's loss against Herbert Lehman with Abraham Lincoln's loss to Stephen Douglas in the 1858 Illinois Senate race. It prepared Dewey for a run for national office. So, as 1940 approached, Dewey, a thirty-seven-year-old whose only elected office was as a local district attorney, was now, remarkably, the leading candidate for the Republican nomination for president.

Dewey would acknowledge late in life that "everything came too early for me," and his first campaign for the White House betrayed his lack of seasoning. The resident curmudgeon of the Roosevelt administration, Interior Secretary Harold Ickes, mockingly announced, "Tom Dewey's thrown his diaper in the ring," while the *New Republic* characterized Dewey's campaign as "Pollyanna for President."

Dewey never really liked campaigning, shaking hands, kissing babies, and posing for photographs. For one thing, he had a phobia of germs. For another, an overbite and two missing teeth from playing football made him reluctant to smile broadly. A photographer once entreated, "Smile, Governor!" Dewey replied, "I thought I was."

A campaign aide from 1940 said Dewey was "brilliant, thoroughly honest...[but] cold as a February icicle." A man who worked on Dewey's farm claimed that Dewey's "greatest fun was finding out someone had made a mistake." Herbert Brownell, one of Dewey's longest-serving advisors, said Dewey's talents were not his charm but that "he'd climbed up the ladder the hard way. He worked harder, studied longer than anyone else. He could take a problem, break it down into component parts, assign it to talented people. He organized people. He was a real fighter. As president, he would have been [the] boss."

Dewey had thought the fight for the 1940 nomination would be with Ohio's new senator Robert Taft, and already the Dewey-Taft rivalry began to define the divisions within the Republican Party: city versus country; East versus Midwest; internationalist versus isolationist; pragmatic against dogmatic. But while Taft and Dewey weren't watching, a third figure, Wendell Willkie, arrived on the scene and, in one of the most improbable events in American political history, snatched the Republican nomination from both men.

Willkie, who had been a Democrat until 1938, was a New Deal critic but a strident internationalist who benefited from a new and growing concern among Americans regarding the war in Europe. Willkie aggressively supported Roosevelt's increasing calls for aid to the British and for enhancing American preparedness should the United States become involved in the fight. "We don't want a New Deal; we want a New World," Willkie proclaimed. Taft took the opposite tack and believed the United States could and should stay out of a foreign conflict where there was no direct American interest. Dewey tried to chart a middle course, supporting some aid to Britain but insisting the United States needed to stay out of war.

The Republican National Convention, however, occurred during the very week in June 1940 when Nazi Germany invaded France, which made Willkie seem prescient. Dewey actually led on the first three ballots during the convention, but with feelings high, party delegates decided to abandon the efficient but seemingly soulless Dewey for the raucous Willkie campaign that one reporter likened to "a whorehouse on a Saturday night."

Roosevelt handily defeated Willkie, and Republicans soon had buyer's remorse. Well before 1944, the party was ready to return to a lifelong Republican to be its standard bearer. Dewey, meanwhile, had been developing a more mature political philosophy informed by real experience. In 1942, he had won the first of his three terms as governor of New York, and he was proving that states could provide for the welfare of the public more efficiently (at least Dewey thought so) than the national government.

Dewey's record included improved mental health care, reform of workmen's compensation, enhanced cancer and tuberculosis screening and treatment, expanded minimum wage coverage, and preventing work stoppages by doubling the funding for labor mediation. He simplified tax forms, cut red tape in many departments, hired management specialists to improve efficiency, and created a new research unit to help with budget forecasting. When Dewey left the governor's office in 1955, state tax rates were 10 percent lower than when he had first been elected, but state revenues had dramatically increased.

During the war, Dewey had shown vision in refusing to spend state budget surpluses, instead setting them aside in a fund he called the "Postwar Reconstruction Fund" that he hoped would ease the transition from a wartime to a peacetime economy. He had also demonstrated the foresight in 1944 to have a state plan in place to help returning veterans quickly access unemployment assistance and prevent delay in their obtaining benefits; the federal government had taken no similar steps to prepare for the end of the war.

At the national level, Dewey called for medical insurance for the poor—but within the framework of private enterprise. As early as 1942, Dewey outlined his own proposal for foreign aid after the war, to allies and foes alike, that anticipated the Marshall Plan that the Truman administration would implement in 1947. He continued to chide Roosevelt for supposed fiscal irresponsibility, saying there needed to be a new beatitude: "Blessed are the young, for they shall inherit the national debt." Government "has nothing it does not take away from the people," Dewey said, but added, "It is our solemn duty . . . to show that government can have both a head and a heart; that it can be both progressive and solvent; that it can serve the people without becoming their master."

With Willkie no longer welcome in Republican circles and Taft temporarily discredited because of his previous isolationism, Dewey easily captured the Republican nomination in 1944 and for the second time in its history (the first being 1864), the United States held a presidential election while the nation was in the midst of total war. Initially, the campaign reflected the soberness of the hour. Dewey essentially began his campaign with a thoughtful and well-received speech on the obligation the United States would have to lead the post-war world in a system of "general international cooperation," which would include the Soviet Union as well as Great Britain. Dewey planned a host of other high-minded speeches, but the campaign turned nasty.

Roosevelt did not like Dewey; intimates said he hated him. Dewey hammered away at the New Deal, claiming it had really never solved the Great Depression nor even "understood what makes a job." After twelve years in office, the Roosevelt administration was simply "old and tired and quarrelsome," Dewey said, and the centralization of federal power under Roosevelt had now led to two dangerous alternatives: Either every aspect of American life would soon be under "complete government regulation" or the public would be so sick of government interference that they would rebel and "take refuge in complete reaction." Polling showed Dewey was within five points of Roosevelt.

Roosevelt had said little publicly during the campaign, but privately he told aides, "The little man makes me pretty mad." Roosevelt believed that most candidates talked too much and that to be successful a candidate had to have the patience to wait until the right moment to strike exactly the right chord. Roosevelt had his opening when an obscure Republican congressman from Minnesota, Harold Knutson, charged that Roosevelt had wasted taxpayer money by allegedly sending a Navy destroyer to pick up his Scottish terrier, named "Fala," that had been accidentally left behind on the Aleutian Islands. In late September, in a speech before a Teamsters meeting in San Francisco, Roosevelt showed why he remained the master campaigner with a sarcastic but hilarious speech in which he said, "I think I have a right to resent, to object to libelous statements about my dog." He added that Fala, being Scotch, did not like to be accused of extravagance. "He hasn't been the same dog since." The audience roared with laughter, but Roosevelt added the unfunny charge that Republicans, without mentioning Dewey by name, were using "propaganda techniques" straight from Hitler's *Mein Kampf.*

Dewey was livid. In a speech a few days later in Oklahoma City, he repeated his critique that, despite twelve years of Roosevelt's policies, ten million Americans were still out of work, but now he added the charge that Roosevelt had failed to adequately prepare the nation for war. Quoting the Army's chief of staff General George C. Marshall, Dewey said only 25 percent of the Army was equipped and in shape to fight when the Japanese attacked Pearl Harbor. It was a "desperately bad" record, Dewey charged.

After the speech, Dewey was mulling whether he might use some additional explosive information that had come to his attention—that Roosevelt had been warned ahead of time of the attack on Pearl Harbor but had not taken action to prevent it or to protect the American fleet. Republicans based this assertion, which has never been proven, on rumors that the United States had broken some key Japanese diplomatic codes. Marshall personally intervened with Dewey, privately urging him not to make the charge because it was true that the United States had broken some Japanese diplomatic codes. Information from the broken codes had indicated the Japanese were planning an attack, but Pearl Harbor was not identified as the target (though it can be argued that both the administration and local commanders were negligent by not being on a higher level of alert). Most importantly, Marshall told Dewey, these diplomatic codes were still being used by the Japanese and were continuing to provide useful information, especially when Tokyo was communicating with Berlin. Dewey was skeptical the Japanese would still be using the same codes three years later, but he agreed to drop the issue in the interests of national security.

Dewey, who by now regretted his intemperate remarks in Oklahoma City, also had to decide in the final weeks of the 1944 campaign whether to make one other spectacular charge—that Roosevelt was a dying man. He decided against making Roosevelt's health an issue, though that was due as much to fear that the charge would cause a backlash, as it was the desire to take the high road. Roosevelt would, in fact, die the following April, making Truman president.

Dewey had waged an aggressive campaign, but organized labor had done a tremendous job in turning out Democratic voters to the polls. Turnout had not been expected to top forty-five million, but forty-eight million people voted. Dewey carried only nine states, and New York was not one of them. Roosevelt received 54 percent of the popular vote to Dewey's 46 percent. It was the narrowest of Roosevelt's four victories and the closest presidential election since 1916, but as with Lincoln in 1864, the key issue was continuity in leadership during war, or as Taft said, a significant number of voters simply decided "we had better not take out a winning pitcher in the eighth inning."

Conservatives thought Dewey was now finished as a presidential contender, and Dewey himself was not certain he would try again. He had a challenging and rewarding job as governor, he noted the Republicans had never renominated a losing candidate, and he thought the war would produce new heroes who would be thrust into politics. Dewey only asked that he be allowed to play the role of the titular head of the party, and he met with Republican congressional leaders in hopes of outlining a Republican program.

But, in a preview of the tensions the party would experience in 1948, the conservatives would have none of it. The *Chicago Tribune* scoffed that it was "pretentious nonsense" that a losing candidate should be allowed to speak for the party. So Dewey focused on winning re-election as governor in 1946, which he did by a record margin, though, with some foresight of what would occur in 1948, he confessed, "I have concluded that it is harder to wage a constructive campaign when you are sure to win, than it is to wage a slugging, aggressive campaign when you are trying to fight your way up."

Dewey continued to pursue progressive, but fiscally prudent, programs and projects in New York. He proposed a 640-mile thruway (now named for Dewey) from New York City to Buffalo that created thirty thousand construction jobs, and he obtained from the legislature the authority to impose rent controls during the post-war housing shortage. Prior planning and the budget surpluses Dewey had hoarded during the war years meant New York had fewer peacetime conversion problems than most states. Post-war unemployment in New York had been expected to top a million, but it turned out to be half that amount as nearly one hundred thousand new small businesses were launched in the state in the two years after the war. Dewey also established another pet project, the State University of New York, now the world's largest university system, which Dewey had envisioned being far less centralized and more locally controlled than typical state university systems.

He also continued to develop his political philosophy, which one observer has maintained, demonstrated "an almost Fabian preoccupation with systems and rationality as the keys that would unlock a better world." In short, Dewey saw governance and politics as a science, and he disdained those who thought that just anyone could do it. "A good many people have the idea that politics is a sordid business, to be left to those who cannot make a living by anything else," Dewey said. "Others have the idea that it is a simple business, in which anyone can become qualified as a sage overnight or with a brief space of speech-making or handshaking. The fact is that politics is the science of government. So far it has defeated all the best minds in the history of the world. At least I have not yet heard of the perfect government."

Compared to Dewey, with his many sterling accomplishments as governor, Roosevelt's successor, Truman, seemed a disaster as president. While later generations would commend Truman for generally making the right decisions during one of the most chaotic periods in world history after the end of World War II, at the time it seemed as if the man who had assumed office less than three months after becoming vice president was being buffeted by one crisis after another. Some suggested that Truman should just resign and let someone more qualified take over. Pundits failed to see the forest from the trees, focusing on Truman's several foibles while ignoring the larger trends that showed unemployment was low, the economy was growing at the rate of 7 percent per year, and corporate profits in 1948 were up a third from the previous year.

Dewey insisted he would have been happy to forego another run at the presidency, but his strong showing in 1944 and his overwhelming re-election as governor in 1946 made him appear a winner who could finally give the Republicans the White House in 1948. For the nomination, he still had to defeat Taft and also former Minnesota governor Harold Stassen, who had not yet become a national joke as a perennial presidential candidate. One of Dewey's key issues in debates with Stassen was his strong opposition to Stassen's proposal to outlaw the Communist Party. "You can't shoot an idea with a gun," Dewey scoffed, adding, "There is no such thing as a constitutional right to destroy all constitutional rights. . . . I am unalterably, wholeheartedly, and unswervingly against any scheme to write laws outlawing people because of their religion, political, social, or economic ideas . . . it is immoral and nothing but totalitarianism itself."

Having dispatched his two rivals and having persuaded the Republicans to adopt a platform that even Roosevelt aide Sam Rosenman said was worthy of the New Deal, Dewey sat back to await his seemingly inevitable election. At least, that is what he would be accused of in hindsight. Dewey, in fact, waged a vigorous campaign. He was "as much a whistle-stop candidate as Truman," said one chronicler of the election, but his demeanor was less folksy than Truman's and his speeches more subdued. There was simply less drama than in the wild and frenetic campaign Truman was waging.

Dewey tried to sound reasonable. He even insisted that Truman was not to blame for all the nation's ills—"only part are deliberately caused for political purposes," he said. He added, in the platitudes that made his campaign seem devoid of any fighting spirit, "The important thing is that as Americans we turn our faces forward and set about curing them with stout purpose and a full heart."

There are several reasons Dewey took a quiet, sensible approach. Dewey was always concerned about dignity, both his own and the dignity of the offices he held or pursued. He found Truman exceedingly unpresidential and thought voters did, too. He also preferred the high road. He sincerely regretted his attacks on Roosevelt in 1944, and when advisors asked him to attack Truman as he had Roosevelt back in Oklahoma City, Dewey moaned that the Oklahoma City address had been the worst speech he had ever given. Finally, he and virtually everyone he consulted were convinced that staying above the fray was good politics. On several occasions, Dewey polled his advisors and party leaders across the country to discern whether he should be more aggressive on the campaign trail. Each time, the unanimous response was that he should continue to ignore Truman as much as possible. Only once, in a speech in Pittsburgh in early October, did Dewey regain his prosecutorial demeanor, lambasting Truman for labor policies that Dewey blamed for a host of strikes. The audience loved it, but when he returned to his campaign train, advisors chastised him, "What are you trying to do, lose the election?"

And for most of the summer and early fall, calm campaigning seemed to be a smart strategy. Polling by Gallup and Roper showed an insurmountable Dewey lead—a lead so large that Gallup announced it would cease regular polling after September, ensuring that a sudden shift in public mood would pass undetected. Newspapers that had traditionally endorsed only Democrats, such as the *New York Times* and a host of Southern papers (upset at the Democrats' newfound interest in civil rights), this time endorsed Dewey. Voters described Dewey in surveys as "able, aggressive, and intelligent," and they described his campaign as "dignified," "sincere," and "clean"; only 6 percent found it cold and only 5 percent thought it dull. A quarter of respondents thought Truman was engaged in mudslinging. Even Truman himself seemed resigned to defeat. At the dedication of the new Idlewild Airport in New York City, Truman whispered into Dewey's ear that he hoped Dewey would fix the White House plumbing when he became president.

Truman was likely joking: The incumbent had a few tricks up his sleeve. Truman understood that for all Dewey's talk of national unity, the Republicans themselves remained badly divided. Truman looked at the Republican platform crafted by Dewey, one that called for action on health care, housing, civil rights, education, and the minimum wage, and he knew that most of the proposals would be unacceptable to the conservative Republicans who ruled Congress, especially Robert Taft. Truman, therefore, in a blatantly partisan maneuver, called Congress into special session on July 29, which Truman said was "Turnip Day" back in Missouri, and dared it to implement all the pledges the Republicans had made in their platform.

Dewey initially thought the special session was "a nuisance but no more." Still, he begged Taft and the congressional Republicans to pass a few bits of legislation to counter Truman's accusation that they were a "do nothing" Congress. Especially helpful politically would be amendments to the Displaced Persons Act, which discriminated against Jewish and Catholic refugees, but Taft said, "We're not going to give that fellow anything." Dewey did not publicly press him to do otherwise, but in private he referred to Taft and his allies as "those congressional bums."

With revelations that summer that Alger Hiss, a high-ranking official in the State Department under Roosevelt and Truman, had given sensitive information to the Soviets, some Dewey advisors urged him to make Communist infiltration of the administration an issue. But Dewey was "no McCarthy," said Pennsylvania congressman Hugh Scott. "He thought it degrading to suspect Truman of being personally soft on communism. He wasn't going around looking under beds." Dewey himself said, "In this country, we'll have no thought police. We will not jail anybody for what he thinks or believes. So long as we keep the Communists among us out in the open, in the light of day, the United States of America has nothing to fear."

Truman, however, was willing to use fear as a tool. Initially, some of Truman's attacks might have been unfair but were hardly libelous. One of his most effective pitches was made in farm country, where a host of commodity prices had suddenly dropped. Truman promised increased price supports for farmers and said the Republicans opposed price supports, which was not true. But as the campaign wore on, Truman's attacks became shrill and unjust. On October 25 in Chicago, Truman gave his most vitriolic speech of the campaign, charging that Republicans paid only "lip service" to democracy itself. He said that the GOP was rife with "powerful reactionary forces, which are silently undermining our democratic institutions," and that Dewey was the "front man" for the same type of cliques that had put Hitler, Mussolini, and Tojo into power.*

Dewey was furious and again polled his advisors as to whether he should respond in kind. Again, the advice was to stay the course and maintain his dignity since most major newspapers and magazines were already referring to him as the next president. Among the advocates for nonconfrontation was his most important advisor, his wife, who, when Dewey began drafting a hard-hitting response to Truman, promised to stay up all night if that was what it took to get Dewey to tear up the speech. Instead, the following day, Dewey simply complained that Truman had "reached a new low in mud-slinging. . . . That is the kind of campaign I refuse to wage." To which a man in the crowd shouted, "You're an American, that's why."

By now, Dewey realized that his election was no longer inevitable. "We are slipping, aren't we?" Dewey asked his staff. Yet, with barely a week left before the election, he decided it was too late to change tactics. With Wall Street complacently expecting a Dewey triumph, Truman ended up raising more money and made particularly effective use of radio. In a final national broadcast the evening before the election, Truman said voting Democratic was the "best insurance against going back to the dark days of 1932." Neither candidate made a truly memorable speech during the campaign, H. L. Mencken concluded, but by appealing to so many special interest groups' self-interest, Truman had at least proven himself to be "a smart mathematician."

On Election Day, Dewey swept the Northeast but lost the usually Republican Midwest. Truman had won 49.5 percent of the popular vote to Dewey's 45 percent, with the rest going to third party candidates Strom Thurmond and Henry Wallace. "You can analyze figures from now to kingdom come and all they will show is we lost the farm vote, which we had in 1944, and that lost the election," said Dewey. Dewey had also been harmed by the belief among potential supporters that his election was a certainty. A full 13 percent of those who had

---

* Some scholars have argued that Truman's incendiary remarks led Republicans to condone the later excesses of Wisconsin senator Joseph McCarthy as retribution for Truman's excesses.

identified themselves as Dewey supporters before the election simply did not bother to vote. Further, Americans had admired Truman's scrappy performance and were thrilled to see an underdog beat the odds. "I have learned from bitter experience," Dewey wrote Eisenhower in 1954, "that Americans somehow regard a political campaign as a sporting event."

While Truman's upset win was thrilling, some of his methods were appalling, yet Dewey was magnanimous in defeat. At a news conference after the election, he said, "When I wished Mr. Truman well, I meant it. I think Mr. Truman is a good man. This nation will go on now; it will prosper and flourish. And so will we." He had vowed that losing the presidency would not scar him as it had Al Smith and Wendell Willkie. Dewey tried to maintain a jocular attitude. Meeting with a group of Boy Scouts, he said, "Remember fellows, any boy can become president—unless he's got a mustache!"*

With his second defeat, Dewey knew his own presidential ambitions had ended. Since Republicans tend to nominate for president the candidate whose "turn" it seems to be, 1952 finally seemed to be Taft's turn. The man known as "Mr. Republican" was an honorable and admirable man, and not the reactionary his critics portrayed. He favored an income floor for the poor, introduced legislation to provide federal aid to education, and his federal housing bill was so progressive it led one real estate industry lobbyist to label Taft a "fellow traveler." Taft also took a courageous stand in criticizing the trials of Nazi war criminals at Nuremberg on the grounds that the Nazis were being tried *ex post facto* in violation of the principles of American justice, and he had been one of the few public figures to oppose internment of Japanese Americans during World War II.

But Dewey could not stand the rigid and often tactless Taft. On more than one occasion, he was heard to suggest that Taft go "screw" himself. Dewey was convinced that a conservative like Taft would lead the party to disaster and that only one man, the Allied commander Eisenhower, could lead the Republicans to certain victory in 1952. Dewey began to recruit Eisenhower to run for president as early as April 1949, first

---

* As of 2008, no presidential nominee had sported facial hair since Dewey.

reaching out to Ike's brother, Milton, and then arranging a private meeting with the general himself.

Eisenhower recorded the private meeting in his diary, noting that he and Dewey were in agreement "that the tendencies toward centralization and paternalism must be halted and reversed," but they also agreed that no Republican candidate could say such a thing aloud and hope to be successful. Dewey counseled Eisenhower to say as little as possible of substance during the campaign, so that after his election he could quietly "lead us back to safe channels."

Eisenhower acknowledged Dewey's key role in his becoming president. The two men never became intimates, but Eisenhower was awed by Dewey's political skills. "It seems that in public he has no appeal, but he is a rather persuasive talker on a tête-à-tête basis," Eisenhower said. And when Dewey made a highly successful thirty-minute commercial for the Eisenhower campaign in the new medium of television, a mildly humorous tour of "Harry's Haunted House" in honor of Halloween, complete with skeletons in closets, Ike wrote Dewey, "I am still lost in wonder at your performance."

Before that, however, Dewey had worked behind the scenes to scuttle Taft's candidacy. Taft had come into the Republican convention in the belief that he had enough pledged delegates to assure his nomination on the first ballot. But Dewey then led the charge to demand "fair play" in seating disputed delegations from the South so that delegates were equitably distributed between Taft and Eisenhower. Passions ran high, and the convention was well aware who was orchestrating Eisenhower's move to the nomination. Westbrook Pegler said it was clear Eisenhower was "just standing around and doing as he is told." Illinois senator Everett Dirksen took the podium to shake his finger at Dewey and proclaim, "We followed you before and you took us down the path to defeat!" Taft supporters distributed flyers, begging delegates to "SINK DEWEY!" and "End Dewey's Control of Our Party!" But a majority of delegates agreed with Dewey that Eisenhower was their best hope for victory, and he slipped past Taft to win the nomination on the first ballot in a very close election.

Eisenhower had not given much thought to his running mate (he thought the convention delegates always chose the running mate), so Dewey convened a meeting of advisors and when all the other possible suspects had been named, it was Dewey who said, "What about Nixon?" Dewey had met Nixon earlier in the year and been impressed by the fact he was a "fine speaker" with a voting record that was "good, intelligent, middle of the road, and . . . [he was] a senator who knew the world was round." He told Nixon that he could be president someday and was, by Nixon's own account, the first person to suggest he would make a good running mate for Eisenhower. At the convention, Dewey even wanted to make Nixon's nominating speech himself, but given the hard feelings in the hall, he left the task to someone else.

Dewey, then, set Nixon on the path that would eventually make him president, and he remained a close advisor and confidant to Nixon until Dewey's death in 1971. When Nixon was accused during the 1952 campaign of tapping a slush fund provided by wealthy supporters, Nixon feared it would be Dewey who would force him from the ticket. But it was Dewey who advised Nixon to respond to the allegations and save his candidacy via television in what became celebrated as the "Checkers speech." Dewey's influence with Nixon was such that nearly twenty years later, when leading Republicans worried that the Nixon White House was headed for political and perhaps legal trouble, the party tapped Dewey as the one man with enough influence to set Nixon straight. But Dewey died in March 1971, before he could talk to Nixon, and fifteen months later the Watergate scandal began to engulf the Nixon presidency.

The 1952 convention had left a bitter aftertaste among conservatives. Taft privately told friends he almost wished Adlai Stevenson had won, that four more years of the New Deal would be preferable to an Eisenhower administration "dominated by Dewey." Five-star generals are not dominated by anyone, but Dewey's stamp was certainly evident. Several Dewey confidants, including John Foster Dulles, Herbert Brownell, and William P. Rogers, held key posts in Eisenhower's administration, though Dewey himself declined any official post, admitting he was too arrogant ever to play second fiddle to anyone, even a former

General of the Army. Dewey even turned down Ike's offer of chief justice of the U.S. Supreme Court—a post Dewey also turned down later when Nixon offered it in 1969.* As he told Kitty Carlisle Hart, the Broadway actress and television personality whom he dated after Frances died, "I'm a warrior. I don't want to be up there judging. I want to be down there in the arena, fighting!"

Dewey regularly offered Eisenhower advice, and it seems clear that Dewey's philosophy of pay-as-you-go liberalism influenced Eisenhower's own thinking, though Eisenhower and his aides preferred the term "Modern Republicanism." In adopting Dewey's philosophy, Ike linked his experience during the war, when government, private business, labor, and other interest groups cooperated, often on a voluntary basis, to further the public interest without the requirement of more federal power. In terms nearly identical to Dewey's, Eisenhower feared increased "statism" would mean the loss of personal freedom and individual initiative, while generating class envy and conflict.

Rolling back the social reforms of the New Deal, however, would be nearly impossible. Echoing Dewey's own conclusion a decade before, Eisenhower told his brother, Milton, "Should any political party attempt to abolish Social Security, unemployment insurance, and eliminate labor laws and farm programs, you would not hear of that party again in our political history." By now, even former president Herbert Hoover was agreeing with Dewey that the best Republicans could hope for was to slow the growth of the federal government.

While Eisenhower was able to take some minor steps to lift wage and price controls, lower some taxes on capital and industry, and return some types of energy development back to the states or the private sector, he also expanded Social Security coverage, advocated extending minimum wage protection to workers in many more categories than previously covered, maintained the highest personal income tax rates in U.S. history, and began the largest public works project in American history, the interstate highway system—all validations of Goldwater's charge that Ike was running a "dime store New Deal." Yet, Eisenhower's shrewd and pragmatic

---

* Eisenhower instead appointed Earl Warren; Nixon appointed Warren Burger.

conclusion, inspired by Dewey's tutelage, that the welfare state cannot be dismantled, only restrained, is still the Republican dilemma today.

If Eisenhower, advised by Dewey, went beyond the New Deal, Nixon, handpicked for the national stage by Dewey and still soliciting advice from Dewey, went beyond Lyndon Johnson's Great Society. "Vigorously did we inveigh against the Great Society," said Nixon speechwriter Pat Buchanan, "enthusiastically did we fund it." Historian Charles Morris argues that Nixon was more liberal than Lyndon Johnson, and Nixon himself once said, "As a matter of fact, to tell you the truth, John F. Kennedy was a little too conservative to suit my taste."

The Nixon administration was the last truly liberal administration of the twentieth century. That legacy is obscured by liberal antipathy toward Nixon because of his history of Red-baiting, his policies in Vietnam, the Watergate scandal, and Nixon's conservative rhetoric. But the words were not matched by deeds. As liberal Republican congressman Hugh Scott, a Dewey ally, said of Nixon's administration, "The conservatives get the rhetoric; we get the action."

Nixon's appeal to conservatives was politically expedient. He needed conservatives to win elections but believed he needed liberal accomplishments to ensure his place in history. Under Nixon, wage and price controls were implemented, the Environmental Protection Agency was created, the food stamp program was begun, affirmative action was put in place, and tax reform essentially freed the poor from having to pay income tax. Nixon even called for comprehensive national health insurance, though he pursued the idea half-heartedly. Conservatives do not embrace Nixon's legacy because it is not theirs; liberals will not embrace it because it belongs to Nixon.

Conservatives do embrace Ronald Reagan, but while Reagan had no direct connection to Dewey, he shared Dewey's pragmatism in a way his conservative hagiographers have ignored. He understood the Republican quandary articulated by Dewey. Reagan may have changed how many Americans feel about the federal government, based on his pronouncement that government is more the problem than the solution, but he did not fundamentally change how we are governed.

While Reagan came into office with a conservative agenda to cut budgets and shift social programs back to the states, he was unable to eliminate a single major federal program or agency. While he cut the highest marginal income tax rates, he then had to raise other taxes in seven of his eight years as president to reduce deficits, and yet was still unable to submit a single balanced budget to Congress. The national debt tripled under his presidency. Rather than eliminate or privatize Social Security, Reagan appointed a commission that successfully ensured Social Security's solvency for decades without trimming benefits. "Americans are conservative," said conservative columnist and Reagan admirer George Will. "What they want to conserve is the New Deal."

This is what Dewey had concluded: Americans are conservative more in temperament than ideology. His imprint on Republican philosophy was still evident when President George H. W. Bush talked about launching "a thousand points of light" to respond to America's social welfare needs; when Bush's son, President George W. Bush, who had campaigned as a "compassionate conservative," greatly expanded Medicare and federal funding on education; and in the 2008 election, when Republicans eschewed more conservative choices and nominated the self-styled Republican "maverick" John McCain, known for working across the aisle with Democrats on issues such as immigration reform.

After 2008, the Tea Party movement agitated to purge the remnants of Republican liberals and moderates from its ranks and pursued the party realignment of pure conservatism that Dewey dreaded and predicted would lead to political disaster. Time will tell if Dewey's prophecy is correct, but Republicans should recall Dewey's legacy and wisdom. He lost the presidency twice, but he pointed the way for many other Republican victories.

CHAPTER SEVEN

ADLAI STEVENSON

1952, 1956

Eggheads of the world, unite! You have nothing to lose but your yolks!

"All the eggheads" were for Adlai Stevenson in his 1952 and 1956 presidential campaigns, and the enthusiasm with which they embraced him has spurred Republicans ever since to argue that the Democratic Party abandoned the values of the middle class to become the party of the elite.

It is certainly true that intellectuals—and many common-man voters—loved the eloquence of Stevenson's speeches, the irony of his wit, the urbanity of his manners, and the contrast he provided to the self-consciously anti-intellectual campaigns waged against him by Dwight Eisenhower and Eisenhower's running mate, Richard Nixon. But while Stevenson was erudite, he was no fringe radical. He was governor of Illinois, located in the middle of America, and if that were not enough, he was raised but five miles from that supposed epicenter of Middle America, Peoria, of which it is said that if it "plays in Peoria" then it will be accepted anywhere in the heartland.

Yet, Republicans have, in virtually every election since 1952, leveled the charge that Democrats are out of touch with this very same Middle America. They point to polling that shows that those who attend religious services regularly, which "average Americans" presumably do, tend to vote Republican, while those who do not tend to vote Democratic.*

---

* A 2010 Gallup poll found 43 percent of Americans claiming to attend church almost weekly.

They argue that while the Democrats once dominated the heartland regions of the Midwest and South, these are now Republican strongholds. And while this formulation presupposes that the East and West Coasts, which are now the centers of Democratic strength, must be lacking in middle class Americans, even some Democrats suggest the charge of Democratic elitism has merit.

Ted Strickland, the Democratic governor of Ohio from 2007 to 2011, fretted that Democrats no longer make the populist appeals that lent the party its nickname, "Party of the People," because of "a sort of intellectual elitism that considers that kind of talk is somehow lacking in sophistication."* And Thomas Frank, the author of several books that question why the Democrats have supposedly lost touch with the middle class, has written that "at the bottom of their hearts, many of the [Democratic] party's biggest thinkers agree with the 'liberal elite' stereotype. They can't simply point to their working-class base and their service to working-class America, because they aren't interested in that base; they haven't tried to serve that constituency for decades."

Conservative critics point to Stevenson's campaign as that point, decades ago, when the Democrats supposedly abandoned the working-class. Conservative political analyst Michael Barone charged that Stevenson "was the first leading Democratic politician to become a critic rather than a celebrator of middle class American culture." Conservative commentator George Will added the charge that the "cultural liberalism" and "condescension" of "the post-Stevenson Democratic Party" drove Southern whites and Northern blue-collar ethnic voters out of the Democratic Party.

Yet, there is no evidence that Stevenson's intellect was anything but an asset during his two campaigns. And while Stevenson was twice defeated for the presidency, Americans have since elected presidents who have been a Rhodes Scholar (Clinton), studied nuclear physics (Carter), and won the Pulitzer Prize (Kennedy). All of these presidents were Democrats, however, so perhaps Stevenson did set "the tone for a new era of Democratic politics" well before the "Camelot" presidency

---

* Strickland lost his bid for re-election to Republican John Kasich, who hosted a program on the Fox News Channel called, interestingly, *Heartland with John Kasich* while Kasich was also a managing director at the Lehman Brothers investment bank.

of John Kennedy. Historian Arthur Schlesinger Jr. argued that it was Stevenson who "made JFK possible." And it was Stevenson's inspirational and high-minded tone, which predates the rhetoric of Kennedy's "New Frontier," that subsequent Democratic nominees from JFK to Barack Obama have emulated.

To contrast themselves against this supposed Democratic elitism, Republican candidates, even if descended from prominent families and holding Ivy League degrees, have aggressively promoted themselves as having middlebrow tastes, much as Eisenhower and Nixon did in their campaigns against Stevenson. President George H. W. Bush, an alumnus of Yale, insisted his favorite snack was pork rinds. His son, President George W. Bush, with degrees from both Yale *and* Harvard, stated that his favorite political philosopher was Jesus Christ. Former Hollywood movie star Ronald Reagan insisted his favorite recreation was clearing brush at his ranch located near Santa Barbara, California.

In turn, Democrats have charged since 1952 that the Republicans have become extreme in their anti-intellectualism, despising experts of all stripes, and espousing a governing philosophy that represents, in a phrase used by former vice president Al Gore, an "assault on reason." So ingrained did this perceived difference in the two parties' intellectual appeals become that one political writer declared that by 2010, American elections were a battle over "who's stupid, and who's a snob." Eloquence was also under assault, as Obama's rhetoric, inspirational to many, was dismissed as a "platitude" by his Republican opponent, Senator John McCain, and "vaporous" by conservative columnist David Brooks.

The debate over whether intelligence and eloquence are assets or liabilities for a political candidate seems to date back to Stevenson, when the question was acknowledged as a "strange, recurring sub-issue" during his 1952 campaign. Those who could be described as intellectuals did embrace Stevenson "with a readiness and a unanimity that seems without parallel in American history," according to historian Richard Hofstadter. So closely did intellectuals identify with Stevenson, Hofstadter added, that they questioned whether his defeat by the bland Eisenhower and the mawkish Nixon represented a rejection of "American intellectuals and of intellect itself."

The excitement Stevenson stirred among intellectuals was so pronounced that it caught the attention of the conservative columnist Stewart Alsop, who is credited with adding the word "egghead" to the English lexicon. The origin of the term began with an argument Alsop had with his brother, John, a Republican official in Connecticut, in which he asserted that "while Stevenson was appealing and appealed strongly to people's minds, Eisenhower, as a man and as a figure, was appealing far more strongly to far more people's emotions." Alsop said his brother then began imagining what a typical intellectual supporter of Stevenson looked like and envisioned someone with a smooth, balding head, like the candidate himself, and said, "Sure, all the eggheads are for Stevenson, but how many eggheads are there?"

Alsop used the word in his column, it stuck, and Republicans pounced on it as a pejorative that they hoped would feed into the perception that Stevenson was removed from the concerns of the average voter. Novelist Louis Bromfield, writing in the conservative publication the *Freeman,* said a future dictionary would define "egghead" as someone of "spurious intellectual pretensions . . . supercilious and surfeited with conceit and contempt for the experience of more sound and able men." Further, an egghead was likely to be a "doctrinaire" socialist and "self-conscious prig, so given to examining all sides of a question that he becomes thoroughly addled while remaining always in the same place."

One of the several ironies of the attacks made by Bromfield and other conservatives on Stevenson's intellectual supporters is that they were occurring at the very time that conservatives were seeking to validate an intellectual tradition of their own. Stung by barbs from academics like Lionel Trilling that there were no conservative ideas worthy of serious consideration, Russell Kirk published *The Conservative Mind* in 1953, which argued that there was, in fact, a coherent conservative intellectual tradition dating to the English philosopher Edmund Burke. Two years after Kirk's book was published, William F. Buckley founded the

National Review as a journal for conservative intellectuals—who presumably did not see themselves as eggheads.

Stevenson professed to be baffled by the word "egghead," joking after the 1952 campaign that it must have been meant to describe "the more intelligensiac members of that lunatic fringe who thought I was going to win." He did not seem to know exactly how to address the unprecedented accusation that he was too smart for the average American voter. He tried to deflect the issue with humor and silly puns. "Eggheads of the world, unite!" he once exclaimed. "You have nothing to lose but your yolks!" At other times Stevenson's humor was more biting. In remarks made a few weeks after his 1952 loss, Stevenson said of the voters, "As to their wisdom, well, Coca-Cola still outsells champagne." Four years later, during his second losing campaign, a woman shouted to Stevenson, "Governor, all the thinking people are for you!" To which Stevenson offered the immediate riposte, "Yes, madam, but I need a majority to win!"

Conservative critics like Barone tut-tut that "it is unthinkable that Franklin Roosevelt would ever have said those things, or that such thoughts would ever have crossed his mind." Roosevelt, despite his Ivy League education and patrician background, delighted in affecting middle class airs, with his "fireside chats" and serving hot dogs to the King and Queen of England when they visited his home. Stevenson preferred the finer things in life, including champagne, and he also seemed a stark contrast to the Democrat still in the White House, Harry Truman, who was widely read but never attended college.

It is easy to accuse Barone and Stevenson's other critics of simply not appreciating Stevenson's postmodern sense of humor. Yet, while Stevenson made jokes about his intellect, there were, in fact, serious discussions within his campaign about whether his intelligence was a handicap. At a strategy meeting late in the 1952 campaign, Stevenson supporter and New York governor Averill Harriman opined that the great problem with the campaign was "that the thinking minority had been convinced but that [Stevenson] had made very little inroad on the unthinking majority." Advisors bemoaned that Stevenson had the ability to persuade those who used reason to make their choice but that he could not excite the multitudes that, they presumed, based their choice on an emotional response. Ike, it was acknowledged, was better at that.

Later in the campaign, longtime CBS newsman Eric Sevareid set aside his professional objectivity and wrote a detailed confidential memorandum to the Stevenson campaign, outlining the problems faced by a candidate who preferred to appeal to voters' reason rather than their emotions:

> *In his almost painful honesty, he [Stevenson] . . . has been analyzing, not asserting; he has been projecting, not an image of the big, competent father, or brother, but of the moral and intellectual proctor, the gadfly called conscience. In so doing he has revealed an integrity rare in American politics, a luminosity of intelligence unmatched on the political scene today; he has caught the imagination of intellectuals, of all those who are really informed; he has excited the passions of the mind; he has not excited the emotions of the great bulk of half-informed voters, nor, among these, has he created a feeling of Trust, of Authority, of Certainty that he knows where he is going and what must be done.*

Harriman's and Sevareid's analyses project the very condescension criticized by Barone and Will, a sense that Stevenson was simply "too good" for the majority of the people whom he sought to lead. Stevenson, himself, would have vigorously disagreed.

Throughout the 1952 campaign, there was a great deal of worry that Stevenson was "talking over the heads of the American people." Of course, no one would admit that Stevenson was talking over *their* heads; they were simply worried about their dimmer neighbor down the street. The journalist Richard Rovere said he overheard a bus driver, whom he felt fit the very definition of the common man, telling some passengers, "I don't suppose the *average* fellow's going to catch on to what he's saying. But I'm telling you, this is just what *I've* been waiting for."

Stevenson, showing more humility than many of his supporters, insisted he had spoken over the heads of the people only once during the campaign—when his train was parked on a trestle and he addressed an audience below. But there is no doubt that Stevenson's speeches were different from those heard during most campaigns before or since.

In most campaigns, at least those that aim to win, the candidate develops a formulaic stump speech and then maintains the discipline to give that speech over and over, never deviating from the central message, in the hope that repetition will work as well for them as it does for a commercial product. But Stevenson refused to be sold like "a box of corn flakes" and insisted on giving a unique address at virtually every opportunity. So intent was he on capturing just the right sentiment that he would order his airplane to circle the landing strip near a campaign rally while he struggled to find just the right phrase or word for the speech he would give to the waiting crowd.

Stevenson himself was a fine writer, extremely sensitive to anyone taking credit for the content of his speeches. He was immeasurably helped, however, by a campaign staff that included four speechwriters who either had won or would win the Pulitzer Prize, including Arthur Schlesinger Jr. and John Kenneth Galbraith. And if Stevenson needed further assistance in word-smithing, he could turn to other advisors such as the Pulitzer Prize–winning poet Archibald MacLeish, theologians Henry Emerson Fosdick and Reinhold Niebuhr, diplomats George Ball and George Kennan, or the British expatriate journalist (and future host of public television's *Masterpiece Theater*) Alistair Cooke.

Perhaps no other campaign in history could boast such an array of intellectual firepower. It is not surprising then that Stevenson is the only presidential candidate in memory whose campaign speeches were bound together as a best-selling book—twice! The first edition came during the 1952 campaign, when publication of such addresses was a common campaign practice. But these and other Stevenson speeches were repackaged a full year after the campaign had ended and once again the collection became a best seller.

Among Stevenson's readers was the novelist and Nobel laureate John Steinbeck, who wrote the foreword to the first book of speeches and said he could never recall reading a political speech for "pleasure" until Stevenson came along. It was solely the power of Stevenson's speeches, he said, that convinced Steinbeck to switch his allegiance from Eisenhower to Stevenson. "As a man, I like his intelligent, humorous, logical, civilized mind," he said. Steinbeck also expressed amazement that the Republicans or anyone else would suggest Stevenson's speeches were too cerebral. Said the author of *The Grapes of Wrath* and *East of Eden*, "I can understand them and I don't think I am more intelligent than the so-called 'people.'"

Stevenson sealed his nomination with an eloquent speech before the Democratic National Convention in 1952, just as a future Illinois politician named Obama would evoke the Stevenson tone at another national convention more than fifty years later.

Having won a landslide victory to become governor of Illinois in 1948, Stevenson seemed a logical candidate for president in 1952 once Truman announced he would not seek re-election. Truman himself actively recruited Stevenson, seeing qualities that he hoped might make voters overlook all the problems of his administration and keep the Democrats in power. "Adlai," Truman said, "if a knucklehead like me can be president and not do too badly, think what a really educated smart guy like you could do in the job."

Stevenson, however, angered Truman and disappointed admirers by resisting calls to become an active candidate. He preferred, he said, to serve a second term as governor of Illinois. (He also thought he would have a better chance at the presidency in 1956.) But in a bit of serendipity that had also benefited the first Illinoisan who was a candidate for president, Abraham Lincoln, the 1952 convention was held in Chicago. Because Stevenson was the host state's governor, he was charged with giving a welcoming speech to the Democratic delegates. This pro forma task on the first day of a convention is usually a sparsely attended affair, but delegates knew Stevenson's reputation for oratory and the Chicago Amphitheater was packed.

"Here, my friends," Stevenson told them, "on the prairies of Illinois and of the Middle West, we can see a long way in all directions. . . . Here there are no barriers, no defenses, to ideas and to aspirations. We want none; we want not shackles on the mind or the spirit, no rigid pattern of thought, and no iron conformity. We want only the faith and conviction that triumph in free and fair contest."

Twenty-seven times Stevenson's brief address was interrupted by wild applause, even for sentiments that would not seem to be obvious crowd pleasers, such as, "What America needs and the world wants is not bombast, abuse, and double talk, but a somber message of firm faith and confidence. St. Francis said, 'Where there is patience and humility, there is neither anger nor worry.' That might well be our text."

Stevenson's was a new style of political oratory that was learned and poignant. Rapt delegates began to believe that they had found the miracle candidate who could overcome the unpopularity of the Truman presidency and maintain the Democrats' twenty-year hold on the White House. Two days later, even though he had actively discouraged the modest draft movement that had been afoot, Stevenson was nominated for president. Because he had not entered a primary, he had no campaign organization in place. He had to start from scratch.

In his acceptance speech, Stevenson famously promised to "talk sense to the American people." He would later complain that most politicians treated American citizens as "fourteen-year-olds." His acceptance speech did not. He was trying to fulfill his pledge to "tell them the truth":

> *Let's tell them the victory to be won in the twentieth century, this portal to the Golden Age, mocks the pretensions of individual acumen and ingenuity. For it is a citadel guarded by thick walls of ignorance and mistrust, which do not fall before the trumpets' blast, or the politicians' imprecations, or even a general's baton. They are, my friends, walls that must be directly stormed by the hosts of courage, of morality, and of vision, standing shoulder to shoulder, unafraid of ugly truth, contemptuous of lies, half truths, circuses, demagoguery . . .*

It was a sterling beginning to what Stevenson hoped would be a campaign conducted upon a high plane. His speech was marred by a gaucherie when Stevenson compared his own deep reluctance to accept the nomination with Christ's prayer at Gethsemane: "If this cup may not pass from me, except I drink it, Thy will be done." Upon hearing Stevenson utter what many Christians would consider a sacrilege, Eisenhower turned off his television set and said, "After hearing that, fellows, I think he is a bigger faker than all the rest of them."

Ike was a rare skeptic that day, however. Liberal columnist Mary McGrory, then a young book reviewer at the *Washington Star,* said Stevenson's acceptance speech was "politically speaking . . . the Christmas morning of our lives."

Before Stevenson's campaigns, intellectualism had not been considered the province of any single political party, and the very phrase "anti-intellectualism" was hardly heard. Certainly, America had seen debates between those who claimed to represent the common people against an economic elite, and this sometimes took on cultural overtones, such as this bit of doggerel from the 1828 presidential campaign, which said the contest was between:

> John Quincy Adams who can write
> And Andrew Jackson who can fight.

But learned men who did not mind being known as learned men could be found in either party, though to the degree there was a cultural elite in America before World War II that disdained popular culture, it was identified with wealthy, conservative Republicans, not liberal Democratic college professors and writers.

Theodore Roosevelt, a Harvard man and the author of serious works of history, attracted the support of numerous intellectuals as a Republican, but then so did Democrat Woodrow Wilson, a professor of political economy who first gained national attention as president of Princeton University. Franklin Roosevelt was celebrated for his "brain trust" of bright young men who came to shape and guide the New Deal, although FDR himself was notoriously charged by Oliver Wendell Holmes with having "a second class intellect." And Roosevelt's Republican opponents—Herbert Hoover,

Wendell Willkie, and Thomas Dewey—were hardly anti-intellectuals. For that matter, neither was Eisenhower.

Ike may have lacked Stevenson's irony, but he was a shrewd and extremely intelligent man who had, as Supreme Allied Commander, successfully managed such egos as Winston Churchill, Charles de Gaulle, George Patton, and Bernard Montgomery in leading the Allies to victory in Europe. After the war, he had briefly served as president of Columbia University, and his wartime memoir, *Crusade in Europe*, which he wrote without help from a ghostwriter, is considered among the finest in the genre.

But like FDR, Eisenhower insisted on cultivating an everyman image and dispelling any notion that he had intellectual pretensions. He let it be known that his preferred reading material was Western pulp fiction such as the work of Zane Grey. Perhaps recognizing he could not match Stevenson's soaring rhetoric, Eisenhower also found it useful to speak in bland phrases, uttering thoughts usually no more provocative than, "The great problem of America today is to take that straight and narrow road down the middle." If, by chance, Ike used a phrase like "status quo" in his remarks, he would apologetically add, "'Course, I'm not supposed to be the educated candidate."

To those who did not understand Ike's true character, he simply sounded boring. But Eisenhower believed that if he stuck to platitudes he would prevent controversy, shield his true intentions from too much scrutiny, and avoid committing to a course of action he was not yet ready to take.

There was method, too, in Nixon's relentless portrayal of himself as an average American. His famous televised "Checkers speech," in which he confronted allegations that he had a secret slush fund provided by rich donors, may have been painfully maudlin to his enemies, but it was also extraordinarily effective. Nixon self-consciously identified with the average American saddled with a mortgage, car payments, and self-pity at being able to afford only a "good Republican cloth coat" for his wife rather than one of mink. If Stevenson was calling young American couples to a higher purpose, Nixon was sharing their middle class struggles, a pose he would continue through his own successful 1968 and 1972 presidential campaigns when he still professed to identify with the "silent majority." Of course, just as Ike graduated in the top half of his class at West Point and became president of Columbia, the supposed anti-intellectual Nixon graduated from Duke University School of Law and, over the course of his life, wrote ten generally well-reviewed books.

Stevenson despised Nixon—and he despised television. He thought both were vulgar. Even though 1952 was the first year television factored in a presidential election, Stevenson was loath to accommodate the new medium. He would not edit his speeches to fit within the thirty minutes of purchased airtime, so he was often cut off in mid-sentence. Ike, by contrast, mimicked Nixon's everyman appeal and adapted to the ways of Madison Avenue, appearing in commercials in which he ostensibly answered questions from average Americans with answers such as, "Yes, my Mamie gets after me about the high cost of living. It's another reason why I say it's time for a change."

Eisenhower accepted and used the power of television. Stevenson felt obliged to critique it. In an article for *Fortune* magazine published shortly after the campaign, Stevenson worried that television was corrupting the ability of the body politic to think critically. "The extensions of our senses, which we find so fascinating, are not adding to the discriminations of our minds, since we need increasingly to take the reading of a needle on a dial to discover whether we think something is good or bad, right or wrong," he wrote.

In critiquing television, Stevenson was also taking aim at Nixon, whose "Checkers speech" had underscored the power of the new medium. Stevenson liked to think of himself as one who bucked popular opinion if for no other reason than to challenge the status quo. He thought Nixon's moral compass was no more than the "needle on a dial" that always pointed where the opinion polls told it to point. Nixon was "the kind of politician," Stevenson said, "who would cut down a redwood tree and then mount the stump and make a speech for conservation." It was a bon mot typical of what came to be known as "the Stevenson wit," and there were those, including members of his own staff, who said it was Stevenson's risky sense of humor, not his intellect, that turned off some voters.

One of his quips became a stock line in many campaigns: "If Republicans stop telling lies about us, we will stop telling the truth about them." He added for good measure, "The Republicans have a 'me, too' candidate running on a 'yes, but' platform, advised by a 'has been' staff." Those were zingers prepared ahead of time, but Stevenson also had a wonderful spontaneous humor. When a young mother walked out of a speech to quiet her crying baby, Stevenson called out, "Please don't be embarrassed. I agree with you, if not my opponent, that it *is* time for a change." There was also his charming response in 1960 to the Protestant clergyman Norman Vincent Peale's attacks on Kennedy's Catholicism: "I have always found the gospel of Paul appealing, but I find the gospel of Peale appalling."

Some of Stevenson's advisors worried that his humor too often seemed to be "inside" jokes between him and his intellectual admirers, while some of it was simply mean-spirited and unfunny. Eisenhower and the Republicans complained that seeking the presidency in a time of global crises was no laughing matter. Stevenson responded, "My opponent has been worried about my funny bone. I'm worried about his backbone."

And it was Stevenson's backbone, as much as his beautiful words, that attracted intellectuals to his campaign, for it was not just the content of his speeches, it was also the courage to give them within context that was so impressive. Far from being a time of triumphalism following the American and Allied victories, the first few years after World War II were a time of deep anxiety. Instead of a world free and at peace, nations were engaged in the Cold War. China had been "lost" to the Communists, much of Europe was in chaos, the Soviets had the hydrogen bomb, and the United States was fighting a war in Korea with uncertain aims and an unforeseeable end. Many Americans—led by demagogues like Wisconsin senator Joseph McCarthy but with strong support from men like Nixon and Indiana senator William Jenner—began to ascribe the course of world events to a large and sinister conspiracy, aided and abetted by traitors here at home.

Unlike the "Red Scare" after World War I, when it was presumed that would-be American Bolsheviks came from the working-class immigrant community, the favored targets for Communist witch-hunting in the 1950s were the intellectual elite. The greatest fear was no longer those inciting revolution among the masses, but espionage facilitated by educated people in positions of authority.

An example of Nixon's attempts to link alleged disloyalty with higher education was his charge that "Stevenson holds a PhD degree from [Truman's secretary of state Dean] Acheson's College of Cowardly Communist Containment." As a congressman, Nixon had led the investigation into whether a State Department official from a prominent family with an Ivy League education named Alger Hiss had been a member of the Communist Party. Hiss was eventually convicted of perjury but not espionage.

Stevenson had worked with Hiss when both were employed in the State Department, so during Hiss's trial Stevenson provided a favorable deposition in which he testified that, as far as he knew, Hiss was an honest and honorable man and that he had never heard any rumors about his former colleague being a Communist. Stevenson said he knew the deposition would be used against him politically, but he felt an obligation as an attorney to provide an honest account when it was requested.

Stevenson had taken a stand against Communist witch-hunting as governor of Illinois, when he vetoed legislation that would have required state employees to take a loyalty oath. "Does anyone seriously think that a real traitor will hesitate to sign a loyalty oath?" he asked. "The whole notion of loyalty inquisitions is a natural characteristic of the police state, not of democracy.... We must not burn down the house to kill the rats."

In perhaps his finest speech of the 1952 campaign, he chose the national convention of the American Legion to attack McCarthyism as the very antithesis of patriotism—and received a warm and enthusiastic ovation when he did. Stevenson told the legionnaires that patriotism "is not short, frenzied outbursts of emotion, but the tranquil and steady dedication of a lifetime.... For it is often easier to fight for principles than to live up to them."

These words and gestures seemed remarkably courageous at the time, especially when contrasted with those of his Republican opponent. In what was certainly the low point of his career, Eisenhower had declined to forthrightly defend his mentor, General George C. Marshall, from attacks by McCarthy and Jenner that Marshall, of all people, was a disloyal American. Marshall, who had been Army chief of staff before becoming Truman's secretary of state, had made Eisenhower's career by appointing him Supreme Allied Commander. Ike never apologized to Marshall for this lapse in loyalty and was so embarrassed by the episode that he refused to discuss the incident or mention it in his memoirs.

McCarthy and others of his ilk, of course, repeatedly implied that Stevenson, too, was a disloyal American, with McCarthy snidely referring to the Democratic nominee as "Alger—I mean Adlai." When speaking of McCarthy and Nixon, Stevenson quoted Aristotle: "History shows that almost all tyrants have been demagogues who gained favor with the people by their accusations of the nobles." When McCarthy and his allies upped the ante and began to make crass insinuations that the divorced Stevenson was a homosexual—the *New York Daily News* referred to Stevenson as "Adelaide"—Stevenson tackled the issue of Communist witch-hunting head on, telling a crowd in Cleveland, "I believe with all my heart that those who would beguile the voters by lies or half-truths, or corrupt them by fear and falsehood, are committing spiritual treason against our institutions. They are doing the work of our enemies."

Moved by such stirring words, liberal intellectuals were prone to overlook the fact that Stevenson was neither as intellectual nor as liberal as they assumed. While Stevenson enjoyed the company and help of scholars and thinkers, his friend and confidant, Alistair Cooke, said that he was skeptical that Stevenson "ever read any books at all"—he didn't have the time. Cooke added that while Stevenson's speeches "were invariably eloquent and noble," they were also "tantalizingly vague about what to do here and now. In fact, I have to admit that much, if not most, of Stevenson's political thought adds up to a makeshift warning to avoid all quick solutions while trusting, in the meantime, to a general outbreak of courage, tolerance, compassion, and universal brotherhood."

This is a too glib assessment, but it is true that Stevenson lacked an aggressive liberal domestic agenda for two reasons: First, he paid far less attention to domestic policy than he did his true love, foreign policy, and second, he was just not that liberal. Stevenson, who had complained that Truman was too liberal for his tastes, had, for example, alienated organized labor by refusing to pledge to repeal the hated Taft-Hartley Act. Stevenson even opposed public housing, which actually put him to the right of conservative Republican senator Robert Taft on that issue. Schlesinger himself ruefully acknowledged that the man he was writing campaign speeches for was the most conservative Democratic presidential nominee since John W. Davis in 1924.

Stevenson was a Democrat primarily by inheritance. His grandfather, also named Adlai Stevenson, had been vice president in Grover Cleveland's second administration and he had also been William Jennings Bryan's running mate in 1900.* Stevenson's father, Lewis, pursued a more modest and less successful political career in Illinois after having worked for the Hearst family, first as manager of some of their mining interests and later as assistant general manager for the Hearst's *Los Angeles Examiner* newspaper. Adlai Stevenson II was born February 5, 1900, in Los Angeles, California, before the family returned to their home in Bloomington, Illinois.

Stevenson's childhood was marred by tragedy when, at the age of twelve, he accidentally shot to death a teenage girl during a party thrown by his older sister. A teenage boy who had been attending military school was eager to show the manual of arms, and so a gun was retrieved from the Stevenson attic. The children thought the rifle was unloaded, but when Adlai took the gun to put it back in the attic, he either (accounts differ) tried to mimic the older boy's manual of arms or he playfully pointed it at the girl, a fifteen-year-old cousin. In either case, the gun went off, a bullet hidden in the chamber having gone undetected because of a rusty spring in the ejecting mechanism.

When reporters doing background on Stevenson uncovered the incident during the 1952 campaign, Stevenson told them he had never

* The name "Adlai" comes from the First Book of Chronicles in the Old Testament as the name of a minor official in the house of King David; it is said to mean in Hebrew "my witness" or "my ornament."

been asked about the incident nor had he spoken of it for forty years. It is impossible to fully know the impact of such an event on a man's life, but one clue was revealed when, in 1955, Stevenson learned of a similar shooting accident involving a family he did not even know. He took the time to write the boy's mother with the advice, "Tell him that he must live for two."

Further belying his intellectual reputation, Stevenson was a mediocre student most of his academic life. He failed in his first attempt to enter Princeton and was sent to the exclusive Choate preparatory school to improve his grades. There, he discovered that out of a student body of two hundred, he was one of only three Democrats. Finally admitted to Princeton, Stevenson maintained the classic "gentleman's C" grade average but enjoyed working on the school newspaper and, later, on a family-owned newspaper.*

Colleagues thought Stevenson was a great natural reporter, but his father insisted he pursue a legal career and so Stevenson went to Harvard Law School, dropped out, and completed his law degree at Northwestern University. After graduation, Stevenson traveled to Europe, visiting fascist Italy and the Soviet Union where, belying future Republican charges that he was soft on the Reds, he said, "I felt that I had seen at first hand what communism meant, in terms of terror and brutality."

When he returned from Europe, he married the beautiful and ebullient Chicago socialite Ellen Borden, ten years his junior, who would grow to detest political life and, twenty years later, despite having three sons with Adlai, divorce Stevenson shortly after he was elected governor. It became increasingly clear that Ellen was suffering from mental illness. Time and again she went out of her way to publicly embarrass Stevenson, leading her own mother to write Stevenson to ask if she should issue a public statement about her daughter's condition. "You must do nothing," Stevenson replied, "except to love her."

In morbid moments, Stevenson would complain that his family history had "doomed" him to a life in politics, but in truth Stevenson

---

* Stevenson had a mother so protective that she moved to Princeton to, like the mothers of Franklin Roosevelt and Douglas MacArthur, be with her son while he attended college.

yearned for public service. When FDR was elected in 1932, Stevenson jumped at the chance to be one of the young New Dealers, working first in the Department of Agriculture, and spending most of the war years as Secretary of the Navy Frank Knox's "principal attorney."

When Knox died in 1944, Stevenson finagled an opportunity to work in the State Department, becoming a deputy to Secretary of State Edward Stettinius. In that capacity, Stevenson was sent to London as part of the American delegation to the committee planning the first general session of the new United Nations organization. Stevenson later served as an alternate American delegate to the first session of the UN, and it was in that role that he forged a close friendship with Eleanor Roosevelt.

Stevenson's interest in foreign affairs drew the scorn of the conservative *Chicago Tribune,* which charged in an editorial that Stevenson "and his kind profess an interest in foreign affairs only because they wish to get away from America and associate with foreigners, to whom they pay fawning obeisance." The kind of opposition that Stevenson would face his entire political life was taking shape even before he had run for office.

On his forty-seventh birthday, Stevenson wrote in his diary that he was "restless, dissatisfied with myself." Despite having "everything"—a wife, children, career—he professed he had "too much ambition for public recognition." He strongly believed public service was honorable and was dismayed when a survey conducted after the war found seven of ten American parents would disapprove of their children going into politics. "Think of it!" Stevenson exclaimed. "Boys could die in battle, but parents did not want their children to give their living efforts toward a better America and a better world. It seems sad to me that 'politics' and 'politician' are so often epithets and words of disrespect and contempt."

Given his background in foreign affairs, Stevenson thought the U.S. Senate was the obvious place to pursue his ambitions, but the leaders of the Illinois Democratic Party had other ideas. They already had an excellent 1948 Senate candidate in Paul Douglas, and they wanted Stevenson to run for governor—once they confirmed that Stevenson had never, contrary to rumor, studied at Oxford, a presumed kiss of death in Illinois politics. "Never went to Oxford, not even to Eton," Stevenson cheerfully telegrammed.

For his campaign announcement, Stevenson was told by party leaders to draft a few notes that would be revised and polished by a party professional. When they read Stevenson's draft, they decided not to change a thing. "We knew then this was a new style of political speaking and it was bound to make an impression upon all those who heard him," said "Colonel" Jacob Arvey, the head of the Cook County Democratic machine.

In his announcement, Stevenson demonstrated that his approach to campaigning would be different from that of the typical pol. "I say simply that our system is on trial; that our example in the years immediately ahead of us will determine the shape of things to come; that unless we continue healthy, strong, and free we will not win many converts; that unless we can lift the hearts of men, unless we can reawaken the hopes of men, the faith of men, in the free way of life, we will be alone and isolated in a hostile world." An old bull of a precinct committeeman, impressed by the high tone of Stevenson's address, turned and whispered to Arvey, "We can go with him. He's got class."

With substantial Republican support, Stevenson won the governorship by the largest plurality in Illinois history. Truman, by contrast, had carried the state by barely thirty thousand votes. Only the third Democratic governor in Illinois since the Civil War, Stevenson focused on cleaning up corruption in state government. He also cracked down on illegal gambling, launched a one hundred million dollar highway program, and nearly doubled state aid to the public schools.

It was a solid, if unspectacular, record for a first termer, which is why Stevenson initially wanted to run for a second term as governor, not for president. He had discovered state government could be a laboratory to experiment with democracy. In answer to those concerned about the concentration of power in the federal government, he called for "effective, responsive, well-operated state and local governments. Too many of the problems of states' rights have been created by states' wrongs."

Even as governor, Stevenson was too conservative for some of his admirers. One of his chief aides, Carl McGowan, said Stevenson hated to spend money, his own or the public's. While Stevenson had instituted some progressive reforms in Illinois, he probably could have done more on such issues as education or mental health. In McGowan's opinion, "Perhaps *the* limiting factor of a Stevenson presidency would have been staying away from new programs that cost a lot of money."

And while his views evolved, Stevenson was not as strong an early leader on civil rights, as, say, Hubert Humphrey was in the same time period. Stevenson did issue an executive order prohibiting discrimination in state parks, and when whites forcibly evicted a black family that had tried to move into the working-class Chicago suburb of Cicero, Stevenson called out the National Guard to quell the rioting when local police refused to take action.

During the 1952 presidential campaign, he tried to appear equally sympathetic to the sensibilities of white Southerners and African Americans and ended up pleasing no one. Four years later, worried about Southern reaction to the Supreme Court's *Brown vs. Board of Education* decision to integrate public schools, Stevenson had suggested in a meeting with liberal supporters that civil rights activists take a one-year moratorium on any further agitation. Stevenson believed prejudice could only be addressed by changing minds, not laws—a position very similar to Barry Goldwater's. After the meeting, Schlesinger sadly wrote in his diary, "It seems evident that he does not feel any strong moral issue in the civil rights fight; that he identifies instinctively with the problems of the Southern white rather than with the sufferings of the Southern Negro."

Stevenson also had a maddening belief that he was somehow above the usual give and take of politics. When Texas governor Allan Shivers asked Stevenson to at least remain neutral in what was then a heated debate on whether the federal government or the coastal states owned offshore mineral rights, Stevenson refused and said he opposed the coastal states' position. Shivers warned Stevenson that such a position could cost him Texas and even the presidency. "But I don't *have* to be president," Stevenson replied loftily.

Whatever his faults, the reluctant candidate Stevenson was the class of the Democratic field when Truman announced he would not seek another term in 1952. But after twenty years of Democrats in the White House, Stevenson thought Eisenhower might make a fine president, and he was skeptical any Democrat had a chance to beat a war hero so popular that he was almost like a "household commodity—the catsup bottle on the kitchen table."

And he was right. Stevenson's campaign was gallant and inspiring, but it never had a chance. While communism and corruption within the Truman administration were millstones for the candidate, his biggest weakness was the Korean War. Stevenson was as baffled as anyone by how to extricate the United States from a conflict whose goal was not total victory. He toyed with the idea of promising to travel to Korea if elected, but dropped it as being too transparent a ploy to win votes. Instead, Stevenson offered this hard truth: "I promise no easy solutions, no relief from burdens and anxieties, for to do this would be not only dishonest, it would attack the foundations of our greatness. I can offer something infinitely better: an opportunity to work and sacrifice that freedom may flourish."

Eisenhower, the nation's most trusted and beloved general, trumped that and the eloquence of all of Stevenson's speeches with five simple words he uttered a week before the election: "I shall go to Korea." If the result had been in doubt before, Eisenhower won the election with that simple declaration in late October. That was the assurance voters were looking for, that the man who engineered America's victory in Europe would find a way to end what seemed an endless war.* Eisenhower won 55 percent of the popular vote and carried all but nine Southern states.

At first, confronted with the bleak prospect of facing Eisenhower again, Stevenson planned not to run for president in 1956, but in 1955 Eisenhower had a heart attack and Stevenson thought Ike might retire. Stevenson relished the thought of running against Nixon, so he announced plans for a second campaign and won the nomination in a hard-fought contest with Tennessee senator Estes Kefauver, made famous by his televised hearings on organized crime. But Eisenhower did not step down.

The 1956 campaign was essentially a replay of 1952, although Stevenson no longer seemed like a fresh, new voice and Ike's health was

---

* Ike's visit did not immediately end the war, of course. Stalin's death in March 1953 plus months of negotiation from the very diplomats Truman had already put in place were necessary before the Korean armistice was signed in late July 1953.

an issue. Stevenson's speeches were not quite as stirring, perhaps because the times were not so dark. The war in Korea was over. McCarthy had been discredited and would soon be dead from the ravages of alcoholism. Then, in the final weeks of the campaign, there were two foreign crises—the uprising against Soviet domination in Hungary and the Suez Crisis in the Middle East—that reminded voters how reassuring it was to have a general in the White House.

Against this backdrop, it is remarkable that Stevenson did as well as he did. Given that popular incumbent presidents with the approval rating enjoyed by Eisenhower usually win re-election with 60 percent or more of the popular vote, Stevenson's 42 percent showing (just two points less than he received in 1952) indicated he was still widely admired—though not by every Democrat.

One of the most memorable episodes during the 1956 campaign was Stevenson's decision to let the Democratic convention choose his running mate for him. Among those who competed for the prize was young Massachusetts senator John F. Kennedy, who was passed over in favor of Kefauver but who made a most favorable impression in his national debut. To appease Kennedy admirers, Stevenson hired Kennedy's brother, Robert, to work on the campaign, but RFK found Stevenson so uninspiring that he quietly voted for Eisenhower.

A few Stevenson acolytes, led by Eleanor Roosevelt, hoped he would make one more try in 1960. Stevenson did not want to actively seek the nomination, but he clearly hoped the Democrats might turn to him once more. As the national convention convened, in a sign of how much he continued to want the presidency, he made a humiliating last-minute call to Chicago mayor Richard Daley to determine if the Illinois delegation might drop its support for Kennedy and lead a convention stampede to Stevenson once more. It was too late—and his effort simply angered the Kennedys.

Stevenson had hoped his stature within the party would make him secretary of state in the Kennedy administration. Instead, he was made ambassador to the United Nations, where he learned to his chagrin that his role was only to enunciate policy, not formulate it. Still, he was an articulate spokesman for the United States in world affairs and earned the country considerable goodwill by treating diplomats from the emerging Third World nations with the same courtesy as that shown to those from the great powers. He also continued to advocate for one of his pet causes, a ban on nuclear testing in the atmosphere, which he had first proposed in 1956, and which was finally approved in 1963.

Kennedy did not particularly like Stevenson; he had bought into the Republican line that Stevenson was not tough enough for realpolitik. When Stevenson was deliberately kept out of the loop on the Bay of Pigs fiasco, he was placed in the position of unintentionally espousing lies before the UN. He was also kept at arm's length during the Cuban Missile Crisis, although it appears one of his suggestions—to remove U.S. missiles from Turkey to help the Soviets save face—was ultimately adopted by JFK.

In the wake of such humiliations, friends kept urging Stevenson to resign and lead a liberal uprising against the perceived conservatism and hard line anti-communism of Kennedy. Stevenson's own conservative nature made it impossible to be a rebel. "That's not how the game is played," he said. Plus, he enjoyed his role at the UN, even if it only provided the appearance of power.

Since his divorce, and with his sons now adults, Stevenson enjoyed the international partying that came with his job and a series of relationships with adoring women. Diplomacy was "one-third protocol, one-third alcohol, and one-third Geritol," Stevenson was fond of saying. Some said his "sybaritic" lifestyle was the cause of the massive heart attack that killed him while walking on the streets of London. He was sixty-five.

On election night in 1952, a supporter told Stevenson, "Governor, you didn't win, but you educated the country with your great campaign." To which Stevenson replied, "But a lot of people flunked the course!" Many agreed with his grading system. Hofstadter said "his political fate was taken as a yardstick by which liberal intellectuals measured the position of intellect in American political life." But that is a false measurement.

Certainly some, then and now, believe Stevenson's intellectual appeal was a handicap. Truman, who privately called Stevenson "a country-club, tweedy snob," had worried that Stevenson lacked the common touch. During the 1956 campaign, when Stevenson came to him for advice, Truman remembered taking Stevenson to a hotel window, pointing down to a random citizen walking on the street below, and saying, "The thing that you have got to do is learn how to reach that man."

As recently as the 2008 presidential campaign, then Pennsylvania governor Ed Rendell publicly expressed his concern that Obama was "a little like Adlai Stevenson. You ask him a question, and he gives you a six-minute answer. And the six-minute answer is smart as all get out. It's intellectual. It's well framed. It takes care of all the contingencies. But it's a lousy soundbite."

The author Garry Wills has suggested that Stevenson represents the "antitype" of an effective electoral leader, as exemplified by FDR. Where Roosevelt "grappled voters to him," Stevenson believed in the "Periclean" model of leadership, where a virtuous man above the pressure of base politics tells the people uncomfortable truths and then waits for the voters to "flock to him."

But perhaps just as Stevenson's intellectual comrades were too hard on the voters for preferring Ike and his supposed blandness, subsequent analysts have been too hard on Stevenson and his supposed elitism. No one can win twenty-seven million votes, as Stevenson did in 1952 (the third-most by a presidential candidate in history), and not reach quite a few so-called common voters—a concept that perhaps carries far more condescension than anything Stevenson ever said.

Some supporters of Stevenson may have, at the time, found it "literally inconceivable . . . that a rational electorate would prefer Ike to Adlai," but given the circumstances of the time—the war in Korea, weariness with Democratic rule, Eisenhower's own shrewd political instincts—it is hard to see how the eventual result could have been different. Further, perhaps the voters' judgment should not be faulted, for Eisenhower is now consistently ranked, even by some of the same scholars who supported Stevenson, as one of our ten best presidents.

After the Soviet Union launched the first space satellite, Sputnik, in 1957, intellectualism was in fashion again as Americans worried about keeping pace in the space race. So they elected Kennedy, who had won (with help from his aide, Theodore Sorensen) the Pulitzer Prize for his own book, *Profiles in Courage*. Kennedy, who had hired Arthur Schlesinger Jr. to serve as a sort of in-house intellectual as well as a host of other Ivy Leaguers to run the government, deliberately maintained a highbrow image. There was even a Stevenson mark on the presidency of Lyndon Johnson, not seemingly an intellectual, but who eschewed the more earthy and colloquial sobriquets like the "New Deal" and the "Fair Deal" to label his own domestic program the Stevensonian-sounding "Great Society."

Whenever Americans believe that the occupant of the White House should possess the intellectual curiosity necessary to meet the current challenges, they have turned to men who wear their intelligence well, whether they were men who did graduate work in nuclear physics, like Jimmy Carter; who studied at Oxford, like Bill Clinton; or who edited the *Harvard Law Review* before becoming a successful and acclaimed author, like Barack Obama. These were all Democrats, and it remains an oddity that Republicans remain resolutely hostile to nominating a candidate whose qualifications include an overt intellectual curiosity.

Stevenson's style could be easily mocked. Peter Sellers reportedly based his character of the balding and cerebral president Merkin Muffley in the 1964 Stanley Kubrick film, *Dr. Strangelove,* on Stevenson. It was a hilarious but devastating portrait of a public official so devoted to rational thought and good manners that he is unable to summon the necessary action to avoid a nuclear apocalypse.

But being easily mocked is not the same as being easily mimicked, which is why Stevenson's appeal has endured. Thousands of young voters in post-war America, many educated on the GI Bill, found something immensely appealing in Stevenson's "fundamental decency." He helped the Democrats shed their image of a party run by big city bosses and Southern reactionaries. As Goldwater would open the South to the Republicans in 1964, Stevenson won Democratic converts in places like

New England, the Midwest, and the Pacific Coast where the party had not been very strong before. They were untroubled that Stevenson asked so many questions and provided so few answers because they thought he was asking the right questions. What kind of country do you want this to be? And what is your role as a citizen in making it that kind of country?

Despite what was said about him during his campaigns and since, Stevenson did not look down on American voters but tried to talk to them eye-to-eye and convince them that they, too, shared the burden of leadership with those whom they put in political office. "I get so sick of the everlasting appeals to the cupidity and prejudice of every group which characterizes our political campaigns," he said. "There is something finer in people; they know that they owe something, too. I should like to try, at least, to appeal to their sense of obligation as well as their avarice."

Chapter Eight

BARRY GOLDWATER
1964

The conservative movement is founded on the simple tenet that people have the right to live life as they please, as long as they don't hurt anyone in the process.

By the 2000s, a time of seemingly unprecedented political polarization, many Americans wondered what had become of bipartisanship? Part of the answer lies in Barry Goldwater's 1964 campaign. Though it ended in a landslide loss to Lyndon Johnson, Goldwater's run dramatically accelerated a partisan realignment that left Republicans and Democrats with less in common than perhaps at any time since the Civil War. Goldwater's candidacy was the tipping point that remade the Republicans into a fundamentally white, conservative party with virtually no liberal and few minority members, while the Democrats were converted into a fundamentally liberal party that draws heavily on the overwhelming support of racial and ethnic minorities.

Such stark ideological and demographic divides between the two parties are without precedent in American history. Before the changes wrought by Goldwater's candidacy, the two major parties were "big tent" parties, and each contained considerable ideological diversity. Each had a liberal wing that advocated for a strong and vital federal government and a conservative wing that sought to limit federal authority, especially in economic affairs and in regulating social relationships.

In those earlier times, bipartisanship was more readily achieved when members of the respective wings of each party would form a coalition, liberal or conservative, which was based on ideological principles rather than partisan identification. Bipartisanship is difficult to achieve when a fundamentally conservative Republican Party can find few conservative Democrats willing to cross party lines to support its agenda and a fundamentally liberal Democratic Party can find even fewer liberal Republicans to help advance its programs.

One issue truly caused this realignment—not tax policy, defense policy, or even abortion. Those issues—and many more—became important partisan markers later on. The initial catalyst for party polarization was the issue of race and whether the federal government has a role in promoting racial equality.

Before Goldwater, the Republican Party platform, dating to the time of Abraham Lincoln, had consistently argued the federal government had such a role. After Goldwater, the GOP began to argue such a role was improper. This had been the Democratic Party's position until shortly after World War II when, under the leadership of men like Harry Truman and Hubert Humphrey, Democrats began to advocate federal expansion and protection of the civil rights of African Americans.

This switch meant that the Republican Party lost what was once the substantial support of racial minorities, particularly African Americans. What the Republicans gained in return was the allegiance of white Southerners who had previously been devoted to the Democratic Party for generations. Both changes in allegiance can be dated to Goldwater's 1964 campaign.

The idea of realigning the two parties so that one party was fundamentally liberal and the other fundamentally conservative did not begin with Goldwater. Franklin Roosevelt, for one, had tried and failed to force a similar political realignment while president. He tried to purge Southern conservatives from the Democratic Party after his court-packing scheme failed in 1938. He then tried to lure liberal Republicans into the Democratic fold in 1944 by suggesting that Wendell Willkie, the Republican candidate Roosevelt had defeated in 1940, rejoin the

Democratic Party, perhaps as Roosevelt's running mate. FDR had thought economic issues alone had the power to force a change in party loyalty, but economics did not trump culture. Southern whites were not yet ready to leave the Democratic Party, and Willkie and other liberal Republicans were not ready to come in. Goldwater, then, would achieve in a landslide loss a feat that a man elected president four times could not, providing one of history's great examples of how losing campaigns, even ones defeated overwhelmingly, can have greater consequences than winning ones.

A number of prominent Republicans, since and including Goldwater, have argued that race was not the issue that turned the South from the center of Democratic power to a bedrock of GOP electoral strength. They instead cite Goldwater's role in founding the modern conservative movement, which reached its apex in the 1980 presidential election of Ronald Reagan. That is certainly a huge part of Goldwater's legacy, but it, too, is rooted in the issue of race. Surveys by the University of Michigan's Survey Research Center suggest, in the words of authors Thomas and Mary Edsall, that the issue of race was still so powerful in the South in 1964 that it "actually produced an *ideological* conversion of poor Southern whites from a deeply held economic liberalism to economic conservatism."

The role race played in prompting this conservative conversion was masked because Goldwater could speak to "white backlash"—white resentment at the assertion of minority rights—in ways that were understood by his audience but that were not overtly or condemnably racist. Goldwater's use of "new political images and code words of racial antipathy," his biographer Robert Alan Goldberg points out, unfortunately, still remains the roundabout way race is generally discussed in our society.

In the half-century after Goldwater's campaign, the Republican Party failed to attract much support from minority groups, not just African Americans. In recent elections, for example, Republicans failed to win even a third of the Hispanic vote. By 2008, the GOP was receiving so little support from Hispanics and African Americans that a Republican candidate for president would need to win 60 percent of the white vote to win election. With non-Hispanic whites scheduled to be in the minority for the first time in the nation's history by 2045, these demographic changes pose a significant long-term challenge for Republicans.

The seminal event in turning the white South from Democratic to Republican was Goldwater's vote against the Civil Rights Act of 1964. Goldwater was one of only six Republican senators to oppose the measure, which passed the Senate by a seventy-three to twenty-seven vote. The legislation was favored by virtually all Republican congressional leaders plus the most recent GOP presidential nominee, Richard Nixon, and the early frontrunner for the 1964 Republican nomination, New York governor Nelson Rockefeller. This landmark legislation, which had dominated national news coverage for more than a year before it was finally approved on July 2, 1964, banned racial discrimination and segregation in public education, employment, and in the use of public accommodations. The bill was a pet project of Lyndon Johnson that was promoted as fulfilling the legacy of the martyred president John Kennedy.

Before casting his "no" vote, Goldwater specifically repudiated the position of segregationists by stating that he was "unalterably opposed to discrimination of any sort." But the problem of discrimination, Goldwater said, "is fundamentally one of [the] heart." He acknowledged, "Some law can help, but not law that embodies features . . . which fly in the face of the Constitution and require for their effective execution the creation of a police state." Goldwater said the act was unconstitutional because nowhere in the Constitution is promoting racial equality listed among the functions of the federal government. On the other hand, he said, the federal system outlined in the Constitution did provide the states wide leeway to "nourish local differences, even local cultures." This seemed an implicit endorsement of the "Jim Crow" laws that enforced racial segregation in the South.

Goldwater was particularly opposed to provisions in the Civil Rights Act that prohibited landlords from refusing to rent to people based on race and that prohibited employers from refusing to hire people based on race. On the campaign trail, Goldwater explained, "No law can make a person like another if he doesn't want to." A few commentators praised Goldwater's political courage in taking what was perceived to be an unpopular stand on civil rights, while others charged he was intent on returning blacks to near servitude. A politically shrewd judgment came from the occupant of the White House who had pushed the legislation through Congress. In signing his civil rights legislation into law, Johnson told his aide, Bill Moyers, "I think we just delivered the South to the Republican Party for a long time to come."

Goldwater certainly hoped so. He had been mulling such a remarkable political development for quite some time. Goldwater once famously declared, with a self-deprecation that charmed many, "You know, I haven't got a really first-class brain," but he possessed exceptional political intuition. As early as 1953, having just arrived in Washington, D.C., as a freshman senator, he wrote in his journal that he was detecting "a cleavage that was new" in American politics and that the opportunity for future Republican growth lay in recruiting Southern Democrats "who believe in states' rights and who believe that the federal government should be out of the state and local government picture entirely, and out of the affairs of business as well."

Goldwater would have observed that South Carolina governor Strom Thurmond's 1948 segregationist "Dixiecrat" campaign for president just a few years before had demonstrated that the civil rights issue had the power to break the century-long hold of the Democratic Party on the South. Thurmond had received only a small fraction of the national popular vote (2.4 percent), but he carried four Deep South states—Alabama, Louisiana, Mississippi, and South Carolina—that Goldwater would carry as well.

Goldwater further recognized that in the post-war period, the South and the Southwest were the fastest-growing regions in the country, and the regions shared not only an abundance of sunshine, but also an antipathy to a federal government that seemed a distant interloper in local cultures and economies. He began to ponder, in his words, "a realignment of Southern conservative Democrats with Democrats and Republicans of the West and Middle West" united in their opposition to federal authority. The new Republican Party Goldwater helped form would be a fusion of Southern race-based populism with Western libertarianism and the remnants of traditional Midwest conservatism.

Interestingly, the South and the West had both once been hotbeds of populist activism that had *demanded* federal intervention to counter the injustices the regions' residents believed they suffered from railroads, banks, and other business interests. But it was another achievement of the Goldwater campaign that it began a process that redefined populism, replacing traditional populist antipathy toward big business with antipathy toward big government. Where the populism of the late nineteenth and early twentieth centuries had seen blacks and whites as suffering from the same economic inequities, the new conservative populism espoused by Goldwater argued that big government was tipping the balance in favor of minorities at the expense of low- and middle-income whites. It was the Democrats' misfortune that where Franklin Roosevelt's "New Deal" had been seen as providing government help based on economic need, Johnson's "Great Society" was perceived as being based on race and providing more benefits to minorities than whites. Goldwater, it was said, had discovered how to exploit the type of populist discontents that "appear in an affluent society, and this he did with unusual self-awareness and clarity," said historian Richard Hofstadter.

The early 1960s were certainly a time of many discontents. Traditional values seemed under assault. The Supreme Court, under the leadership of Chief Justice Earl Warren, an Eisenhower appointee, had issued a number of controversial decisions. The court ruled that mandatory prayer in the public schools was unconstitutional at a time when pornography and a perceived decline in sexual morality was a growing concern. The civil rights of accused criminals were expanded at the very time Americans were increasingly concerned about rising street crime.

The push by African Americans to assert their civil rights was perceived as more than just another sign that the traditional norms of society were under assault. An influential study published in 1991 by Thomas and Mary Edsall argues that the high profile issue of civil rights triggered a "chain reaction" that exposed middle class white anxieties on a host of issues, all of which had a racial component—even the surge of rock 'n' roll and the youth culture that frightened many parents was blamed on the infusion of wanton and promiscuous black culture into an otherwise polite white society.

Goldwater saw the civil rights protests, the coddling of criminals, and the increasing burden of the welfare state as all of one package, and he was able to address the collective anxiety around these issues, the Edsalls noted, "without the liability of being labeled a racist."

As a Westerner from Arizona, Goldwater was not saddled with the South's history on race. It is notable that all the Republican presidential nominees since Goldwater, with the exception of Michigan's Gerald Ford in 1976, have identified themselves as Westerners even as they have built upon the Republicans' so-called Southern strategy. Even both presidents Bush, each born in New England but hailing from Texas, emphasized the Western nature of that state, never its legacy as a member of the old Confederacy. With no Southern vice presidential nominees either, the GOP's "Southern strategy" seems to refrain from placing any true Southerners on the national ticket lest the issue of race become too explicit.

Goldwater also averted the racist tag because he demonstrated no racism in his personal life. Some of his relations with minority groups smacked of paternalism, but at an individual level, Goldwater enjoyed positive personal relationships with African Americans, Native Americans, and Hispanics. He did take some provocative stands on race during his career, such as when he argued in 1968 that apartheid should be given time to work in South Africa. Yet, a friend said, "nothing was more distressing to Goldwater" than to be accused of being a racist.

He admonished his children to never use the word "nigger"; his family's stores, called Goldwater's, were among the first in Arizona to hire black clerks (though they could only wait upon white customers during the Christmas rush); and when approached by black veterans of World War II, Goldwater, as a senior officer, personally desegregated the Arizona Air National Guard two years before Truman desegregated the U.S. Armed Forces. He even expressed empathy for the impatience felt by black civil rights protesters in the early 1960s. He simply argued that the federal government had no constitutional authority to do anything for their plight beyond guarantee their right to vote.

What seemed genuinely shocking about Goldwater's narrow view of the federal role in enforcing civil rights is that it was at odds with the more than one-hundred-year-old tradition of the Republican Party (although it must be acknowledged that from Reconstruction on, the GOP mostly paid lip service to civil rights for blacks, appearing enlightened only when matched against the Democrats; "The Party of Lincoln" was more slogan than a commitment to a set of policies that might elevate the status of African Americans).

Still, Republicans had maintained the allegiance of a significant number of African-American voters through the 1960 election. From Reconstruction until the New Deal, those relatively few African Americans who were allowed to vote overwhelmingly supported the Republican Party. Most African Americans, however, still lived in the South, where more than 90 percent of eligible blacks were denied their right to vote by a host of state initiatives, including poll taxes and literacy tests, as well as outright intimidation.

Between 1915 and 1970, six million African Americans migrated out of the South and into the North, where they were slowly recruited into the urban Democratic political machines. They began switching party allegiance during the New Deal, which offered some hope for unemployed blacks as well as whites. Roosevelt captured an estimated 60 percent of the African-American vote in 1936. Black movement into the Democratic Party accelerated in 1948 when Truman desegregated the federal work force, including the Armed Forces, and Democrats finally adopted, at Hubert Humphrey's urging, a strong civil rights plank to their party platform—the act that led Thurmond to launch his independent candidacy.

But Republicans had maintained a commitment to civil rights, at least as stated in their party platforms, through 1960. So Eisenhower received 39 percent of the black vote in 1956 and Nixon received 32 percent in 1960. But African Americans took Goldwater's nomination as a sign that the Republicans had abandoned them. The break was decisive. Goldwater received but 6 percent of the African-American vote, and no Republican presidential candidate has been able to win even 15 percent of the black vote since.

It was extraordinary how rapidly Goldwater's candidacy changed perceptions of the two parties in regard to race and civil rights. In 1962, a survey conducted by National Election Studies found that the public saw virtually no difference between the two parties on the issue of civil rights. Asked which party would most likely ensure blacks received fair treatment in jobs and housing, 23 percent said Democrats, 21 percent said Republicans, and 56 percent felt there was no difference. Just two years later, the same survey found 60 percent of the respondents believed Democrats would do more to ensure fair treatment for African Americans, 33 percent felt there was no difference between the parties, and just 7 percent thought the Republican Party would do more to help blacks.

Since most other Republican leaders remained at least publicly committed to civil rights, it seems that the new perception of the Republican Party's position on the issue was due mostly to Goldwater's nomination and candidacy. Former New York congressman Jack Kemp, who was the party's 1996 vice presidential nominee, has called the GOP's "Southern strategy" a "disgrace," adding, "The Democrats had a terrible history [on civil rights] and they overcame it. We had a great history, and we turned aside."

Goldwater understood his views would cost the Republican Party the support of African Americans, but he had made the calculation the GOP could win far more white votes than it would lose black votes. In 1961, Goldwater told a group of Georgia Republicans that a GOP organized along conservative principles was "not going to get the Negro vote . . . so we ought to go hunting where the ducks are."

Some, including Goldwater himself, have suggested that the Republican appeal below the Mason-Dixon Line was centered in the less racially restricted and more economically diverse states of the so-called New South. Yet, Goldwater failed to carry the New South states of Florida, Tennessee, and Texas that Eisenhower and Nixon had carried in their campaigns. Rather, all five states that Goldwater won in the South were in the Deep South, and no Republican presidential candidate had won Alabama, Mississippi, Georgia, and South Carolina since Reconstruction. Yet Goldwater carried these states by overwhelming percentages, winning nearly 60 percent of the vote in South Carolina, 70 percent of the vote in Alabama, and 87 percent of the vote in Mississippi—which, not coincidentally, was the same percentage that Thurmond had won in 1948.

Goldwater won 55 percent of the total white vote in the South in 1964, but given the scope of his landslide loss, Johnson was able to win a majority of the white vote nationally. LBJ was, however, the last Democratic candidate for president to win the white vote. Ronald Reagan carried 61 percent of the Southern white vote in 1980 even while running against a Southerner; in 1984, Reagan won 71 percent of the Southern white vote.

The Goldwater campaign's seminal role in triggering this dramatic racial shift has been obscured by three subsequent events. First, George Wallace's independent campaign for president in 1968 carried the states of the Deep South that would otherwise likely have gone to the Republican Nixon. Second, Nixon's 1972 rout of George McGovern was so overwhelming that race was not an obviously identifiable factor in such a landslide.* Third, the Democrats' nomination in 1976 of a Southerner, former Georgia governor Jimmy Carter, made it appear as if Democrats would again aggressively compete in the South at the presidential level. After Carter, however, no Democrat has been able to win more than four Southern states, and Democrats did not carry a single Southern state in the presidential elections of 1984, 1988, 2000 (even though their nominee that year was from Tennessee), or 2004.

Republican success in the South is not limited to presidential races. By the 1990s, Southern Republicans dominated the party's congressional leadership, and in 2010, Republicans swept away the last vestiges of Democratic power in the South by winning a majority of the region's

---

* Worth noting is that Nixon's 1972 vote totals were remarkably close to the sum of his and Wallace's totals in 1968, indicating that Wallace voters had switched their support to Nixon's re-election en masse and further reinforcing the supposition that Nixon would have carried the South in 1968 had Wallace not been in the race.

state legislatures. A disheartened Democratic 2010 U.S. Senate candidate in Louisiana said, "White male Democrats in the South are becoming extinct." African Americans make up 20 percent of all voters in the South, but they represent a majority of Democrats in the region. In the South, the two parties are stratified along racial lines just as they were during Reconstruction—only the parties have switched roles.

Republicans and Goldwater admirers are understandably reluctant to acknowledge that this realignment, which has helped Republicans win seven of the eleven presidential elections between 1968 and 2008, was rooted in opposition to the struggle for black equality. In a 2010 interview, Mississippi Republican governor Haley Barbour insisted that those "who really changed the South from Democrat to Republican were a different generation from those who fought integration." Goldwater had made the same claim in a 1971 letter to *Business Week* magazine, where he said that the growing Republican strength in the South "has nothing to do with busing, integration, or any other of the so-called closely held concepts of the Southerner. The South began to move into the Republican ranks because of the influx of new and younger businessmen from the North who were basically Republican. And they were aided by young Southern Democrats who were sick and tired of the Democratic stranglehold on the South and switched over to the Republican Party."

This was certainly not the prevailing view then, and it does not seem supported by the facts now. Kevin Phillips, a campaign aide for Richard Nixon in 1968 who published the influential study *The Emerging Republican Majority* that promoted a "Southern strategy," declared Goldwater's presidential campaign to be the South's "final battle against Negro voting rights." Columnist Robert Novak, in a 1965 book on the Goldwater campaign, *The Agony of the GOP 1964,* said that Goldwater's strategy was clearly to "forget all the sentimental tradition of the party of Lincoln" and to "soft-pedal civil rights" without "actually endorsing racial segregation."

Novak also said that Northeastern Republicans still committed to the GOP's civil rights tradition were shocked by the "unabashed hostility toward the Negro rights movement" expressed at a 1963 convention of Young Republicans dominated by pro-Goldwater conservatives. "For the Young Republicans . . . their party was now a White Man's Party," Novak wrote. Nixon was equally blunt. He said flatly that Goldwater "ran as a racist candidate," and Nixon, who had nonetheless stumped for Goldwater, resented insinuations that his campaigns in 1968 and 1972 were a continuation of Goldwater's "Southern strategy." Nixon saw his own efforts as far subtler and less crude than Goldwater's.

Despite Goldwater's attempts to distance himself from overt racism, Southern segregationists were drawn to him. South Carolina's Strom Thurmond, even though still nominally a Democrat, had been one of the first persons to urge Goldwater to run for president as far back as 1959. When Goldwater won the Republican nomination in 1964, Thurmond not only endorsed him, he switched parties, becoming the first Republican senator from the South since Reconstruction.* Thurmond said he was "not under any false illusions that [Goldwater] is a segregationist," but Johnson's choice of civil rights advocate Hubert Humphrey to be his vice presidential nominee was a clear signal that segregationists were no longer welcome in the Democratic Party. Thurmond's hometown newspaper, the *Charleston News and Courier*, saw that Goldwater had opened the way for "a realignment of political power in this country, with the South, Middle West, and Far West joined together in a new alliance."

George Wallace even imagined an alliance that would make him Goldwater's running mate in 1964. Far more an economic populist than a conservative, the Alabama governor found common cause with Goldwater on the issue of race. Wallace told an aide it would be "apparent to a one-eyed nigguh who can't see good outa his other eye that me and Goldwater would be a winning ticket. We'd have the South locked up, then him and me could concentrate on the industrial states and win." There was some basis for Wallace's bravado. He had run as a protest candidate against Johnson in the Democratic primaries and had won more than a third of the vote in the Wisconsin primary, 30 percent of the vote in the Indiana primary, and 43 percent in Maryland where, as Wallace put it, "If it hadn't been for the nigger bloc vote, we'd have won it all."

---

* Republicans also won an unprecedented nine congressional seats in the South in 1964 and would have won more if they had been able to field candidates in several more districts.

Goldwater was uncomfortable embracing the overt racism practiced by Wallace. When an intermediary advised Goldwater of Wallace's desire to be his vice presidential running mate, an observer said Goldwater "looked as though someone had just reported a death in the family." Goldwater rejected Wallace's gambit. He did not need Wallace to win the Deep South, while Wallace would drive away all hope of support from racial moderates. Besides, Wallace was a Democrat, not a Republican. But Goldwater did talk Wallace into abandoning an independent presidential campaign that would have ruined the GOP candidate's chances of taking the South.

Even without Wallace, Goldwater had difficulty keeping some of the most noisome racists in the country from jumping on his bandwagon. Robert Creel, Alabama Grand Dragon for the Ku Klux Klan, made headlines when he endorsed Goldwater, saying, "I like Barry Goldwater. I believe what he believes in. I think the same way he thinks." Goldwater's vice presidential running mate, the conservative and irascible New York congressman William Miller, said, "Senator Goldwater and I will accept the support of any American citizen who believes in our posture, who believes in our principles, who believes in our platform." Only after considerable public criticism did the Goldwater campaign rebuff Creel's endorsement.

Goldwater campaign advisor J. William Middendorf II, who would later serve in the Nixon, Ford, and Reagan administrations, acknowledged, "It was not Barry's intention, but indeed was a fact, that racists thought he was their friend. While [the Goldwater campaign] tacitly accepted their support, to charge Barry with consciously appealing to racism was specious."

Goldwater, however, had always seemed ambivalent about race. Back in Arizona, he had been a member of the Tucson chapter of the National Association for the Advancement of Colored People. He also made significant contributions to the Phoenix chapter of the Urban League, but he funneled the contributions through a friend so that his involvement could remain anonymous. Later in life, Goldwater seemed embarrassed that he had not done more to further the cause of black equality in his community. In his 1988 autobiography, Goldwater takes credit for integrating Phoenix's lunch counters. In truth, the only action the Phoenix City Council took while Goldwater was a member in the early 1950s was to order the restaurant at the city-owned airport to serve black customers—and Goldwater was not present for either the deliberations or the vote on that issue.

At other times, Goldwater claimed to have been unaware that Arizona had any racial problems, even though his own African-American butler said that Phoenix in the 1940s and 1950s was as segregated as any city in the South, and another local African-American businessman said Phoenix in the 1950s was "just like Mississippi."

Adding a layer of complexity to Goldwater's views on prejudice was his Jewish ancestry on his father's side. Raised an Episcopalian in a prominent family, he claimed never to have experienced anti-Semitism in Arizona. His best friend, a practicing Jew, did, however. Yet, when his friend was barred from the University of Arizona fraternity where Goldwater was a member, Goldwater neither left the fraternity nor made an effort to get his friend admitted. Later in life, when that same friend was prevented from joining the restricted Phoenix Country Club where Goldwater served as president, he forced the other members to admit his friend—but made no effort to get the club to lift its anti-Semitic restriction and no other Jew joined the club for another decade.

Goldwater could empathize with an individual who experienced prejudice and could be moved to do something about it personally, if it was within his power. But he had, in the words of his biographer, Robert Alan Goldberg, "an inability to conceptualize prejudice and discrimination beyond the individual experience to institutional or societal conditions."

This view was certainly shaped by Goldwater's own privileged background. The man who became the epitome of the politics of self-reliance guilelessly noted, "You might say I was a success by being born into a successful family."

Equally incongruous for the man who despised government handouts, Goldwater's family dry goods business struggled on the Arizona frontier until the government moved to aggressively subdue the local Apache tribe, which proved to be a tenacious adversary. By the 1880s, a full 20 percent of the U.S. Army's soldiers were stationed in Arizona and the Goldwater's store provided a large share of their food and clothing. Later, federally funded dam and reclamation projects created the booming state's agricultural industry. By the 1920s, 15 percent of Arizona's gross domestic product was from federal spending. Yet, later in life, Goldwater was in no way being intentionally ironic when he said, "We didn't know the federal government. Everything that was done, we did it ourselves."

Goldwater said his motto for employee relations was, "Treat people right and they will treat you right." Goldwater provided his workers with good wages, a forty-hour week, health insurance, paid sick leave, profit sharing, a pension, and a host of other perks that included use of a Goldwater-owned recreation area just outside of town. This had the intended result of discouraging his employees to unionize. Goldwater believed unions were in league with racketeers and infringed on his rights as a businessman. It was apparently the New Deal's promotion of organized labor that led Goldwater to conclude he was a conservative Republican when his parents had been Democrats.

Goldwater had little interest in business, though he had a flair for merchandising, starting a national fad when he designed and sold men's underwear printed with red ants and marketed under the slogan: "You'll rant and dance with ants in your pants!" Goldwater preferred to pursue his primary interests: photography and flying. Goldwater was such a fine photographer, with Arizona's Native American culture a particularly favored subject, that he was elected to the Royal Photographic Society of London. He was an even more avid flyer, owning a multitude of planes throughout his life. When war came in 1941, poor eyesight kept Goldwater from becoming a fighter pilot, but he later flew dangerous supply missions in South Asia over the Himalayas. He remained in the Air Force Reserve until he retired as a major general in 1967.

He cut a dashing figure in Arizona, and his place in Phoenix's business community ensured he would become active in civic affairs. He had a tremendous aptitude for politics. He managed local campaigns and served on the Phoenix City Council before emerging as a national figure because of his stunning upset victory over Senate Majority Leader Ernest McFarland in 1952.* By 1955, most leaders of the conservative GOP old guard had departed, and Goldwater was already a leading national spokesman for the conservative cause. General Douglas MacArthur had retired from public life, Ohio senator Robert Taft had died in 1953, and Wisconsin senator Joseph McCarthy had been censured and discredited in 1954. Most other party leaders were following the Thomas Dewey–inspired "Modern Republicanism" of the Eisenhower administration, which Goldwater derided as "a dime store New Deal."

But it was not just by default that Goldwater became the nation's leading conservative, it was also the Goldwater persona, the "tanned, square-jawed, ex-Army Air Corps pilot with horn-rim glasses, straight talk, and sardonic humor," that set conservative hearts aflutter. In a period when Westerns represented virtually all of the top-rated shows on television, Goldwater, sans glasses, wearing a cowboy hat and sometimes holding a rifle, seemed to embody the mythic West that enthralled the rest of the nation. His emergence as a national personality coincided neatly with the growing conservative intellectual movement, which included William F. Buckley's founding of the *National Review* in 1955. Buckley, too, was smitten with Goldwater, later recalling that he "brought a supernal charm and utterly American savoir-faire into twentieth-century politics."

When Goldwater made such pronouncements as, "I would rather see the Republicans lose in 1960 fighting on principle, than I would care to see us win standing on grounds we know are wrong and on which we will ultimately destroy ourselves," conservatives knew they had found their man. Clarence Manion, the former dean of the law school at the University of Notre Dame and a wildly popular conservative commentator on radio, was one of those most strongly urging Goldwater to become a presidential candidate in 1960. While flattered by Manion's attentions, Goldwater thought Nixon was a near shoo-in for the nomination. He told Manion he would do nothing to encourage or discourage a "draft Goldwater" effort but would actively campaign for the nomination only

---

* One result of Goldwater's defeat of McFarland was that it opened the way for Lyndon Johnson to become the new Senate Democratic leader, the post that made his own national reputation.

if it appeared that Rockefeller was poised to take the nomination from Nixon. Privately, Goldwater expressed doubt that Americans would elect a candidate of Jewish descent.

Goldwater, however, did like Manion's idea that he write a book. He approached L. Brent Bozell, Buckley's brother-in-law, to serve as his ghost-writer because, he acknowledged with charming humility, "my complete incapacity to be an author is well known to everybody." Goldwater provided Bozell with some general thoughts and a rough outline, and Bozell did most of the rest of the work. Goldwater did not even come up with the title. He was fine with Manion's suggestion: *The Conscience of a Conservative.*

The slim, 124-page book was a publishing sensation. Even though Manion had it published through a small "vanity house," by November 1960 it had sold a half-million copies (with the help of bulk purchases by various conservative groups), and it would go on to sell three million more copies over time, making it one of the most successful political treatises in American history. The book's slimness emphasized its theme, encapsulated by the following excerpt:

> *I have little interest in streamlining government or in making it more efficient, for I mean to reduce its size. I do not undertake to promote welfare, for I propose to extend freedom. My aim is not to pass laws, but to repeal them. It is not to inaugurate new programs, but to cancel old ones that do violence to the Constitution, or that have failed in their purpose, or that impose on the people an unwarranted financial burden. I will not attempt to discover whether legislation is "needed" before I have first determined whether it is constitutionally permissible. And if I should later be attacked for neglecting my constituents' "interests," I shall reply that I was informed their main interest is liberty and that in that cause I am doing the very best I can.*

Popular scholarship in the post-war period had been insisting that America had finally reached a liberal consensus and that there were no conservative ideas in circulation worthy of serious consideration. Now, here came Goldwater with a conservative creed that seemed both fresh and defiant. As such, it had a near electric appeal to young conservatives. Largely ignored while the media lavished attention in the 1960s on the youth movement from the left, the kids on the right represented a counterculture to the counterculture. Many young Goldwater supporters would later report that they felt a "thrill" in being part of what seemed almost a conspiracy against the prevailing liberal mindset. Goldwater's campaign became "a Woodstock of the right" that attracted a host of clean-cut young people, among them a seventeen-year-old "Goldwater girl" in Park Ridge, Illinois, named Hillary Rodham who attended rallies wearing cowboy boots, a red, white, and blue sash, and an "AuH_2O" button. Eight years later, she worked on the George McGovern campaign with her future husband, Bill Clinton.

The Conscience of a Conservative also directly addressed the issue of civil rights, tipping Goldwater's hand on where he would stand on future legislation. Goldwater would note elsewhere that he had voted in favor of civil rights legislation in 1957 and 1960 because, he said, those bills were narrowly focused on protecting the right of African Americans to vote and the guarantee of the right to vote could be found in the Fifteenth Amendment to the Constitution. But nowhere in the Constitution, Goldwater argued, was there anything that mandated integration, most particularly in the public schools, where jurisdiction was strictly a local, not a federal, affair.*

It might be "wise and just" to have black children attend the same schools as white children, Goldwater acknowledged. "I am not prepared, however, to impose that judgment of mine on the people of Mississippi or South Carolina, or to tell them what methods should be adopted and what pace should be kept in striving toward that goal. That's their business, not mine." Goldwater even questioned whether the U.S. Supreme Court's ruling in *Brown vs. the Board of Education,* desegregating the nation's public schools, "is the law of the land." For Goldwater, states' rights trumped even the right of black children to receive an equal education.

---

* Bozell and Buckley had both been students of Yale University professor Willmoore Kendall, a particularly influential thinker in the conservative movement, who developed the argument adopted by Goldwater that promoting racial equality is not a conservative principle because it is not mentioned in the Constitution.

While *The Conscience of a Conservative* was a runaway best seller and dramatically increased Goldwater's national profile, Nixon was, as Goldwater predicted, the Republican nominee in 1960. Of conservatives, Nixon said, "They don't like me, but they tolerate me." Goldwater allowed his name to be put in nomination at the Republican National Convention and then withdrew with a challenge to his followers: "Let's grow up, conservatives. If we want to take this party back, and I think we can someday, let's get to work."

Goldwater was already hard at work, particularly as the chair of the Republican Senatorial Campaign Committee, the person designated by the Republican Senate caucus to help elect more Republican senators. The chair of the complementary National Republican Congressional Committee was Goldwater's future running mate, William Miller, and together they poured money into a Republican initiative that was called "Operation Dixie," whose goal was to build a Republican Party worthy of the name in the South.

Operation Dixie showed results in 1962. In South Carolina, William D. Workman Jr., a recent GOP convert who was a popular columnist and television commentator, astonished observers by receiving 44 percent of the vote, an extraordinary total for a Republican in South Carolina. Workman had argued that his opponent, three-term Democratic senator Olin D. Johnston, was a "fine segregationist," but Johnston was hindered in those views by his allegiance to a national Democratic administration that was becoming increasingly pro–civil rights. In Alabama, another Republican recruit, oil distributor James Martin, did even better, losing to thirty-seven-year congressional veteran Lister Hill by less than a single percentage point. Goldwater could see that his theories were correct: Gains could be made in the South if Republicans accommodated the segregationist sympathies that dominated the region.

Despite these successes, Goldwater was not the front-runner to win the 1964 Republican presidential nomination. Nixon had eliminated himself from a potential rematch with Kennedy by virtue of his 1962 loss in the California governor's race. Rockefeller, therefore, seemed the likely GOP nominee, and he continued to support a strong civil rights plank in the Republican platform. But Rockefeller critically wounded his prospects when, in the spring of 1963, he divorced his wife of thirty years and a month later married Margaretta "Happy" Murphy, a family friend nearly twenty years his junior who was also a recent divorcée with four small children. No divorced man had been elected president, and Rockefeller was not only divorced but accused of breaking up another man's marriage.

Goldwater had believed he would be a stronger candidate against Kennedy than Rockefeller anyway. Kennedy's weaknesses played to the strengths of a conservative opponent, thought Goldwater, not a liberal one. Further, he saw Kennedy's particular weakness in the South as an opening to unseat the young president.

Kennedy's martyrdom has obscured the reality that he was once a flesh and blood politician, facing a host of political challenges in late 1963. Since Johnson defeated Goldwater in a landslide in 1964, the conventional assumption is that Kennedy would have done the same had he lived. But Kennedy had felt politically vulnerable going into the 1964 campaign. He had not forgotten that his margin of victory over Nixon was razor-thin and fell short of an outright majority.[*] Beginning with the Bay of Pigs fiasco, his first two years in office had been blighted by an amazing string of foreign policy mishaps and disasters. The uneasy coalition of Southern conservatives and liberal Northerners that had made him president was rapidly deteriorating over the civil rights issue. His tepid response to the civil rights challenge was eroding support among his liberal base, while most Southern whites fervently concluded he was moving too fast on the issue.

Kennedy, of course, had the power of incumbency, and he was certainly growing in the job, but he acknowledged in the fall of 1963 that he faced a tough fight for re-election the following year. In the South, Kennedy's approval rating had dropped from 64 percent in 1962 to 35 percent in 1963. Robert Kennedy, his brother's chief political advisor, conceded that Kennedy might lose every Southern state in 1964—including Texas, even with Johnson on the ticket. Kennedy's prospects in the Plains and Mountain states were equally dim.

---

[*] Kennedy received 49.7 percent of the popular vote to Nixon's 49.6 percent.

The media thought he was vulnerable, too. Nationally syndicated columnist Marquis Childs had taken a tour of the South and Southwest and told Kennedy he was "startled" by the level of "hatred" he found for the president—as great as had been experienced by FDR, Childs told a rattled Kennedy. A Georgia theater had advertised the movie *PT-109* with a marquee that read, "See How the Japs Almost Get Kennedy." *Look* magazine ran a banner headline that said, "JFK COULD LOSE," while *Time* magazine did a state-by-state survey, backed up by several reputable national polls, that concluded Goldwater could give Kennedy "a breathlessly close race."

Goldwater was further heartened by a growing and exceedingly well-financed movement on the right that included the notorious John Birch Society, whose founder, Massachusetts candy maker Robert Welch, had accused Eisenhower of being a "conscious agent" of the Communist conspiracy. Goldwater told Welch he should drop that nonsense but otherwise welcomed the support of the Birchers and their allies, despite urgings from some supporters to repudiate them. "I am impressed by the type of people in it," Goldwater said of the Birchers. "They are the kind of people we need in politics," adding that "the finest people in my community" were members.

Then, on November 22, 1963, while on a trip to mend an intra-party feud in Texas between liberal and conservative Democrats, Kennedy was assassinated in Dallas and Vice President Johnson ascended to the presidency. Even though Kennedy's murderer was a deeply troubled pseudo-Marxist, many blamed the far right for creating "a conspiratorial atmosphere of violence" that led to the assassination. All forms of extremism, especially conservative extremism, were now suspect, and Johnson's strategy would be to ensure that America considered Goldwater an extremist—a strategy with which Goldwater obligingly cooperated.

Goldwater, meanwhile, was deeply saddened by Kennedy's murder. He had looked forward to campaigning against Kennedy, not just because he thought he had tactical advantages in such a race, but also because he and Kennedy genuinely liked each other. Goldwater said they had even talked about barnstorming across the country, engaging in

Lincoln-Douglas–style debates in which they would offer a stark contrast in philosophy and provide voters with a clear choice.

With Kennedy dead, Goldwater considered ending his presidential bid, knowing that the assassination would ensure a Johnson victory in 1964 as a memorial to the dead president. But Goldwater realized that he remained the great hope of conservatives and stayed in the race, now less to win the presidency than to capture the soul of the Republican Party.

Republican moderates tried to stop Goldwater, but competing egos prevented them from rallying around a single candidate. Rockefeller had one last chance to derail the Goldwater movement by winning the California primary, but a week before the election his new wife gave birth to their first child, reminding voters of "Rocky's" indiscretions. Goldwater partisans gleefully held up signs that asked, "Do You Want a Leader or a Lover" in the White House? Rockefeller had carried fifty-four of California's fifty-eight counties, but Goldwater's support was so strong in Los Angeles, Orange, and San Diego Counties that he won the primary with 51 percent of the vote. The conservative movement was not derailed, and the nomination was his.

With little hope of winning the general election against Johnson, Goldwater felt no need or desire to conciliate with the moderate and liberal wings of the party. Unlike 1960, the party platform did not have a strong civil rights plank, nor did the platform address any of the interests of the party's liberal wing. "The spirit of compromise and accommodation was wholly alien" to the Goldwater forces, journalist Richard Rovere wrote. "They came for a total ideological victory and the total destruction of their critics."

When it came time to pick a running mate, Goldwater felt no need to balance the ticket ideologically and chose his congressional partner Miller, largely, he said, because he knew Miller drove Johnson "nuts." Nor would Goldwater even offer words of conciliation to party members. At the Republican convention in San Francisco, when the word "extremist" was, in the wake of Kennedy's murder, an anathema, Goldwater defiantly declared, "I would remind you that extremism in the defense of liberty is no vice. And let me remind you that moderation in the pursuit of justice is no virtue." A reporter present blurted out, "My God, he's going to run as Barry Goldwater!"

A campaign aide later explained, "We were talking about the good extremists, not the idiots." It was a distinction lost on many voters. Goldwater did not help his own cause, uttering impolitic, even outrageous, things. He suggested that Social Security be made voluntary and that the federal government sell off the Tennessee Valley Authority, a position that greatly eroded his support in large parts of the South. He wanted to end crop subsidies and the income tax, and he spoke of using nuclear weapons with a casualness that was reckless, such as his suggestion that perhaps the United States ought to "lob one [nuclear missile] into the men's room at the Kremlin."

Such remarks led his opponents to suggest that Goldwater might be more than an extremist. Goldwater's slogan, "In your heart, you know he's right," was cunningly countered with, "In your guts, you know he's nuts." Publisher Ralph Ginzburg, who had served eight months on an obscenity conviction before turning from pornography to political commentary, enterprisingly sent surveys to twelve thousand psychiatrists, asking their opinion as to whether Goldwater was psychologically fit to be president. Remarkably, eighteen hundred psychiatrists returned the survey, concluding by a two-to-one margin, based on no clinical evidence or personal observation, that Goldwater was indeed crazy—and "uneasy about his masculinity" and anti-Semitic, too, because he denied his Jewish ancestry. The stunt made Goldwater angry enough that he later sued Ginzburg, winning one dollar in compensatory damages and seventy-five thousand dollars in punitive damages in a landmark case that proved public officials can be libeled if "actual malice" can be proven.

But the efforts to unravel Goldwater's psyche were not limited to partisans and pornographers. The historian Richard Hofstadter authored an article in 1964 for *Harper's Magazine* based on an earlier lecture in which Hofstadter suggested that Goldwater and other ultra-conservatives practiced a "paranoid style" of politics. Unlike Ginzburg's psychiatrists, Hofstadter said he was not making a clinical diagnosis but said he used the word "paranoid" because "no other word adequately evokes the qualities of heated exaggeration, suspiciousness, and conspiratorial fantasy that I have in mind."*

The lowest blow was a television commercial developed by the Johnson campaign, in which the image of a young girl pulling petals from a flower is obliterated by the mushroom cloud of a nuclear blast. The commercial ran only once and Goldwater was not mentioned by name, but he didn't have to be. The point was clear: Goldwater was crazy enough to start a nuclear war.

Given Johnson's commanding lead (he would win a record 61 percent of the popular vote to Goldwater's 39 percent), the commercial seemed like overkill. But Johnson remained wary, for there was one issue that—if it could not defeat him—could still dramatically reduce his vote totals and the mandate to govern that Johnson was grasping for: That issue was race.

Even when African Americans had used only the tactics of nonviolence to advance their cause, there had been a growing "white backlash." A national Harris poll from July 1964 found 58 percent of white Americans concerned that blacks might "take over" their jobs, while significant pluralities worried blacks would want to move into their neighborhoods or attend their children's schools. Now, just a few weeks after the Civil Rights Act became law, blacks began rioting in Harlem, and over the next several weeks rioting spread to other cities in New York and New Jersey, as well as Philadelphia. Johnson campaign aides glumly called the riots "Goldwater rallies," and a campaign analysis concluded, "There is considerable evidence to show that every time there is violence by Negroes, Goldwater gains supporters." Pollster Sam Lubell added, "The racial issue is the only one that can elect Goldwater."

Goldwater was tempted to use the riots to his advantage. He said the rioting proved his point that laws were ineffective in addressing a problem like prejudice. No state had tougher civil rights legislation than New York, and yet it was in that supposedly tolerant Northern city, not the South, where rioting was occurring—a fact that baffled Johnson and other civil rights advocates.

---

* Nearly forty years later, in the May 2003 issue of *Psychological Bulletin*, some scholars were still debating whether ultra-conservatism was a political belief or a psychological pathology.

But then Goldwater, despite having a rare tactical advantage at his command, again displayed his ambivalence about racial issues. He asked for a private meeting with Johnson to discuss whether they could mutually agree to take both race and the Vietnam War off the table for discussion. Johnson, suspicious of nearly everyone, was skeptical of Goldwater's motives: "He wants to encourage the backlash, that's where his future is; it's not in peace and harmony." Johnson, engaging in his own paranoid style of politics, even had the FBI investigate whether it could prove Goldwater supporters were helping to incite the riots for political gain.

Goldwater, however, was genuinely troubled by the bloodshed. He believed the nation's big cities were "just tinderboxes," and said in later years that he had thought, "I'll be darned if I will have my grandchildren accuse their grandfather of setting fire to it [sic]." Johnson, fully realizing his two greatest weaknesses in the campaign were racial unrest and growing American military involvement in Southeast Asia, readily agreed to Goldwater's astonishing suggestion.

Goldwater now suggested the nation give the civil rights legislation that he had opposed "a real chance to work." Goldwater even cancelled his campaign's plan to release a film called *Choice,* which linked black rioting to what he called the nation's general moral decay. Images of rioting blacks were interspersed with women in topless bathing suits, teenage gangs, and striptease shows. Goldwater thought the film appealed to racist sentiment, which had been the point.

Bound by his own suggestion not to talk about race explicitly, yet knowing it was the only issue that could help Republicans avoid a total debacle in November, Goldwater focused on the themes of law and order, personal safety, and dependency on the dole—legitimate issues, certainly, but issues in which race was a clear subtext never addressed directly. And while he cancelled his campaign film, Goldwater still talked about the riots as another manifestation of moral decay. "Why do we see riot and disorder in our cities?" Goldwater asked, answering his own question by claiming, "The moral fiber of the American people is beset by rot and decay." He did not interpret the riots as the result of a frustrated underclass, yearning for economic, political, and social equality.

Instead, he talked about the new prevalence of "the sick joke, the slick slogan, the off-color drama, and the pornographic book." And he decried the Supreme Court's ruling that banned mandatory prayer in the public schools, while saying of the Democrats: "You will search in vain for *any* reference to God or religion in the Democratic platform." Goldwater was pioneering the use of "social issues," a tactic that would evolve into the "culture wars" twenty years later, though by then, Goldwater would be on the other side of the war to the dismay of his fellow conservatives. Such issues would lead to GOP victories in later decades but not in 1964 when Johnson trounced Goldwater by the largest percentage in history.

Goldwater was only fifty-five years old in 1964 and still cut a dashing figure, but no one considered Goldwater a potential presidential contender in 1968. Conservatives had transferred their affections to another: movie star Ronald Reagan. One of the most important developments of the 1964 Goldwater campaign was making Reagan a national political figure. Reagan and Goldwater were longtime acquaintances through Reagan's second wife, Nancy Davis, whose parents lived in Phoenix. Goldwater recalled that when he first met Reagan, the actor-turned-politician was still an orthodox New Deal liberal, and he got into such heated arguments with Goldwater that he once called the Arizonan "a black fascist bastard." Under the Davis family's tutelage, Reagan moved politically to the right and, his movie career in decline, became primarily known as a television host and a favorite speaker at corporate events.

Late in the 1964 campaign, it was suggested that Reagan be featured in a thirty-minute Goldwater campaign commercial, giving a speech on conservative values that had been garnering Reagan high praise on the speaking circuit. Later known simply as "The Speech," Reagan's address generated more than six hundred thousand dollars in contributions to a campaign badly in need of cash. Goldwater never thanked Reagan for his efforts. Those who knew him said Goldwater was likely jealous to see the mantle of conservative leadership passed on to someone else. By January 1965, many of the same men who had drafted Goldwater to run for president now approached Reagan and started plotting his new political career, which began with Reagan's election as governor of California in 1966.

Elected president in 1980, Reagan completed what Goldwater had started by greatly broadening the appeal of conservatism, most particularly in the South where, by the end of his term in office, 45 percent of white Southerners identified themselves as Republican and just 34 percent still called themselves Democrats. Reagan's appeal transcended Goldwater's. Where Goldwater's manner was strident and frightening to nonbelievers, Reagan was sunny, optimistic, and soothing. Or as one conservative admirer put it, Reagan was "Goldwater mutton, dressed up as lamb." Goldwater neither appreciated the comparison or Reagan's political gifts. Asked to participate in a commemorative film near the end of Reagan's presidency, Goldwater repeatedly muttered, "He's just an actor."

Choosing Republican orthodoxy over conservative ideology, Goldwater refused to support Reagan's conservative insurgent campaigns for president either in 1968 against Nixon or in 1976 against Gerald Ford. In the latter campaign, he added the gibe that it was a "toss-up" whether Reagan was more conservative than Ford. Conservatives were aghast. William Rusher spoke for many on the right when he said, "Goldwater's grip on conservative principles just isn't (and perhaps never was) the absolutely dependable thing we believed it to be." Goldwater further ensured his invitations to the Reagan White House would be few and far between when he criticized the Reagans for their "ostentatious" inaugural festivities. He also criticized Reagan for increasing, not reducing, the federal debt and for a radical increase in defense spending that Goldwater believed included a lot of waste.

Goldwater, who had returned to the Senate in 1968, no longer felt fully at home in the new Republican Party, one he had done as much as anyone to create. Even though he had pioneered the use of social issues in his own campaign, Goldwater, given his social caste and acquaintances, was not at heart a culturally conservative man. Nor was he a particularly religious man, and he was uncomfortable with the assertive role conservative Christians were playing in the GOP. He referred to them as "a bunch of kooks." Goldwater's wife, Peggy, had helped form the Arizona chapter of Planned Parenthood, and the Goldwaters had helped their daughter procure an illegal abortion in 1955. After the Supreme Court's *Roe v. Wade* decision, Goldwater expressed his belief that abortion should be legal, but a few years later, facing a tough Senate re-election campaign in 1980 (his last), Goldwater signed an anti-abortion rights pledge to win the support of Arizona's growing pro-life movement. After he narrowly won his fifth Senate term, he essentially repudiated his pledge, lamenting, "The radical right has nearly ruined our party."

Goldwater had already become the liberals' favorite conservative in 1974, during the Watergate scandal, when he was chosen to head the Republican delegation that told Nixon he could not survive an impeachment trial in the Senate. Now he was winning their further admiration while diminishing his standing among conservatives. Goldwater's increasingly libertarian bent was at odds with the beliefs of largely Southern evangelical Christians and other conservative traditionalists who were now the base of the Republican Party. That portion of the Southern populist tradition that looked to the government to enforce certain moral standards now populated the GOP.

Goldwater had been the catalyst of this new populist conservatism, but he did not like all aspects of it. "The conservative movement is founded on the simple tenet that people have the right to live life as they please," he said, "as long as they don't hurt anyone in the process." He said he was "damn tired" of the role evangelical ministers were playing in the new Republican Party. When the Reverend Jerry Falwell was misquoted as criticizing Reagan's choice of former Arizona legislator Sandra Day O'Connor, a Goldwater protégé, to be the first woman on the Supreme Court because of her views on abortion, Goldwater said, "Every good Christian ought to kick Falwell right in the ass." He further distanced himself from the religious right and the bulk of his party when he endorsed allowing homosexuals to openly serve in the military. "You don't need to be 'straight' to fight and die for your country; you just need to shoot straight," said Goldwater, whose views were influenced by the fact that he had a gay grandson and a lesbian grandniece. Unlike his views on civil rights thirty years before, Goldwater was now linking the individual experience of prejudice with the need to provide a broader group with government protections.

In the years since his defeat and more so since his death in 1998, two years after he suffered a massive stroke, Goldwater has occupied a strange place in American politics, admired by liberals as well as conservatives, but fully embraced by neither. A 2007 reissue of *The Conscience of a Conservative*, which features a foreword by conservative commentator George Will and an afterword by liberal environmental activist Robert F. Kennedy Jr., exemplifies this. Will focuses his praise on Goldwater as a catalyst of conservative ideas, particularly the argument that conservatism, not liberalism, preaches ideals higher than simple material gain. Kennedy specifically absolves Goldwater of any role in the formation of the new, Southern-oriented Republican Party, instead citing the "thuggery" of a host of power-mad Republican consultants who are guilty of "the hijacking of Goldwater's rational conservatism" and interjecting divisive social issues into the American political debate, neglecting Goldwater's role in the very same.

Goldwater remains a great example of how we misread the impact of losing presidential campaigns. In the wake of his historic loss, some said that Goldwater had both destroyed the Republican Party and "broken the back" of the conservative movement. Of course, the opposite turned out to be true. The Goldwater campaign, Kevin Phillips wrote, "was a Rubicon for the Republican Party," and in crossing that line, Goldwater fundamentally altered both who and what the Republican and the Democratic Parties stood for.

CHAPTER NINE

GEORGE McGOVERN
1972

Thoughtful Americans understand that the highest patriotism is not to blindly accept official policy but to love one's country deeply enough to call her to a higher standard.

Conservative Republicans trace the genesis of the Ronald Reagan presidency back to Barry Goldwater's landslide loss to Lyndon Johnson in 1964. Likewise, liberal Democrats should view George McGovern's landslide loss to Richard Nixon in 1972 as the precursor to the presidency of Barack Obama—and, for that matter, the 2008 presidential candidacy of Hillary Clinton, too.

That anything positive could come out of McGovern's 1972 campaign would have struck those who lived through the debacle as miraculous. Surveying the enormity of his defeat, in which he carried only Massachusetts and the District of Columbia, McGovern himself quipped, "I opened the doors of the Democratic Party—and twenty million people walked out." McGovern exaggerated—but not by much. An estimated third of all registered Democrats—ten million—abandoned McGovern to vote for Nixon.

But those same doors through which many longtime Democrats walked out also remained open to let other newer Democrats march in. The McGovern campaign may have marked the end of the Democrats' old New Deal coalition, as urban ethnics and organized labor were among those who exited the party in droves, but the reforms McGovern instituted within the Democratic Party created a new Democratic base. Just as Goldwater's "Southern strategy" pointed the way for Republican conservative majorities in the 1980s and 1990s, McGovern's "New Politics" coalition of women, minorities, young voters, and highly educated activists may provide a blueprint for Democrats to build a new liberal majority in the twenty-first century.

McGovern's critics, then and now, have derided this new coalition as "identity politics" and a motley collection of "special interests," but the potential of this coalition, first envisioned by McGovern, was finally realized with Obama's election in 2008. That year, Obama joined LBJ as the only Democrats since Franklin Roosevelt to win more than 50.1 percent of the popular vote. Where McGovern won only 37.5 percent of the vote in 1972, Obama won 53 percent in 2008 by appealing to roughly the same demographics. Those demographics had grown between 1972 and 2008, and trends in the U.S. population suggest that Obama's vote total may not be an anomaly, but a benchmark for future liberal candidacies willing to join Obama in following the trail blazed by McGovern.

Of course, when McGovern was labeled "the Goldwater of the left," it was not meant as a compliment to either man. Just as pundits in 1964 incorrectly forecast that Goldwater had left conservatism in shambles, even some liberals believed the McGovern campaign had "discredited liberalism." The magnitude of McGovern's loss was such that the Democratic Party spent the better part of four decades actively distancing itself from the South Dakota senator who was unfairly labeled "the candidate of the three As—acid, amnesty, and abortion."*

Rather than embrace McGovern's "New Politics," most subsequent Democratic presidential candidates have looked back with nostalgia to Franklin Roosevelt's New Deal coalition, but with little success in reassembling it. Between McGovern in 1972 and Obama in 2008, the high-water mark for a Democratic presidential candidate was Jimmy Carter, who received 50.08 percent of the popular vote in 1976. Between Carter and Obama, no Democratic candidate for president received

---

* McGovern did favor amnesty for Vietnam-era draft dodgers, but he did not favor nationally legalized abortion or legalization of even marijuana, let alone LSD.

even 50 percent of the vote—not even Bill Clinton in his perceived rout of Bob Dole in 1996. Walter Mondale tried to rebuild the New Deal coalition in 1984, and he won back the support of organized labor but lost the youth vote and ended up winning the same number of states as McGovern: one. And yet, as poor a showing as Mondale made, it is still the McGovern campaign that is cited as the greatest Democratic disaster of all, and to be called "another McGovern" is considered an enormous millstone around the neck of any candidate.

There were repeated attempts by conservative commentators to tie Obama to McGovern during the 2008 campaign. One labeled Obama "the most liberal Democrat running for the presidency since McGovern." Another said, "Obama comes to us from a background farther to the Left than any presidential nominee since George McGovern, or perhaps ever." They also noted that Obama's early opposition to the Iraq War mirrored McGovern's opposition to American involvement in the Vietnam War and McGovern's campaign theme, "Come Home, America."

The intent was not only to label Obama a radical but to dispirit Democrats still haunted by the specter of the McGovern campaign's supposedly woeful legacy. Some Democrats feared the McGovern label might indeed be affixed to Obama with dire results. Early in 2008, a *New Republic* writer fretted that in Obama's supporters "you begin to see the outlines of the old George McGovern coalition that haunted the Democrats during the '70s and '80s, led by college students and minorities."

The writer was correct. There were "striking similarities" between Obama's coalition and McGovern's (as McGovern himself noted), and Obama won precisely by appealing to the new Democratic coalition that McGovern had first put together in 1972 but that other Democratic candidates, "haunted" by the fiasco of 1972, had declined to embrace as enthusiastically.*

---

* The party was so eager to move on after 1972 that perhaps the single most valuable legacy of the McGovern campaign—a list of six hundred thousand donors—was lost. New Democratic National Committee Chair Robert Strauss said he never received the list. McGovernites believe Strauss threw out the list on purpose to diminish the influence of the McGovern supporters in the party going forward. Lost was the basis for a new model of raising money, and instead the Democrats rejoined the Republicans in soliciting large, wealthy donors who have left the party beholden to many of the interests it purports to oppose.

What McGovern understood in 1972 was that key pieces of the old New Deal coalition were shrinking in size and influence and their remnants were increasingly attracted to the conservatism and cultural traditionalism of the Republican Party. To replace these lost Democrats, McGovern reached out to voters who had not been actively courted in previous elections but whose level of political participation could be expected to grow: women (particularly working women), young voters, African Americans, Hispanics, other minorities, and gays. The difference between 1972 and 2008 is that these elements of the new Democratic coalition grew to a size in which they could form a real majority, and in Obama the Democrats found a candidate who could rally and inspire these varied elements. Obama did so, in part, by using McGovern's "grassroots" campaign style—though by 2008 the grassroots would be supplemented by the "netroots."

McGovern can take some credit that Obama, as an African American, was taken seriously as a candidate at all. Reforms pressed by McGovern, beginning in 1969, when he chaired a Democratic Party commission, and continuing through his 1972 campaign, greatly advanced the role minorities have since played in the Democratic Party and significantly increased the number of elected black officeholders. Without those reforms, minority participation in Democratic politics might have been years behind what it was in 2008, and the time for a major African-American candidate to run for president might have been years or even decades away.

Women received the same boost. For the 2008 Democratic nomination, Obama had, after all, defeated former McGovern campaign worker and New York senator Hillary Rodham Clinton, wife of the former president. That the first African-American and the first woman candidates with realistic chances to become president were both Democrats is not a coincidence but was due in large part to the work of McGovern in opening up the party to nontraditional voices. Indeed, two pundits who had been predicting "an emerging Democratic majority" even before Obama was elected have described the party's early twenty-first century makeup as "George McGovern's revenge."

Racial and ethnic minorities were a key component of the McGovern coalition, and they proved essential to Obama's election. As noted in the previous chapter on Goldwater, African-American voters abandoned the Republicans when the GOP abandoned federal guarantee of their civil rights as a core party philosophy. McGovern won more than 85 percent of the African-American vote; Obama, as the first African-American major party nominee, won nearly 95 percent.

While "Brother McGovern," as the Reverend Jesse Jackson dubbed him, had simply continued a trend of overwhelming black support for Democratic presidential candidates, he made new inroads with America's Hispanic population. McGovern tried to address the specific concerns of Hispanic voters and sought and received the endorsement of the legendary Mexican-American farm labor leader César Chávez. In states with significant Hispanic populations, McGovern insisted his convention delegations include a proportionate number of Hispanic delegates.

McGovern and Obama each won roughly two-thirds of the Hispanic vote in their respective races. The difference: In 1972 there were fewer than ten million Hispanic Americans while in 2008 there were nearly fifty million, and by 2050 it is projected there will be more than one hundred million people of Hispanic heritage in the United States.

Another group critical to both McGovern and Obama were women voters. Women had traditionally strongly favored Republican presidential candidates from the passage of the Nineteenth Amendment in 1920 through the 1960 election. Dwight Eisenhower had won 63 percent of the women's vote in 1956 and Nixon 53 percent in 1960. But that was still when the Republican Party was seen as the party of civil rights—an issue important not just to African Americans. Thomas Dewey, for example, was the first major national politician to endorse the Equal Rights Amendment for women.

As the Republican Party ended its identification with civil rights, many women joined African Americans in searching for a new political home. McGovern did his best to ensure they found one in the Democratic Party. At the 1968 Democratic National Convention, just 13 percent of the delegates were women and the party platform made no mention of issues specifically important to women. In 1972, thanks largely to party reforms pushed by McGovern, 39 percent of the delegates were women and the party platform included a fifteen-point "Rights of Women" plank that included such thereafter mainstream proposals as equal pay for equal work, paid maternity leave, appointment of women to key government posts, ending sex discrimination in employment, and including gender discrimination in the enforcement of civil rights.

Not included in the platform was anything about legalized abortion. Despite the taunts of his rivals and critics, McGovern did not favor national legalization of abortion. Running for president in the year before the U.S. Supreme Court's *Roe v. Wade* decision, McGovern believed the issue of abortion legalization should be left to the individual states to decide.

While it would be incorrect to label McGovern a "feminist," he had "a wonderful instinct for fairness," said his women's outreach coordinator, Amanda Smith. He also provided women with real positions of authority. While his senior campaign staff was uniformly male, McGovern did select Jean Westwood to become chair of the Democratic National Committee, the first woman to head either major party.

McGovern did not win a majority of the women's vote in 1972 (if he had, he wouldn't have lost in a landslide), but he did receive a large share of the votes of single women, working women, and college-educated women. More importantly, after McGovern's campaign, "women had to be at the table," said Doris Meissner, the first executive director of the National Women's Political Caucus.

In successive campaigns, Democrats continued to whittle away at the previous Republican advantage with women voters, so that by the late 1980s Democrats benefited from a significant "gender gap." Exit polls in 2008 showed Obama winning 56 percent of the women's vote, including an extraordinary 70 percent of the vote of unmarried women, one of the fastest-growing demographics in the United States. Particularly beneficial to Democrats, women make up a larger percentage of the voting population than men and turn out to vote in higher percentages. In 2008, an astonishing ten million more women than men voted in the presidential election.

A third component of the McGovern coalition was a hodgepodge of "issue-oriented voters" whose passion was not around partisanship but individual issues, such as the environment. These movement voters, as they were called, tended to be highly educated, which further distanced the Democrats from their working-class roots. But McGovern was aware that the number of white collar workers was increasing in the United States while the number of blue collar workers was in decline. In 1900, barely 5 percent of high school graduates went on to attend college. By 1970, more than 50 percent of high school graduates went on to attend college, and that number had increased to 70 percent by 2009.

Well-educated professionals had previously voted overwhelmingly for Republicans, primarily on the issue of tax and social welfare policies. But the post-industrial economy, with its focus on the production of services and ideas rather than on manufactured goods, has placed a higher value on diversity and equality than the old, hierarchical, male-dominated industrial economy. As social issues became more central to presidential campaigns, large numbers of educated professionals moved to the left in their politics. McGovern won a significantly higher percentage of the vote of college graduates (42 percent) than previous Democratic candidates, while Obama won 47 percent of the votes of college graduates.

One group of movement voters previously ignored by both parties, and never targeted for inclusion in politics until McGovern's campaign, were gays and lesbians. The McGovern campaign had issued a statement, courageous for the time and likely still controversial in some quarters, that said, "Sexual orientation should cease to be a criterion for employment by all public and governmental agencies, in work under federal contracts, for service in the United States armed forces, and for licensing in government-related occupations and professions."

It is impossible to know what percentage of gay and lesbian voters supported McGovern in 1972—no one in those days would have polled such a question or even known whom to poll, even though we now know that roughly 3 percent of voters are gay or lesbian. But it was clear to many gay activists that McGovern had at least given them a voice at a time when they were expected to stay silent and in the closet. While the number of gays who voted for McGovern is unknown, polling data suggests that Obama won about 80 percent of the gay vote in 2008.

One group that proved to be a disappointment to McGovern, however, was the youth vote. The Twenty-Sixth Amendment, which lowered the legal voting age to eighteen, was approved in 1971. The McGovern campaign believed that millions of young voters, motivated by opposition to the Vietnam War, would flood the polls and give him a decided advantage. It was an illusion.

Young voters were no more a monolithic bloc than any other age group. Among young voters not attending college, McGovern was no more popular than Nixon or even Alabama governor George Wallace. While anti-war protesters, hippies, Yippies, and dissidents of all stripes received most of the media coverage, there was an unnoticed concurrent increase in conservative activism among other young people, as exemplified by the founding of such groups as the Young Americans for Freedom. McGovern did win the eighteen- to twenty-one-year-old age group, but with only 55 percent of their support—and that age group had the lowest voter turnout of any demographic. In what must have been a shock to McGovern and his aides, Nixon won the twenty-one- to twenty-four-year-old age group. Obama, by contrast, won 66 percent of the votes of those under age thirty. While young voters still have the lowest turnout of any age group, it is estimated that more than 50 percent of all Americans under thirty voted in 2008, accounting for nearly a third of Obama's total vote, and voters under thirty in 2008 were almost twice as likely to identify themselves as Democrats than Republicans.

While younger voters, women, activists, and minorities provided a large part of the McGovern campaign's energy and volunteer base, their involvement also caused headaches. The McGovernites learned that issue-oriented voters often cared more about their causes than the candidates. Some McGovern aides thought the movement people "were crazy," pushing McGovern to take positions that would clearly cost him support from more traditional voters in the general election.

The cost of assembling this new coalition was McGovern's failure to receive the endorsement of that critical Democratic constituency, organized labor, most particularly the AFL-CIO, whose leadership became one of McGovern's chief nemeses. Organized labor had been in decline prior to 1972. In 1955, 33 percent of the nonagricultural labor force belonged to unions, but by 1972 that number had slipped to 27 percent. Urban Democrats, the ethnic voters who typified the New Deal coalition, were also a smaller factor. Urban Democrats had represented 21 percent of the vote in 1952, but just 14 percent in 1968.

Labor was, therefore, already feeling defensive and protective of its status within the party even before McGovern further limited labor's influence by squelching the type of backroom deal-making in which labor excelled. Then there was the growing cultural divide. Labor represented men who did not want to see women enter the workforce and compete for jobs, who did not approve of a perceived assault on traditional moral values, and who were sending a seemingly disproportionate share of their own sons to fight in a war that McGovern was proclaiming to be morally wrong.

While there were dissenters who stayed loyal to the Democratic ticket, labor attacked McGovern privately and publicly. The AFL-CIO anonymously put out anti-McGovern literature, implying he was a Communist sympathizer and questioning his alleged "Blind Trust in Moscow." In a speech before the United Steelworkers, AFL-CIO president George Meany expressed outrage that the 1972 Democratic National Convention included "the gay lib people—you know, the people who want to legalize marriage between boys and boys and legalize marriages between girls and girls."

Labor's refusal to endorse McGovern "dramatically influenced the perception of McGovern" as a radical far outside the American mainstream, said McGovern campaign organizer Carl Wagner. McGovern's Democratic competitors, particularly Hubert Humphrey, were first to hammer home that perception, and Republicans gleefully picked up the theme in the general election.

The conservative magazine *First Monday* hyperbolically charged that McGovern was "a dedicated radical extremist who as president would unilaterally disarm the United States of America and open the White House to riotous street mobs." The *National Review* added that though McGovern's "quiet demeanor, flat dull voice and square clothes is not like the standard caricature of the demagogue ... when we look more closely we see that he is in the classic American demagogic tradition."

It was a wildly distorted portrait of a man who was the son of a fundamentalist minister, who had himself been a war hero, and who enjoyed political success representing a predominantly Republican and conservative state in the Midwest. As McGovern put it, "Ordinarily, we don't send wild-eyed radicals to the United States Senate from South Dakota."

If not a radical, McGovern was certainly a moralist. Born July 19, 1922, and growing up in Mitchell, South Dakota, McGovern was the son of a strict Wesleyan Methodist minister. "Movies were off-limits to good Wesleyan Methodists, as were dancing, card-playing, smoking or drinking," McGovern recalled. But McGovern rebelled, sneaking off to movies at a young age, yet retaining his father's Manichean view of the world, a trait that seldom endeared him to those on the other side of an argument.

Interested, even as a young man, in the problems of hunger and world peace, McGovern read widely on the Social Gospel and briefly attended seminary before deciding a ministerial career was not for him. He instead turned to the study of history. McGovern did not subscribe to the mid-twentieth-century consensus view of American history. He saw the arc of American history as a series of conflicts and wrote his doctoral dissertation on the bloody Colorado coal strike of 1913–1914.

He earned a PhD at Northwestern University where his faculty advisor was Arthur Link, one of the nation's foremost scholars on Woodrow Wilson. Wilson was also a historian (and a moralist), and he and McGovern remain the only two presidential nominees to have earned a PhD. Foreshadowing his approach to the Vietnam War, McGovern deeply admired Wilson's attempts to apply moral principles to foreign policy.

World War II interrupted McGovern's undergraduate studies at Dakota Wesleyan University. Even though he had a fear of flying, McGovern had taken flying lessons while a student, and when war broke out, he volunteered to be a bomber pilot. Nixon, who never saw combat himself during the war, later directed his presidential campaign to try to portray McGovern as a coward, making the claim that McGovern had refused to fly his final mission. This was a lie. McGovern flew thirty-five missions in his B-24 in the Italian campaign, the number required before a pilot earned a ticket home, and he earned the Distinguished Flying Cross. McGovern's heroism and that of his colleagues is chronicled in the Stephen Ambrose book *The Wild Blue*.

McGovern, despite his opposition to the Vietnam War, was no pacifist. He never regretted his role in the fight against fascism, and later in life he would support President Clinton's decision to use force to stop genocide in Bosnia and Kosovo. Yet, he seldom used his war record to full political effect, making no mention of it in his nomination acceptance speech. It was 1972, and his young campaign advisors convinced him it was incongruous, even hypocritical, for the anti-war candidate to boast of his military record, so many Americans remained unaware that the anti-war candidate was a war hero.

McGovern's willingness to fight for causes he believed in is what drew him into politics. Inspired by Adlai Stevenson's 1952 presidential campaign and determined to battle the followers of Wisconsin senator Joseph McCarthy, McGovern abandoned his teaching career and became the executive secretary of the South Dakota Democratic Party, a job with extraordinary challenges. In 1953, Democrats held only two of South Dakota's 110 legislative seats. After two years of McGovern's fundraising, speechwriting, candidate recruiting, organizing, and strategizing, Democrats in 1954 picked up an additional twenty-two state legislative seats. Two years later, in 1956, McGovern used the party organization he had built to defeat a three-term incumbent congressman by a comfortable margin, and he won re-election in 1958 by an even wider margin. South Dakota voters forgave McGovern his unconventional foreign policy views as long as he fought in Congress for farm subsidies and policies that promoted high crop prices.

In 1960, McGovern ran for the U.S. Senate but lost to longtime Republican senator Karl Mundt by a single percentage point in a year when Nixon walloped John F. Kennedy in South Dakota's presidential voting. As consolation, Kennedy made McGovern his special assistant in charge of an upgraded Food for Peace program. McGovern gained national attention by expanding the program's Third World development program six-fold and developing a humanitarian school lunch program that fed thirty-five million children around the world.

In 1962, McGovern ran for the Senate again, this time winning by just 597 votes out of a quarter million ballots cast. He would always be wary of his precarious position in heavily Republican South Dakota and, belying his image as a radical, carefully avoided taking positions that ran counter to his constituents' interests. Always looking out for South Dakota's agricultural interests, he persuaded the Senate to establish a Select Committee on Nutrition and Human Needs. Co-chaired by Kansas senator and future Republican presidential candidate Bob Dole, the committee greatly expanded the school lunch program, making it free to low-income students, added a federally funded school breakfast program, and expanded and improved the food stamp program, all humanitarian programs that also benefited Midwestern farmers.

Taking care of his farming constituents allowed McGovern to stake out risky foreign policy positions without too much fear of ballot box retribution. McGovern, along with Oregon senator Wayne Morse, became an early critic of President Kennedy's policies in Southeast Asia, and he heightened that criticism as President Lyndon Johnson escalated American military involvement in Vietnam. In March 1965, McGovern predicted in an interview on CBS News, "I think there will be a staggering loss of human life out of all proportion to the stakes involved, and I see no guarantee that once we go through that kind of a murderous and destructive kind of military effort that the situation out there will be any better. In fact, I think it will be a lot worse." Later that year, McGovern made his first trip to Vietnam, and said that after visiting military and civilian hospitals filled with amputees and overworked staffs, he "left . . . determined to redouble my efforts against the war . . . to do whatever might persuade Congress and the American people to stop the horror."

What set McGovern apart from other politicians opposed to the war was his visceral anger; his belief that war was corrupting the soul of America; and his equal anguish at American casualties and the suffering of Vietnamese civilians, "like us, children of God." The certainty that he was right, and the moralistic streak he inherited from his father, made him a modern-day Jeremiah whose uncompromising rhetoric unsettled many Americans, including his fellow senators. Failing to persuade the Senate to cut off funding for the war, McGovern gave a remarkable speech before a packed Senate chamber on September 1, 1970, that offended a good many of his colleagues and their constituents:

> *Every senator in this chamber is partly responsible for sending 50,000 young Americans to an early grave. This chamber reeks of blood. Every senator here is partly responsible for that human wreckage at Walter Reed and Bethesda Naval (hospitals) and all across our land—young men without legs, or arms, or genitals, or faces, or hopes. There are not very many of these blasted and broken boys who think this war is a glorious adventure. Do not talk to them about bugging out, or national honor, or courage. It does not take courage for a congressman, or a senator, or a president to wrap himself in the flag and say we are staying in Vietnam, because it is not our blood that is being shed. But we are responsible for those young men and their lives and their hopes. And if we do not end this damnable war, those young men will some day curse us for our pitiful willingness to let the Executive carry the burden that the Constitution places on us.*

McGovern's deep hatred of the war led anti-war activists to first approach him about running for president in 1968. He initially deferred to the candidacy of another war opponent, Minnesota senator Eugene McCarthy. But after Robert Kennedy had entered the race and was then assassinated, McGovern was prevailed upon to become a candidate in order to be a rallying point for Kennedy delegates, who were reluctant to switch their support to McCarthy.

McGovern's token candidacy was quickly forgotten in the turmoil of the 1968 Democratic National Convention in Chicago. Riots by anti-war protesters and what was later described in an official report as a riot by the police against the anti-war protesters split the party in two and so damaged its prospects that a Nixon win in the fall seemed inevitable.

Despite the fact that he had not entered a single primary, the Democratic presidential nomination went to Vice President Hubert Humphrey, which outraged both reformers who wanted a more open nomination process and also those opposed to the war, for at this point Humphrey was still supporting Johnson's war policies. Only in late September did Humphrey break with LBJ in calling for an end to the bombing of North Vietnam and the resurrection of peace talks in Paris. His new position allowed Humphrey to close the gap, but in the end he lost to Nixon by less than six-tenths of a percentage point in a three-way race that included George Wallace. Despite the narrowness of Humphrey's defeat, the Democrats seemed in complete disarray.

To help heal the wounds and bridge divisions within the party, Humphrey had agreed to let the Chicago convention's delegates vote on and approve a proposal to create a Commission on Party Structure and Delegate Selection that would soon be known as the "McGovern Commission." Humphrey had chosen McGovern to head the task force because he had credibility with the insurgents but was also a loyal Democrat who, unlike other insurgent leaders like McCarthy, had enthusiastically campaigned for Humphrey during the general election. McGovern was also acceptable to all party factions because no one thought he would be a serious presidential contender in 1972.

Party regulars had no concept of how thoroughly the commission would change the Democratic Party. Organized labor declined to participate at all, thinking it a waste of time. Much of labor felt contempt for the insurgents, who were seeking to reduce labor's traditional influence within the party, and they were convinced the college kids and highly educated professionals behind the mass movements felt contempt for them as well.

With the party regulars sitting on the sidelines, McGovern and the insurgents dominated the commission, determined to open up the delegate selection process. In the commission's final report, members listed expanding the level of popular participation as "more than a first principle. We believe that popular control of the Democratic Party is necessary for its survival." In a period of intense social turmoil, over the war, over race, over gender, over morality, the commission warned that if the

Democratic Party did not provide an avenue for people committed to change to find expression within the political system, the danger was not that they would become Republicans but that "they will turn to third and fourth party politics or the anti-politics of the street."

State parties were encouraged to hold primaries rather than caucuses, but if the caucus was the method of selecting national convention delegates, then the meetings had to be adequately advertised so that any interested party member could attend. No longer could party chairs just decide who the delegates to the national convention would be, and no longer could a fee be charged as a requirement for a party member to be a convention delegate. Proxy voting was disallowed, and the unit rule, which bound delegates to back the candidate supported by the majority of their delegation, was ended—though an exception was made for states that selected delegates through a primary. This would prove to be an especially important exception in the state of California.

The most controversial recommendation of the commission was to establish numerical targets for the inclusion of women and minorities in convention delegations. At the 1968 Democratic National Convention, in addition to only 13 percent of the delegates being women, only 6 percent had been African Americans, and just 2 percent were under the age of thirty. Party regulars on the commission argued that party rules should simply ensure that no representative of any group could be specifically excluded from participating, but McGovern and the insurgents did not want a passive plan of no exclusion, they wanted an aggressive program of inclusion.

Under McGovern's chairmanship, the commission recommended that each future convention delegation include women, minorities, and young voters "in reasonable relationship to their presence in the state as a whole." After McGovern had left the commission to run for president, and a new chair took over, feminists pushed through additional language that committed the party to specific numerical targets for each previously underrepresented group—essentially quotas that have been ridiculed by critics ever since, but which over time increased the allegiance of women and minorities to the Democratic Party.

The immediate impact of the commission's work was clear at the 1972 convention. Eighty percent of the delegates were attending their first convention, and women now made up nearly 40 percent of all delegates. But the greatest initial impact of the commission's work was that it allowed McGovern to win the nomination, a feat that, given the antagonism of the regulars to his candidacy, would likely have eluded him had the old rules remained in effect.

Early polling showed McGovern receiving less than 3 percent of the Democratic vote, and the famous odds-maker Jimmy "The Greek" Snyder put McGovern's chances of winning the party's nomination at 200-1.* But under the new rules, having high profile endorsements, the support of powerful special interest groups, or even a lot of money mattered far less than being able to organize supporters and get them to turn out for caucuses and primary elections. Because attendance for caucuses and primary elections was generally low, a cadre of dedicated supporters could easily determine the outcome. The organizing phrase was "grassroots"—which, not coincidentally, became the title of McGovern's autobiography. The other Democratic candidates for president in 1972 did not seem to realize the rules had changed. McGovern, co-author of the new rules, did, and he surrounded himself with aides who knew everything there was to know about the new delegate selection process.

McGovern's chances were also boosted because the man who might have dominated the nomination process in 1972, Massachusetts senator Edward Kennedy, had disqualified himself to run because of his bizarre behavior following a 1969 traffic accident that had killed a young woman on Chappaquiddick Island. The remaining favorite for the nomination was Maine senator Edmund Muskie, who had been Humphrey's running mate in 1968. Some have attributed Muskie's later fall from frontrunner status to a series of sophomoric "dirty tricks" played on the Muskie campaign by Nixon operatives, but in truth Muskie proved, as McGovern had predicted he would be, "a bland and unexciting campaigner" who was out-hustled by McGovern and his grassroots army.

---

* Snyder made Ed Muskie the prohibitive favorite at 2-5 with Humphrey second at 4-1.

McGovern made a stronger than expected showing in the opening Iowa caucuses, and it was soon clear that Muskie was simply not attuned to the electorate's new mood, which demanded more openness from candidates. When McGovern made all his public and personal finances public, Muskie declined to follow suit; when McGovern challenged Muskie to debate, Muskie refused. Muskie also misplayed the expectations game. A campaign staffer had guaranteed that Muskie would get 50 percent of the vote in the New Hampshire primary, but he received 46 percent, so even though he won, the media spun it as a loss.

With Muskie no longer seeming the inevitable nominee, Humphrey got into the race, joining a host of other candidates that also included Wallace, who was still running a racially divisive campaign but who won the Florida primary and finished a strong second in Wisconsin. After McGovern defeated Muskie in the Massachusetts primary, and after Wallace was shot and paralyzed on the eve of the Maryland primary, the race for the nomination came down to McGovern and Humphrey.

McGovern, who considered Humphrey a political mentor and a friend, expected a civil, even friendly, contest. But Humphrey, now sixty-one years of age and seeing yet another opportunity to become president slip away, went on the attack. He pummeled his fellow Democrat as a dangerous leftist radical whose supporters included even more dangerous radicals.

After McGovern narrowly defeated Humphrey in the California primary and won all the state's delegates (because the unit rule had been left in place for primary states), Humphrey challenged the "winner-take-all" results. McGovern was astonished that he was now mired in an intraparty squabble when it was clear he had won enough delegates overall, even without California, to be the nominee. He needed time before the convention to pull the party together and prepare for the general election, but all his campaign's energy was now spent on beating back the Humphrey challenge.

While Humphrey and the other regulars within the party resented that the new politics meant their own influence was reduced, many also sincerely believed that McGovern was not only unelectable, but he would also be a disaster for down-ticket races. This fear turned out not to be true; while Nixon won in a landslide, Democrats actually gained two Senate seats in 1972.

Nor did McGovern believe himself unelectable. He and his advisors, who included his thirty-five-year-old campaign manager, future Colorado senator and presidential aspirant Gary Hart, had concluded that McGovern had an excellent chance to defeat Nixon based on six assumptions that proved to be mostly false. As author Bruce Miroff outlined them, they were:

One, there was a widespread feeling of political alienation among the electorate;

Two, Nixon was an unpopular president;

Three, George Wallace would eventually become a third-party candidate, as he had in 1968, and siphon votes away from Nixon in the South and Midwest;

Four, the Twenty-Sixth Amendment lowering the voting age to eighteen would spur a huge turnout among youth, most of whom were anti-war;

Five, the Democrats were the natural majority party; and

Six, Democrats were united in their animosity toward Nixon—no matter whom the nominee might be.

McGovern and his advisors could not have foreseen, of course, the assassination attempt that ended Wallace's presidential bid. But the other assumptions suggested that McGovern's team was out of touch with the prevailing sentiments in America.

In addition to misreading the youth vote, McGovern also misread the public attitude toward Nixon. Because McGovern had despised Nixon since the latter's Red-baiting days began in the late 1940s, he assumed most Americans shared that feeling. The hard part of the election, McGovern thought, would be winning the Democratic nomination. After that, "it should be comparatively easy to defeat Richard Nixon by appealing to the decency and common sense of the American people." One of the cruel twists of McGovern's campaign was that the election ended up, as *Time* magazine noted, "turning not on Nixon's character and credibility, but on McGovern's."

This was thanks to the way McGovern mishandled the Thomas Eagleton affair.

Prior to the Democratic National Convention, McGovern and his campaign had been consumed with Humphrey's challenge of the California primary results. They were left little opportunity to consider whom McGovern's running mate should be. Despite Chappaquiddick, McGovern still wanted Ted Kennedy as his running mate and was certain he could persuade Kennedy to accept the nomination. He couldn't. Kennedy declined, and so did Walter Mondale.

Because McGovern failed to finally put the California challenge to rest until the national convention was well under way, he found he had only a single day to decide whom his running mate would be before presenting the name to the convention. That day, July 13, would be among the worst in the history of presidential campaigns.

Weary campaign staffers gathered early that morning and developed a list of three dozen potential running mates, a sign of how little forethought had gone into the decision to date. The ridiculously lengthy roster was finally winnowed down, and McGovern first focused upon Boston mayor Kevin White. An urban Catholic, White might have appealed to the old guard of the party and been a force for party unification. Ted Kennedy, however, did not want the nomination to go to a rival Massachusetts politician.

McGovern then offered the nomination to an old friend, Wisconsin senator Gaylord Nelson, founder of Earth Day, but, like Kennedy and Mondale, he, too, declined. It was then, with only an hour left before the deadline to give the convention a name, that the campaign concentrated on Thomas Eagleton, a senator from Missouri and another urban Catholic with appeal to labor who had also been a Muskie supporter. Eagleton immediately accepted the invitation to join the ticket.

Eagleton had been asked point-blank by a McGovern aide if he had any skeletons in his closet that should cause the campaign concern; Eagleton said no. His nomination went forward. What Eagleton failed to mention was that he had previously undergone treatment, including electro-shock therapy, for a mental illness. He later explained that he felt he had been cured and so felt no more need to disclose that condition than he would have mentioned he had once had a broken leg that healed.

Because Eagleton was a last-minute selection, convention delegates had not had time to rally around him and make his nomination pro forma. Punchy delegates decided to have some fun instead and nominated or cast votes for nearly eighty vice presidential nominees. Some were serious offerings, such as the feminists' nomination of Texas state legislator Frances "Sissy" Farenthold. Other votes for Archie Bunker or Mao Zedong were pure silliness.

To that point in the process, the McGovernites had done their best to ensure an orderly convention to counter their image as radical amateurs. The convention had adopted a moderate platform, and the most radical ideas and unsettling images had been kept out of the convention's television coverage. *Washington Post* columnist David Broder praised the type of delegates and convention the McGovern reforms had created: "Purposeful, decent, demonstrative, good-humored, indefatigable, and, above all, diverse."

But this single lapse in discipline concerning the selection of a running mate had two fateful consequences.

First, the "convention horseplay" around the vice presidential choice threw off the convention schedule, and McGovern was not able to give his nomination acceptance speech until 2:45 a.m. EDT. Instead of a prime time television audience of seventy million who might have heard McGovern give one of the best speeches of his campaign, his audience was estimated at fifteen million—and, except for insomniacs, these were likely only die-hard Democrats who were going to vote for McGovern anyway.

But a botched opportunity to deliver his most considered pitch to the largest possible audience was only the second worst outcome of July 13. Within a day, rumors about Eagleton's history of mental illness were circulating widely. Eagleton insisted to McGovern aides that he had only been hospitalized once for exhaustion, but it was soon confirmed that he had been hospitalized three times for what appeared to be severe depression and that part of his treatment involved electro-shock therapy.

It seemed to most observers, then, that McGovern would have no choice but to dump Eagleton from the ticket, not only out of concern for his mental stability should he be elevated to the presidency, but also because he had misled McGovern and withheld the truth. Yet, McGovern continued to back his choice publicly, at one point issuing a statement that he was "a thousand percent behind Tom Eagleton," even as he privately sent out feelers to reporters to determine what the reaction would be if he dropped Eagleton. Six days after issuing his "a thousand percent" statement, McGovern asked Eagleton to withdraw from the ticket.

This complete reversal badly damaged McGovern's credibility and remade Eagleton into a sympathetic figure. Eagleton was angry both at the damage done to his reputation and at how McGovern had publicly backed him while privately expressing doubts to others. In a face-to-face meeting, McGovern denied to Eagleton that he was the source of any of the stories that suggested McGovern was considering dropping him from the ticket. "Don't shit me, George," Eagleton responded.

In no mood to do McGovern any favors, Eagleton said he would resign only on the condition that he write McGovern's statement announcing the decision. He told McGovern that if there were any mention of his alleged mental illness, he would refuse to resign and would fight for his place on the ticket all the way to November. McGovern, then, was forced to say only what Eagleton allowed him to say, which was that Eagleton was an able public servant who was in fine physical and mental health. McGovern explained that he was removing Eagleton from the ticket only because the furor over his past medical treatment "continues to divert attention from the great national issues that need to be discussed." Such a disingenuous statement made McGovern appear indecisive and untrustworthy.

McGovern's reluctance to drop Eagleton from the ticket was, he said later, deeply personal. McGovern had a daughter, Terry, who had battled depression and became an abuser of drugs and alcohol. Terry would later freeze to death in 1994 at age forty-five after passing out outside a Madison, Wisconsin, bar on a cold winter night, and McGovern would chronicle his daughter's tragic life in a book titled *Terry: My Daughter's Life-and-Death Struggle with Alcoholism*. McGovern later said that he felt that if he had jettisoned Eagleton, he would be sending a message to Terry that mental illness made a person a pariah.

McGovern had not only lost the character issue to Nixon, but the whole mess with Eagleton was considered the political story of the year, drawing media attention away from Nixon's Watergate scandal.

Whatever small chance (and it was almost certainly infinitesimal) McGovern had had for victory in the general election was lost with the Eagleton fiasco. The search for Eagleton's replacement was a farce played out in public view. Once again, a steady stream of prominent Democrats refused to board a rapidly sinking ship. Finally, Kennedy brother-in-law Sargent Shriver accepted. Shriver had run the Peace Corps under JFK and the "War on Poverty" under LBJ. Had he been a first choice, Shriver, who proved to be an effective campaigner, would have pleased party regulars and attached some of the Kennedy glamour to a charisma-challenged candidate now branded a "hapless loser." Instead, Shriver was a bandage applied to a patient who had already bled to death.

When looking at 1972 in retrospect, McGovern aides have conceded that a McGovern victory would have been highly unlikely even if they had run a near perfect campaign. But had it not been for the Eagleton debacle, those same aides believe that McGovern would have carried ten or twelve states, instead of one, and he would have won 45 percent of the vote, instead of 37.5 percent.

Perhaps, but while Watergate would eventually color the view of what Nixon accomplished in 1972, his landslide win was not all about political dirty tricks and subversion of the Constitution. Nixon ran a masterful, disciplined campaign, and the first six months of 1972 were the high point of his presidency. In that time period he made his remarkable visit to the People's Republic of China, he bombed Hanoi in response to a North Vietnamese offensive, and did so without scuttling a summit with the Soviets in Moscow where he signed the first Strategic Arms Limitation Treaty (SALT). At the beginning of the year, Nixon's job approval rating had been just below 50 percent, but by mid-year it had soared to 61 percent.

McGovern's belief that he could unify the party around a shared antipathy toward Nixon was a gross miscalculation. He couldn't. And it was not just jealousy by the party regulars; McGovern's moralistic tone, delivered as a jeremiad to a nation that prefers sunny optimists, was as offensive to Cold War Democrats as it was to conservative Republicans.

Returning to the Senate after his defeat, McGovern overheard Georgia senator Herman Talmadge explain to other senators, "You know, what was wrong with George in that campaign was that he gave the impression that he was mad at the country. . . . This is a great country. It makes mistakes, but by God if you get up there and preach day and night against America, you're not going to be elected."

Washington Post reporter William Greider had written during the campaign that "McGovern's moral message is repugnant to a great many American voters who not only disagree with it, but are outraged that a major party presidential candidate should even be saying such things." *Newsweek* added that McGovern, "the preacher's boy from Mitchell, S.D.," had "turned more furiously evangelical than any major-party candidate since William Jennings Bryan . . . [and had] returned more and more to the old moral absolutism—and to the harshest rhetoric of any campaign in memory."

But where Bryan had railed against Wall Street and the Eastern establishment, McGovern's anger at the war in Vietnam, and his consuming desire to end it at almost any cost, was received by many voters as an indictment of the American people for their complicity in the conflict. He certainly said things no presidential candidate had said before or since.

McGovern had begun his campaign in January 1971 with the high-minded idea that "thoughtful Americans understand that the highest patriotism is not to blindly accept official policy but to love one's country deeply enough to call her to a higher standard." McGovern was then intent on ensuring Americans knew how far below that standard American behavior in Vietnam had fallen and how they were complicit in that failure. In one campaign speech, he said:

> *For what we now present to the world is the spectacle of a rich and powerful nation standing off at a safe distance and raining down a terrible technology of death on helpless people below—the most incredible and murderous bombardment in all the history of*

mankind. . . . We have steel fleshettes that penetrate the skin and cannot be removed. We have napalm—jellied gasoline that sticks to the skin as it burns. We have white phosphorus that cannot be extinguished until it burns itself out.

McGovern's opponent may have been Nixon, but he was campaigning as fiercely against the apathy of the American people, and was desperately trying to get the American public to confess and atone for their own culpability as passive witnesses and active participants. In one particularly exasperated moment, McGovern said:

I do not honestly know whether the war weighs as deeply on the minds of the American people as it does on mine. I do not honestly know whether the blunt words I have said tonight will help me or hurt me in this election. I do not really care. For almost a decade, my heart has ached over the fighting and the dying in Vietnam. I cannot remember a day when I did not think of this tragedy.

What he learned, gonzo journalist Hunter S. Thompson wrote, was that "we are not a nation of truth-lovers. McGovern understands this, but he keeps on saying these terrible things anyway."

Dissent is an honored American tradition, but it is seldom popular in the moment and opens up the dissenter to charges from opponents that he or she is unpatriotic. McGovern would later admit that his harsh moral tone had been a mistake. Moral critiques, as Jimmy Carter learned and put to use in his own campaign, are only effective when directed at the Washington establishment. What voters want to hear, McGovern aide Greg Craig said ruefully after the campaign, is that America is a great country filled with good people.

McGovern's complete dedication to extricating America from Vietnam also made voters wary that he could end the war in a way that protected American pride, honor, and interests. Polling showed most Americans believed Nixon was satisfactorily winding down the war and, in a paradox that deeply troubled McGovern, polls showed that, by a better than two-to-one margin, Americans believed Nixon would do a better job of withdrawing the United States from Vietnam than the anti-war candidate. While more than twenty thousand of the roughly fifty thousand U.S. combat deaths in Vietnam occurred during Nixon's first term, Nixon did finally withdraw most U.S. troops from Vietnam in 1973, a year that saw fewer than two hundred U.S. combat deaths.

Nixon was so disliked in so many quarters that he received scant praise for his overwhelming victory. Rather than credit Nixon for running a brilliant campaign, which would have triumphed without the dirty tricks, the narrative that came out of 1972 was that McGovern had run a lousy campaign and that he proved that liberalism was no longer ascendant in American politics.

Yet over time much of McGovern's domestic program, such as expanded rights for women and gays, became mainstream, and some scholars argue McGovern was well within the tradition of the Democratic Party's Jacksonian and New Deal past in "its commitment to economic security for the average American." Nor have subsequent Democratic presidents and presidential candidates abandoned all liberal reform impulses. Carter proposed tax reforms that were very similar to McGovern's own wealth redistribution programs. Mondale ran as a very conventional liberal—he even pledged to raise taxes to reduce the federal deficit. Clinton tried to reform national health care, and Obama did just that. Even McGovern's proposal of amnesty for "draft dodgers," considered extreme in 1972, was not a particularly divisive issue when President Ford granted conditional amnesty in 1974 and President Carter granted unconditional amnesty in 1977.

Yet, despite all this, the McGovern campaign is not remembered among Democrats as a prophetic venture in the same way that Republicans venerate the equally hapless Goldwater campaign. McGovern and Goldwater were both insurgents attacking the established order. Goldwater inspired a movement that took control of the Republican Party; four decades later, it is still considered "toxic" for a Democrat to be known as the "next McGovern." Why has McGovern's campaign been interpreted as the last gasp of a dying liberal movement that had once dominated American politics, while Goldwater's sounded like the first breath of a newborn?

The notoriety of McGovern's campaign is due to his anti-war stance and his legacy as "the ultimate peace candidate" in a society that still esteems martial virtues.* This is where subsequent Democratic candidates have tried to draw a distinction between themselves and McGovern—not over any alleged radical domestic agenda. They have wanted it understood that they are not "soft" on defense issues.

In 1984, Mondale and McGovern's former campaign manager, Gary Hart, each called for modest increases in the U.S. defense budget. In 1988, Michael Dukakis explicitly insisted that he was "not another McGovern" when it came to foreign affairs.

Clinton had joined in protests against the Vietnam War and was the Texas coordinator for the McGovern campaign, yet he dissembled during his own presidential campaigns on whether he did or did not try to avoid the draft. "I think he winced every time it was mentioned that he was a McGovern worker in '72," said a McGovern campaign colleague who also knew Clinton as president. In a bizarre twist, John Kerry had made his national reputation as a Vietnam veteran who ended up opposing the Vietnam War, yet in his 2004 campaign Kerry played down his brave and prescient role as dissenter and instead played up his war record, only to see that record distorted and used against him.

The message is clear: Candidates cannot hope to be elected president if they talk about war as McGovern talked about war. Indeed, they must seem to be eager for the role of commander-in-chief.

McGovern had hoped that Obama, with his opposition to the Iraq War, had perhaps demonstrated that an anti-war candidate could win the presidency. But Obama was no peace candidate. He said he only opposed "a dumb war" and labeled himself "a hawk when it comes to defeating terrorism." He pledged during the campaign to actually increase the U.S. military presence in Afghanistan and shocked his liberal supporters when he did just that as president.

McGovern, of course, as noted, was not a pacifist either, but he opposed the Cold War liberalism that had taken over the Democratic

---

* "Ultimate peace candidate" was the label applied by mock commentator/comedian Stephen Colbert in a 2008 interview with McGovern, who had written a book on how the United States should also extricate itself from Iraq. Overlooking McGovern's World War II service, Colbert asked, "Is there any kind of war you *would* support?"

Party after World War II and that emphasized a strong national defense while muting the party's reform instinct. McGovern, for example, had supported Henry Wallace over Harry Truman in 1948 and never regretted it. "My mission," McGovern had said, "was to try to show the American people that we didn't have any mission to police the world."

Many Americans agree. Three-fifths of Americans, even in 1972, agreed with McGovern that sending troops into Vietnam in the first place had been a mistake. But McGovern's language was so harsh and uncompromising that it disturbed the fundamental belief of most Americans that the United States only engages in "good" wars that are fought by humane means for the best of intentions.

Because McGovern challenged this fundamental American belief, some challenged his masculinity. *First Monday*, the now-defunct conservative magazine, called McGovern "a sort of benign political Liberace." Matching McGovern with the flamboyant entertainer who most assumed was gay was hardly subtle. The supposed effeminacy of being a peace candidate was reinforced by McGovern's outreach to women and his support of gay rights, which further alienated those who want our leaders to possess a machismo that Barry Goldwater flaunted but that McGovern lacked. Like AFL-CIO president George Meany, they expressed disgust that McGovern's convention had attracted "people who look like Jacks, acted like Jills, and had the odors of Johns about them."

The year before McGovern's presidential campaign, the movie *Patton* won the Academy Award for Best Picture. It was Nixon's favorite film. He watched it many times and ordered his staff to watch it too. To prepare for Nixon's visit to China, Premier Chou En-Lai watched *Patton* to better understand his guest. It was also the fourth-highest grossing film of 1970 at more than sixty-one million dollars.

Some critics, perhaps because a young Francis Ford Coppola wrote the screenplay, have argued that *Patton* can also be seen as satire, but it is safe to say that neither Nixon nor the vast majority of other Americans who viewed the film saw it as such. In the iconic opening scene, George C. Scott portrays American World War II general George S. Patton, standing before a massive flag, and offers Patton's take on the American attitude toward war:

Americans, traditionally, love to fight. All real Americans love the sting of battle. . . . Americans love a winner and will not tolerate a loser. Americans play to win all the time. I wouldn't give a hoot in hell for a man who lost and laughed. That's why Americans have never lost and will never lose a war because the very thought of losing is hateful to Americans.

If the screenwriters for *Patton* accurately captured an essential part of the American character, and the success of the movie suggests they did, then McGovern's antipathy toward war put him at odds with the feelings of many voters. In a nation where the first president was the former general of our national army and our greatest presidents are those who led us to victory in great wars, it is a routine test for every presidential aspirant to demonstrate that they are "tough enough" to order our troops into war.

McGovern aspired to a different kind of toughness, a toughness that enables leaders to avoid and to end wars, even when the end means withdrawal without the victory Americans crave. Woodrow Wilson, the fellow moralist whom McGovern aspired to emulate, had said in trying to avoid American entry into World War I, "There is such a thing as a nation being too proud to fight." Public opinion led Wilson to abandon that noble sentiment and seek a declaration of war.

Perhaps, as the movie *Patton* suggests, Americans do love "the sting of battle." For while much of McGovern's critique of the Vietnam War has, in hindsight, been proven correct, as author Bruce Miroff noted, "it has been the heirs of Nixon who have had the upper hand on national security issues in subsequent presidential campaigns, and it has been the heirs of McGovern who have been caught up in an identity crisis of American patriotism."

Chapter Ten

ROSS PEROT

1992, 1996

It's that simple.

For a nation so enamored with capitalism and industry, it is striking
that so few businessmen have been
tapped to be president. No person
has moved directly from the business world into the White House.
Of those presidents who had a
background in business before they
entered politics, there were as many
business failures (Grant, Truman,
George W. Bush) as successes, and
those who enjoyed success in business before entering politics—and
none could be labeled tycoons—had unsuccessful presidencies (Harding,
Hoover, and George H. W. Bush).

The bulk of our presidents and presidential candidates have been
attorneys, generals, or educators. Perhaps, as Harry Truman noted, the
reason more business executives don't enter politics is that "after they've
had a successful business career . . . they want to start at the top." Most
businessmen scorn the drudgery of practical politics and conclude that
the worlds of politics and business, however entwined they may be, have
different purposes and require different skills.

The business titans of America's past, such as John D. Rockefeller,
Cornelius Vanderbilt, J. P. Morgan or Henry Ford, thrilled the nation
with their exploits, but no one seems to have thought that the skills that
created their extraordinary fortunes were transferrable to politics. Even

without elective office, these men were politically powerful, of course, and used sympathetic and often indebted politicians to protect their corporate interests. As Vanderbilt once exclaimed, "What do I care about the law? Hain't I got the power?"

A few tycoons dabbled in broader issues of public policy; Andrew Carnegie tried to purchase the independence of the Philippines from the U.S. government, and Ford led a much-ridiculed civilian delegation to Europe to try to end World War I. But when someone with a name renowned in business, like Rockefeller or Kennedy, does run for office, it is usually a second- or third-generation family member who did not build up the family fortune themselves but turned to public service relatively early in life.

The handful of moguls who have entered politics have come from the news media.* Perhaps William Randolph Hearst, James M. Cox, or Michael Bloomberg simply thought public office was good business since politics and the media often seem one industry. But generally, businessmen find the compromises and general messiness of electoral politics unappealing—and unprofitable. A business executive might accept the occasional Cabinet post, but he shuns too much involvement in partisan politics for fear of offending customers, shareholders, or powerful public officials. As one automobile executive explained to *Time* magazine in 1956, "We sell cars to both Republicans and Democrats."

Not until the 1980s were prominent businessmen pushed to consider national office. Then, admirers touted as possible presidential candidates both Lee Iacocca, who had reversed Chrysler's sagging fortunes as its CEO, and Peter Ueberroth, the travel industry executive who managed the successful 1984 Los Angeles Olympics. The two demurred from running at the time, though each remained an active commentator on current events, and Ueberroth, after serving as commissioner of Major League Baseball, did eventually run for governor of California during the 2003 recall election but finished sixth out of 135 candidates.

Then came Ross Perot, incongruously described by his admirers as a "down to earth . . . billionaire," who became the most successful

---

* Wendell Willkie, the utility executive who became the Republicans' presidential nominee in 1940, is the rare non-media businessman to run for president, but the circumstances of his nomination were very unusual. He was also nominated more for his foreign policy views than for his business acumen.

third party candidate for president since Theodore Roosevelt bolted the Republican Party in 1912. While Perot is a unique personality, what truly separates him from the industrialists of yore is the time in which he has lived. Perot arrived on the scene when businessmen and those of great wealth were held in high public esteem, which has not always been the case in our history, and he entered politics when new technologies allowed those who could afford it the opportunity to bypass the traditional political process. Perot also offered himself as a candidate for president when people had lost faith in traditional political institutions and the wisdom of experts, and when the end of the Cold War made foreign policy experience less important in selecting a president.

The Cold War had established an easily understood framework— "us vs. them"—that defined our politics for a half century. The collapse of the Soviet Union thrust a new set of issues before the nation, which made the world seem a much more complicated place. Many voters yearned for simpler times and for a "man on horseback" who could come in and solve our problems with a minimum of fuss. Perot, as one scholar noted, was more than happy to sell himself as "a political Lone Ranger, a lonely hero able to ride into Washington and single-handedly clean up the mess."

Perot's 1992 campaign for president occurred at a time when businessmen were as exalted in America as they had been at any time in history. Unlike previous business booms, such as the Gilded Age of the late 1800s, there was no accompanying backlash against the rich. The excesses of the Vanderbilts, the DuPonts, and the other so-called robber barons, when contrasted with the misery experienced by much of the working poor, led to the reforms of the Progressive Era. The "Roaring Twenties, when President Calvin Coolidge had said, "The man who builds a factory builds a temple," was followed by the Great Depression and the reforms of the New Deal. Businessmen blamed for the crash were considered near criminals, and some were criminals, such as Richard C. Whitney, the president of the New York Stock Exchange, who ended up in prison for embezzlement and fraud. President Franklin Roosevelt regularly castigated "blind economic forces and blindly selfish men," as he did in his second inaugural address, for leaving "one-third of a nation ill-housed, ill-clad, ill-nourished."

But by the time Perot became part of the national consciousness, World War II had allowed the corporate world to rehabilitate its reputation by once again demonstrating the United States' industrial genius, which was crucial to the Allied victory. The following decades witnessed continued economic growth that seemed, except for the occasional hiccup of a mild recession, to have no end. Moreover, social programs first implemented during the New Deal began to ensure that the new wealth was no longer contrasted with widespread poverty, and there had been no severe economic contraction that would, have caused a backlash against business. Business seemed to have mastered the business cycle; great wealth was tolerated because it occurred in a time of general prosperity.

Meanwhile, new industries were emerging, exciting the public imagination. They were led by men who had the cachet of being entrepreneurs and innovators, not bland corporate managers. Perot was an early pioneer in the high-tech business world, and he demonstrated, to great public fascination, that this new industry allowed those who mastered it the opportunity to amass extraordinary fortunes.

Perot had begun Electronic Data Systems (EDS) in 1962. As late as 1965 the company's annual earnings were still less than one million dollars, and even though it was a computer company, it still didn't own a single computer. But then Perot secured government contracts to manage data for Medicare and Medicaid, and revenues soared. The company made its first public stock offering in 1968, and the share price rose to $23 on the first day, meaning that Perot, who owned ten million shares in the company, became worth $230 million literally overnight. A year-and-a-half later, the share price peaked at $162.50—an extraordinary 50,000 percent of earnings—and Perot was now worth $1.5 billion. Since he had accumulated that wealth primarily by providing data services to the government in support of social programs, one wit noted he was America's first "welfare billionaire."

By the 1970s (and especially by the 1980s), there were some who began to think that such spectacular success in business promised similarly spectacular results in public service. With government becoming ever more complex financially, there were also those who argued that government could and should be operated like a business. Meanwhile, as the attitude toward business was ascendant, the reputation of public service was in decline. A succession of calamities, among them the supposed shortcomings of Lyndon Johnson's Great Society program, the Vietnam War, Richard Nixon's Watergate transgressions, and Jimmy Carter's warnings of a national malaise had badly discredited government. An indicator of the positive status of business in the public mind has historically been the election of a Republican president, and Carter was followed by Ronald Reagan, who declared government was no longer the solution to the nation's problems, but in large measure the cause. The answers to America's increasingly complicated problems (or so it appeared) now seemed to lie in the dynamic private sector as Americans were becoming increasingly disenchanted with the static political system.

One sign of that political disenchantment was that fewer Americans identified themselves as either Republicans or Democrats. The growing number of unaffiliated voters seemed to create an opening for candidates outside the two-party system. Since its peak in the late nineteenth century, partisan political affiliation has been in a steady decline, a decline Perot's candidacy would exacerbate. According to Gallup's annual surveys, in 1988, 36 percent of American voters identified themselves as Democrats, 33 percent as Republicans, and 31 percent as independents. By 1993, the year after the Perot campaign, 32 percent of Americans considered themselves Democrats, 30 percent Republicans, and 38 percent as independents.*

Political parties were not the only institutions to lose the confidence of many Americans. Experts and professionals of all stripes were no longer given the deference they had enjoyed in previous times. There was a growing belief that the opinion of experts had no more validity than that of any reasonably educated, thoughtful person. Conservative journalist William F. Buckley, himself a Yale graduate, captured the sentiment when he said, "I should sooner live in a society

---

* While the 2004 and 2008 campaigns increased voter identification with one of the two main parties, by 2010 the partisan affiliation numbers were back to being remarkably similar to those from 1993.

governed by the first two thousand names in the Boston telephone directory than in a society governed by the two thousand faculty members of Harvard University."

Deference to experts diminished also because more Americans were becoming better educated themselves. By the 1990s, two-thirds of adult Americans had attended at least some college and roughly one-third had earned a four-year degree. More importantly, new technologies allowed average citizens to bypass the traditional gatekeepers of information and have greater access to the public square. People who were used to being talked *to* could now talk *back*. After Perot would come the Internet and blogging, but shortly before Perot announced his candidacy, the rise of talk radio hailed the public's new respect for the opinions (informed or otherwise) of the average citizen.

Talk radio had its origins in New York City in the 1940s as a local phenomenon, but it got a huge boost in terms of tackling political content in 1987 when the Federal Communications Commission repealed the so-called Fairness Doctrine. Without the requirement that broadcasters provide free airtime for a response to any controversial opinion that had been aired on the station, the door was opened for "increasingly partisan discussions without rebuttal." Rush Limbaugh began his first national broadcast in late 1988, and by late 1990 he was the most popular figure on radio. Like Perot, the message of Limbaugh and a host of primarily conservative commentators who commanded the airwaves was that average citizens, usually defined as their followers, needed to take back the country from an ineffectual elite.

Yet, even as modern society celebrated the wisdom of the common man in the finest Jeffersonian tradition, there was also a new fascination with the uncommon man or woman, the celebrity. *People* magazine had debuted in 1974, the first of a variety of magazines, television shows, and websites devoted to celebrating the art of being famous for being famous. *People* was such a publishing success that its focus on personality was soon being mimicked even by business magazines, such as *Forbes* and *Fortune*. In 1989, television shows focused on celebrity, such as *Inside Edition* and *Hard Copy*, made their debut.

Perot had begun his career at IBM as a salesman, and through the years he remained a salesman whose favorite product was Ross Perot, but he was still an odd candidate for celebrity. He was, as a *Newsweek* reporter described him, "a banty rooster of a man with question mark ears, a mangled nose, a barber-college haircut, and an East Texas drawl as thin and sharp as wine gone to vinegar." His life story offers few clues as to what fueled his massive ambitions or his need for public recognition. He was born June 27, 1930, in Texarkana, Texas, the son of a successful cotton broker and a mother who was a devout Methodist. By all accounts, it was a loving home where Perot received plenty of attention from his parents. Physically small, Perot played few sports but expressed his competitive nature in other endeavors, such as being the first in his Boy Scout troop to attain the rank of Eagle Scout. Even as a teenager, a friend recalled, Perot had "a very healthy ego."

Perot attended the U.S. Naval Academy, where he was an average student academically but a champion debater, and his leadership skills were acknowledged by his election as class president in his final two years. Perot did not smoke, drink, or chase women. He loved the rigorous ethical standards at the academy, but when assigned to active duty, he professed to be appalled by the lax moral standards of what he termed the "fairly godless" regular Navy. His request for early dismissal was rejected. Later, as his naval commitment was ending, he met a touring IBM executive who was impressed by Perot's confidence in directing a series of naval maneuvers. He offered Perot an interview, which Perot jumped at, telling the executive, "And I don't even know what you do."

Perot became one of IBM's star salesmen, popular with managers, less so with co-workers. But he grew frustrated at IBM. He felt the company was capping his earning potential and was not interested in his ideas for IBM to move beyond selling computer hardware and begin offering computer services, such as helping companies with data management. In 1962, he made the decision to leave IBM and form his own company after reading a quote from Henry David Thoreau in the *Reader's Digest:* "The mass of men lead lives of quiet desperation."

His success at EDS garnered an introduction to Richard Nixon in 1968 when he was invited to give a presentation on how computers could enhance political campaigns. After Nixon's election, the administration repeatedly turned to Perot as a potential donor for various administration initiatives, though Perot got the reputation of overpromising in order to gain access to the president and then underdelivering. Perot "actually thought he knew what to do, better than anyone else," a Nixon aide said. "He never considered the possibility that anyone else could be right."

In late 1969, Perot complained that the Nixon administration was ignoring the plight of U.S. prisoners of war in North Vietnam. He then gained international attention when he proposed to deliver Christmas dinners and other supplies to POWs. After weeks of negotiation, the North Vietnamese finally flatly refused to accept the supplies, though reports that treatment of POWs improved after the attempt greatly enhanced Perot's reputation—but not at the White House. "Some of us started to think that the trip had been more about Perot than about the POWs," a Nixon aide said.

While his POW gambit had made him a national figure, it was Perot's upstaging of another president ten years later that would make his reputation as a man who could do what others—including presidents—could not. In late December 1978, two EDS employees were arrested in Iran as the Shah's government was crumbling before the Iranian Revolution. The Shah's government, which had demanded bribes from EDS in return for government contracts, reportedly made the arrests to demonstrate it was cracking down on the government corruption that was helping to fuel the revolution.

Perot was furious. Discounting the U.S. State Department's struggle to evacuate twenty-five thousand other American citizens in Iran, Perot grew impatient with supposed government inaction and hatched his own plan to send a privately financed commando team to Tehran to break the men out of jail. EDS employees with military experience—"preferably in Special Forces–type action"—volunteered for a rescue team that was led by an old Perot acquaintance, Colonel Arthur "Bull" Simons, who had once led a celebrated attempt to rescue American POWs in North Vietnam and who had assisted in Perot's ongoing quest to determine if any American POWs remained alive in Southeast Asia after the end of the war. Simons, by then sixty, was so eager to help with the Iranian rescue that he refused compensation for his services.

Seven EDS employees, all of them military veterans, all in their mid-thirties, and all who had worked in Tehran at one time or another for EDS, joined Simons on January 3, 1979, to begin a week of training before heading to Iran. The initial plan to break the EDS prisoners out of a Tehran jail was foiled when the prisoners were transferred to Gasr, the main Iranian prison for political prisoners. But the revolution was gaining momentum, and Simons was an experienced hand, who knew that all revolutions feature a mob storming the toppled regime's prisons in order to release its prisoners. He counseled patience. Perot, meanwhile, had personally traveled to Tehran with remarkably little difficulty, even using his own name and passport, to give instructions and advise his imprisoned employees that rescue was imminent.

On February 11, ten days after the Ayatollah Khomeini made his triumphal return from exile to Iran, a mob did storm Gasr. The two now freed EDS employees walked to a nearby Tehran hotel, the designated meeting place, where they were picked up by Simons and other members of the team and driven to safety in Turkey. The story was front-page news around the world. Perot deserved enormous credit for the effort and determination he showed in trying to protect and rescue his employees, yet he felt the need to embellish the story. He insisted that an Iranian EDS employee had instigated and fomented the mob's storming of Gasr, which no independent report could verify. When U.S. undersecretary of state David Newsom telephoned Perot to question the facts of the operation relayed in news stories, Perot reportedly replied, "Well, the press never gets it right."

Perot's "can do" image was later contrasted with the agonizing 444 days U.S. Embassy employees in Tehran (a group Perot had consistently and unfairly maligned while plotting the rescue of his own people) were held hostage after having been captured by mobs sympathetic to the Ayatollah. President Jimmy Carter's failure to secure the release of the hostages, either by diplomacy or military rescue, was a key reason he was defeated for re-election.

But Perot, ever the salesman, was not through embellishing his hostage rescue story. While retaining full editorial control, Perot hired Welsh novelist Ken Follett, and together in 1983 they published *On Wings of Eagles*. It became a number one best seller, selling more than three hundred thousand copies in hardcover. Three years later, NBC television produced a five-hour miniseries based on the book that drew an audience of twenty-five million. Perot demanded and received full script and casting approval. Perot was portrayed by Richard Crenna while Simons was played by Burt Lancaster. This newest version of the story included a shootout between the rescue team and the Iranian guards, and an Iranian prosecutor madly pursuing the rescued prisoners across Iran until Simons blows up an ammunition dump at the Turkish border. The story also had Perot greeting the rescued men at the border when he was, in fact, still in Istanbul. "Now, in creating a miniseries, there is always a little dramatization," Perot explained, though the show's producer noted that all the new drama had been inserted by Perot.

The book and the miniseries catapulted Perot's fame to new levels and prompted dozens of people to begin writing Perot to suggest he run for president. "Do you think I should run for president?" Perot asked an employee. "President? No," the employee replied. "King? Yes."

Before he did either, Perot was busy with his business interests. In 1984, Perot sold EDS to General Motors, though Perot acted as if he had purchased GM. His battles with GM management, which he was happy to make public, led GM to pay him $750 million—twice the value of Perot's stock—just to go away. GM executives considered it a bargain. To his admirers, it was another example of Perot battling a stagnant and entrenched bureaucracy.

This reputation was further enhanced when Perot was asked to chair two public policy commissions in Texas during the late 1980s, one on drug abuse and the other on education reform. One of Perot's favorite phrases during his presidential campaigns was "It's that simple," and as chair of these commissions Perot was already demonstrating his faith that complex problems would yield to straightforward solutions. On drug abuse, Perot's ideas, an aide said, were generally limited to "tougher and longer sentences and more aggressive law enforcement." In coming to that view, Perot had at least gone through the motions of meeting with experts in the field. When he chaired the commission on education policy, Perot did not bother to meet with teachers or students. He dismissed the opinions of educators by claiming, "The dumbest folks in college are studying to be teachers." Consultants hired by the commission did develop a plan that included such ideas as reduced class size, more preschool education, merit pay for teachers, and student achievement tests, but the only issue that really held Perot's attention was his insistence that Texas adopt a program by which students could not play athletics unless they were passing all their courses. In football-mad Texas, Perot's "no pass, no play" proposal created shockwaves, as it was something easily understood and easily implemented. When he ran for president, Perot would take the same approach.

Perot had also not abandoned his interest in whether the United States had left behind POWs still alive in Southeast Asia after the end of the Vietnam War, funding several missions that turned up no hard evidence. Still, he was convinced that the government was hiding the truth in order to protect its involvement in the region's illicit drug trade. He also became convinced that the Reagan administration was spying on him and that elements within the government were plotting his assassination. He became so paranoid that when traveling to Washington, D.C., he would check into one hotel, then sneak out and register in another hotel, all while traveling around town in what he thought was the "perfect disguise," a beat-up Volkswagen. He grew so frustrated by the administration's failure to accept his conspiracy theories that he withdrew his $2.5 million pledge for President Reagan's presidential library, and he concluded Vice President George H. W. Bush was "a wimp."

Perhaps it was his enmity for Bush that led Perot to harshly criticize the then-president's decision to rally an international army to oppose the Iraqi invasion of Kuwait. Perot charged the Gulf War was only a war over oil. "We rescued the emir of Kuwait," he said. "Now, if I knock on your door and say I'd like to borrow your son to go to the Middle East so that this dude with seventy wives, who's got a minister for sex to find him a virgin every Thursday night, can have his throne back, you'd probably hit me in the mouth."

This unconventional candor earned Perot even more admirers, particularly from a growing group of individuals who hoped to find someone who could lead a challenge to the two-party political system. Perot was invited to speak at the 1991 convention of a group called THRO (Throw the Hypocritical Rascals Out). His speech electrified many in the independent political movement, and they began a months-long seduction of Perot to convince him that he was the man the country needed in the White House.

The idea of calling out a virtuous citizen who can rise up from outside an allegedly corrupt political system to lead a nation in time of peril—and then walk away from power once the crisis has passed—is one of the most cherished of all democratic myths. It is most closely associated with the myth of Cincinnatus, a real person who was a consul in the early Roman republic. Cincinnatus, an experienced general, was persuaded to abandon his farm and assume the power of a dictator in order to lead the army to repel the invaders. This Cincinnatus accomplished in just sixteen days, after which he voluntarily relinquished his power as dictator and quickly returned to his farm in time to bring in the harvest.

As the Founding Fathers struggled to build an enduring and functioning republic on the Roman model, George Washington was cast as the American Cincinnatus when he, too, had the opportunity to assume dictatorial powers at the end of the Revolutionary War. Instead, he resigned his generalship to return to his home at Mount Vernon—an act of faith in the fledgling democracy that led Britain's King George III to reportedly acclaim Washington "the greatest man in the world." Washington's selflessness inspired his officers, among them Alexander Hamilton and Henry Knox, to form the Society of the Cincinnati, whose motto is "He relinquished everything to save the Republic."

Perot was acting in the tradition of Cincinnatus by insisting that he, too, was a simple man reluctant to assume the burden of political power. Perot's own wife, unaware of the months-long recruitment of her husband to run, claimed to be "stunned" when Perot went on CNN's *Larry King Live* show on February 21, 1992, to announce that he would become a presidential candidate—but *only* if his supporters could get his name on the ballot in all fifty states. If they could achieve that miracle, then Perot said he knew he was truly wanted and needed. As that process went forward, Perot continued to insist, "I don't want to do the job" of president.

Perot's reluctance seemed believable. He already had the fame, wealth, and honor that the cynical assume is the secret reason all politicians pursue high office, so the perception was that Perot would have no need to engage in the grubby behavior of the "typical" politician and would have no incentive to do anything but focus on the greater public good. Since Perot, this same rationale has been used to advance the political careers of a variety of other independently wealthy and famous candidates, including action movie star and former California governor Arnold Schwarzenegger; media mogul and New York City mayor Michael Bloomberg; unsuccessful California gubernatorial and senatorial candidates Meg Whitman and Carly Fiorina, both high-tech CEOs; and entrepreneur and reality television star Donald Trump, who toyed with running for president in 2000 and 2012. As a sign of the appeal wealthy celebrity business tycoons can hold for voters, Trump led in early polls for the 2012 Republican nomination before it became clear his candidacy was more a publicity stunt than a serious campaign and he again opted out of running.*

For Perot and these other celebrity candidates, their great wealth was perceived by many as a virtue. Because of the 1976 U.S. Supreme Court decision, *Buckley v. Valeo*, no limits are placed on personal campaign spending. This allowed Perot and the other super-rich to self-fund their campaigns, which supporters found appealing because their candidates then owed no favors to special interests as an exchange for needed campaign contributions. Not lost on their admirers was how this wealth

---

* In announcing his entry into the 2003 race to recall and replace California governor Gray Davis, Schwarzenegger also professed to be a reluctant candidate, saying, "I came to the conclusion that even though there are great sacrifices to make, I felt in the end it is my duty to jump in the race." Schwarzenegger had been politically active and contemplating a political career for some time, but most voters, perhaps rightly, assumed being governor was a step down from being an action movie star. As he left office, Schwarzenegger insisted his seven years as governor had cost him two hundred million dollars in expenses and lost income.

also freed the supporters from a good deal of hard work. Large sums of money could immediately put in place the type of political infrastructure it would take a true grassroots movement years to develop.

Lack of prior experience in elected office was perceived as an equal or greater virtue than wealth. "Thank God he has no political experience!" one supporter told a pollster, as Perot had never run for any elected office before running for president. Perot, his supporters believed, could enter public office with "clean hands" and no prior commitment to a course of action based on party loyalty or a particular ideological bent. Perot ran as a political independent, but even the rich and famous who have run as Republicans or Democrats have joined Perot in offering the promise, implicit or explicit, that they were not typical partisan politicians, but rather offered the opportunity to move "past partisanship, past bipartisanship to postpartisanship," as Schwarzenegger phrased it in his second inaugural address as governor.

Perot's campaign, according to one political scientist, was not merely against partisan politics but against the very "*idea* of partisanship, and indeed, against the idea that politics is a profession." While experience is considered a plus in almost any other profession, Perot argued that too much experience in politics is corrupting, with the United States being ruled by a "political class" that is "out of touch" with most American voters. He amplified this message with one of his key proposals: term limits for all elected offices. The belief that a career in politics neither offered nor required any particular accumulation of knowledge or development of talent resonated in a culture that one could argue is devoted to finding shortcuts to success—a society where most state governments operate lotteries promising instant wealth, where Las Vegas became the nation's most popular tourist destination, and where television "infomercials" promised the opportunity to earn thousands if not millions from the privacy of your home—though by doing what, exactly, was never made clear.

In a culture of instant gratification, large segments of the population rejected the worldview that our problems and challenges were complicated and nuanced, and instead subscribed to the view that there were always simple, common-sense (perhaps even pain-free) answers whose implementation would be thwarted by a government composed of mandarins more concerned with their own status than the public welfare. If Perot offered few specific proposals on how to fix an economy perceived to be in recession in early 1992—beyond his pledge to "get under the hood" and see what needed to be "fixed"—it did not bother his admirers. They had no doubt that the man who had beaten IBM and GM at their own game would find solutions to the nation's economic woes, answers beyond the grasp of the lawyers and lifelong politicians who had never met a payroll.

While Perot was vague on what he might do to stimulate economic growth, he had some specific proposals for the issue he made his own during his first presidential campaign, the federal budget deficits and the national debt. The budget deficit issue played into Perot's strengths—and his and his audience's prejudices. The deficit was prima facie evidence that traditional politicians were in over their heads when it came to finance, and the issue cried out for leadership from someone, like Perot, who knew how to make and manage money. Perot likened the deficit to "a crazy aunt you keep down in the basement. All the neighbors know she's there, but nobody talks about her." When Reagan took office in 1981, the national debt was just over nine hundred billion dollars. By 1992, the national debt had soared to four trillion dollars. Complicit in the failure to address the government's deficit each year was a tax code that Perot compared to "an old inner tube that's been patched by every special interest in the country."

Perot argued his business skills would allow him to reduce federal spending through efficiencies without the need for dramatic cuts in government services. But, to his credit, he was not proposing pain-free deficit reduction. He advocated a fifty-cent-a-gallon tax on gasoline to reduce the deficit, plus higher income tax rates, higher tobacco taxes, and reduced exemptions for mortgages and business expenses. Washington insiders, Perot argued, because they were only interested in lining their own pockets at the expense of the national good, could never implement such common sense solutions. Implementing his common sense fiscal agenda would also require a political reform agenda that would include term limits for elected officials, campaign finance reform, and a ban on former officials lobbying for foreign governments.

The public response to Perot's qualified announcement on Larry King's program that he might run for president was electric, triggering an amazing groundswell of support. His office reported receiving an average of two thousand phone calls an hour from people who wanted to help. Almost overnight, volunteers organized in all fifty states to begin the process of getting Perot on the ballot. Reflecting the near religious fervor that ensued, one volunteer called Perot's conditional promise to run his "covenant with America," while another likened all the volunteers circulating ballot access petitions to "peaceful freedom fighters . . . who had come to take their country back." What seemed to really thrill Perot supporters was the sense that he had empowered them to take charge of his campaign. One Perot volunteer recalled an interview in which Perot was asked, "'What could be done to fix the country and the path on which it was headed?' 'Look in the mirror' was his response. Indeed I did."

The Perot volunteers had a formidable task ahead of them. Getting an independent candidate on the ballot in all fifty states is extraordinarily difficult, and once on the ballot independent and third party candidates face skepticism that they can actually win an election.

There is no national standard for ballot access. Each of the fifty states has its own rules and procedures, some remarkably picayune down to the color of ink required for petition signatures. Ballot access laws had been toughened in many states during the 1930s when legislators were determined to keep Communist candidates from qualifying for the ballot. Just determining what the fifty different standards are is expensive and time-consuming, let alone then gathering the thousands of signatures and paying thousands of dollars in filing fees. The magnitude of the task is demonstrated by the fact that, as of this writing, even relatively established third parties in the United States, such as the Green and Libertarian Parties, have never qualified to be on the ballot in all fifty states in the same election year.

Nothing in our Constitution ordains our two-party system. The Founding Fathers had hoped to avoid the creation of political parties entirely. Yet, even as the two-party system took hold for good in 1832, there arose the first "third party" in the United States, the Anti-Masons, whose members believed the Masons were secretly conspiring to rule the country. That the first third party was based on a conspiracy theory will have special resonance when we return to the story of the Perot campaign. Third parties devoted to ending slavery, imposing Prohibition, opposing immigration, or promoting an expansion of the money supply and regulation of the railroads followed. Few of the candidates of these third parties received even 10 percent of the popular vote, and fewer still earned the only votes that matter—the ones cast in the Electoral College.*

In the twentieth century, the most successful third party candidacy before Perot was that of former president Theodore Roosevelt. Disgusted by the conservative policies of his handpicked successor, William Howard Taft, TR bolted the Republican Party to lead the Progressive Party in 1912. Roosevelt finished second in the presidential contest behind Woodrow Wilson and collected more than 27 percent of the popular vote in a race that also saw a strong showing by the Socialist Party, whose candidate, Eugene Debs, collected 6 percent of the vote.

Three more times after Roosevelt, third party candidates managed to win electoral votes, but all were primarily regional candidates. Progressive senator Robert LaFollette carried only his home state of Wisconsin in 1924. South Carolina governor Strom Thurmond in 1948 and Alabama governor George Wallace in 1968, both running either explicitly or implicitly opposed to racial integration, won states only in the South. Between Wallace and Perot, the only other third party candidate to make a credible showing was Illinois congressman John Anderson in 1980, who won nearly 7 percent of the vote nationally but failed to carry a single precinct anywhere in the nation.

Most third parties, before Perot's campaign, had followed historian Richard Hofstadter's dictum that their role in U.S. politics "has not been to win or govern but to agitate, educate, generate new ideas, and supply the dynamic element in our political life." Like bees, he added, "Once

---

* The Republican Party is sometimes called the only successful third party in American history, but the truth is that the Whig Party had already disintegrated before the Republican Party was formed and the Republicans simply filled the void.

they have stung, they die." But the rationale for Perot's campaign was not promotion of a single cause or issue; it was based on the belief that he personally possessed the character traits needed for national leadership.

Perot's image contrasted sharply with his two opponents, neither of whom inspired much public trust. George Bush Sr. had an approval rating of 90 percent during the Gulf War, but there was a widespread perception that he had no solutions to the recession, and he seemed removed from the economic concerns of struggling Americans. Meanwhile, the Democratic nominee for president, Bill Clinton, had character issues, highlighted by his admission on national television that he had been unfaithful to his wife—a charge that particularly bothered Perot, who would fire his employees if he thought them guilty of adultery.

Perot was seen as a breath of fresh air, endearing himself to voters with his plain talk (usually accompanied by easy-to-understand graphs and charts), his candor, his seeming lack of pretense, and his refusal to play the usual political games. When asked by Larry King if Bush should attend an environmental conference in Brazil, Perot happily acknowledged, "I don't know a thing about it," and when interviewed later about federal funding for abortions, Perot (who favored abortion rights) said he had not "spent ten minutes thinking about it."

Perot was discovering that the usual rules did not apply to him, especially when it came to engaging the news media. He found that he could avoid the grilling by political reporters that the typical presidential candidate faced and that when he pushed back against the media it simply enhanced his reputation of not suffering fools gladly. When a national correspondent asked Perot if he had ever used illegal drugs, Perot responded, "No. Why, have you?" This belligerence delighted admirers who saw it as yet another sign that Perot shared their disdain for traditional elite institutions, above all the national news media.

Meanwhile, Perot found an alternate media universe in which to promote his candidacy, a universe that had not been opened to politicians before. He reached millions of voters with his message by submitting to amiable and nonconfrontational interviews conducted by the likes of Larry King and Oprah Winfrey. The talk show format also helped convey a sense of intimacy with his audience. During the relatively abbreviated 1992 campaign, Perot appeared on thirty-three such programs, in which he was able to convey that while fabulously wealthy, he was still, as those who admired him maintained, an ordinary man who had never lost "the basic East Texas values of compassion, patriotism, and hard work." Every presidential candidate since has emulated his use of these nontraditional venues for political talk.

Perot tended to avoid traditional political talk shows in large part because he was not used to—and did not tolerate—being challenged. He became so upset by Tim Russert's questioning on NBC's *Meet the Press* that, while he kept his cool during the interview, afterward he threatened to end his campaign. But if he could avoid hard interviews, he could not avoid the media scrutiny given to anyone who has a genuine chance to be elected president, and it seemed that Perot might have that chance.

Within weeks of his conditional announcement in February, Perot was at 16 percent in early presidential preference polling, trailing Bush's 44 percent and Clinton's 31 percent; by May, a CNN/*Time* survey showed Perot in the lead at 33 percent, with Bush at 28 percent and Clinton at 24 percent. But it was the beginning of the end. Reporters were dredging up old stories about his fights with GM, his conspiracy theories regarding the POWs and MIAs, his efforts to scuttle the Vietnam War Memorial because he did not like its design, and many more. Perot discovered he could not control what the media wanted to discuss. He gave a speech on how to revitalize the American automobile industry, but afterward reporters wanted to ask him to clarify remarks he had made the day before on gay rights. Perot favored gay rights but had given an interview where he said he would probably not appoint an openly gay person to his Cabinet because the controversy would distract from more important issues.

He was also certain that he was again under government surveillance and that the Republicans, particularly, were planning to sabotage his campaign. He may have been "projecting," for many among his campaign staff believed that *Perot* had tapped *their* phones and done extensive background checks on each of them. Perot did not deny it and instead justified it by saying he had a right to know who was working for him and acting as a representative of his campaign.

As Perot moved up in the polls, his key advisors, most from Perot Systems, the company Perot founded after he sold EDS to GM, believed the campaign needed professional help. Perot was persuaded to hire two high-profile consultants, one Democrat and one Republican. The Democrat was Hamilton Jordan, who had managed Jimmy Carter's successful 1976 campaign and then served as Carter's chief of staff. The Republican was Ed Rollins, who had managed Reagan's 1984 re-election. Their hiring gave Perot yet another bump in the polls. With two political winners on board, more and more voters began to consider that Perot truly had a chance to take the White House.

The addition of traditional political consultants to the Perot campaign proved as dysfunctional as Perot's union with GM. Perot vetoed most of Rollins's and Jordan's ideas. He was furious when Rollins went on the Sunday talk shows without his permission and suspected Rollins of leaking negative information to the press. While Rollins and Jordan said Perot told them he would be willing to spend whatever it took to win, he rebelled against their strategy and its one hundred fifty million dollar price tag.* Despite his inclination to occasionally tap his great fortune for quixotic ventures, Perot was actually quite careful with his money. As one associate noted, "Ross Perot did not get to be a billionaire by giving people blank checks."

Mostly, Perot just did not want to run a conventional campaign. When Jordan pressed Perot to begin running television commercials in the summer, which Perot did not want to do until fall, he gave Jordan such a dressing down that the former presidential chief of staff suffered an anxiety attack so severe that Rollins worried he was having a heart attack. When Perot began yelling at Rollins for some similar transgression, Rollins walked out on Perot, saying he would not be "treated like one of your busboys here."

---

* While the actual Bush and Clinton campaigns would each spend "only" about seventy million dollars each, when expenditures by their respective party organizations and affiliated groups are also taken into account, the total would be close to the one hundred fifty million dollars Jordan and Rollins believed Perot needed to spend to be competitive.

In short, Perot wasn't having any fun. Plus, all the negative media coverage, including rumblings about disharmony within his campaign, had dropped him into third place in the polls. Having fired Rollins on July 15, the next day, just as the Democrats were meeting to officially nominate Clinton, Perot announced he was withdrawing from a presidential race he had actually never officially entered. He said he could quit with a clear conscience because the "Democratic Party had revitalized itself." He also expressed the fear that his candidacy would only throw the election into the House of Representatives, where he could not possibly win.

And yet . . . Perot did not close down operations in states where petitions were still being circulated to get him on the ballot. Back on CNN's *Larry King Live,* King asked Perot if he wasn't still holding out the possibility he might get back in the race. "That's the magic, Larry," Perot replied. In mid-September, it was announced that Perot had finally qualified to be on the ballot in all fifty states, should he run for president. Rumors that he would get back in the race swirled. Perhaps, some surmised, this had been his master strategy all along. But first, Perot decided to have some fun at the expense of the Republicans and Democrats.

He invited representatives from each party to come to Dallas and make presentations to Perot supporters in a bid for their support. The dog-and-pony show occurred on September 28 with Democrats doing their best to woo Perot and keep him out of the race, while Republicans seemed to muff their presentation deliberately as they had decided Bush's only chance at victory, given that he seemed stuck at 40 percent in the polls, was to get Perot back in the race where 40 percent could win the election.*

Once more playing the role of Cincinnatus, seemingly reluctant to take power, Perot announced the next day that he had received 1.5 million telephone calls, urging him to re-enter the race, and that "I have, accepted their request." As he re-entered the race on October 1, he was down to 7 percent in the polls.

But now, with barely a month left before the election, Perot could run the type of campaign he had wanted to. He declined to give public speeches and continued to avoid news interviews. He appeared mostly in

---

* Clinton would win with 43 percent of the popular vote to Bush's 37 percent and Perot's 19 percent.

thirty-minute or hour-long infomercials that, according to Perot biographer Gerald Posner, looked like "low-budget corporate training films," but which cost as much as five hundred thousand dollars per half hour slot. (Perot would eventually spend seventy million dollars of his own money on his campaign, half what Jordan and Rollins had suggested.) The infomercials, with Perot wielding a series of charts while talking directly into the camera, were parodied mercilessly on comedy shows, but they were remarkably effective with voters. His first infomercial, titled *The Problems—Plain Talk about Jobs, Debt, and the Washington Mess*, drew 16.5 million viewers in winning its time slot in the Nielsen ratings.

More important, Perot was included in the televised presidential debates. Both the Republicans and Democrats, still unsure who Perot's supporters were, wanted Perot to participate in the belief that he would either draw votes from the other side or self-destruct. Perot did well in the debates, his outsized personality contrasting nicely against the familiarity of Clinton and ennui of Bush. After the first debate, polls found 70 percent of Americans more inclined to vote for Perot based on his debate performance, and his standing in the polls rose to 13 percent. He did equally well in the next two debates, and he now had climbed to 19 percent in the polls with growing momentum. The negative publicity that dogged him after his withdrawal from the race, the headlines that called him "The Quitter," and "The Yellow Ross of Texas," were now forgotten, and his negative ratings had dropped in half to 33 percent.

Then, he made the disastrous decision to explain why he had dropped out of the race back in July. On Sunday, October 25, Perot appeared on the CBS news show *60 Minutes* and declared that he had dropped out of the race because he had been warned that Republican operatives intended to engage in a campaign of dirty tricks against him that would include disrupting his daughter's wedding and publicizing a doctored photo that would purport to show his daughter engaging in lesbian sex. The FBI was quoted saying it had looked into Perot's allegations, and there was no evidence to support them.

Public reaction to the interview and a subsequent news conference was "catastrophic," in the words of a Perot aide. Perot's favorable-unfavorable ratings flipped overnight from 56 percent positive and 34 percent negative to 44 percent positive and 46 percent negative. With only a week until Election Day, there was no time left to repair the damage.

Yet, on November 4, Perot still collected 19 percent of the popular vote. Only Theodore Roosevelt in 1912 had done better as a third party candidate. Perot won no states but finished second in two, behind Bush in Utah and behind Clinton in Maine. His level of support was remarkably consistent across the nation, and post-election surveys found 40 percent of voters would have considered voting for Perot if they had thought he could actually have won. This led Perot's running mate, Admiral James Stockdale, to declare, "Ross showed you don't have to talk to [ABC News political reporter] Sam Donaldson to get on television. Ross has shown that American candidates can now bypass the filters and go directly to the people."*

It was now clear, too, that Perot voters, despite their claim to being "zealots of the center," were generally disaffected Republicans. While Perot supporters professed to be equally turned off by the cultural conservatism of the Republicans and the economic liberalism of Democrats, post-election surveys discovered that more than 70 percent of Perot voters had voted for Bush in 1988, and another poll found 62 percent of Perot voters had supported Reagan in 1980 or 1984 or in both years.

What truly distinguished Perot's supporters was that, while they may have been consistent voters, usually supporting conservative candidates, they were not typically active in partisan politics as volunteers or donors. Not being active in a political party fed their sense of alienation from the political system as a whole and reinforced their belief that traditional politics had not been responsive to their concerns.

In 2010, the question arose whether the "Tea Party" movement was a descendant of the Perot movement. There were similarities in demographics, with both movements being overwhelmingly white, attracting

---

* Admiral Stockdale's role as Perot's running mate should be explained, given the mirth Stockdale's own vice presidential debate performance ("Who am I? Why am I here") caused. In order to get on the ballot in some states, Perot had to have a running mate listed. Stockdale, a courageous Vietnam POW and longtime acquaintance of Perot's, had been drafted into service as a surrogate running mate on the understanding he would later be replaced on the ticket. Perot had just begun to consider who his running mate might be when he dropped out of the race in July. When Perot got back in the race in October, there was no time to change the names on the ballots, so Stockdale stayed on the ticket.

more men than women, and involving people with income levels slightly above average. There were also shared concerns. Each began during times of economic distress, identified the budget deficit as a symbol of government failure, and professed to be composed of angry Washington outsiders who were previously not politically active.

But there was a considerable difference in ideology and purpose. While leaning Republican, Perot voters identified themselves as being far more ideologically diverse than the Tea Party movement. Exit polls found that 53 percent of Perot voters in 1992 described themselves as moderate, 27 percent called themselves conservative, and 20 percent liberal. Surveys of Tea Party adherents found three-quarters declared themselves conservative and one-quarter moderate. The Tea Party seemed an adjunct wing or more likely, as commentator E. J. Dionne said, "right-wing Republicans organized under a new banner," rather than an independent or third party movement. While the Tea Party, as of this writing, has been critical of past Republican leadership, its goal appears to be ensuring conservative control of the Republican Party, not mounting a challenge to the two-party system.

While Perot had run as an independent in 1992, he decided in 1995 to create the Reform Party as a credible and enduring alternative to the Republicans and Democrats. At first, it was not clear whether Perot intended to use the Reform Party to run again for president himself in 1996. He still had many devoted followers from the 1992 election—and he still had several billion dollars at his disposal. In May 1993, *U.S. News and World Report* announced, "Ross Perot may be the most important force in American politics." An economic nationalist, Perot was critical of the proposed North American Free Trade Agreement (NAFTA). With congressional ratification of NAFTA expected to be a near-run thing, the Clinton White House concluded it had to confront Perot directly. They challenged him to debate Vice President Al Gore on *Larry King Live* on November 9, 1993, before a record cable television audience of sixteen million viewers.

Gore, who tried to rattle Perot by sitting so close to him that their shoulders touched throughout the debate, projected calm, while Perot came across as testy, sarcastic, and evasive. Surveys showed support for NAFTA rose from 37 to 54 percent following the debate, while Perot's favorable rating plummeted from 66 to 29 percent. Perot's national political chances, born on Larry King's show in February 1992, basically died on Larry King's show twenty months later.

But Perot still had national ambitions. In 1996, the day after former Colorado governor Richard Lamm announced he would seek the Reform Party nomination, Perot announced his candidacy. Part of his rationale for entering the race was that the Federal Election Commission ruled the Reform Party would receive federal matching campaign funds only if Perot was the party's nominee since it was Perot who had qualified for the funds by running as an independent in 1992. But many in the party worried the Reform Party could not grow into a viable party as long as it was seen as a vanity vehicle for Perot. Continuing to experiment in how to engage voters outside the normal political process, the Reform Party did not hold a nominating convention but allowed interested party members to cast ballots for their nominee. Nearly fifty thousand participated and chose Perot over Lamm by a 65 to 35 percent margin. Lamm alleged the election was rigged, and so began years of legal wrangling that would ultimately ruin the Reform Party.

Perot intended to reprise his 1992 campaign strategy, but he suffered a large blow when he was excluded from the presidential debates this time. The Clinton campaign was happy to include Perot, believing he would siphon votes away from Republican nominee Bob Dole, but the GOP was adamant that Perot should not participate. Perot complained bitterly about being excluded from an event that would attract eighty million viewers, calling the decision "a blatant display of power by the Republicans and the large donors who fund their campaign."

More importantly, the political ground had shifted. The Republicans in Congress, led by Newt Gingrich, had made a bold play for Perot voters in the 1994 mid-term elections, winning back the House for the first time in forty years in large part by adopting key elements of Perot's reform agenda, including a call for term limits and a balanced budget amendment. The Republicans' "Contract with America" even mimicked

Perot's checklist for candidates that he had included in his materials for "United We Stand America," the formal name he had earlier given his reform movement. The disaffected Republicans who had made up the bulk of Perot's supporters had come home to the GOP. But there were other factors, too, that explain his diminished support. The economy was again prosperous, reducing voter discontent; NAFTA had not proved to be the disaster he had predicted; the Clinton administration had joined congressional Republicans in reforming the welfare system, a sign that it was not business as usual in Washington; and budget deficit projections were shrinking. Perot continued to air his infomercials, just as in 1992, but the campaign generated none of the excitement of four years before. Perot and his running mate, economist Pat Choate, received only 8.4 percent of the vote, less than half the 1992 count.

The Reform Party seemed as if it might yet remain a viable entity when, in 1998, former professional wrestler and talk radio host Jesse Ventura was elected governor of Minnesota with 37 percent of the vote as the Reform Party candidate. But Ventura had a rocky tenure as governor and declined to run for a second term. Still, Perot had done well enough in 1996 that the Reform Party was again qualified to be on the ballot in at least forty-eight states in 2000.

Were this book written in 2000, the Perot legacy would look much different from what it does today. Perot would be receiving credit not only for creating what seemed to be an ongoing viable third party, he would also be credited for being a driving force behind the remarkable budget deficit reductions that occurred during the 1990s. The Clinton administration, working with a predominantly Republican Congress, had picked up on Perot's deficit reduction theme. A smaller federal workforce, tax increases, and an economic boom fueled by the high-tech industry all combined to eliminate annual budget deficits and create annual budget surpluses. There was even talk of reducing the accumulated national debt, and what to do with the projected budget surpluses was a key issue during the 2000 presidential campaign.

But the 2000 election was the last hurrah for the Reform Party. Real estate developer Donald Trump initially announced he was interested in the party nomination but changed his mind, and the nomination instead went to conservative commentator Patrick Buchanan, who had sought the Republican nomination in 1992 and 1996. Buchanan tried to adopt some of Perot's economic nationalism for his platform, but he remained best known for his conservative views on social issues, such as abortion. Those Perot voters wanting nothing to do with the "culture wars" fought to form rival Reform Party entities in their respective states. Despite appearing on forty-eight state ballots, Buchanan won less than a half percent of the popular vote, and even Perot announced he had voted for Republican George W. Bush.

The ongoing legal battles among various local parties, each vying over which had the right to identify themselves as the official Reform Party entity, continued the party's decline. With Perot no longer funding the effort, the remnants of the Reform Party in 2004 simply chose to endorse the independent candidacy of Ralph Nader, who won barely a third of a percent of the popular vote. In 2008, the Reform Party qualified for the ballot in only a single state, Mississippi, where its presidential candidate, a local businessman, received fewer than five hundred votes.

More disheartening than the demise of the Reform Party was the reappearance of budget deficits. During the George W. Bush administration and the early years of Barack Obama's administration, a combination of events—the bursting of the tech and housing "bubbles," the terrorist attacks of September 11, 2001, the two ensuing costly wars waged in response to those attacks, large tax reductions, increased spending on entitlements, and the collapse of the world financial markets—conspired to balloon federal deficits once more and increase the federal cumulative debt to fourteen trillion dollars in 2011. Fourteen trillion dollars was more than twice the debt a decade before and more than three times the level that had alarmed Perot and his followers back in 1992.

Yet, Perot said virtually nothing publicly about the issue. He had all but disappeared from public view. In January 2008, he contacted *Newsweek* magazine to announce he was supporting former Massachusetts governor Mitt Romney, a successful businessman and the son of the founder of American Motors, instead of former POW and Arizona senator John

McCain in the Republican primary. He was still angry that McCain had called him "nuttier than a fruitcake" for persisting in his belief that there had been live POWs left behind in Southeast Asia.

Perot also told *Newsweek* that he had launched a website with the kind of charts and graphs he had used to such great effect in 1992 to again educate Americans about the problems he had talked about in his two presidential campaigns but were still not resolved. As of 2011, it did not seem the site was being regularly updated, except for a counter that showed the national debt increasing at the rate of one hundred thousand dollars per second. A polarized political establishment seemed unable to address the issue, leading conservative *New York Times* columnist David Brooks to wonder if what the nation needed now was "a saner Perot."

Chapter Eleven

AL GORE, JOHN KERRY, AND JOHN McCAIN

2000, 2004, 2008

"I'm the ... loyal opposition. And both words, I think, are operative."
—*John McCain*

In a nation that has fretted for decades over whether it has properly honored its Vietnam War veterans, it is ironic that the three presidential nominees who served in Vietnam—Al Gore, John F. Kerry, and John McCain—were all defeated, while the two men of the Vietnam generation who were elected president did not serve in Vietnam. Bill Clinton avoided military service entirely, while George W. Bush spent the war stateside as a member of the Texas Air National Guard.

At one level, it is remarkable that Gore, Kerry, and McCain served overseas during an unpopular war, since many sons from wealthy, prominent, or well-connected families successfully avoided service. Each of the three was, after all, in the words of the Creedence Clearwater Revival anti-war song, a "fortunate son," born into privilege. Gore was the son of a three-term U.S. senator; Kerry, a descendant of two of Massachusetts's most prominent families; and McCain was the son and grandson of admirals.

Yet each bucked the conventional wisdom of the time to serve, partly out of family obligation, partly out of idealism, and partly under the misapprehension that a military record would be necessary to pursue

a career in public service. When Gore sought advice about whether to enlist in the army and risk being sent to Vietnam, one of his Harvard professors, Richard Neustadt, told him, "If you want to be part of the country twenty-five years from now, if you want any future in politics, you've got to serve." Neustadt later ruefully acknowledged that he had given that advice from "a World War II perspective that didn't prove to be exactly right."

While their status as veterans may not have been key to their later political success, their service certainly helped define Gore, Kerry, and McCain as different from other politicians of their generation who avoided service and as individuals who struggled with concepts of honor and duty more familiar to earlier generations of Americans. Similarly, these unsuccessful presidential candidates are, each in their own way, bucking the recent convention that losing presidential candidates should quietly fade from view. Instead, as they did in their decision to serve in Vietnam, they are looking to past traditions to reclaim a level of influence and power that losing presidential candidates once enjoyed. For this reason, this chapter looks at their experiences collectively to see if the role of presidential loser is being redefined.

Gore, who won the popular vote but lost the presidency to Bush in 2000, traded in the role of politician for prophet. Like William Jennings Bryan nearly a century ago, Gore has used his prestige to promote a cause in which politics intersects with science. The difference between the two is that Bryan staked his legacy on persuading the public to *be wary of* scientific consensus around the theory of evolution, while Gore's struggle is to persuade the public simply to *accept* scientific consensus around the issue of global climate change and do something about it.

In 2007, for his work in sounding the alarm to the danger of global climate change, Gore won the Nobel Peace Prize—an unprecedented honor for a losing presidential candidate. Indeed, only four presidents have ever won the Nobel Prize: Theodore Roosevelt, Woodrow Wilson, Jimmy Carter, and Barack Obama. But Gore also won prizes that no president has ever won: a Grammy for the spoken word version of his book, *An Inconvenient Truth*, and an Emmy for his global television network, Current TV, an "interactive television service" that gives viewers the power to create and influence content. Gore was also the subject of the Academy Award–winning documentary on climate change, *An Inconvenient Truth*, and he has authored several best-selling books.

Defeated by Bush in 2004, Kerry defied expectations by returning to the Senate in the unusually prominent and influential role of chair of the Senate Foreign Relations Committee. Some suggested that Kerry, because of his exceptionally proactive efforts to promote free and fair elections in the Muslim world, had become a "de facto" secretary of state. As Jimmy Carter once earned the reputation of being the most active ex-president in recent American history, admirers said Kerry was determined to become the "best ex-presidential nominee."

Kerry's role during President Barack Obama's administration parallels Adlai Stevenson's relationship with President John F. Kennedy—though Obama seemed more receptive to Kerry's mentoring than Kennedy was to Stevenson's. Both Stevenson and Kerry had hoped to be appointed secretary of state but were passed over by the young presidents they wished to serve. So they assumed different influential roles regarding foreign policy, though again, Kerry seemed to have the better arrangement as chair of Senate Foreign Relations, while Stevenson held the less effective post of ambassador to the United Nations.

McCain, who lost to Obama in 2008, spurred considerable comment when he broke with recent tradition and became an immediate, prominent, and harsh critic of Obama and many of his policies. McCain's decision to attack Obama's policies within weeks of Obama assuming office led the *New York Times* to comment in a front-page article in March 2009 that McCain was "rewriting the part of presidential loser." McCain responded, "I'm the, as I said, loyal opposition. And both words, I think, are operative."

During the second half of the twentieth century, losing candidates generally afforded the winning candidate at least a short grace period during which they withheld criticism. But McCain was not "rewriting" the part of presidential loser as much as he—like Kerry and Gore— was returning to an older script. In attacking Obama for "leading an extreme, left wing crusade to bankrupt America," McCain evoked memories of Henry Clay's denunciations of Andrew Jackson's supposed pretensions to monarchy or Al Smith's excoriating Herbert Hoover for the ills of the nation's Great Depression. There was a time when a losing candidate stayed in the fray, and McCain's attacks only seemed shocking when compared with the way our more recent losing presidential candidates quietly absented themselves from the public arena.

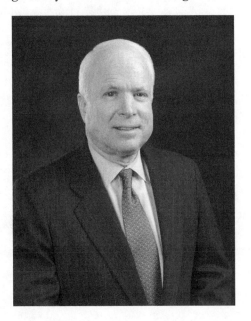

Bob Dole resigned from the Senate during his 1996 presidential campaign and was only modestly involved in politics after his loss to Clinton. Michael Dukakis finished out his final term as governor of Massachusetts but then devoted most of his time following his 1988 defeat to teaching at colleges in Massachusetts and California. Walter Mondale was urged to run for the Senate again after his defeat in 1984, but he declined. He had noted the cool reception George McGovern and Hubert Humphrey had received from their peers when they returned to the Senate following their defeats. "It's never the same when they come back," Mondale said. Mondale served as U.S. ambassador to Japan under Clinton and was finally drafted back into the senatorial election arena in 2002 as a last-minute replacement when Senator Paul Wellstone died, but he lost.

McGovern, who returned to the Senate after losing to Richard Nixon in 1972, and Humphrey, who returned to the Senate two years after losing to Nixon in 1968, had hoped to be acknowledged leaders and spokesmen for their party. They had plenty to say, but few were interested in their opinions. After Humphrey's loss to Nixon in 1968, he was not invited to speak at any Democratic Party function for almost a year. He was even rejected by his colleagues in his bid to become Senate majority leader, despite his previous prominence as a senator and vice president. His peers felt so guilty about the rebuff that they created a new honorary post, deputy president pro tempore, just for Humphrey.

McGovern famously gave a speech at Oxford University on the day of Nixon's second inauguration in which he claimed "the United States is closer to one-man rule than at any time in our history." McGovern was chastised for what he was told was "unsportsmanlike conduct toward my victorious rival," and *New York Times* columnist Joseph Kraft added that McGovern should have had "the grace to keep quiet for a while."

But this notion that the presidential loser should keep quiet is relatively new. Clay was merciless in his attacks on Jackson whom he believed to be, as McCain was said to believe of Obama, unqualified for the presidency. Bryan led the campaign against President William McKinley's "imperialist" ambitions in the Philippines. Thomas Dewey, after first excoriating the conservative wing of his own party for wanting to "turn back the clock" to the "good old days of the nineteenth century," turned his fire on the Democrats by charging in the summer of 1949 that Truman seemed determined to "throw China into the bottom of the Pacific Ocean."

Stevenson, too, had no qualms about challenging the policies of Eisenhower and the Republicans weeks after Ike took office. On February 11, 1953, Stevenson gave a highly regarded speech in New York City, which he concluded with an attack on Wisconsin senator Joseph McCarthy and his supporters for laying "rough hands" on the Bill of Rights. Traveling on to Washington, D.C., the next day, Stevenson was greeted by hundreds of cheering Democratic congressmen and their aides—a different welcome from what McGovern or Humphrey received.

In making public attacks so soon after an election, Clay, Bryan, Dewey, and Stevenson were acting in the unofficial capacity as the titular leader of their party, a post that seems to have disappeared in recent decades, though it seemed McCain was trying to resurrect the title. Being the titular leader of a political party is unique to the American form of democracy. Unlike a parliamentary democracy, there is no official leader of the opposition party in American politics who can speak on behalf of the party. That duty is often split among the opposition party leaders in Congress, the party chair, and those most likely to obtain the party nomination the next election cycle.

But there was a time when the most recent presidential loser was automatically considered the de facto spokesperson for the party out of power until the party nominated someone else. But the last person generally acknowledged as the titular leader of a nonpresidential party was Stevenson, who held that title from 1952 until the Democrats nominated Kennedy in 1960. Richard Nixon had disqualified himself for the role by his behavior following his loss in the California governor's race in 1962, and the dimensions of Barry Goldwater's defeat in 1964 sent Republicans immediately searching for a new standard-bearer.

Observers debated whether McCain attempted to resurrect the title following his 2008 loss to Obama. The news media seemed intent on bestowing it upon him. In the first two years after his loss to Obama, McCain appeared on the prestigious Sunday morning news interview shows more than two dozen times—far more appearances than any other official, Republican or Democrat, during the same time period. Also, in contrast to McGovern's and Humphrey's return to relative anonymity, McCain returned as the ranking Republican on the powerful Senate Armed Services Committee, which made him a particularly sought-after spokesman for the Republican Party on foreign and military affairs.

Because the concept of a titular head of a party had disappeared for a half-century, McCain's behavior was carefully scrutinized. Commentators debated whether McCain was speaking out on principle or whether he was simply bitter and envious of Obama's victory.

While the McCain-Obama race was not particularly vitriolic by the standards of past presidential campaigns, Obama's status as the first African-American presidential nominee added a new tension to the contest, as did the economic crisis that engulfed the globe during the final months of the campaign. As noted in chapter one, there was genuine concern during the campaign that the ill will would not abate following the election, but McCain then gave his exceptionally gracious concession speech and tempers seemed to cool almost at once. Then there were some commentators who went too far the other way and suggested that McCain and Obama might develop a partnership similar to that enjoyed between Franklin Roosevelt and Wendell Willkie.

That alliance did not happen in the first few years after the campaign in part because McCain had developed a negative opinion of Obama well before their campaign began. While both were in the Senate, McCain accused Obama of reneging on a deal for the two of them to work together on Senate ethics reform. He questioned whether Obama had the courage to stand up to the special interests in his party as McCain had proudly dissented from Republican positions on so many occasions. But there were also those who thought that McCain was simply jealous of the news media's infatuation with Obama. Obama, meanwhile, sensed McCain's disrespect and returned it in kind.

Obama had been in the Oval Office less than a month when McCain began complaining that the administration was not reaching out in the spirit of bipartisanship, and friends said McCain was miffed that Obama did not reach out to him as the leader of the opposition party to help craft legislation. McCain became an especially harsh critic of Obama's proposals to reform the nation's health insurance system, a measure that received virtually no Republican support. When Obama convened a summit with Republican and Democratic members of Congress to discuss how to forge a bipartisan compromise, McCain attended and chided Obama for failing to live up to his campaign promises. Obama interrupted, saying "the election's over," to which McCain testily responded, "I'm reminded of that every day."

McCain was known for having a sharp temper. Further, friends have said that McCain's survival through more than five horrific years as a prisoner of war in North Vietnam left him with the conviction that he had a destiny to fulfill. Having also lost to Bush in the 2000 Republican presidential primaries, McCain was twice denied the presidency by men he deemed less deserving than himself.

Following the 2000 election, McCain had been a thorn in the side of Bush's presidency, too, and seemed to relish thumbing his nose at Republican orthodoxy. He pushed his McCain-Feingold campaign finance legislation into law over Republican objections, he broke from the GOP position to support a patient's "bill of rights" in the regulation of health management organizations, supported more stringent background checks for certain gun purchases, and initially opposed significant elements of Bush's proposed tax cuts. McCain's unorthodox positions even led Kerry to send feelers out to determine if McCain would consider being his running mate in 2004 on a type of "national unity" ticket—an idea McCain quickly dismissed as unfeasible.

Realizing that his "maverick" status, if unabated, could alienate the Republican base and cost him his last chance at the Republican presidential nomination, McCain began altering a number of his positions during the 2008 campaign. The McCain who had once advocated reform that included a path to citizenship for illegal immigrants now focused almost exclusively on border security. The McCain who had initially voted against the Bush tax cuts now favored extending them. The McCain who had once opposed repeal of the *Roe v. Wade* Supreme Court decision on abortion now said repeal "wouldn't bother me any"— and he claimed to no longer even favor rape and incest as exceptions where abortion might be appropriate.

McCain seemed to have abandoned even his signature issue, campaign finance reform, and dropped his support for a cap and trade system to combat climate change and instead strongly supported more domestic drilling for oil. Most disconcerting of all to many of his admirers, given the moral authority on which he, as a former POW, could talk about torture, he brokered a "compromise" with the Bush administration on how it could treat detainees accused of terrorist activities. Critics said the policy allowed the administration to ignore the Geneva Convention if it chose to do so.

After Obama's election, McCain continued to tack to the right. He had previously said he would favor allowing gay men and women to serve openly in the military once the joint chiefs of staff endorsed the idea, yet when the joint chiefs did so in 2010, McCain maintained his opposition. McCain even denied that he had ever considered himself a political "maverick," when that had been a key theme of his presidential campaigns. Some credited this shift to the political right to McCain's having a strong Senate primary challenge in 2010 from someone even more conservative than he. Friends also say the 2008 campaign changed McCain. A former chief of staff, Grant Woods, acknowledged that McCain's views on immigration, for example, changed in part because he felt betrayed by Hispanic voters, who overwhelmingly supported Obama despite McCain's years of championing immigration reform. "When you carry that fight at great sacrifice year after year and then you are abandoned during the biggest fight of your life, it has to have some sort of effect on you," he said.

Others insist it was all a manifestation of McCain's ornery temperament. *Washington Post* columnist Dana Milbank said it was McCain's "antipathy toward President George W. Bush [that] led him to seek common cause with Democrats to thwart a Republican president. Now his antipathy toward President Obama has made him a leading Republican hardliner." McCain allies countered that a liberal news media had been quick to applaud McCain's differences with a Republican president as "courageous" but now expressed disapproval when he did not offer uniform support to a Democratic one. Some observers believe he took certain positions just to earn media coverage, and others simply believe he enjoyed "being a pain in the ass." There was "an element of truth in each charge," McCain said.

It may also be true that a news media awed by McCain's Vietnam experience simply misjudged McCain's fundamental political philosophy, that while he cast some votes counter to Republican orthodoxy he was, as one friend said, "fundamentally . . . very conservative." Perhaps, but the record indicates McCain became far more conservative after Obama's election. A *National Journal* analysis of one hundred key votes found McCain tied with four other senators as the most conservative member of the Senate in 2010. More typically in his career, the *National Journal* said, McCain had ranked as "near the 45th" most conservative member of the Senate, which meant that he had previously been one of the least conservative Republican members of the Senate.

If McCain's visibility was due to a sense of obligation to lead opposition to the Democratic agenda because he was the most recent Republican standard bearer, then he was simply returning to a tradition only recently abandoned. But even though McCain, seventy-two years old when he ran in 2008, is unlikely to seek the presidency again, aides said McCain intended to stay politically relevant. One aide told *Vanity Fair* in 2010 that service in the Senate is "McCain's whole life, his reason for being," and another said there is no chance McCain will one day "go off and set up a global education foundation."

No losing presidential nominee has been named secretary of state since Charles Evans Hughes in 1921. Kerry had hoped to become Obama's first secretary of state, a post that went instead to Hillary Clinton. Descended from the prominent Winthrop and Forbes families, Kerry's father was a career Foreign Service officer, giving young Kerry an interest in foreign affairs almost from birth. His family moved around the world, including time spent in divided Berlin, where an adolescent Kerry once snuck into the Communist half of the city. In part to keep young John out of such trouble, Kerry was sent to boarding school in Switzerland.

While this background enhanced Kerry's deep interest in foreign affairs, it also left him without a sense of place, of being from some-where.* Back in the States, Kerry continued to struggle to fit in at the exclusive St. Paul's preparatory school in New Hampshire, where his relative lack of wealth, his Catholic faith, and his Democratic politics stood out among the preppie WASP student body. Kerry would later bond with Obama, friends said, as a "fellow outsider."

---

* This was a problem that McCain and Gore faced as well, with McCain attending roughly twenty schools as the son of a roving naval officer and Gore being raised primarily in a Washington, D.C., hotel.

Their shared politics, faith, and initials led Kerry to adopt John F. Kennedy as his political hero. Kerry even once had the opportunity while still a schoolboy to go sailing with Kennedy, and he had briefly dated Jackie Kennedy's half-sister. Kerry joined the Navy after a Kennedy aide came to Yale following Kennedy's assassination and told the students that serving in Vietnam would help fulfill Kennedy's legacy. Kerry even became skipper of patrolling gunboats known as "Swift boats," similar to the PT boats Kennedy had commanded during World War II.

Kerry's war record would be a matter of some dispute during his presidential campaign, but official records label him an aggressive commander who earned three Purple Hearts, the Silver Star, and a Bronze Star. Disenchanted with the war, after his discharge he became active in the Vietnam Veterans Against the War. Well spoken and well groomed, Kerry, the former champion debater, was viewed by the Nixon administration as perhaps the most dangerous anti-war protester in the country.

In testimony before the Senate Foreign Relations Committee in April 1971, Kerry famously asked, "How do you ask a man to be the last man to die for a mistake?" But he also earned the enmity of many veterans and others when he alleged that American atrocities in Vietnam were not isolated incidents, but were widespread, systemic war crimes that represented the "accepted policy" of the U.S. military and government.

Kerry used his renown as an anti-war activist to launch a political career. He chose Massachusetts as his home, though in his second bid for Congress he betrayed his lack of roots by establishing residence in three separate congressional districts while he mulled which one to run in. Choosing the Fifth Congressional District, Kerry tried to connect with district residents when he proclaimed, "I learned to walk in the Fifth District," a reference to the year his family lived there when he was a toddler.

After losing congressional races in 1970 and 1972, Kerry took a ten-year break from electoral politics while he finished law school and became a prosecutor. In 1982, he was elected Massachusetts's lieutenant governor and two years later was elected to the U.S. Senate. For twenty-five years, Kerry seemed "the perpetual junior senator from Massachusetts" as he served in the shadow of the state's senior senator, Edward Kennedy.

Never particularly interested in legislation, Kerry instead led investigations into U.S. foreign policy. His efforts helped spur congressional inquiry into what became known as the Iran-Contra scandal. Later, he and McCain, bonded by their war experience, spearheaded the effort to normalize relations with Vietnam.

Kerry's fascination with foreign affairs led to some snide remarks back in Massachusetts that Kerry had become "senator for the world." At times, he seemed the caricature of a senator, a man with a stentorian speaking style that struck many as pompous. His positions were often so nuanced that it seemed he could argue both sides of an issue with equal conviction with one journalist concluding, "He lacks a center of gravity." In 2004, however, he seemed the ideal presidential nominee for the Democrats.

The circumstances around the 2000 election immediately gave Democrats high hopes of recapturing the White House in 2004 as George W. Bush entered office in controversy and his term began sluggishly. Then, on September 11, 2001, Islamic extremists from the group Al-Qaeda flew hijacked commercial airliners into the twin towers of the World Trade Center and the Pentagon, while a fourth plane crashed in rural Pennsylvania. All told, some three thousand people were killed in the terrorist attacks, and the nation rallied to Bush and his call to take the fight to the perpetrators of this evil act.

Bush had widespread support for attacking Afghanistan, where Al-Qaeda's leaders were believed to be hiding with the support of that nation's Taliban government. But when Bush then expanded the war to include Iraq, even though there was no provable link between Iraq and the terrorist attacks, his support began to erode. American forces had quickly overrun Iraq and deposed its dictator, Saddam Hussein, but the United States government seemed unprepared for what to do with Iraq once it was conquered. An insurgency against the American occupation would eventually claim the lives of more than four thousand American servicemen and women.

But the Democrats were wary of being too aggressive in challenging Bush and the wars. In 2002, Republicans had made electoral gains by charging Democratic candidates with being weak on what Bush termed "the war on terror." Even Georgia Democratic senator Max Cleland, who lost both legs and an arm as a soldier in the Vietnam War, was defeated for re-election after his patriotism was challenged because he had questioned the constitutionality of some Bush policies. Democrats wanted a presidential candidate who could correct the course of U.S. foreign policy but be inoculated against charges of being unpatriotic. Kerry, the former war hero turned anti-war activist, fit the image.

Kerry reinforced the desired narrative in his nomination acceptance speech at the Democratic National Convention, which he began with a sharp salute and the greeting, "I'm John Kerry and I'm reporting for duty." Not surprisingly, the service records of Kerry and Bush immediately were scrutinized. Kerry seemed dumbfounded that his record was challenged by veterans still angry about his earlier allegations of atrocities committed by U.S. GIs, while Bush seemed to get a pass for sitting out the war while in the National Guard.

Kerry's greater problem, however, was public unease about his authenticity. Most famously, in explaining his nuanced position on the war in Iraq, Kerry explained, "I voted for the bill before I voted against it," which might be understood in the context of a discussion of Robert's Rules of Order, but which in a presidential campaign made Kerry seem indecisive and insincere. Still, Kerry would have been president had he been able to carry Ohio. Instead, Bush eked out a narrow win with 50.7 percent of the popular vote.

Having come so close, Kerry intended to seek the Democratic nomination again in 2008, but, as recent presidential losers have discovered, there was little enthusiasm for a second Kerry candidacy and what little there was evaporated as a result of what Kerry called "a botched joke." Speaking to a group of California college students in October 2006, Kerry said, "You know, education, if you make the most of it, you study hard, you do your homework and you make an effort to be smart, you can do well. If you don't, you get stuck in Iraq." Republicans immediately charged Kerry with insulting American troops by suggesting that they were serving only because they were poor students. Kerry explained that he had left out the key word "us," as in "you get us stuck in Iraq," an allusion to Bush allegedly lacking the smarts to avoid an unnecessary war. But even Democrats criticized the remark and distanced themselves from Kerry, going so far as to cancel campaign appearances with him. A few months later, Kerry announced he would not be a candidate for president in 2008.

Instead, he became a key early supporter of Obama, who was engaged in a tremendous battle for the Democratic nomination with New York senator and former first lady Hillary Clinton. Obama aides gushed that Kerry was "doing everything he's asked and keeping his advice confidential." Kerry even became a point man in attacking McCain, the man he had asked to be his running mate just four years before. He charged McCain with taking "the low road express" in his campaign against Obama. Pundits were amazed that the usually circuitous and long-winded Kerry now spoke for Obama "in more forceful terms than he'd ever used during [his own] presidential campaign."

Kerry had hoped his service in the campaign would lead to his appointment as secretary of state. But, like Stevenson, he was passed over for the post when Obama tapped Hillary Clinton instead. Kerry then threw himself into his duties as chair of the Foreign Relations Committee. In explaining his new sense of purpose, a Kerry advisor said, "I think he's decided that he wants to be a senator." Kerry received kudos for his deftness in handling a variety of foreign policy crises. In 2009, he personally helped avert even more chaos in Afghanistan when he persuaded Afghan president Hamid Karzai to agree to a runoff election after an earlier election had been marred by allegations of fraud. The result was hailed as a "diplomatic triumph" for Kerry and led some to suggest that Obama was now using him as a "de facto secretary of state," an assertion that Kerry, formerly known for his tendency toward "self-aggrandizement," dismissed as inappropriate.

Kerry continued to represent American interests in additional crises, including the popular uprisings against Arab dictatorships in 2011, and he was widely credited with playing a critical role in finally securing Senate ratification of a new arms control treaty with Russia. These efforts and their results led to speculation that Kerry might yet join Hughes,

Bryan, James G. Blaine, Lewis Cass, and Clay by someday becoming the first losing presidential candidate in more than three-quarters of a century to serve as secretary of state.

~

Born into privilege, Gore, Kerry, and McCain were also born with extremely high expectations that they would make their mark upon the world. Friends and observers even speculated that the loss of the presidency was actually a liberating experience for each man. Freed from the weight of obligation their upbringing had forced upon them, they could now do what they wanted to do and pursue their interests and passions unfettered by political calculation. This theory seemed especially true of Gore, who was molded from birth by his ambitious parents to become president of the United States just as surely as Tiger Woods was groomed to be a golf prodigy. When Gore was tapped to be Bill Clinton's running mate in 1992, his beaming father, former three-term Tennessee senator Albert Gore Sr., gushed, "We raised him for it!"

Earnest, dutiful, and clean-cut, Gore has been described as "an old person's idea of a young person." It was to serve and please his father that Gore entered the Army. His father was facing a tough fight for re-election in 1970, and Gore did not want his father having a son of draft age who avoided military service to be a campaign issue. Gore was one of only about a dozen young men out of a graduating class of more than eleven hundred at Harvard who would serve in Vietnam. Gore did not see combat but served in Vietnam as a military journalist. After the war, he worked as a reporter and editor at the *Nashville Tennessean*, earned his law degree, and studied at divinity school. He won his first congressional seat in 1976, moved up to the Senate in 1984, and was pressured by his father to run for president in 1988 even though he was only thirty-nine years old. Gore Sr., then eighty years old, did not want to die before seeing his son elected president.

Having lost the 1988 Democratic presidential nomination to Dukakis, Gore was mulling whether to pursue the presidency again in 1992 when he experienced what he described as a life-altering event. In

April 1989, while leaving a Baltimore Orioles baseball game with his family, his six-year-old son Albert broke free from his grasp, ran into the street, and was hit by a car, sustaining life-threatening injuries. While helping to nurse his son back to health, Gore thought more deeply about what moved him and what he wanted to accomplish in the world. He had once considered himself a leading congressional expert on environmental issues. He realized that environmentalism was the international concern he most cared about, and so he began researching and writing a book with the working title *The New World War*.

Gore had first learned about the problem of global warming as an undergraduate at Harvard from professor Roger Revelle, the first scientist to catalogue the amount of carbon dioxide in the atmosphere and to chart its apparent impact. The theory, endorsed by the bulk of the world's climatologists, is that greenhouse gases, most especially carbon dioxide, are entering the earth's atmosphere at record levels because of humans burning carbon fuels for energy and transportation. These gases trap heat in the atmosphere, raising the average global temperature, which has a number of potential impacts, including melting the polar ice caps, thereby raising the world's sea level, and changing weather patterns to devastating effect.

Working without a ghostwriter, Gore began what came to be titled *Earth in the Balance* in the fall of 1989, and the book was published in January 1992. Drawing on his time in divinity school, Gore, a Baptist, infused the work with spiritual musings and biblical quotations that direct humanity to care for creation. His main recommendation was for the multinational creation and funding of a "Global Marshall Plan" to educate the public about the dangers of climate change and overpopulation, and to fund investment in new technologies to replace the internal combustion engine. The book was well reviewed and became a best seller.

But his father's dream intruded again when Clinton chose Gore to be his vice president. Following the model established by Mondale, Gore was an active and influential vice president. Clinton had chosen him, not only because they were in sync as moderate, young, Southern Democrats, but also because he was told Gore was loyal and would never embarrass him in public. Gore could not say the same of Clinton. While publicly he remained loyal to the president during the Monica Lewinsky scandal and ensuing impeachment trial, privately Gore indicated to aides that he knew Clinton had lied to him when he said he had not had sex with Lewinsky, a White House intern.

When it was confirmed that Clinton had lied about having an affair with Lewinsky, Gore, partly out of political calculation and partly because of his own rectitude, made the fateful decision to disassociate himself from Clinton when he ran for president in 2000. He declined to involve Clinton in campaign strategy, and he declined to have Clinton campaign on his behalf. His choice of a running mate, Connecticut senator Joe Lieberman, the first practicing Jew to ever serve on a national ticket, was also seen as a rebuke to Clinton because Lieberman had been among the most vocal Democrats in condemning Clinton's behavior. Gore even declined to run on Clinton's record of peace and prosperity that he could have plausibly argued was his record as well. Gore, after all, had done an especially fine job heading up the administration's "reinventing government" initiative that reduced the size of the federal civilian workforce by more than four hundred thousand positions. Instead, Gore rejected Clinton's governing philosophy of centrist "triangulation" and adopted an aggressive populist tone, which he labelled—in shades of Bryan—a fight between "the people vs. the powerful."

In hindsight, it was the wrong strategy for the wrong time. The 1990s had been a time of exceptional economic growth and one of the key points of debate in 2000 was how to spend (or not spend) the new federal budget surplus. It was not a period of deep class resentment. Gore had also misjudged public sentiment regarding Clinton. Certainly, almost everyone disapproved of the president's dalliance with a young woman half his age—and doing so right in the White House—but in impeaching the president, a majority of the public believed Republicans in Congress had gone too far. Gore's populist message also did not match up well against his opponent. The affable Bush had pledged to govern as a "compassionate conservative"; he was not a reactionary who spurred deep anxiety among the working-class.

Yet, Gore still won! The popular vote, that is, by a margin of a half-million votes. He did not win the presidency, however.

On election night, it all came down to the state of Florida. More than six million ballots had been cast in the state. Initially, the television networks called the state for Gore, then reversed themselves a few hours later and called it for Bush. Gore immediately placed a congratulatory call to Bush. Perhaps he was simply trying to do the right thing, the gracious thing. Perhaps he understood that he was only fifty-two years old and would have time to try again, and did not want to be labeled a sore loser. Whatever his motivation, the call was reported in all the news outlets and it appeared the election was over.

But as Gore was travelling to downtown Nashville to give his public concession speech, his staff intercepted him with news that Bush's winning margin in Florida had been shrinking throughout the night and early morning hours. The last count had Bush ahead by only a few hundred votes. Further, there were reports of widespread problems during balloting, particularly in Palm Beach County, where the design of the ballot had confused elderly voters and had reportedly prevented them from casting their votes as they intended for Gore. Gore retracted his telephoned concession to Bush.

The premature concession was probably Gore's largest tactical mistake. Once he had conceded, in the public's mind, it was now up to Gore to provide the incontrovertible evidence that the result already reported by the networks should be reversed. Gore, repeating the mistake made by Samuel Tilden in 1876, also initially tackled the problem as if it were technical or legal in nature, rather than an extension of the political campaign. The Republicans were much more successful in characterizing the dispute as sour grapes from a Democratic ticket they gleefully labeled "Sore-Loserman." Gore also faced a serious obstacle in that the chief election official in Florida, Secretary of State Katherine Harris, was an ambitious Republican and the state's governor, Jeb Bush, was Bush's brother.

Democratic appointees, however, dominated the Florida Supreme Court. That court was willing to allow a recount of ballots in three counties selected by Gore as having the greatest likelihood of ballot problems.

This was a third tactical mistake. In not simply calling for a statewide recount, it appeared Gore was trying to "cherry pick" those counties where he expected to pick up votes, while Republicans said Gore was passing over counties where a recount might favor Bush.

Unlike 1876, when there had been an electoral commission consisting of members of Congress and the U.S. Supreme Court, this time the Supreme Court alone intervened in the case. On a partisan 5-4 vote, the court halted the Florida recount, allowing the Republican-controlled Florida Legislature to award the state's electoral votes to Bush, ending the election on December 12, 2000. The court indicated that its decision was "limited to the present circumstances" and created no precedent for how future courts might decide a similar impasse.

The next day, Gore gave a remarkably cheerful and upbeat concession speech. He said he had called Bush to congratulate him on "becoming" president, adding, "And I promised I wouldn't call him back this time." Gore quoted Stephen Douglas's pledge to Abraham Lincoln upon losing the 1860 presidential election, "Partisan feeling must yield to patriotism. I'm with you Mr. President, and God bless you." After urging his supporters and the nation to rally around the new president, Gore announced, "It's time for me to go."

For the first year after his loss in 2000, Gore "disappeared so completely from national life that people thought of putting his face on milk cartons," joked a *New York Times* writer. He grew a beard and gained weight. According to one of his key political consultants, Bob Shrum, Gore had already decided he would never again run for president, but publicly he insisted he was keeping his options open. By late summer 2001, he prepared to re-enter the debate and planned to attack some of Bush's policies in a speech to Iowa Democrats when the terrorists attacked on 9/11. Gore changed his speech to pledge his support for Bush "in this time of crisis."

He remained restless. He and his wife, Tipper, published a book on the American family in 2002. (The couple would separate in 2010.) Asked in 2007 when she and her husband got over the disappointment of 2000, Mrs. Gore looked at her watch and laughed, "What time is it now?" Trying to get her husband out of his funk, Mrs. Gore suggested he resurrect the slideshow he had originally prepared while writing *Earth in the Balance*. Always interested in new technology, Gore replaced the slideshow with computer graphics and began traveling the country, warning of the danger of global climate change that he attributed to humans spewing trillions of tons of carbon dioxide into the atmosphere through our burning of carbon fuels.

The presentations were not reaching a large audience, and in the wake of 9/11, Americans seemed more concerned about security than a potential environmental catastrophe that few understood. Then, in April 2005, Gore gave his slideshow in Beverly Hills at the request of Hollywood producer Laurie David. In the audience was another producer, Lawrence Bender. Upon seeing Gore's presentation, Bender thought, "This has got to be a movie." As the movie was being filmed in the summer of that year, Hurricane Katrina devastated the Gulf Coast and generated public debate on whether the world's weather patterns were changing. The movie, *An Inconvenient Truth*, was shown at the Sundance Film Festival in January 2006, and by May it was widely distributed throughout America, becoming a surprise hit. It won the Oscar for best documentary film, and the companion book sold one million copies.

"Al Gore may have done for global warming what 'Silent Spring' did for pesticides," wrote James Hansen, then director of the NASA Goddard Institute for Space Studies. Admirers gushed that the formerly stiff and reserved Gore had undergone a "rediscovery of his hidden self." No longer "a hamster locked in the cage of a broken political process," Gore, who had so long played the role of "Dudley Do-Right," was "generating far more political capital by breaking the political rules than he did by obeying them."

He also seemed to be having fun. To continue to raise awareness of climate change, Gore helped produce "Live Earth," a concert broadcast to all seven continents (including Antarctica) via satellite that featured some of the most popular music performers in the world. Seen in more than one hundred countries, it was estimated that one billion people saw at least part of the event.

Gore had long been interested in how new media could link people together as a community, particularly in the cause of democracy.*

---

* Gore was famously ridiculed for allegedly claiming to have "invented" the Internet. He made no such claim. He did author legislation, signed into law in 1991, that expanded access to the Internet, which had been solely the province of the federal government, to libraries and schools.

Gore has called democracy a "conversation," and he has charged television with destroying that conversation because it involves only one-way communication. He has noted that 80 percent of the money raised in political campaigns is spent on thirty-second television ads that are "a manipulative exercise utilizing the tools of persuasion." Gore has said the goal of his Current TV project is the "democratization" of television news by providing alternative viewpoints to what is normally heard on network and cable news, including from the viewers themselves.

Here, Gore was echoing William Jennings Bryan as a sophisticated user and critic of the news media. Bryan, in order to have his own message delivered unfiltered to the masses, created his own newspaper, the *Commoner*. In one of his first editorials, Bryan, like Gore, said his use of the media was designed to urge the average citizen to join the cause and "contribute by brain and muscle to the nation's strength and greatness." The *Commoner* grew so large in circulation that, adjusted for the change in population, if around today it would dwarf the readership enjoyed by such influential publications as the *Nation*, the *New Republic*, and the *National Review*. Current TV has had a more modest start. Critics said some programming was so crude that it appeared to have been produced in someone's basement, like the *Saturday Night Live* skit "Wayne's World." In prime time, in early 2011, its programming was viewed by only an average of twenty-six thousand households, but Gore announced plans to broaden the network's appeal, in part by hiring populist broadcaster Keith Olbermann and populist filmmaker Michael Moore.

Gore's faith in the project could not be discounted, for he had already attained the highly improbable when, in 2007, he won the biggest prize of all, the Nobel Peace Prize, which he shared with the Intergovernmental Panel on Climate Change. Gore's winning the prize seemed to provide considerable momentum to address climate change in the United States. A significant number of states, particularly in New England and on the West Coast, were moving forward to develop a "cap and trade" program designed to put a price on carbon in order to reduce emissions.

There was optimism in 2008 that the federal government would also take action during the next administration as both the Republican presidential nominee, McCain, and the Democratic nominee, Obama, stated that they accepted the scientific explanation that climate change was occurring, that it was at least partially human-caused, and that, unabated, climate change could have devastating effects. But the world financial collapse and subsequent efforts to stimulate economic growth put climate change on the back burner. In addition to his attempts to stimulate the economy, President Obama used the bulk of his political capital to push through legislation to reform the nation's health insurance system and dropped administration efforts to address climate change through legislation, though he did direct the Environmental Protection Agency to outline how carbon emissions could be reduced through regulation.

Meanwhile, McCain changed his view on climate change during the 2008 election and joined an increasing number of conservative Republicans who questioned the science—or who concluded the cure would be worse than the disease. Gore soldiered on, continuing his slideshow but with less acclaim than he had enjoyed a few years before.

The questioning by others of what he believed to be incontrovertible science particularly exasperated Gore. In 2007, he wrote a book titled *The Assault on Reason* in which he charged that, whether the issue was the environment or foreign policy, "reason, logic and truth seem to play a sharply diminished role in the way America now makes important decisions." This rejection of reason in favor of "the politics of fear" was one cause of an alleged decline in participation in the democratic process, Gore said. In the book's conclusion, Gore quotes the Book of Proverbs, "Where there is no vision, the people perish." It was an interesting bookend to Bryan's planned summation at the Scopes Trial, which he ended up publishing as a newspaper editorial and which cited Christian dogma for another purpose: "It is not scientific truth to which Christians object, for true science is classified knowledge, and nothing therefore can be scientific unless it is true."

The final legacies of Gore, Kerry, and McCain are unknown because they remain so active in public service as of this writing. If they continue to follow the forceful examples of Clay, Bryan, Stevenson, and the other men featured in this book, their legacies may be substantial indeed. More important, by resurrecting the notion that the loss of a presidential election should not be the end of an influential career in public service, they hopefully herald a renewed tradition in which the expertise of our unsuccessful presidential candidates continues to be tapped for the national benefit.

We have in our history often lamented that we do not make full and good use of our former presidents. They have learned so much from their experience in the White House as leader of the free world yet are so seldom sought out for further duty. The same can be said of our former presidential nominees. They, too, have had a unique experience. They have been tested by the rigors of a national campaign. They have traveled throughout the country and discussed issues and concerns with thousands of their fellow citizens. They enjoyed successful, even stellar careers as public servants before they were nominated, and they earned the political allegiance of tens of millions of voters while a presidential candidate.

And yet, for these past several decades, they have not been valued as elder statesmen and have seldom been asked to re-enter the debate with vigor in order to share their wisdom and expertise. More often, they have been shunted aside, ignored even by their own party like crazy uncles, and ridiculed simply because they did not win the greatest political prize, more likely to be seen on late night television as the butts of jokes than on Mount Rushmore as paragons of American achievement and citizenship. This was not always so. Before the age of television created the image of failure, a losing presidential candidate remained a revered figure, still venerated by many followers and still holding the promise of what might have been.

Al Smith once suggested that former presidential nominees be made honorary U.S. senators. Perhaps there is no need for something so formal. Perhaps, they simply need the cue from us, the public, that we respect what they have accomplished and that we want them to find other opportunities for continued service to the nation. That does not require us to wait for an act of Congress.

APPENDIX

Not every presidential nominee has had as great an impact on contemporary politics as those profiled in the previous chapters. Yet each man nominated for president was a distinguished public servant whose life is worthy of study. The following are sketches of these other men who were "almost president."

The Three Federalists
1804, 1808, 1812, 1816

Because George Washington ran unopposed and Thomas Jefferson lost to John Adams but was later elected president, the United States did not have its first presidential "also ran" until 1804, when Jefferson walloped Charles Pinckney of South Carolina by a tally of 162–14 electoral votes. (The popular vote would not be widely used to help select the president until 1824.) Pinckney was the first of a series of essentially token presidential candidates put forward by the Federalists, who would be defunct a dozen years later as the United States drifted into one-party rule by Jefferson's Democratic-Republicans.

Active in South Carolina politics, Pinckney declined offers from Washington to be secretary of war and secretary of state, though he was Adams's vice presidential running mate in 1800. Nominated by the Federalists for president again in 1808, he modestly improved his showing but was still defeated by James Madison by a better than two-to-one margin. Madison, a brilliant constitutional scholar and legislator but a mediocre president, had more difficulty winning re-election in 1812 over New York City mayor DeWitt Clinton.

Clinton, a renaissance man and visionary politician best known as the driving force behind the development of the Erie Canal, was also actually a Jeffersonian Republican, not a Federalist. But he had had a falling out with local Tammany Hall leaders and was lukewarm in supporting the War of 1812. Falsely viewing Clinton as a peace candidate (Clinton supported the war once it was declared), anti-war Federalists decided to put Clinton forward as their own presidential candidate.

Clinton won more than 40 percent of the Electoral College vote, but after the election he returned to the Democratic-Republican fold and later became a strong supporter of Andrew Jackson.

The last Federalist candidate to run for president was former New York senator Rufus King in 1816. King had been the Federalists' vice presidential nominee back in 1804 and was an early anti-slavery activist. King carried a handful of New England states in his losing campaign against James Monroe, but the Federalists were in such disarray that they could not even settle on a single vice presidential candidate, with votes split among three men.

The Federalists put forward no candidate in 1820, allowing Monroe to join Washington as the only people to run unopposed for president.

The Federalists' demise has been blamed on many things. Skeptical of the wisdom of ordinary citizens, the party lost touch with the growing democratic sentiment in the nation. The Adams presidency, marred by passage of the Alien and Sedition Acts, had been unsuccessful. The Federalists' political and tactical genius, Alexander Hamilton, was killed in an 1804 duel with Vice President Aaron Burr. Jefferson and Madison also absorbed some Federalist support as they federalized their own views when an exigency demanded it, such as Jefferson's purchase of the Louisiana Territory without consulting Congress.

The Federalists were badly discredited in January 1815, when Federalists vehemently opposed to the War of 1812 concluded a weeks-long convention in Hartford, Connecticut, where they discussed the possible secession of the New England states. Unfortunately for the Federalists, their convention coincided with Jackson's great victory over the British at New Orleans and word that American diplomats had simultaneously concluded a peace treaty on honorable terms with Great Britain. The Federalists' secessionist talk at the very moment of an American victory led their last few adherents to abandon the Federalists' banner, and Federalist thinking would not emerge again as a distinct political philosophy until Henry Clay and Daniel Webster revived its nationalist elements within the new Whig Party.

Stanley Elkins and Eric McKitrick, *The Age of Federalism: The Early American Republic, 1788–1800* (Oxford University Press, Oxford, 1995).

Shaw Livermore, *The Twilight of Federalism: The Disintegration of the Federalist Party, 1815–1830* (Gordian Press, New York, 1972).

Gordon S. Wood, *Empire of Liberty: A History of the Early Republic, 1789–1815* (Oxford University Press, Oxford and New York, 2009).

Lewis Cass

1848

Lewis Cass was considered the nation's leading expert on Native Americans, which remains a sad commentary on how little we understood (or still understand) our indigenous peoples. Cass's writings on the subject led to his election to the American Philosophical Society, and his notes on Michigan's tribes inspired Longfellow to write his poem, "Hiawatha." Cass correctly lamented that Native Americans had suffered badly from contact with whites, through disease, alcoholism, and cultural demoralization, yet he was not above using whiskey to help secure lopsided treaties, such as persuading the Ottawa and Ojibwa to sell six million acres of land for three thousand dollars and the use of a blacksmith.

Initially, Cass argued against Indian removal as complicated, expensive, and inhumane. But he was a loyal Democrat. Selected as Andrew Jackson's secretary of war, by 1830 he was forcefully arguing that separation *was* the humane course of action since Native Americans allegedly lacked the capacity to reason and assimilate into "civilization." Cass oversaw Jackson's brutal "Trail of Tears" Indian removal policy.

Born in New Hampshire in 1782, Cass moved west, studied law, and served in the Ohio Legislature, beginning fifty years in public service. He served with distinction during the War of 1812, earning the moniker of "General Cass." In 1813, President Madison appointed him governor of the Michigan Territory, and it was in this post, held for eighteen years, that he did his most important work. As historian Walter A. McDougall has said, Cass "all but invented Michigan." Curious, able, and courageous, Cass led expeditions that mapped the Michigan wilderness and its immense natural resources. Honest in the discharge of his duties, Cass nonetheless made a fortune in Detroit real estate.

Dedicated to learning, he founded the University of Michigan in 1817 and established a model public school system. By 1837, Michigan became a state, but only after a skirmish between Michigan and Ohio militia settled which state claimed Toledo. The incident led Ohioans to label their feisty neighbors "wolverines," an appellation Michiganders enjoyed so much they made it their university's mascot.

Having also served as President Martin Van Buren's minister to France, Cass was given the Democratic nomination for president in 1848. Opposed to slavery in the abstract but believing it necessary to maintain the Union, Cass, not Stephen Douglas, first developed the doctrine of "Popular Sovereignty." Cass's acceptance of slavery led Van Buren to bolt the party and run as the Free Soil Party candidate for president, which assured Whig candidate Zachary Taylor's victory in the general election, although Cass carried as many states (fifteen) as Taylor did. Cass later served in the Senate and then as President Buchanan's secretary of state. He died in 1866.

Willard Carl Klunder, *Lewis Cass and the Politics of Moderation* (Kent State University Press, Kent, Ohio, 1996).

Walter A. McDougall, *Freedom Just Around the Corner: A New American History, 1585–1828* (Perennial, New York, 2004).

Andrew C. McLaughlin, *Lewis Cass* (Chelsea House, New York and London, 1980).

Joel H. Sibley, *Party Over Section: The Rough and Ready Presidential Election of 1848* (University of Kansas Press, Lawrence, 2009).

WINFIELD SCOTT

1852

Few presidential losses have been of greater benefit to the United States than General Winfield Scott's to Franklin Pierce in 1852, and not because Scott would have made a poorer president (Pierce was one of that office's greater nonentities). Rather, the loss freed Scott to go back to what he did best: leading the Army of the United States and ultimately developing the Union strategy that won the Civil War.

Scott is not only arguably the greatest soldier America ever produced, but the Duke of Wellington, conqueror of Napoleon, deemed him the *world's* "greatest living soldier" after learning of Scott's masterful capture of Mexico City against overwhelming odds during the Mexican-American War. Scott essentially created the modern American army and was the first soldier since Washington to earn the rank of lieutenant general. His rapid rise through the ranks was aided by his commanding physical presence; he stood six-feet-four-inches tall and in his prime weighed 230 pounds. Scott credited his mother, who raised Scott after his father died when he was six, for instilling in him the discipline and perseverance that made him a success.

His devotion to military correctness earned him the unfortunate nickname "Old Fuss and Feathers." That reputation, plus his habit of putting into writing his resentment at not being fully appreciated for his military genius, prevented him from winning political office. Twice before 1852, the Whig Party passed him over as its nominee in favor of two other generals, "Tippecanoe" William Henry Harrison and "Rough and Ready" Zachary Taylor, a reminder that when Americans choose generals as presidents they prefer those who eschew military decorum and who thereby earn a more folksy nickname—like "Ike."

When Scott suffered what he called his "third and greatest humiliation in politics," he blamed his staunch Unionist and anti-slavery views and said the South rejected this son of Virginia because it was filled with "wiseacres" already preparing for "rebellion and ruin." When the rebellion came, there was no doubt Scott would stay with the Union, though he could not persuade his acolyte Robert E. Lee to do the same.

Understanding that conquest of the South would take years and hundreds of thousands of men, Scott developed the "Anaconda Plan": a naval blockade of the South, dividing the Confederacy east and west along the Mississippi River, and slowly strangling it to death economically, politically, and militarily. Scott was forced into retirement in 1861 by age, illness, the impatience of political leaders hoping for a quicker victory than Scott's plan promised, and the connivance of disciple George McClellan. Scott lived until 1866, long enough to see the Union he had served for more than fifty years restored.

John S. D. Eisenhower, *Agent of Destiny: The Life and Times of General Winfield Scott* (Free Press, New York and London, 1997).

Timothy D. Johnson, *Winfield Scott: The Quest for Military Glory* (University Press of Kansas, Lawrence, 1998).

Allan Peskin, *Winfield Scott and the Profession of Arms* (Kent State University Press, Kent, Ohio, 2003).

Winfield Scott, *Memoirs of Lieut.-General Scott, LL.D. in Two Volumes* (Sheldon and Co., New York, 1864).

JOHN C. FRÉMONT

1856

Celebrity is always a valued commodity in politics. The explorer John C. Frémont was one of the most famous men in the world in his time, revered for his exploration of the West. Frémont was so celebrated that he was offered the nominations of *both* the Democratic and Republican Parties. Because he opposed the expansion of slavery, he took the Republican offer and campaigned under the stirring slogan "Free Soil, Free Men, Frémont!" In choosing Frémont, the Republicans passed over more experienced politicians such as William Seward or Charles Sumner for fear that their images as radicals would limit their appeal, while Frémont's renown would broaden the young party's prospects.

The dashing forty-three-year-old Frémont lost to James Buchanan in 1856 but ran a more than credible campaign, carrying eleven Northern states and ensuring that the Republican Party would not quickly disappear as had so many other minor parties during the antebellum period. Instead, the Republicans succeeded the Whigs as the second major party, and Frémont, "The Pathfinder," led the political way for the election of the first Republican president, Abraham Lincoln, four years later.

Presaging their reaction to Lincoln's election, Southern politicians had warned that Frémont's election would have meant "the end of the Union." That threat badly damaged Frémont's chances for victory, as did gossip about the circumstances of his birth. Frémont was the illegitimate child of a French expatriate and the young wife of an elderly cuckolded Virginia planter. In a remarkable coincidence, while still an infant living with his family in Tennessee, Frémont was nearly struck in his crib by gunfire from a nearby duel between Andrew Jackson and Frémont's future father-in-law, Thomas Hart Benton.

A gifted mathematician, Frémont caught the eye of several benefactors and won civilian appointment to the military as an officer and aide to the French-born Joseph Nicollet, then the world's leading geographer, who was working on the first comprehensive map of the United States. Frémont joined Nicollet on several expeditions to map the West before leading expeditions of his own. His descriptive and meticulous reports fired the imagination of the American public and opened the way for settlement in the West.

One of those intrigued by Frémont's work was Benton, a powerful senator from Missouri since 1821 and the nation's foremost exponent of Manifest Destiny. On a visit to the Benton home, the handsome Frémont, then twenty-seven, met the senator's beautiful and brilliant daughter, Jessie, then fifteen. The two fell in love and eloped two years later, creating a lifelong estrangement with the senator. Her father's favorite, Jessie had been educated far beyond the norm for women of her day. With beauty and charm coupled with fiery ambition and great political acumen, today political observers might label her a cross between Jacqueline Kennedy and Hillary Clinton. Women had become politically active in the anti-slavery movement, which in turn inspired the suffragette movement. The 1856 election was the first to capture the wide attention of women. Aware of Jessie's role in her husband's career, the public loudly cheered her name during the campaign.

Few have led a life so adventurous and odds-defying as Frémont. In mapping much of the Oregon Trail, he cheated death a dozen times. Frémont led an expedition that prematurely annexed California before the Mexican-American War was declared, though he was later cleared of misconduct charges. Frémont resigned his commission and returned to California. He had given money and instructions to purchase property near San Francisco, but his agent swindled him and instead purchased a remote property at the foot of the Sierras—which turned out to possess a fabulous gold mine. But Frémont lost most of his wealth in bad investments.

During the Civil War, while military commander of Missouri, Frémont issued an unauthorized order freeing slaves in his district—the first emancipation proclamation—and was reprimanded by Lincoln.

Late in life, Frémont was appointed governor of the Arizona Territory as a sinecure for his many services to the nation, while Jessie, to help the family finances, wrote books that often chronicled one of the most fascinating political couples in American history.

~

H. W. Brands, *The Age of Gold: The California Gold Rush and the New American Dream* (Doubleday, New York and London, 2002).

Sally Denton, *Passion and Principle: John and Jessie Frémont, the Couple Whose Power, Politics, and Love Shaped Nineteenth-Century America* (Bloomsbury, New York, 2007).

Eric Foner, *Free Soil, Free Labor, Free Men: The Ideology of the Republican Party Before the Civil War* (Oxford University Press, New York and Oxford, 1995).

Allan Nevins, *Frémont: Pathmarker of the West* (University of Nebraska Press, Lincoln, 1992).

George B. McClellan

1864

General George B. McClellan is primarily remembered for his insubordination toward President Lincoln and his failure to use the Army of the Potomac, which he had trained into a magnificent fighting force, to win a decisive victory for the Union in the Civil War. While lacking in some aspects of generalship, McClellan should be more fondly remembered for his role in demonstrating that American democracy is strong enough to hold a national election even in the midst of civil war.

McClellan, the precocious son of a Philadelphia doctor, received special permission to enter West Point at the age of fifteen. A brilliant engineer, he rose quickly through the ranks with his successes in the Mexican-American War and later as a surveyor for railroad routes to the West. McClellan left the Army to become vice president of the Illinois Central Railroad, but when the Civil War broke out, he was called back into service and was soon asked to command the dispirited Army of the Potomac, which had suffered a humiliating defeat at the First Battle of Bull Run.

McClellan was exceptionally talented at training and equipping his soldiers. His troops loved him and McClellan loved his troops—perhaps too much. Lincoln accused him of having a bad case of the "slows" because McClellan, always imagining he was outnumbered by Confederate forces, was reluctant to fully commit his beloved army to a battle or campaign that might win the war. Worse, McClellan, just thirty-four years old when given command of the army, took to heart his nickname, "The Young Napoleon," and treated his superior officers, including Lincoln, with open disdain. After McClellan failed to exploit an opening for an offensive following the Battle of Antietam, Lincoln relieved McClellan of command in November 1862. Some urged McClellan to disobey the order, but McClellan rebuked them, a sign that his disloyalty to the administration did not extend to disloyalty to country.

Remaining in the army but with no real duties, McClellan became the rallying point for those opposed to Lincoln's policies and became the Democrats' presidential nominee in 1864. Lincoln was certain, with the North weary of war, that he would lose to McClellan. But then, as the highlight of a series of Union victories that suddenly made Union victory seem within reach, General William T. Sherman took Atlanta. Meanwhile, Democrats saddled McClellan with a "Copperhead" running mate and platform that urged peace with the Confederacy at any price.

McClellan repudiated his party's platform, stating that while emancipation of the slaves should not be a precondition for peace, reunion had to be. Otherwise, he said, "I could not look in the face of my gallant comrades . . . and tell them that their labors, and the sacrifice of so many of our slain and wounded brethren had been in vain." The troops, however they may have admired their former chief, could not bring themselves to cast a vote that might be interpreted as a vote for the Democratic platform. Amid some controversy over the fairness of balloting, Lincoln ended up winning three-quarters of the soldier vote and McClellan carried just three states. He had run a dignified but passive campaign, making only two public speeches and refraining from personal attacks on the president.

The new commander of the Union Army, Ulysses S. Grant, told Lincoln the election result was a "double victory" because the election had been conducted without "bloodshed or riot"—to the dismay of the Confederacy. McClellan accepted the result without public complaint, but private disappointment led him to Europe, where he lived for three years before he returned to later serve as governor of New Jersey. While overseas, he expressed "horror" at Lincoln's assassination and joy at the Union victory, while urging a "magnanimous" peace toward the South. McClellan proclaimed that the Union victory "completely vindicated our national strength." So, too, did holding a free and peaceful election in the midst of civil war.

~

Charles Bracelen Flood, *1864: Lincoln at the Gates of History* (Simon and Schuster, New York, 2010).

Stephen W. Sears, *George B. McClellan: The Young Napoleon* (Ticknor and Fields, New York, 1988).

John C. Waugh, *Lincoln and McClellan: The Troubled Partnership between a President and His General* (Palgrave Macmillan, New York, 2010).

John C. Waugh, *Reelecting Lincoln: The Battle for the 1864 Presidency* (Da Capo Press, Cambridge, Mass., 1997).

HORATIO SEYMOUR

1868

Horatio Seymour is supposedly the only person truly compelled to run for president against his will, when he was drafted to be the Democratic nominee against Republican Ulysses S. Grant in 1868. Of course, Seymour *always* claimed reluctance to being the nominee for any office, yet he still served two separate terms as governor of New York and was nominated for governor four other times.

Seymour, whose real passions were farming and promoting improvements to the Erie Canal, professed to be "annoyed" that his unwillingness to seek public office was "looked upon as a strategic movement." While his sincerity was questioned but never disproved, the regular efforts to draft him for public office do indicate that Seymour, once called "a gentleman disguised as a Democrat," was one of the most highly regarded public servants of his day.

Seymour had refused to allow his name to be placed in nomination in 1868, but he was the chair of the Democratic convention. After eighteen ballots, when no other candidate seemed capable of securing the nomination, Seymour began receiving votes. He stopped the balloting and reminded the delegates that under no circumstances could he be their nominee. Flustered, he turned over the gavel and stepped outside for some air. If sincere in his desire not to run, it was foolish; if a ploy to win the nomination, it was genius. While absent, he was nominated by acclamation.

His strong showing against Grant astonished many. Running as a Democrat three years after the Civil War against the greatest Union military hero, Seymour won 47 percent of the vote. It is likely he won a majority of the white vote nationally as Grant carried five states of the Confederacy on the votes of freed black men. Four Southern states not yet "redeemed" could not participate in the election. Seymour benefited from the Ku Klux Klan's use of violence to suppress black voter turnout in the two Southern states he carried: Georgia and Louisiana. In eleven Georgia counties where blacks were in the majority, Grant received not a single vote.

Seymour's showing is remarkable given that Republican newspapers had questioned his wartime loyalty. A War Democrat who opposed secession, Seymour also opposed emancipation and was critical of how Lincoln's administration prosecuted the war, particularly its infringement of civil liberties in stifling Northern dissent. Seymour was governor in 1863 when riots broke out in New York City to protest military conscription. Mobs lynched African Americans and burned down a black orphanage. More than one hundred people were killed, most of them rioters shot by troops called in to quell the disturbance. Seymour had rushed to New York City to give a speech at City Hall where he reportedly addressed the crowd as "my friends." Most newspapers reported that the crowd in attendance was peaceful—and not the rioters—but Horace Greeley's Republican *New York Tribune* insisted then and during the 1868 campaign that Seymour had been addressing a violent mob.

How, then, did Seymour fare so well against Grant? Stephen Douglas and George McClellan had maintained the integrity of the Democratic Party, while many Americans, North as well as South, had no commitment to racial equality and were wary of the Radical Republican agenda. They wanted less excitement in their politics, and Seymour promised that.

Eric Foner, *Reconstruction: America's Unfinished Revolution, 1863–1877* (Harper and Row, New York, 1988).

Stewart Mitchell, *Horatio Seymour of New York* (Harvard University Press, Cambridge, Mass., 1938).

HORACE GREELEY
1872

No losing presidential candidate suffered more from his loss than crusading newspaper editor Horace Greeley. Five days before he decisively lost his 1872 race against President Ulysses S. Grant, Greeley's wife of thirty-five years, Mary, a brilliant but often disagreeable woman, died. Within a week of the election, Greeley learned he had lost control of his beloved newspaper, the *New York Tribune*. On November 29, just twenty-four days after the election, Greeley died of what was described as "brain fever." His last words were, "It is done."

At Greeley's funeral, the renowned minister Henry Ward Beecher eulogized: "He was the feet for the lame; he was the tongue for the dumb; he was an eye for the blind; and had a heart for those who had none to sympathize with them." So great was his influence among the American masses that Ralph Waldo Emerson, one of many writers whom Greeley made famous, said the blunt "Uncle Horace" did many Americans' thinking for them, and for just the two dollars per year it cost them to subscribe to the *Tribune*—which by 1860 had the largest circulation of any newspaper in the world and which still exists as the *International Herald-Tribune*.

Described by *Harper's Weekly* as "the most perfect Yankee the country ever produced," Greeley was a Universalist who believed everyone could achieve salvation. He was so odd and angular in appearance that one wag said Greeley made Lincoln appear "debonair." His views were as eccentric as his looks; he advocated such social reforms as vegetarianism, temperance, the abolition of capital punishment, and various social utopian experiments, including one in Colorado named for him. He likely never said the quote most attributed to him—"Go West, young man!"—even though he wholeheartedly agreed with the sentiment.

First a Whig, he was a founding member of the Republican Party. He cheered the North into war and was initially extremely critical of Lincoln for dawdling on emancipation. Midway through the conflict, he seemed to change course and urged Lincoln to seek a negotiated peace with the South, even personally seeking out a foreign mediator. After the war, he helped make bail for jailed Confederate president Jefferson Davis out of what he said was Christian compassion and anger that the government was holding Davis, in violation of his constitutional rights, without any specific charges.

Supportive of Grant's presidency at first, Greeley became disillusioned by Reconstruction and corruption within Grant's administration. He helped form a splinter group, labeled the Liberal Republicans, which held a rump convention and nominated for president the incorruptible Greeley. But he was no third party candidate; the Democrats could find no one better and shockingly chose Greeley, their longtime adversary, to be their standard-bearer as well. The Republican campaign against the "traitor" Greeley was merciless and he carried only six states, but because he died before the Electoral College convened, he technically received not a single electoral vote.

~

Kenneth Cmiel, *Democratic Eloquence: The Fight over Popular Speech in Nineteenth-Century America* (William Morrow and Co., New York, 1990).

Horace Greeley, *Recollections of a Busy Life* (J. B. Ford and Co., New York, 1868).

William Harlan Hale, *Horace Greeley: Voice of the People* (Harper & Bros., New York, 1950).

Robert C. Williams, *Horace Greeley: Champion of American Freedom* (New York University Press, New York and London, 2006).

Samuel J. Tilden
1876

A presidential candidate who averted a second civil war would seem heroic, but Samuel J. Tilden was instead criticized for not forcefully claiming a presidency many believed was rightfully his. Our leaders, it seems, are valued more for their aggressiveness than their restraint.

The 1876 election, held during the national Centennial, had the highest voter turnout rate in history at 82 percent. Tilden, then governor of New York, won 51 percent of the popular vote to Republican Rutherford B. Hayes's 48 percent. But Tilden was denied the presidency when he lost the Electoral College by a single vote.

Tilden had gone to bed election night certain that he was the next president. He had already won 184 of the 185 electoral votes he needed for victory. He had carried the South except for three states that had not yet reported their returns: Florida, Louisiana, and South Carolina. Winning any one of the three would ensure victory.

Election Night, most Republican Party officials had gotten drunk to dull the pain of expected defeat when Dan Sickles, a former New York congressman and Union general once acquitted of murder, walked into Republican headquarters and grasped the opportunity at hand. Without any authority to do so, Sickles wired Republican election officials in the three outstanding states and demanded, "Hold your states!" Republican election officials announced the next day that Hayes had eked out razor-thin victories in all three places.

State Democratic officials were outraged by this apparent fraud and submitted slates of rival electors pledged to Tilden. But if the Republicans committed fraud, they did so with a clear conscience. Tilden's margin of victory in the South was due in considerable part to violence and intimidation by armed whites to keep freed blacks from voting.

This infringement on the constitutional rights of African Americans did not trouble Democrats, South or North. To their mind, their candidate had been robbed. Mobs gathered across the country to chant "Tilden or blood!" President Grant fortified the nation's capital with additional troops, and gunboats patrolled the Potomac. Armed clubs, called "Tilden Minutemen," formed in a dozen states, ready to march on Washington whenever Tilden gave the word. But he never did.

A bookish, sickly child, prone to hypochondria and never married, Tilden, it was said, had admirers, not friends. He had displayed great courage and ingenuity in bringing down Boss Tweed as part of a reform campaign in New York. But after the presidential election, Tilden went into seclusion, saying no more than to urge calm. He occupied his time by preparing a legal brief on the precedent for counting presidential ballots, certain he would win the presidency on the legal merits. Tilden's "fatal flaw," says a character in Gore Vidal's novel about the election, *1876,* was that he possessed the "curious notion that men can be compelled by good argument to be honest."

Tilden declined to sanction mass protests on his behalf, let alone armed insurrection. His "sphinx-like" behavior befuddled his supporters. A Southern Democrat complained Tilden was "a bag of mush."

The Constitution is silent on what happens when the Electoral College votes are in dispute. Congress's solution in 1876 was the creation of an unprecedented election commission composed of members of Congress and the Supreme Court. The commission began politically balanced but lost its one allegedly independent member, Justice David Davis, when he suddenly accepted election by the Republican-controlled Illinois Legislature to the U.S. Senate. Another Republican jurist replaced Davis, and on a straight 8-7 party-line vote the commission gave all three outstanding states' electors to Hayes.

Yet, Southern Democrats no longer threatened renewed civil war, and it was clear a secret deal had been made when Hayes, shortly after assuming office, pulled federal troops out of the South and ended Reconstruction. Though he, too, believed that he had been defrauded, Tilden told supporters to "be of good cheer. The Republic will live." He thought he would get another chance in 1880, but Democrats, disillusioned by Tilden's lack of fight, chose General Winfield Scott Hancock instead.

Tilden had made a fortune as a Wall Street attorney and he bequeathed the majority of it to help start the New York Public Library. When he died, he asked that his tombstone carry the inscription, "I Still Trust in The People."

Eric Foner, *Reconstruction: America's Unfinished Revolution, 1863–1877* (Harper and Row, New York, 1988).

Michael F. Holt, *By One Vote: The Disputed Presidential Election of 1876* (University Press of Kansas, Lawrence, 2008).

William H. Rehnquist, *Centennial Crisis: The Disputed Election of 1876* (Vintage Books, New York, 2004).

Gore Vidal, *1876: A Novel* (Vintage International, New York, 2000).

WINFIELD SCOTT HANCOCK

1880

Americans love bestowing nicknames, particularly on politicians. Those unfortunate enough to have been tagged "Tricky Dick" or "Slick Willie" would certainly envy Winfield Scott Hancock for being known as "The Superb." George McClellan gave that handle to Hancock for his work at the relatively minor Battle of Williamsburg during McClellan's Peninsula campaign in the second year of the Civil War. Few men could carry such a title without embarrassment or irony, but such was Hancock's character that it seemed a natural and honest description of the man.

He was a corps commander throughout the war without responsibility for devising strategy, but his performance and personal courage at Chancellorsville, Gettysburg, and Spotsylvania won plaudits and the deep affection of his troops. Ulysses S. Grant claimed in his memoirs that Hancock never made a blunder in battle, while William T. Sherman called Hancock "one of the greatest soldiers in history."

When he died in 1886, the *New York Evening Post,* which had supported James Garfield over Hancock in the 1880 presidential election, said Hancock was the most beloved and admired commander on either side during the Civil War. The affection felt for Hancock in the South was due largely to his tour of duty as military commander of Louisiana and Texas during Reconstruction, where he announced, to the anger of Radical Republicans, his goal of restoring civil liberties and returning civil authority as quickly as possible back to reconstructed Confederates.

Why Hancock had been named after a military hero is unclear, because when the local congressman nominated Hancock for West Point, his father, a devout Christian and Democrat, opposed the idea. He yielded when convinced that if the world needed soldiers, they should at least be Christian ones.

Based on his service during the war and on the frontier, and because of his appeal in the South, Hancock was considered a strong presidential candidate who could neutralize the Republicans' post-war campaign strategy of "waving the bloody shirt." But he lost the nomination in 1868 and again in 1876. His turn finally came in 1880.

Sensitive to his good reputation, Republicans acknowledged Hancock was a good soldier—but no more. Hancock did not hold complex political views. He once suggested the party platform should simply read, "An honest man and the restoration of the Government." During the 1880 campaign, Hancock was mocked by Republicans for asserting the issue of federal tariffs was primarily a local issue, which as one observer noted, either indicated no understanding or a very profound understanding of the issue, depending upon how it was interpreted.

Generally, however, issues were secondary to political affiliation. This was a period of extraordinary parity between Republicans and Democrats. Hancock lost the popular vote to Garfield by less than ten thousand votes out of more than nine million cast, the closest popular vote in history. Awakened, his wife told him of his defeat. "That is all right. I can stand it," said The Superb, and then, with the same coolness he had demonstrated when wounded while defending against Pickett's charge at Gettysburg, he went back to sleep.

John W. Forney, *Life and Military Career of Winfield Scott Hancock* (H. N. Hinckley and Co., Chicago, 1880).

David M. Jordan, *Winfield Scott Hancock: A Soldier's Life* (Indiana University Press, Bloomington and Indianapolis, 1996).

James G. Blaine
1884

Despite being the state's only presidential nominee, James G. Blaine is not memorialized with a statue anywhere in Maine. But Blaine achieved literary immortality in two renowned works of fiction as the very model of the cynical and corrupt "Gilded Age" politician.

He inspired the characters of Colonel Beriah Sellers in Mark Twain's *The Gilded Age* and Senator Silas P. Ratcliffe in Henry Adams's *Democracy*. In the latter book, the heroine asks Senator Ratcliffe whether democracies are doomed to be corrupt. Ratcliffe's pragmatic response is, "No representative government can long be much better or much worse than the society it represents. Purify society and you purify government."

There is no doubt that the sentiment was inspired by Blaine. He was the master political operator—often operating on the edge of propriety. Tall, commanding, and eloquent, Blaine was, with the exception of Ulysses S.

Grant, the most popular Republican politician of the late nineteenth century. Yet, he was the first Republican nominee to lose the presidency after the Civil War, and while he served admirably as secretary of state twice, Blaine had few great achievements as a legislator. One of his biographers wrote, "No man in our annals has filled so large a space and left it so empty."

Blaine came within 1,047 votes of becoming president—his margin of loss in New York to Grover Cleveland in 1884. It was an ugly campaign that revolved around questions about each man's character; Cleveland had fathered a child out of wedlock, and Blaine, while a faithful family man, was engulfed in personal financial scandals.

A one-time schoolteacher, Blaine was a Maine congressman who rose swiftly to become Speaker of the House and later senator. He had been implicated but cleared in the infamous Crédit Mobilier scandal in 1872, but four years later, it came to light that he had used worthless bonds in a troubled Arkansas railroad to leverage a sixty-four-thousand-dollar "loan" from the Union Pacific Railroad that he never repaid.

He defused that crisis in a dramatic speech before the House in which he selectively read from letters that purported to exonerate him, while leaving out such parts as his own admonition to his correspondents to "Burn this letter!" Blaine was so deft in rebuffing these assaults on his character that he was dubbed the "Plumed Knight," but money and politics were more closely entwined than usual in this period, and Blaine was continually charged with some new malfeasance involving money and influence.

Two events in 1884 are usually cited for Blaine's defeat. Blaine had a Catholic mother and had, as secretary of state, pushed Great Britain for Irish home rule, but when a Protestant minister supporting Blaine proclaimed that the Democrats were the party of "rum, Romanism, and rebellion," Blaine lost much Catholic support.

The day after that fiasco, and just a week before the election, Blaine provided political cartoonists of the day with irresistible fare when he attended a lavish dinner at the posh New York eatery Delmonico's to solicit funds from black-tied and well-fed millionaires—while most of the nation was reeling from a deep economic recession.

Henry Adams, *Democracy: An American Novel* (Henry Holt and Company, New York, 1933).

Neil Rolde, *Continental Liar from the State of Maine: James G. Blaine* (Tilbury House, Gardiner, Maine, 2007).

David Saville Muzzey, *James G. Blaine: A Political Idol of Other Days* (Dodd, Meade, and Company, New York, 1934).

Mark Twain and Charles Dudley Warner, *The Gilded Age* (Oxford University Press, New York, 1996).

ALTON B. PARKER

1904

As a young schoolteacher, Alton B. Parker had signed a contract with a school in a small town in his native New York only to find out when he arrived home that his father had secured him a higher-paying job the same day. When Parker proposed to take the better-paying job, his father said he could not do that; he had signed a contract and must honor it. So began a record of impeccable public propriety.

Never the subject of a biography, Parker may be the most obscure of all losing presidential candidates. He had the misfortune of being over-shadowed by his larger-than-life opponent in 1904, Theodore Roosevelt. And while active in Democratic Party politics, except for one county-level position, the only elected office he held was as chief judge of the New York Court of Appeals, the highest judicial office in the state.

Parker was plucked from the bench to be the Democratic nominee for president as a result of Democratic infighting in New York. William Jennings Bryan, having suffered two consecutive defeats, was (reluctantly) persuaded to step aside in 1904. Rushing to take up Bryan's mantle was newspaper mogul William Randolph Hearst, whom the *New York Times* charged with "greater recklessness" than even the populist Bryan. To stop Hearst, prominent conservative New York Democrats rallied to Parker.

While Parker's nomination for president is usually described as a tri-umph of the conservative wing of the Democratic Party (mostly because Parker supported the gold standard), Parker had a moderately progres-sive record on the bench. His rulings upheld the right of unions to strike and of legislatures to outlaw child labor and to establish the eight-hour workday. He was actually a good match for Roosevelt. Fifty-two years old, six feet tall, and a robust two hundred pounds, Parker exuded the same vitality for which Roosevelt was known. He began every morning at his farm with a swim in the Hudson River followed by an hour's ride on horseback. But Parker was reluctant to wage a vigorous campaign. When Democratic convention delegates demanded Parker express his positions on the issues of the day, he replied that as long as he was a sitting judge it was inappropriate for him to express political opinions. If that dissatisfied the delegates, Parker said, he was content to "let the nomination go."

Even though Bryan and TR had established a new tradition of candidates vigorously campaigning on their own behalf, Parker disappointed Democrats by sticking to the nineteenth-century tradition of staying home and saying little. He did strongly criticize mistreatment of local citizens during the American occupation of the Philippines, and charged Roosevelt and his campaign with shaking down big business for contributions even as TR campaigned as a "trust-buster." Parker's liberal record on the bench was downplayed so that he would seem a safe alternative to the "lunatic" Roosevelt. But TR was wildly popular, and Parker carried the South and nothing else.

Parker returned to private practice, and some said his run for president derailed his dream of being appointed to the Supreme Court. That is probably not true. President Woodrow Wilson might have appointed him, but Parker had opposed Wilson's nomination in 1912. Owing Parker no favors, Wilson passed him over on the three occasions when he made a court appointment. Parker died in 1926.

~

Because there is no biography of Parker, material for this essay was derived from Irving Stone, *They Also Ran*, and Leslie H. Southwick, *Presidential Also-Rans and Running Mates, 1788–1980*.

CHARLES EVANS HUGHES
1916

Charles Evans Hughes is the only U.S. Supreme Court justice to have resigned to run for president. Fourteen years after Hughes lost an extraordinarily close race to Woodrow Wilson in 1916, President Herbert Hoover reappointed him to the court as chief justice, when it was routine to appoint politicians to the Supreme Court—a practice that is now unusual.

Hughes, the son of an abolitionist Baptist minister, never wanted to be a politician. His love was the study, teaching, and practice of law. But his brilliance was obvious, and he was tapped to help the New York Legislature investigate reports of inflated utility rates. The legislature, now cognizant of Hughes's remarkable ability to unravel financial intricacies, then asked him to lead a second investigation into fraud and manipulation within the insurance industry.

Hughes uncovered a particularly cozy relationship between key leaders of his own Republican Party and big business, so GOP leaders, including President Theodore Roosevelt, pressed Hughes to run for governor as the party's only hope as a reform candidate in 1906. Hughes defeated newspaper tycoon William Randolph Hearst in a close and bitter race.

His progressive record, which included implementing solutions to the scandals his investigations had uncovered, won Hughes national acclaim. In 1910, President William Howard Taft appointed Hughes to the Supreme Court, where his legal reasoning on such complicated issues as railroad regulation was so sound that of the 150 majority opinions he wrote in his first six years on the Court, his fellow justices offered dissents to only nine.

There was already talk of nominating Hughes for president in 1912 as a compromise candidate who could heal the rift within the GOP between Roosevelt and Taft, but Hughes said it was improper for a justice to become involved in politics. Then, having observed the split that did occur between Taft and Roosevelt in 1912, Hughes changed his mind and agreed to be a unifying nominee for the Republicans in 1916. His ambivalence was noticeable in a lackluster campaign that cost him the presidency. While Wilson won the popular vote, 49 to 46 percent, had Hughes won California, a state he lost by less than five thousand votes, he would have been elected president.

After his loss, Hughes served as secretary of state under Harding and Coolidge before being named chief justice in 1930. A strong record on civil liberties distinguished his eleven years as chief justice, and he led the court as it reviewed various legal challenges to the New Deal.

The Hughes court upheld many key portions of the New Deal, but rulings striking down such initiatives as farm price controls led Franklin Roosevelt to try his foolish and unsuccessful "court packing" plan in 1938.

Hughes was instrumental in thwarting Roosevelt's plan, and his political savvy showed the benefits that practical political experience can provide in interpreting the law. Until recently, politicians routinely served on the court. Hughes's predecessor as chief justice had been former president Taft, and among his successors was former California governor Earl Warren. Of the 112 justices who served on the Supreme Court through 2010, nearly thirty had once served in Congress and several more had been governors. But the last justice with any experience in elected office was Sandra Day O'Connor, appointed the court's first woman justice in 1981 and retired in 2006. She had served in the Arizona State Senate. None of the current nine justices, as of this writing, have ever held elective office and all are former appellate court judges.

It has led to concern about the lack of professional diversity on the court, which brings to mind the story of Vice President Lyndon Johnson raving to House Speaker Sam Rayburn about the brilliance and educational qualifications of John Kennedy's aides, some of whom were helping push the United States ever more deeply into the Vietnam War. This led Rayburn to respond, "I hope you're right, Lyndon, but I just wish one of them had ever run for county sheriff."

꒰꒱

Henry Julian Abraham, *Justices and Presidents: A Political History of Appointments to the Supreme Court* (Oxford University Press, New York and Oxford, 1992).

Merlo John Pusey, *Charles Evans Hughes, Vols. 1 and 2* (Macmillan, New York, 1951).

JAMES M. COX
1920

John McCain is not the only presidential candidate who some say was upstaged by his vice presidential nominee. In 1920, Ohio governor James M. Cox was the Democratic nominee for president, and his running mate was thirty-eight-year-old Franklin Delano Roosevelt.

Roosevelt had little political experience at the time, having been a New York state senator with some reform credentials and having served as assistant secretary of the Navy during World War I. But Cox personally chose Roosevelt to be his running mate. He thought Roosevelt could help carry the battleground state of New York (he didn't); as a member of the Wilson administration he could help unify the party (the Democrats stayed split); and the Roosevelt name would bring cachet to the campaign (the children of Theodore Roosevelt, FDR's fifth cousin, actively campaigned for Republican nominee Warren Harding).

It was also thought that Roosevelt, like McCain's running mate, Sarah Palin, had sex appeal. He was young, energetic, and very handsome—a great asset, it was thought, in 1920, which would be the first year when women in all states would be allowed to vote. While Roosevelt was not able to perform all the miracles that Cox had hoped he might, he was an asset to the campaign, even in a losing cause, and his future seemed limitless. Then, in August 1921, barely nine months after the election, Roosevelt contracted polio.

The 1920 presidential contest pitted two small town Ohio newspaper publishers against each other. Harding was a U.S. senator, while Cox had been a popular three-term governor. Cox established a remarkably progressive record his first term, creating workers' compensation and a citizen referendum process, among other things, but as governor during World War I he was more conservative, cracking down on labor violence that impeded the war effort. That crackdown, plus his success in business, led conservative Ohioans to consider Cox "a 'safe' kind of liberal," he said.

Cox won the Democratic nomination in 1920 after the forty-fourth ballot. The Democrats tapped Cox in part because it was clear Wilson was no longer popular and Cox's distance from the administration was considered an asset. Then Cox surprised and appalled many Democrats when, after an emotional meeting with a very ill Wilson, he made American membership in the League of Nations the centerpiece of his campaign. Joining the league might have been a popular campaign issue in 1919; it was no longer in 1920. Americans wanted to put the tumult of the war and the Wilson years behind them and responded instead to Harding's promise of a "return to normalcy." Cox lost in a rout, carrying eleven Southern states and nothing else, winning only 34 percent of the popular vote to Harding's 60 percent.

Cox had been worried his personal life would become an issue during the campaign. He was a rare divorced politician, his wife having accused Cox of mental cruelty and neglect shortly after he was elected to Congress in 1908. But Harding and the Republicans had no interest in making the candidates' personal lives an issue; Harding himself had married a divorcée and, as few others knew, had fathered children with two other women who were not his wife.

After his defeat, Cox remained active as a party power broker but spent most of his time building up what was first a newspaper and then a multimedia empire. Still a family-owned company, what is now known as Cox Enterprises is one of the nation's ten largest media companies whose holdings include the company's original newspaper, the *Dayton Daily News*, plus the *Atlanta Journal-Constitution*, the *Austin American-Statesman*, and, as of 2011, fifteen television stations, eighty-six radio stations, and cable television and Internet service providers.

While Cox returned to the newspaper business, Roosevelt stayed in politics. He overcame his disability to become governor of New York and president of the United States—the only unsuccessful vice presidential candidate to ever win the presidency.

James M. Cox, *Journey Through My Years* (Mercer University Press, Macon, Ga., 2004).
David Pietrusza, *1920: The Year of the Six Presidents* (Carroll and Graf, New York, 2007).

John W. Davis
1924

The 1924 Democratic National Convention in New York City, which nominated "lawyer's lawyer" John W. Davis after a record-breaking 103 ballots, was so arduous that Will Rogers imagined this father-son conversation: "Father, were you in the big war?" And the father would reply, "No, son, but I went through the New York convention."

The surface argument that dominated the convention was over whether the party platform should condemn the reborn Ku Klux Klan by name. A compromise condemned all secret organizations without singling out the Klan, but the debate exposed deeper fissures within the party: urban vs. rural, North vs. South, conservative vs. progressive, Protestant vs. Catholic, and, as Prohibition was in full swing, "Drys" vs. "Wets."

Davis, a former West Virginia congressman, was a long shot among the nineteen men nominated until it was clear no candidate had a prayer of getting the two-thirds vote necessary to win. As balloting wore on, Davis's appeal grew because he had progressive credentials, having been Wilson's solicitor general and ambassador to Great Britain, *and* conservative credentials as a Wall Street attorney and counsel for J. P. Morgan.

Davis understood his nomination was "an empty honor." The party was split, the nation was prosperous under Republican Calvin Coolidge's administration, and Davis was saddled with William Jennings Bryan's brother, Charles, as his running mate, an accommodation that cost him a good deal of the Catholic vote. Still, Davis ran an honorable campaign, repeatedly condemning the Klan by name. But with Progressive Wisconsin senator Robert LaFollette in the race as a third party candidate, Davis ended up receiving less than 29 percent of the popular vote, the second-lowest total for a major party candidate, after William Howard Taft's 23 percent in 1912.

So Davis returned to his pride and joy, the law, becoming known as the greatest legal advocate in American history. He made oral arguments before the U.S. Supreme Court 140 times—more than anyone since Daniel Webster—and justices such as Oliver Wendell Holmes and Hugo Black praised him as the most persuasive advocate they had ever heard.

Asked to explain Davis's greatness as a lawyer, a contemporary noted his courtesy, his dignified, commanding appearance, confidence, and perfect diction. He made forceful, logical arguments, never making emotional appeals to win over judge or jury. He was so revered that future Supreme Court justice Thurgood Marshall claimed that he tried to emulate Davis and did so most effectively when he opposed Davis as counsel in the most celebrated Supreme Court case of the twentieth century.

Davis often represented the underdog, defending a conscientious objector during World War II, and arguing successfully that President Harry Truman had no right to nationalize the steel industry to prevent a strike. But he also represented, without fee, the State of South Carolina when it was sued, along with school districts in Virginia and Kansas, by African-American parents who were challenging the "separate but equal" standard for public schools that the Supreme Court had established in *Plessy v. Ferguson* in 1896. Because of a quirk in the chronology of when the several lawsuits were filed, the new case demanding desegregation of the public schools was known as *Brown v. Board of Education of Topeka.*

While Davis was not a virulent racist, he ridiculed the notion that segregation harmed black children and believed both races were better off separated. Davis was certain precedent was on his side; Marshall agreed, but he also understood that in order to reverse settled law a lawyer needed to "convince both [the justice's] . . . mind and his emotions." To argue the law was unchangeable, legal scholar Alexander Bickel observed, "was to deny the essence of the Court's function."

Having already struck down segregation in housing, public transportation, and higher education, the court now unanimously struck it down in the most emotionally laden venue possible: public schools. Davis at first predicted turmoil, and there was some of that, but upon reflection he later decided that if the court were to order such a sea change, he was glad it was on a unanimous decision. It was a rare loss for America's greatest attorney, but a loss that served the cause of equal rights.

꜀꜀

William H. Harbaugh, *Lawyer's Lawyer: The Life of John W. Davis* (Oxford University Press, New York, 1973).

Alfred M. Landon
1936

Many people believed that Kansas Republican governor Alfred M. Landon would defeat Democratic president Franklin Roosevelt in a landslide in

1936. They really did. They based that belief, at least in part, on the *Literary Digest*, which had surveyed millions of Americans and predicted in its October 1936 issue that Landon would win by a 57 to 43 percent tally.

A young pollster just starting out named George Gallup had also done a survey, but with a much smaller, random sample, and he predicted Roosevelt, not Landon, would win in a landslide. People laughed at Gallup. After all, the *Digest* had, as its editors proudly noted, "been right in every Poll" since 1916. The *Digest* had mailed its survey to more than ten million Americans whose names were drawn from lists of automobile and telephone owners. An extraordinary 2.3 million people responded to the survey, an extremely large sample, especially compared to Gallup's sampling of fifty thousand.

The problem with the *Digest* sample was that automobile and telephone owners in 1936 were the well-to-do, and the country was still in the grips of the Great Depression. The wealthy were more likely to vote Republican. Further, the *Digest* depended upon a voluntary response, which increased the bias because those angry at the status quo have a greater incentive to respond. The angry turned out to be in the minority.

Landon, an oil man who had served two terms as an effective progressive governor, ended up winning only two states, Vermont and Maine. He believed many New Deal programs were poorly executed and wasteful but supported their and Roosevelt's aims. While surrogates charged FDR was leading the nation into socialism, Landon said, "I do not believe the Jeffersonian theory that 'the best government is the one that governs the least' can be applied today." He was therefore criticized for a lack of passion and for a lack of effort on the campaign trail. Landon later looked at the results, with Roosevelt winning nearly 61 percent of the vote, and countered, "I don't think that it would have made any difference what kind of a campaign I made.... That is one consolation you get out of a good licking."

Landon never ran for office again but remained a progressive voice in the Republican Party, later endorsing portions of Lyndon Johnson's "Great Society," particularly Medicare. Known as the "Grand Old Man of the Grand Old Party," Landon lived to be one hundred, old enough to enjoy watching his daughter, Nancy Landon Kassebaum, be elected to the U.S. Senate in 1978.

Meanwhile, Americans still argue over polls, baffled that a sample of as few as five hundred voters can usually accurately predict a presidential election and wondering when a new development, such as the failure to poll people with only cell phones and not landlines, will cause some pollster today to suffer the humiliation the *Literary Digest* felt in 1936. The *Digest*, by the way, failed in 1938 after nearly fifty years in business.

⌒

Donald R. McCoy, *Landon of Kansas* (University of Nebraska Press, Lincoln, 1966).

WENDELL WILLKIE
1940

In his novel, *The Plot against America*, Philip Roth paints a frightening portrait of what might have happened had America elected an isolationist for president in 1940. In the novel, the president is Charles Lindbergh, who is unrealistically portrayed as a Nazi sympathizer. In reality, there were no men running for president in 1940 who sympathized with the Nazis. But there were men intent upon taking decisive steps to keep America out of the growing war in Europe—men thwarted by Wendell Willkie's improbable capture of the Republican presidential nomination, an event that newspaper columnist Walter Lippmann called "the decisive event, perhaps providential," in ensuring an Allied victory in World War II.

This mildly extravagant claim is based on the key support Willkie gave President Franklin Roosevelt's relatively modest preparations for American entry into World War II. Several of Willkie's primary opponents, including Robert Taft and Arthur Vandenberg, were determined, at least before Pearl Harbor, to not only prevent American entry into the war, but also to block any assistance FDR intended to provide Great Britain and other allies in the fight against fascism.

The Republicans' nomination of Willkie was improbable because he had never run for any elected office before, he was virtually unknown

outside the business community, and, until 1938, he had been a registered Democrat! But Willkie had gained Republican admirers through
his strong but thoughtful critiques of the New Deal. Willkie, an attorney
who had risen to become president of utility giant Commonwealth and
Southern Corporation, was particularly critical of the Tennessee Valley
Authority and won impressive concessions from the Roosevelt administration, protecting Commonwealth and Southern's shareholders.

Willkie also had a magnetic personality. A large bear of a man who
had sophisticated tastes, he nonetheless liked to play the part of the
Indiana country boy, which led Roosevelt's curmudgeonly secretary of
the interior Harold Ickes to memorably label Willkie "a simple, barefoot,
Wall Street lawyer." Still, a survey taken in April 1940, just six weeks
prior to the Republican National Convention, found that only 15 percent of the American people knew who Willkie was.

But the week the GOP convention was held was also the week France
fell to German troops. Suddenly, the isolationists' stock fell, too, and delegates
yielded to the packed galleries that incessantly screamed, "We want Willkie!"
Willkie won on the fifth ballot and undertook a memorably vigorous campaign that still failed to deny Roosevelt an unprecedented third term.

Roosevelt liked and admired Willkie and was determined to enlist his
help in ending American neutrality. Shortly after the election, Roosevelt
sent Willkie to Great Britain as a symbol of American unity and then
called Willkie back to testify before Congress on behalf of the proposed
"Lend-Lease Act." Willkie's riveting testimony was crucial to the passage
of legislation that allowed Britain to fight on. Later, Willkie used his prestige to persuade Congress to maintain the military draft, which Congress
came within one vote of ending six months before Pearl Harbor.

Returning from a world tour in 1943, Willkie wrote the influential best-selling book, *One World*, which argued for creation of a United
Nations. Roosevelt allegedly tried to persuade Willkie to return to the
Democratic Party and be his running mate in 1944. Whether Roosevelt
was serious or simply toying with Willkie and the Republicans remains
a matter of debate. Willkie was still weighing his political options when
he died unexpectedly of a heart attack in October 1944.

Conservative Republicans were furious at Willkie's hijacking of the party and his alliance with Roosevelt. One disillusioned follower was the objectivist novelist Ayn Rand, who said Willkie was "the guiltiest man of any for destroying America, more guilty than Roosevelt." Far more believed he helped prepare America for the fight that destroyed fascism.

<hr>

Mary Earhart Dillon, *Wendell Willkie: 1892–1944* (J. B. Lippincott Company, Philadelphia and New York, 1952).

James H. Madison, ed., *Wendell Willkie: Hoosier Internationalist* (Indiana University Press, Bloomington and Indianapolis, 1992).

Steve Neal, *Dark Horse: A Biography of Wendell Willkie* (Doubleday and Company, Inc., Garden City, N.Y., 1984).

Charles Peters, *Five Days in Philadelphia: 1940, Wendell Willkie, and the Political Convention That Freed FDR to Win World War II* (Public Affairs, New York, 2005).

Philip Roth, *The Plot against America* (Houghton Mifflin Company, Boston and New York, 2004).

Wendell Willkie, *One World* (University of Illinois Press, Urbana and London, 1966).

HUBERT H. HUMPHREY
1968

Hubert H. Humphrey was vice president, one of our nation's most influential and productive senators, the Democratic nominee for president in 1968 (losing to Richard Nixon), and three other times a serious candidate for his party's nomination. His most important contribution to the nation occurred, however, while still a young mayor of Minneapolis. At the 1948 Democratic National Convention, Humphrey changed the course of the Democratic Party and the nation when, against all odds, he persuaded the Democrats to finally adopt a platform strongly in favor of civil rights for African Americans, an issue Humphrey would champion throughout his career.

Humphrey was an unusual choice to lead the cause of civil rights. Born above his father's drugstore in a small town in South Dakota where there were few African Americans and only slightly more Democrats, young Hubert inherited his father's gift of gab and a commitment to help the underdog. After graduating from the University of Minnesota, Humphrey pursued his graduate studies at Louisiana State University.

There, he was "dismayed" by the discrimination he saw—"stately homes on manicured lawns in the white sections, the open sewage ditches in black neighborhoods."

One biographer likened Humphrey's awakening to that experienced by young Abraham Lincoln, when he had rafted down the Mississippi and witnessed a New Orleans slave auction. "My abstract commitment to civil rights was given flesh and blood during my year in Louisiana," Humphrey said, adding that the experience "also opened my eyes to the prejudice of the North."

Humphrey parlayed his experience as assistant director of the Minnesota War Manpower Commission and a strong relationship with organized labor into election as mayor of Minneapolis in 1945 when he was only thirty-four years old. Franklin Roosevelt had died weeks before Humphrey's election, making Harry Truman president. Truman had appointed a civil rights commission but, for fear of alienating the South and ruining his chances for election in 1948, he dragged his feet in implementing the commission's recommendations, including a call to desegregate the armed forces.

Attending the Democratic National Convention in 1948, Humphrey was on the platform committee, but his bid to include a strong civil rights plank, opposed by the Truman administration, was rebuffed by a vote of seventy-eight to thirty. Despite fears it would split the party and doom his own senatorial race that year, Humphrey pledged to bring the issue to the floor of the convention the next day.

Having lost fifteen pounds that week from not eating, Humphrey stayed up all night to lobby convention delegates, consult with allies, and craft an eight-minute address that would become the most dramatic speech given at a convention since William Jennings Bryan's "cross of gold" speech in 1896. In a stroke of political genius, Humphrey and his friends decided not to criticize Truman for inaction, but to credit Truman for the action he had taken to date.

Sweating profusely in the ninety-three-degree heat in the Philadelphia convention hall, Humphrey put forward his four proposals: outlaw lynching, ensure black voting rights, guarantee fair employment, and integrate the military. He told the crowd:

To those who say that we are rushing this issue of civil rights—I say to them, we are 172 years late. To those who say this bill is an infringement on states' rights, I say this. . . . The time has arrived for the Democratic Party to get out of the shadow of states' rights and walk forthrightly into the bright sunshine of human rights.

A raucous demonstration followed, and when the roll was called, even though minority planks are always doomed to failure, Humphrey's proposal was approved by a vote of 651½ to 582½. Southern delegates from four states, led by South Carolina governor Strom Thurmond, walked out to prepare an independent presidential campaign.

Twelve days later, Truman embraced the Democrats' new position on civil rights and finally issued his executive order, directing the armed forces to integrate. The process was laborious, and the real catalyst to integration was the Korean War. Large numbers of African-American enlistments proved vital in plugging holes in previously segregated units that had suffered appalling casualties. By October 1953, the Army was finally able to announce that 95 percent of African-American soldiers served in integrated units. It took a long time, but it would have taken much longer without Humphrey.

Lewis L. Gould, *1968: The Election That Changed America* (Ivan R. Dee, Chicago, 1993).

Hubert H. Humphrey, *The Education of a Public Man: My Life and Politics* (Doubleday and Company, Inc., Garden City, N.Y., 1976).

Carl Solberg, *Hubert Humphrey: A Biography* (W. W. Norton and Co., New York, 1984).

WALTER MONDALE
1984

A wag once said Walter Mondale was born to be vice president. Unkind, perhaps, but Mondale's legacy is tied to the vice presidency, both for his own role in redefining the office while serving as Jimmy Carter's vice president and for picking the first woman vice presidential candidate during his own campaign for the presidency in 1984.

When Daniel Webster was offered the vice presidential nomination, he quipped, "I do not propose to be buried until I am dead." Webster's belief that the vice presidency was a dead end was well founded. While nine vice presidents have succeeded to the presidency upon a president's death or resignation, after Martin Van Buren succeeded Andrew Jackson in 1836 it was another 124 years before a former vice president even received his party's nomination for president.

Mondale agreed to be Carter's vice presidential running mate only after Carter agreed to make it "a useful instrument of government." Mondale, son of a poor Methodist minister, was well aware of the abuse and humiliations suffered by his fellow Minnesota liberal and mentor Hubert Humphrey when Humphrey served as Lyndon Johnson's vice president.

Mondale became the first vice president in history to have an office inside the White House. He regularly participated in administration policy meetings, was granted access to the same intelligence the president received, and he and Carter lunched together weekly. Every vice president since has followed the "Mondale model."

After Carter and Mondale lost decisively to Ronald Reagan and George H. W. Bush in 1980, Mondale had high hopes for his own presidential run. Reagan seemed vulnerable in 1982 with unemployment near 10 percent and a majority of Americans believing Reagan should not run for a second term. But the economy improved, and Mondale led a fractured Democratic Party, fending off a challenge for the nomination from Colorado senator Gary Hart, of whose policies he famously asked: "Where's the beef?"—though Mondale had never seen the television ad from which the quip was taken.

Mondale hoped candor might carry the day. He said the federal deficit needed to be brought under control no matter who was elected. "Mr. Reagan will raise taxes, and so will I," Mondale said. "He won't tell you. I just did." A pledge to raise taxes did not improve his standing in the polls, so Mondale was determined to make a bold choice, either a woman or a minority, for his running mate in order to prove he was a bridge between the old and the new in Democratic politics.

Mondale was pained when the National Organization for Women publicly demanded he pick a woman. Now, instead of looking bold, it would look as if he had caved to a special interest group. Still, he chose New York congresswoman Geraldine Ferraro, not only the first woman but also the first Italian-American to be on a major party ticket. He liked her résumé. She epitomized the American dream, a schoolteacher who had attended law school at night and then become a tough criminal prosecutor before her election to Congress. But Mondale almost immediately regretted the choice.

Ferraro declined to study issue papers, wanted to take a vacation instead of campaign in California, accused Mondale's staff of condescension and chauvinism, and then drew unwelcome headlines when her husband's messy financial dealings were made public. When she complained she would be treated differently if she were a white male, Mondale later told aides she was right: If she had been a man, he would have dropped her from the ticket.

Given America's general prosperity, Reagan's landslide re-election was a foregone conclusion. Mondale carried only his home state of Minnesota and the District of Columbia. Following a stint as U.S. ambassador to Japan, in 2002 the seventy-four-year-old Mondale was hastily drafted to run for the U.S. Senate seat vacated by the death of Paul Wellstone. But for the first time in a forty-two-year public career, Mondale failed to win a statewide race in Minnesota. It was a disappointing end to a distinguished career best captured by the sentiment of a poor Hispanic man in Texas who, during the 1984 campaign, brought his daughter just to "see Walter Mondale. He is the last of a dying breed. The breed that cares for people."

⌐⌐

Steven M. Gillon, *The Democrats' Dilemma: Walter F. Mondale and the Liberal Legacy* (Columbia University Press, New York, 1994).
Finlay Lewis, *Mondale: Portrait of an American Politician* (Harper and Row, New York, 1980).

Michael Dukakis
1988

Michael Dukakis disappeared from the public arena as completely as any losing candidate since Alton B. Parker. His low profile was partly by choice and partly by circumstance. Because he was the only governor to be a presidential also-ran since Adlai Stevenson, Dukakis did not, as a senator would, return to the national media spotlight in Washington, D.C., after his loss to George H.W. Bush. Instead, he finished out the remaining two years of his gubernatorial term in Massachusetts.

Voters like executive experience. Seven of the nine presidential elections from 1976 to 2008 were won by governors, and many felt that Dukakis should have won in 1988, as he held a seventeen-point polling lead over Bush coming out of the Democratic National Convention in July. Of course, the country was relatively prosperous and at peace in 1988, which always helps the incumbent party, but Bush, tainted by the Iran-Contra scandal, was having trouble improving his favorable ratings with voters. So, he decided to drive down Dukakis's favorable ratings instead.

Dukakis, who served as governor when Massachusetts experienced a tremendous burst of economic growth known as the "Massachusetts Miracle," insisted the 1988 election would be "not about ideology, [but] about competence." Bush and campaign manager Lee Atwater, however, found a host of "wedge" issues with which to paint Dukakis as a wild-eyed liberal. Dukakis was attacked for declining to support constitutional amendments that would ban the burning of the American flag or allow prayer in the public schools. He was attacked for once vetoing a bill that would have required the Pledge of Allegiance to be recited in Massachusetts's classrooms. Most famously, he was attacked because a Massachusetts prison inmate named Willie Horton had raped a woman and stabbed her fiancé while on furlough under a program that predated Dukakis's tenure as governor and that was common in most other states.

The barrage of negative advertising was "ugly, brainless," wrote Richard Ben Cramer in his epic study of the 1988 campaign, *What It Takes*. Even Atwater, who lay dying from a brain tumor three years later, felt obliged to publicly apologize for some of the "naked cruelty" of the attacks made against Dukakis.

When Bill Clinton was under the same type of attacks from Bush's re-election campaign in 1992, Dukakis volunteered to defend Clinton as a campaign surrogate. But the Clinton campaign viewed Dukakis as a loser. They never found a time or a place for Dukakis to speak, not even at that year's Democratic National Convention. The irony is that Clinton went on to win the presidency with only 43 percent of the popular vote, while the shunned Dukakis had won nearly 46 percent of the vote in 1988.

Dukakis had loved being governor. An unassuming man, he was the only governor in America who took public transportation to work, paying the sixty-five-cent fare to ride the trolley and arriving every day by 8:15 a.m. The day after his presidential defeat in 1988, Dukakis was back at work, arriving by 9:00 a.m. and preparing for next year's Massachusetts budget. A few months later he announced he would not run for elective office again.

Instead, he took up teaching public policy, splitting his time between Northeastern University in his native Boston and the University of California, Los Angeles. Dukakis called teaching "the best work I've ever done. It's impossible not to have faith in the system when you work with these kids." His only foray into public policy was to serve on the national board of directors for Amtrak, where he could continue to push for investments in rail and mass transit.

No one has been harder on Dukakis for his defeat than Dukakis, the first Greek-American nominated for president. "I blew it," he said many times. He shouldn't have posed for photographs riding in a tank, he has acknowledged, which made the Army veteran look too much like Snoopy ready to battle the Red Baron. And asked at one presidential debate if his opposition to the death penalty would change if his own wife were raped and murdered, he has recognized that he should have shown some real passion in his response.

Dukakis has said the legacy of his defeat stung even more when Bush's son, George W. Bush, won the presidency in 2000 and served two controversial terms that included America's war in Iraq, noting, "If I had taken care of the pop, we wouldn't have had to worry about the kid."

—

Richard Ben Cramer, *What It Takes* (Vintage Books, New York, 1993).
Brad Koplinski, *Hats in the Ring: Conversations with Presidential Candidates* (Presidential Publishing, North Bethesda, Md., 2000).

Bob Dole

1996

Bob Dole inherited his deadpan sense of humor from his father and perfected it while a teenager, working as a soda jerk in a Russell, Kansas, drugstore. Times were tough in the Dust Bowl, and soda jerk was one of many odd jobs Dole worked to earn extra money for his family. Dole's father, too, tried many means to provide for his family. He'd run a restaurant, operated a cream and egg business, and managed a grain elevator. Bob Dole dreamed of a life in which you did more than get by. He wanted to go to college and then medical school.

He had a chance, too. A strapping six-feet-two-inches tall and weighing nearly two hundred pounds, he was the best athlete in town. The great Coach "Phog" Allen invited him to play basketball at the University of Kansas, but then the war came and Dole enlisted. As a lieutenant in Italy, he led his platoon on a raid to take out a German machine gun. They shot him up, nearly blew his right arm completely off, and he was left paralyzed for months. His weight dropped to barely 120 pounds, they took out one of his kidneys, and his life was touch and go. But thanks to the then-experimental drug streptomycin and the generosity of the good people in Russell, who raised eighteen hundred dollars for an operation to rebuild his arm with other body tissue, Dole recovered, though his right arm remained maimed. Dole used sheer force of will to hold it up across his chest during public appearances to hide its uselessness.

Back in college on the GI Bill, Dole studied law instead of medicine. He discovered his drive, and the patter he had perfected back at the drugstore made him a pretty good politician. He was elected to the Kansas Legislature while still a law student, won his first congressional race in 1960, and was elected to the U.S. Senate in 1968. He was a conservative, but pragmatic and open-minded, joining George McGovern in sponsoring legislation to combat hunger and malnutrition.

In 1976, President Gerald Ford, to appease the GOP right, dropped Vice President Nelson Rockefeller and chose Dole as his running mate. Dole's tough style of campaigning and often sarcastic humor made him seem a hatchet man, and he caused an uproar when he labeled World Wars I and II, Korea, and Vietnam "Democratic wars." The day after he and Ford narrowly lost to Carter and Mondale, Dole claimed he had slept like a baby the night before—"Every two hours, I woke up and cried."

Dole ran for president in 1980 and lost the Republican nomination to eventual winner Ronald Reagan. He ran again in 1988 and lost the nomination to eventual winner George H. W. Bush. Dole became majority leader in the Senate, and in 1996, Republicans decided it was finally his turn. Like Henry Clay, Dole wasn't nominated by his party until he was sure to lose. The nation was prospering and mostly at peace, and Bill Clinton was handily re-elected.

Less than two weeks after the election, Dole went on the satirical television program *Saturday Night Live*, to spoof his loss and his alleged tendency to speak of himself in the third person, complaining, "That's not something Bob Dole does. It's not something Bob Dole has ever done, and it's not something Bob Dole will ever do!"

He wrote a memoir of his war experience and put together two books on political humor: *Great Presidential Wit: (Wish I Was in the Book)* and *Great Political Wit: Laughing (Almost) All the Way to the White House.* They sold well, and Dole's second wife, Elizabeth, had a good job running the American Red Cross. But Dole never forgot the hardscrabble times of his youth, and perhaps he succumbed to the envy that many politicians feel as they solicit contributions from the rich and peek into their world while still earning a public servant's salary. So, Dole became a spokesperson for the treatment of erectile dysfunction, and then he spoofed that spokesmanship in an ad for Pepsi in which the then seventy-eight-year-old politician feigned lust for teen pop starlet Britney Spears. A lot of people thought it was undignified, but if Bob Dole hadn't earned the right to make a few bucks making people guffaw, who had?

~

Richard Ben Cramer, *What It Takes* (Vintage Books, New York, 1993).
Robert J. Dole, *One Soldier's Story: A Memoir* (HarperCollins, New York, 2005).

ACKNOWLEDGMENTS

All good books (I hope this qualifies) are the product of many people, not just the author. I have been fortunate to receive the assistance of many good friends.

Special thanks go to two "Buds." William H. "Bud" Moore, friend and mentor, gave me many excellent and extensive suggestions for improving the manuscript and also the foundation in history that allowed me to tackle this project. Friend and colleague Egil "Bud" Krogh, a man who has been at the center of presidential history, provided great encouragement and direction and introduced me to my wonderful agent, Laura Dail.

Laura took a personal interest in this project, making the right edits and prodding me with provocative questions. Most especially, I thank Laura for selling our project to a fine company, Lyons Press, and partnering me with an exceptional editor, Keith Wallman. Keith, too, improved this book immeasurably. He and his colleagues at Lyons treated me, a first-time author, with all the courtesy due a Pulitzer Prize winner.

Among the many talented and generous friends who reviewed my proposal or drafts of the manuscript, or assisted in the various other tasks necessary to complete and market a book were: Karen Deike, former boss and beloved friend; fellow wire-service veteran Hank Stern; poet and professor Jerry Harp; friend and fellow political junkie Gary Conkling; politico Steve Novick, one of those who shouted "Gore or blood!" during the 2000 recount; another superb former boss, Jim Wieck, who helped secure the photographs used in the book; Courtney Kerr, friend and photographer; critic and confidant Rick Thamer; and the creative Austin advertising mogul and *New York Times* blogger M. P. Mueller.

I am fortunate to live in the very literate city of Portland, Oregon, and I thank the staffs at Multnomah County Public Library, Reed College library, and Portland State University library for their help and assistance. And what a treat to live in the city that is home to Powell's City of Books, where you can find a 130-year-old biography of Winfield Scott Hancock *on the shelves*.

I want to thank the great presidential scholar Richard Norton Smith for his kindness. He is one of many writers, some famous, others not, who offered encouragement and assistance in this process. They will never know how many times their kind words helped me persevere.

This being my first book, I have thought about all the people who helped nurture my love of history and writing: my teachers in Lander, Wyoming, and at the University of Wyoming; the many editors and colleagues in journalism who made me a better writer; and my political bosses—Malcolm Wallop, Bill Budd, Mike Sullivan, Gray Davis, and Vera Katz—who gave me lessons in practical politics.

Then, there are my first teachers, my mother and late father, who raised me in a house filled with books, newspapers, and lively discussions of current events.

Most important, I want to acknowledge those to whom this book is dedicated. My two children, William and Grace, were infinitely patient and inspiring. My wife, Patti, was a great partner in this as in all our endeavors. Sharing my love of history, she helped with research, talked me through my various bouts of writer's block, and was an extraordinarily valuable editor, identifying gaps in my arguments and reining me in when my prose went seriously awry. Without her, there would be no book, and life would be very dull.

BIBLIOGRAPHY

The most authoritative comparable book to *Almost President* is Leslie H. Southwick, *Presidential Also-Rans and Running Mates* (Second Edition), (McFarland and Company Inc., Jefferson, N.C., and London, 2008). Southwick has compiled a remarkable amount of data on all those who ran for president (and vice president) and fell short, and has authored a series of essays on each that includes Southwick's own take on the qualifications of each candidate.

Livelier essays on losing candidates can be found in Irving Stone, *They Also Ran: The Story of the Men Who Were Defeated for the Presidency* (Doubleday and Company, Inc., Garden City, N.Y., 1945). Stone's provocative assessments demonstrate how the context of the present influences our interpretation of the past. Stone wrote most of the essays immediately following the Great Depression, when Jefferson and Jackson were enjoying revivals and the Scopes Monkey Trial was a recent memory. He is therefore far too hard on Bryan and Clay and too generous to Greeley, Tilden, and Cox.

Paul F. Boller Jr. includes anecdotes about losing candidates in *Presidential Campaigns* (Oxford University Press, New York and Oxford, 1984), a follow-up to Boller's immensely popular *Presidential Anecdotes*. Most helpful in thinking about what it means to be a loser in our society is Scott A. Sandage, *Born Losers: A History of Failure in America* (Harvard University Press, Cambridge, Mass., and London, 2005), which is worthy of the several prizes it has won for its insight into the evolving American attitude toward success and failure.

An invaluable online resource used throughout the writing of this book is Dave Leip's Atlas of Presidential Elections (www.uselectionatlas.org), which has detailed information on every presidential election.

Chapter One. The Concession

An extraordinary collection of concession speech excerpts is found in John R. Vile, *Presidential Winners and Losers: Words of Victory and Concession* (CQ Press, Washington, D.C., 2002). I drew from several of political scientist Paul Corcoran's published articles, including "Presidential Concession Speeches: The Rhetoric of Defeat," *Political Communication* 11 (April-June 1994), pp. 113–117, and an updated version of that article, which appeared in a U.S. State Department publication as "Democracy's Rhetoric of Defeat," *eJournalUSA*, Vol. 15, No. 1 (January 2010), pp. 13–15. Also quoted in this chapter is Corcoran's "Saying Uncle and Mouthing Bromides," *Los Angeles Times*, November 7, 2004.

Most helpful in assessing the loser's role in promoting a stable democracy is, Christopher J. Anderson, André Blais, Shaun Bowler, Todd Donovan, and Ola Listhaug, *Losers' Consent: Elections and Democratic Legitimacy* (Oxford University Press, Oxford and New York, 2005), a series of enlightening essays aimed at academics, which draws on the research of political scientists from three nations.

In understanding the crafting of concession speeches, I drew upon Robert Schlesinger, *White House Ghosts: Presidents and Their Speechwriters* (Simon and Schuster, New York, 2008). Some of the anecdotes were drawn from texts and memoirs cited elsewhere in this bibliography or included in the appendix, some from contemporary news reports, primarily the *New York Times*, but some of the discussions on the candidates' reaction to defeat were found in Brad Koplinski, *Hats in the Ring: Conversations with Presidential Candidates* (Presidential Publishing, North Bethesda, Md., 2000).

On the role of religion in concession speeches: David Domke and Kevin Coe, *The God Strategy: How Religion Became a Political Weapon in America* (Oxford University Press, Oxford, 2008); Russel B. Nye, *This Almost Chosen People: Essays in the History of American Ideas* (Michigan State University Press, East Lansing, 1966); and Stephen H. Webb, *American Providence: A Nation with a Mission* (Continuum International Publishing Group, New York, 2004).

Finally, two general political reference books consulted not only for this chapter, but also throughout the book, were William Safire, *Safire's Political Dictionary* (Oxford University Press, New York and Oxford, 2008), and Charles Henning, *The Wit and Wisdom of Politics* (Fulcrum, Inc., Golden, Colo., 1989).

CHAPTER TWO. HENRY CLAY

Robert V. Remini, also perhaps Andrew Jackson's greatest biographer, produced *Henry Clay: Statesman for the Union* in 1991 (W.W. Norton and Co., New York and London). Remini, the official historian of the U.S. House of Representatives, is the leading expert on the politics from 1825 to 1850. *Statesman for the Union* remains the definitive study of Clay and benefits from Remini's studies of Jackson, which allow Remini to appreciate Clay's essential role as Jackson's bête noire. Remini also penned a slimmer volume focused on Clay's role in the Compromise of 1850, *At the Edge of the Precipice* (Basic Books, New York, 2010).

David S. and Jeanne T. Heidler wrote *Henry Clay: The Essential American* (Random House, New York, 2010), a lively, affectionate portrait of Clay whose judgments are similar to Remini's. The authors spend more time than Remini on Clay's home life and flesh out his usually overlooked wife, Lucretia.

Clement Easton, in *Henry Clay and the Art of American Politics* (Little, Brown and Co., Boston and Toronto, 1957), did a fine character study as part of the Library of American Biography series edited by Oscar Handlin. One must then go back to the 1930s for published biographies of Clay. The best from that period is Glyndon Van Deusen, *The Life of Henry Clay* (Greenwood Press, Westport, Conn., reprinted 1979).

Former *Newsweek* editor-in-chief Jon Meacham won the Pulitzer Prize for *American Lion: Andrew Jackson in the White House* (Random House, New York, 2008), though he may not have appreciated the role Jackson's feud with Clay played in shaping the policies of both men. Another recent Jackson biography consulted was H. W. Brands, *Andrew Jackson: His Life and Times* (Doubleday, New York, 2005). Despite their merits, neither book will boast the influence that Arthur M. Schlesinger Jr. had in *The Age of Jackson* (Little, Brown and Co., Boston, 1945). Schlesinger later acknowledged in his Pulitzer Prize–winning memoir, *A Life in the 20th Century: Innocent Beginnings, 1917–1950* (Houghton Mifflin Co., Boston and New York, 2000), that his groundbreaking study gave Clay and the Whig Party short shrift. Despite his own work, Schlesinger has labeled Remini as Jackson's finest biographer. I confess that I did not consult Remini's full three-volume study of Jackson, but I do highly recommend his abridged one-volume version, *The Life of Andrew Jackson* (Harper and Row, New York, 1988).

A superb condensed assessment of how Clay and Jackson's rivalry defined American politics in the period is Harry L. Watson, *Andrew Jackson vs. Henry Clay: Democracy and Development in Antebellum America* (Bedford/St. Martin's, Boston and New York, 1998), which contains original source speeches, letters, and other documents that provide further insight into the two men's contrasting characters. To judge Clay against his other rivals, Calhoun and Webster, I consulted Merrill D. Peterson, *The Great Triumvirate: Webster, Clay, and Calhoun* (Oxford University Press, New York, 1987).

In exploring Clay's role in the formation of the Whig Party, I relied on two superb studies. One is Michael F. Holt's twelve-hundred-page *The Rise and Fall of the American Whig Party: Jacksonian Politics and the Onset of the Civil War* (Oxford University Press, Oxford and New York, 1999). Holt underscores Clay's central role in the formation and continuation of the Whig Party and aptly notes that when Clay died, so did the only man still able to unite the Whigs. Equally instructive is Daniel Walker Howe, *The Political Culture of the American Whigs* (University of Chicago Press, Chicago, 1984).

Howe has also written the definitive general history of the era: *What Hath God Wrought: The Transformation of America, 1815–1848* (Oxford University Press, Oxford and New York, 2007). The brilliant book gives Clay his due as perhaps the most important American statesman of the age. Conversely, Sean Wilentz, *The Rise and Fall of American Democracy: Jefferson to Lincoln* (W. W. Norton and Co., New York and London, 2005), like Schlesinger sixty years before, gives Clay a clearly secondary role and sees Jackson's expansion of the franchise to all white males as the more important development in American democracy than the Whigs' role in growing a civic-minded middle class. A third recent book, David S. Reynolds, *Waking Giant: America in the Age of Jackson* (HarperCollins, New York, 2008), is a more offbeat study but helps bring to life the richness of the period.

Great help in assessing Clay's impact on Lincoln came from Michael Lind, *What Lincoln Believed: The Values and Convictions of America's Greatest President* (Doubleday, New York, 2004), while a slim monograph by Edgar DeWitt Jones, *The Influence of Henry Clay upon Abraham Lincoln* (The Henry Clay Memorial Foundation, Lexington, Ky., 1952) has anecdotes that reinforce the close ties between the two men. Maurice G. Baxter, *Henry Clay: The Lawyer* (University Press of Kentucky, Lexington, 2000) argues that if Clay had done no more than practice law, he would still be a historically significant figure.

CHAPTER THREE. STEPHEN DOUGLAS

Until a new substantial biography comes along, we can give thanks for Robert W. Johannsen, *Stephen A. Douglas* (Oxford University Press, New York, 1973). As editor of Douglas's papers, *The Letters of Stephen A. Douglas* (University of Illinois Press, Urbana, 1971), Johannsen has kept Douglas before the academy and uncovered and organized the material that should help historians appreciate Douglas's key role in American history. Johannsen also supplies an incisive essay on the 1860 Democratic National Convention in Norman A. Graebner, ed., *Politics and the Crisis of 1860* (University of Illinois Press, Urbana, 1961)

A smaller, more specialized monograph recently came with James L. Huston, *Stephen A. Douglas and the Dilemmas of Democratic Equality* (Rowman and Littlefield Inc., Lanham, Md., 2007). An economic historian, Huston provides insight into why Douglas believed territorial expansion was more critical to the nation's well-being than resolving the debate over slavery.

Another shorter Douglas biography is Gerald M. Capers, *Stephen A. Douglas: Defender of the Union* (Little, Brown and Co., Boston and Toronto, 1959). Part of a series of biographies on key non-presidential figures in American history, the book highlights Douglas as a man of principle, but is hampered because the Douglas papers had not been organized yet when it was being written, the civil rights movement had not yet come to the fore, and it does not focus on Douglas's role in preserving the Democratic Party.

A particularly helpful book in the development of this chapter on Douglas was Roy Morris Jr., *The Long Pursuit: Abraham Lincoln's Thirty-Year Struggle with Stephen Douglas for the Heart and Soul of America* (HarperCollins, New York, 2008). Morris particularly emphasizes Lincoln being spurred to greatness partly by his envy of Douglas, and Lincoln being forced to grow because Douglas made such a worthy adversary. A fine new account of the presidential election of 1860 is Douglas R. Egerton, *Year of Meteors: Stephen Douglas, Abraham Lincoln, and the Election That Brought on the Civil War* (Bloomsbury Press, New York, Berlin, and London, 2010).

Of course, Lincoln and Douglas are linked in popular memory mainly by their series of debates, an excellent recent study of which is Allen C. Guelzo, *Lincoln and Douglas: The Debates That Defined America* (Simon and Schuster, New York, 2008). Original transcripts plus some superb accompanying essays appear in Robert W. Johannsen, ed., *The Lincoln-Douglas Debates of 1858: The 150th Anniversary Edition* (Oxford University Press, New York and Oxford, 2008).

One of the great early Civil War scholars, Allan Nevins, devotes considerable space to Douglas in three of the six volumes of his history of the Civil War era: *Ordeal of the Union: A House Dividing, 1852–1857* (Charles Scribner's Sons, New York and London, 1947); *The Emergence of Lincoln: Douglas, Buchanan, and Party Chaos, 1857–1859* (Charles Scribner's Sons, New York and London, 1950); and *The Emergence of Lincoln: Prologue to Civil War, 1859–1861* (Charles Scribner's Sons,

New York and London, 1950). Nevins admires the courage Douglas showed in campaigning in the South against secession in 1860 but spends little time on how Douglas's goal of maintaining a legitimate Democratic Party impacted either the conflict or the restoration of the Union. Too skeptical of Douglas's role, in this author's opinion, is Damon Wells, *Stephen Douglas: The Last Years, 1857–1861* (University of Texas Press, Austin, 1971).

Allegedly, more books have been written about Lincoln than any other person except Jesus Christ. I relied primarily on what is generally accepted as the finest one-volume biography of Lincoln, David Herbert Donald, *Lincoln* (Simon and Schuster, New York, 1995). To understand the rise of the Republican Party, in part as a response to Douglas's Kansas-Nebraska Act, the definitive study probably remains Eric Foner, *Free Soil, Free Labor, Free Men: The Ideology of the Republican Party before the Civil War* (Oxford University Press, Oxford and New York, 1995). Foner recognizes that Douglas Democrats' increasing animosity toward the South created the united front in the North as the Civil War began. Foner also explores Douglas's pragmatic brand of politics in *Politics and Ideology in the Age of the Civil War* (Oxford University Press, New York and Oxford, 1980).

Interestingly, Foner does not even mention Douglas in his *Reconstruction: America's Unfinished Revolution, 1863–1877* (Harper and Row, New York, 1988). Foner emphasizes, not inappropriately, the Democrats' interest in keeping freed African Americans disenfranchised after the war but does not emphasize that the Democratic Party seemed to play a role as envisioned by Douglas and his followers, which was to be a legitimate vehicle for sectional reconciliation when the war ended. That task is left to Joel Sibley, *A Respectable Minority: The Democratic Party in the Civil War Era, 1860–1868* (W. W. Norton and Co., New York, 1977), which shreds the cliché, pushed by Republicans for decades after the war, that Democrats were broken into two distinct groups: War Democrats who set aside all partisan activity and Copperheads who favored peace at any price, even if it undermined the Union cause. Jules Witcover, *Party of the People: A History of the Democrats* (Random House, New York, 2003) does not discuss the Democrats' positive role in Reconstruction but does claim Douglas joined the National Union Party, which is not correct.

Two other books that influenced my thinking in this chapter were James M. McPherson, *Battle Cry of Freedom: The Civil War Era* (Oxford University Press, New York and Oxford, 1988), and Doris Kearns Goodwin, *Team of Rivals: The Political Genius of Abraham Lincoln* (Simon and Schuster, New York and London, 2005). Both books have earned immense praise, and while neither spends a great deal of time on Douglas, they acknowledge his key contribution as expanded upon in this book. Douglas's probable influence on Ulysses S. Grant was gleaned from Jean Edward Smith, *Grant* (Simon and Schuster, New York, 2001).

CHAPTER FOUR. WILLIAM JENNINGS BRYAN

A superb recent William Jennings Bryan biography is Michael Kazin, *A Godly Hero: The Life of William Jennings Bryan* (Anchor Books, New York, 2006). Kazin acknowledges that, as a secular liberal, he has a "certain ambivalence" regarding Bryan's religious beliefs, but the book is admiring of its subject and fair on all the key points. Three slimmer volumes on Bryan are also recommended: LeRoy Ashby, *William Jennings Bryan: Champion of Democracy* (Twayne, Boston, 1987); Robert Cherny, *A Righteous Cause: The Life of William Jennings Bryan* (University of Oklahoma Press, Norman, 1994); and Kendrick A. Clements, *William Jennings Bryan: Missionary Isolationist* (University of Tennessee Press, Knoxville, 1982). The latter, as the title implies, especially focuses on Bryan's views on foreign policy.

To compare Woodrow Wilson's own infusion of morality into foreign affairs, there is John Morton Blum, *Woodrow Wilson and the Politics of Morality* (Little, Brown, Boston, 1956). On one of Bryan's harshest critics and putting that criticism in perspective, a fine biography is Fred Hobson, *Mencken: A Life* (Random House, New York, 1994).

Perhaps the most influential study of Bryan in recent times is Lawrence W. Levine, *Defender of the Faith: William Jennings Bryan, The Last Decade, 1915–1925* (Harvard University Press, Cambridge, Mass., 1987), which first came out in 1965, five years after *Inherit the Wind* was made into a film, and which offers a fresh assessment of Bryan's motivations for embarking on his crusade against the teaching of evolution. A collection of essays edited by Paul W. Glad, *William Jennings Bryan: A Profile* (Hill and Wang, New York, 1968) is extremely illuminating. This book includes Richard Hofstadter's essay on Bryan, "The Democrat as Revivalist," which can also be found in Hofstadter's *The American Political Tradition and the Men Who Made It* (Alfred A. Knopf Inc., New York, 1948). Glad also includes a wonderful essay by Ray Ginger on the Scopes Trial that comes from Ginger's book, *Six Days or Forever?: Tennessee v. John Thomas Scopes* (Oxford University Press, London and New York, 1974). The best complete study of the Scopes trial is likely Edward J. Larson, *Summer for the Gods: The Scopes Trial and America's Continuing Debate over Science and Religion* (Basic Books, New York, 1997). Two other Hofstadter books have been key in painting both Bryan and the Populists in negative terms: *The Age of Reform: From Bryan to F.D.R.* (Vantage Books, New York, 1960), and *The Paranoid Style in American Politics and Other Essays* (Harvard University Press, Cambridge, Mass., 1965).

A nice antidote to Hofstadter is an article by Robert M. Collins, "The Originality Trap: Richard Hofstadter on Populism," *Journal of American History* 76 (1989: pp. 150–167), as are these key books on Populism: John D. Hicks, *The Populist Revolt: A History of the Farmers' Alliance and the People's Party* (University of Minnesota Press, Minneapolis, 1931), C. Vann Woodward, *Origins of the New South* (Third Edition) (Louisiana State University Press, Baton Rouge, 1994), and the most influential contemporary overview of Populism, Lawrence Goodwyn, *The Populist Moment: A Short History of the Agrarian Revolt in America* (Oxford University Press, Oxford, London, and New York, 1978).

Bryan himself was a fine writer, as was his wife, Mary Baird Bryan, who finished Bryan's memoirs after his death. Memoirs are never objective, of course, but these at least appear guileless: *The Memoirs of William Jennings Bryan, Volumes 1 and 2* (Kennikat Press, Port Washington, N.Y., and London, 1971).

For a more detailed look at the 1896 campaign, the University Press of Kansas continues its superb series on pivotal presidential elections with R. Hal Williams, *Realigning America: McKinley, Bryan, and the Remarkable Election of 1896* (University Press of Kansas, Lawrence, 2010). It is the finest account since Paul W. Glad, *McKinley, Bryan, and the People* (J. B. Lippincott Co., Philadelphia and New York, 1964).

On Bryan's role in the period in which the Fundamentalist movement was born, I have relied on Ferenc Morton Szasz, *The Divided Mind of Protestant America: 1880–1930* (University of Alabama Press, Tuscaloosa, 1982). Other works consulted include Willard H. Smith, *The Social and Religious Thought of William Jennings Bryan* (Coronado Press, Lawrence, Kans., 1975); Susan Curtis, *A Consuming Faith: The Social Gospel and Modern American Culture* (John Hopkins University Press, Baltimore and London, 1991); and Ronald C. White and C. Howard Hopkins, *The Social Gospel: Religion and Reform in Changing America* (Temple University Press, Philadelphia, 1976).

Recent books that explore the intersection of faith and populism in contemporary politics include Garry Wills, *Head and Heart: American Christianities* (Penguin Press, New York, 2007); Amy Sullivan, *The Party Faithful: How and Why Democrats Are Closing the God Gap* (Scribner, New York and London, 2008); E. J. Dionne, *Souled Out: Reclaiming Faith and Politics after the Religious Right* (Princeton University Press, Princeton, N.J., 2008); Jim Wallis, *The Great Awakening: Reviving Faith and Politics in a Post-Religious Right America* (HarperOne, New York, 2008); and Thomas Frank, *What's the Matter with Kansas: How Conservatives Won the Heart of America* (Henry Holt and Co., New York, 2004).

CHAPTER FIVE. AL SMITH

Al Smith is the subject of two excellent recent biographies: Robert A. Slayton, *Empire Statesman: The Rise and Redemption of Al Smith* (Free Press, New York and London, 2001); and Christopher M. Finan, *Alfred E. Smith: The Happy Warrior* (Hill and Wang, New York, 2002). Slayton particularly focuses on Smith's Lower East Side upbringing as key to understanding the man, while Finan is intrigued by the real motivation behind Smith's rupture with Roosevelt. One of the few earlier biographies of Smith, Oscar Handlin, *Al Smith and His America* (Little, Brown and Co., Boston and Toronto, 1958), is less satisfying, perhaps because it seems to be less critical—perhaps in deference to the aspirations of the man whose recommendation appears on the book's dust jacket: John F. Kennedy. Smith also receives insightful treatment in Robert Caro, *The Power Broker: Robert Moses and the Fall of New York* (Vintage Books, New York, 1975), which chronicles the long partnership between Smith and Moses, dating to Smith's time in the New York Legislature.

The four books I most relied upon in regard to Smith's legacy and how Kennedy's Catholic faith impacted the 1960 election were W. J. Rorabaugh, *The Real Making of the President: Kennedy, Nixon, and the 1960 Election* (University Press of Kansas, Lawrence, 2009); Shaun A. Casey, *The Making of a Catholic President: Kennedy vs. Nixon 1960* (Oxford University Press, Oxford and New York, 2009); Michael Sean Winters, *Left at the Altar: How the Democrats Lost the Catholics and How the Catholics Can Save the Democrats* (Basic Books, New York, 2008); and Richard Nixon, *Six Crises* (Touchstone, New York and London, 1990). Nixon is obviously biased but had a knack for political analysis, and his own view of how religion played as an issue in 1960 seems right.

The most accessible history of the Roman Catholic Church in America is Charles R. Morris, *American Catholic: The Saints and Sinners Who Built America's Most Powerful Church* (Times Books, New York, 1997). Also excellent is Jay P. Dolan, *The American Catholic Experience: A History from Colonial Times to the Present* (University of Notre Dame Press, Notre Dame, 1992), which describes how Catholicism evolved as a church for poor immigrants into a church of the middle class. Also recommended is Dolan's *The Irish Americans: A History* (Bloomsbury Press, New York, Berlin, and London, 2008).

An especially interesting book is George J. Marlin, *The American Catholic Voter: 200 Years of Political Impact* (St. Augustine's Press, South Bend, Ind., 2004). Marlin has compiled reams of data and anecdotes in arguing that Catholics have always been a pivotal (and often controversial) voting bloc, and that the shift of many Catholics to the Republican Party is one of the key partisan developments of the last half-century. Though it also seems true to me, from reading Marlin, that it can also be said there is no "Catholic vote" anymore and that Catholics are now so fully assimilated and so diverse that their votes are divvied up in the same proportion as the overall vote.

In offering my thesis on how Smith's loss changed how Catholics interacted with the mass media, I was fortunate that a fine book had just been published: Anthony Burke Smith, *The Look of Catholics: Portrayals in Popular Culture from the Great Depression to the Cold War* (University Press of Kansas, Lawrence, 2010). Smith, however, believes the Great Depression was the impetus for the glowing portrayals of Catholicism in films and on radio because Catholic teaching on community resonated during this period. Since I am skeptical that even many of my fellow Catholics know much about Catholic social teaching, I will stay with my own thesis that the overt bigotry faced by Smith was the more likely stimulant. More closely aligned with my own thinking is Thomas Doherty, *Pre-Code Hollywood: Sex, Immorality, and Insurrection in American Cinema, 1930–1934* (Columbia University Press, New York, 1999), which described the Production Code as being such a Catholic effort.

Regarding other issues raised in the chapter, I thought Nancy MacLean, *Behind the Mask of Chivalry: The Making of the Second Ku Klux Klan* (Oxford University Press, New York and Oxford, 1994), does a fine job of describing what the second iteration of the Klan was all about. For Prohibition, I relied on one of the more influential studies, Norman H. Clark, *Deliver Us from Evil: An Interpretation of American Prohibition* (W. W. Norton and Co., New York and London, 1976), which makes the observation that not only were many Catholics active in the Anti-Saloon League, but many Catholics were leaders in that group and the Prohibition effort. Regarding the "Radio Priest," Father Charles Coughlin, there is no better book than Alan Brinkley, *Voices of Protest: Huey Long, Father Coughlin and the Great Depression* (Vintage Books, New York, 1983). To place Smith in the context of the 1920s, I used Geoffrey Perrett, *America in the Twenties: A History* (Touchstone, New York, 1982), and the classic by Frederick Lewis Allen, *Only Yesterday: An Informal History of the 1920s* (Wiley, New York, 1997).

Persuasive data that the magnitude of Smith's defeat was due to his Catholicism can be found in Allan J. Lichtman, *Prejudice and the Old Politics: The Presidential Election of 1928* (Lexington Books, Lanham, Md., 2000).

CHAPTER SIX. THOMAS E. DEWEY

Dewey is fortunate to have a particularly excellent and comprehensive biography by Richard Norton Smith, *Thomas E. Dewey and His Times* (Simon and Schuster, New York, 1982). Smith's exuberance for his subject is indicated by his lively prose, though his judgments are sober.

Dewey himself explained his political thinking in a series of lectures that were captured in John A. Wells, ed., *Thomas E. Dewey on the Two-Party System* (Doubleday and Company, Inc., Garden City, N.Y., 1966). Also influential in how I thought about Dewey and his development of "Modern Republicanism" was an article published in 1982, Robert Griffith, "Dwight D. Eisenhower and the Corporate Commonwealth," *American Historical Review*, Vol. 87, No. 1 (February), pp. 87–122.

Dewey's career as a prosecutor is well chronicled in Mary M. Stolberg, *Fighting Organized Crime: Politics, Justice, and the Legacy of Thomas E. Dewey* (Northeastern University Press, Boston, 1995), though Stolberg is critical of the prosecutorial techniques pioneered by Dewey and emulated by most prosecutors today to the detriment of defendants' civil liberties.

The 1948 upset campaign has garnered quite a bit of attention, and I consulted both Harold I. Gullan, *The Upset That Wasn't: Harry S. Truman and the Crucial Election of 1948* (Ivan R. Dee, Chicago, 1998), and Zachary Karabell, *The Last Campaign: How Harry Truman Won the 1948 Election* (Alfred A. Knopf, New York, 2000). I particularly enjoyed Karabell's insight that Dewey's campaign was made for the age of television just *before* television was much of a factor. By 1952, Eisenhower mimicked Dewey's strategy to great effect.

On major contemporary figures and placing Dewey's contributions in context, see James T. Patterson, *Mr. Republican: A Biography of Robert A. Taft* (Houghton Mifflin Company, Boston, 1972); Alonzo L. Hamby, *Man of the People: A Life of Harry S. Truman* (Oxford University Press, Oxford and New York, 1995); David McCullough, *Truman* (Simon and Schuster, New York, 1992); John Robert Greene, *The Limits of Power: The Nixon and Ford Administrations* (Indiana University Press, Bloomington and Indianapolis, 1992); Richard Nixon, *Six Crises* (Simon and Schuster, New York, 1962); Stephen E. Ambrose, *Eisenhower: Soldier and President* (Simon and Schuster, New York, 2003); and Michael Korda, *Ike: An American Hero* (Harper, New York, 2007).

CHAPTER SEVEN. ADLAI STEVENSON

So many Stevenson books were written by friends and admirers that an objective view of the man is not easy to find. Fortunately, many of Stevenson's friends were scholars and students of history, unafraid to offer a more nuanced portrait of the man.

There are George W. Ball, *The Past Has Another Pattern: Memoirs* (W. W. Norton and Company, New York and London, 1982); Alistair Cooke, *Six Men* (Alfred A. Knopf, New York, 1977); and Arthur M. Schlesinger Jr., *Journals: 1952–2000* (Penguin Press, New York, 2007). Each offers extraordinarily helpful insights into Stevenson's character, the authors having been with him in every conceivable situation and environment.

The more obviously laudatory memoirs that were helpful include: Edward P. Doyle, ed., *As We Knew Adlai: The Stevenson Story by Twenty-two Friends* (Harper and Row, New York, 1966), and Alden Whitman, *Portrait: Adlai E. Stevenson: Politician, Diplomat, Friend* (Harper and Row, New York, 1965).

Full-scale biographies that strive mightily to provide an even-handed treatment of Stevenson include: Jeff Broadwater, *Adlai Stevenson and American Politics* (Twayne, New York, 1994); Kenneth S. Davis, *The Politics of Honor: A Biography of Adlai E. Stevenson* (G. P. Putnam's Sons, New York, 1967); John Bartlow Martin, *Adlai Stevenson of Illinois* (Doubleday and Company, Garden City, N.Y., 1976); and Porter McKeever, *Adlai Stevenson: His Life and Legacy* (Quill William Morrow, New York, 1989).

More critical of Stevenson's role in allegedly unmooring the Democratic Party from its blue collar, middle class roots are Michael Barone, *Our Country: The Shaping of America from Roosevelt to Reagan* (Free Press, New York, 1990); and Garry Wills, *Certain Trumpets: The Call of Leaders* (Simon and Schuster, New York, 1994). The most influential book to address the role of intellectualism in American political life is Richard Hofstadter, *Anti-Intellectualism in American Life* (Vintage Books, New York, 1963), though Hofstadter's tone is sometimes so condescending it seems to reinforce the reputation of intellectuals as snobs disconnected from ordinary Americans.

Putting the Stevenson era in broader context are: David Halberstam, *The Fifties* (Villard Books, New York, 1993); Alonzo L. Hamby, *Liberalism and Its Challengers: FDR to Reagan* (Oxford University Press, New York and Oxford, 1985); and William O'Neill, *American High: The Years of Confidence, 1945–1960* (Free Press, New York, 1986).

Of course, the most eloquent voice on Stevenson is Stevenson, and like John Steinbeck, I enjoyed reading Adlai Stevenson, *Speeches* (Random House, New York, 1952).

CHAPTER EIGHT. BARRY GOLDWATER

Many write about Goldwater, but most are partisans. The only truly scholarly biography of Goldwater is Robert Alan Goldberg, *Barry Goldwater* (Yale University Press, New Haven and London, 1995). Goldberg, a Goldwater volunteer as a teenager in New York City whose politics moved to the left later in life, is tough but fair in assessing Goldwater's career, particularly his personal attitudes on race. Not a biography, but a (justifiably) highly lauded recent study of Goldwater's place in the rise of the modern conservative movement is Rick Perlstein, *Before the Storm: Barry Goldwater and the Unmaking of the American Consensus* (Hill and Wang, New York, 2001).

Then, there is the host of tributes to Goldwater, particularly those that came after his death. As with Stevenson, Goldwater had friends and admirers whose academic integrity would not allow them to offer an only one-sided assessment of the man. Four worthy of recommendation are William F. Buckley Jr., *Flying High: Remembering Barry Goldwater* (Basic Books, New York, 2008); Lee Edwards, *Goldwater: The Man Who Made a Revolution* (Regnery Publishing Inc., Washington, D.C., 1997); J. William Middendorf II, *A Glorious Disaster: Barry Goldwater's Presidential Campaign and the Origins of the Conservative Movement* (Basic Books, New York, 2006); and Bill Rentschler, *Goldwater: A Tribute to a Twentieth-Century Political Icon* (Contemporary Books, Chicago, 2000).

Goldwater himself produced two memoirs: *With No Apologies: The Personal and Political Memoirs of United States Senator Barry M. Goldwater* (William Morrow and Company, Inc., New York, 1979), and *Goldwater* (Doubleday, New York, 1988). And no one can profess to have studied twentieth-century American politics without having read Goldwater's manifesto, *The Conscience of a Conservative* (Princeton University Press, Princeton and Oxford, 1960 and 2007). To see how that seminal book fits into the broader pattern of post-war conservative thought, see the dry but comprehensive George H. Nash, *The Conservative Intellectual Movement in America Since*

1945 (Basic Book Publishers, New York, 1979). Goldwater's son also helped develop a collection of speeches, articles, interviews, and public papers that tell Goldwater's story quite well in John W. Dean and Barry Goldwater Jr., *Pure Goldwater* (Palgrave Macmillan, New York, 2008). To understand the right and Southern turn made by the Republican Party in the 1960s, most particularly around the issue of race, I consulted John A. Andrew III, *The Other Side of the Sixties: Young Americans for Freedom and the Rise of Conservative Politics* (Rutgers University Press, New Brunswick, N.J., and London, 1997); Earl Black and Merle Black, *The Rise of the Southern Republicans* (Belknap Press, Cambridge, Mass., and London, 2002); Mary Brennan, *Turning Right in the '60s: The Conservative Capture of the GOP* (University of North Carolina Press, Chapel Hill and London, 1995); John E. Chubb and Paul E. Petersen, eds., *The New Direction in American Politics* (Brookings Institution, Washington, D.C., 1985); the particularly influential study by Thomas Byrne Edsall and Mary D. Edsall, *Chain Reaction: The Impact of Race, Rights and Taxes on American Politics* (W. W. Norton and Company, New York and London, 1991); Richard Hofstadter, *The Paranoid Style in American Politics and Other Essays* (Harvard University Press, Cambridge, Mass., 1965); Jeremy D. Mayer, *Running on Race: Racial Politics in Presidential Campaigns, 1960–2000* (Random House, New York, 2002); Kevin P. Phillips, *The Emerging Republican Majority* (Arlington House, New Rochelle, N.Y., 1969)—another critical book in understanding late-twentieth-century American politics; Nicol C. Rae, *The Decline and Fall of the Liberal Republicans: From 1952 to the Present* (Oxford University Press, New York and Oxford, 1989); William A. Rusher, *The Rise of the Right* (William Morrow & Co., New York, 1984); and Louis M. Seagull, *Southern Republicanism* (John Wiley and Sons, New York and London, 1975) For a broader overview on the Republican Party and the 1960s, helpful books included Lewis L. Gould, *Grand Old Party: A History of the Republicans* (Random House, New York, 2004); Jon Margolis, *The Last Innocent Year: America in 1964, the Beginning of the "Sixties"* (William Morrow and Company, Inc., New York, 1999); and Allen J. Matusow, *The Unraveling of America: A History of Liberalism in the 1960s* (Harper Torchbooks, New York, 1984), while two important Goldwater Southern supporters are profiled in Dan T. Carter, *The Politics of Rage: George Wallace, the Origins of the New Conservatism, and the Transformation of American Politics* (Simon and Schuster, New York and London, 1995); and Nadine Cohodas, *Strom Thurmond and the Politics of Southern Change* (Simon and Schuster, New York and London, 1993).

CHAPTER NINE. GEORGE MCGOVERN

The best single volume on McGovern, the 1972 campaign, and its legacy is Bruce Miroff, *The Liberals' Moment: The McGovern Insurgency and the Identity Crisis of the Democratic Party* (University Press of Kansas, Lawrence, 2009). Miroff makes a compelling case that a supposedly radical "McGovernism" is a bugaboo that did not exist but that McGovern was a thoughtful, often conventional liberal.

John B. Judis and Ruy Teixeira, *The Emerging Democratic Majority* (A Lisa Drew Book, New York and London, 2002) joins Miroff in urging the Democratic Party to take a fresh look at the McGovern legacy and to build upon the McGovern coalition, rather than the long-gone New Deal coalition.

Theodore H. White, *The Making of the President 1972: A Narrative History of American Politics in Action* (Atheneum, New York, 1973) was the last of the "making of the president" series that White began in 1960. White is a gifted storyteller who offers a particularly riveting account of the whole Eagleton mess. White's 1972 book was not as influential as his previous books, in part because he was then being imitated by other journalists, and because there was a new style of campaign reporting on the scene that got lots of attention, primarily gonzo journalist Hunter S. Thompson, *Fear and Loathing: On the Campaign Trail '72* (Warner Books, New York, 2006, c. 1973). McGovern aide Frank Mankiewicz called Thompson's account "the least factual, most accurate account" produced.

An interesting collection of essays, primarily authored by South Dakota academics, on various aspects of McGovern's life can be found in Robert P. Watson, ed., *George McGovern: A Political Life, a Political Legacy* (South Dakota State Historical Society Press, Pierre, S.D., 2004). The essays emerged from a conference held on McGovern and his legacy in 2004 at Dakota Wesleyan University.

With a PhD in history, McGovern wrote one of the more insightful and candid candidate memoirs, *Grassroots: The Autobiography of George McGovern* (Random House, New York, 1977). Also worth reading are McGovern's other works, including *Abraham Lincoln* (Times Books/Henry Holt and Co., New York, 2009), a compact study of Lincoln that breaks no new ground, and *Terry: My Daughter's Life-and-Death Struggle with Alcoholism* (Villard Books, New York, 1996), his tragic story of his daughter's battle with mental illness and substance abuse.

To understand the man McGovern ran against, two superb but disturbing portraits emerge in Richard Reeves, *President Nixon: Alone in the White House* (Simon & Schuster, New York and London, 2001), and Rick Perlstein, *Nixonland: The Rise of the President and the Fracturing of America* (Scribner, New York and London, 2008).

CHAPTER TEN. ROSS PEROT

Gerald Posner, *Citizen Perot: His Life and Times* (Random House, New York, 1996) is the finest biography of Perot, written with his cooperation but not authorized. It is a scrupulously fair assessment of the man. Ted G. Jelen, ed., *Ross for Boss: The Perot Phenomenon and Beyond* (State University of New York Press, Albany, 2001) is a series of essays developed by political science professors from thirteen universities that assess the Perot phenomenon from the perspective of the year 2000. The essays cover such topics as the religious affiliation of Perot voters, his pioneering use of television in his campaigns, and an explanation of why his support plummeted between 1992 and 1996.

Pat Benjamin, *The Perot Legacy: A New Political Path* (iUniverse, Inc., New York, Lincoln, and Shanghai, 2007), is written by a Perot volunteer who wanted to correct "misperceptions" regarding the Reform Party movement. Benjamin focuses on all the legal travails and disputes that helped bring the Reform Party down, but the book is also helpful in understanding the mindset of a Perot activist. Ronald B. Rapoport and Walter J. Stone, *Three's a Crowd: The Dynamic of Third Parties, Ross Perot, and Republican Resurgence* (University of Michigan Press, Ann Arbor, 2008) makes the argument that the great impact of the Perot candidacies was in revitalizing the Republican Party, which, having absorbed a significant portion of the agenda in its 1994 "Contract With America," took back the U.S. House of Representatives for the first time in forty years.

Peter Goldman, Thomas M. DeFrank, Mark Miller, Andrew Murr, Tom Mathews, *Quest for the Presidency 1992* (Texas A&M University Press, College Station, 1994) is a lively and lengthy summation of the 1992 campaign with some excellent reporting by a team of *Newsweek* reporters.

To ascertain Perot's place within the history of American capitalism, consulted were H. W. Brands, *American Colossus: The Triumph of Capitalism, 1865–1900* (Doubleday, New York and London, 2010), and John Steele Gordon, *An Empire of Wealth: The Epic History of American Economic Power* (HarperCollins, New York, 2004). For information on the rise of talk radio, consulted was Randy Bobbitt, *Us against Them: The Political Culture of Talk Radio* (Lexington Books, Lanham, Md., and Boulder, Colo., 2010).

CHAPTER ELEVEN. AL GORE, JOHN KERRY, AND JOHN McCAIN

Given that all three men, as of this writing, are still in the midst of their public careers, sources for this chapter include a number of newspaper and magazine articles and profiles. However, each man has also been the subject of some fine books.

The profile of Al Gore usually deemed to be the most comprehensive look at the former vice president is Bill Turque, *Inventing Al Gore: A Biography* (Houghton Mifflin, Boston, 2000). Turque, a reporter for *Newsweek* at the time he wrote the book, does a particularly fine job exploring the way Gore was groomed by his father specifically to run for president one day with all the psychological baggage that entailed. A serviceable study of Gore is David Maraniss and Ellen Nakashima, *The Prince of Tennessee: The Rise of Al Gore* (Simon and Schuster, New York and London, 2000), which contains some interesting anecdotes. Alexander Cockburn and Jeffrey St. Clair, *Al Gore: A User's Manual* (Verso, London and New York, 2000) is an attack on Gore from the left, questioning even his environmental credentials.

Gore himself, befitting his journalistic background, has authored several books referenced in this chapter, including *Earth in the Balance: Ecology and the Human Spirit* (Houghton Mifflin Co., Boston, 1992); *An Inconvenient Truth: The Crisis of Global Warming* (Viking, New York, 2007); and *The Assault on Reason* (Penguin Press, New York, 2007). The account of the 2000 election that I used as my primary source was Jeffrey Toobin, *Too Close to Call: The Thirty-Six-Day Battle to Decide the 2000 Election* (Random House, New York, 2001). Toobin unravels a complicated situation with clarity and fairness to both parties. The Republican take on the recount can be found in James A. Baker III (with Steve Fiffer), *"Work Hard, Study . . . and Keep Out of Politics!": Adventures and Lessons from an Unexpected Public Life* (G.P. Putnam's Sons, New York, 2006). An entertaining overview of the 2000 election controversy is the HBO film *Recount*, available on DVD through HBO Video [2008].

The most comprehensive and fair account of Kerry's life and career (at least up through 2004) seems to be Michael Kranish, Brian C. Mooney, and Nina J. Easton, *John F. Kerry: The Complete Biography by the* Boston Globe *Reporters Who Know Him Best* (Public Affairs, New York, 2004). The book offers probably the fullest and fairest explanation of Kerry's war record that we are likely to find. What should be the definitive study of Kerry's service by a highly regarded historian, Douglas Brinkley, *Tour of Duty: John Kerry and the Vietnam War* (William Morrow, New York, 2004), has correctly been labeled a little too laudatory and, while beautifully written, contained so many initial factual errors that the publisher had to issue a revised edition. Kerry's own obligatory campaign tome, *A Call to Service* (Viking, New York, 2003), is, as most such books are, not very illuminating.

John McCain has a fine co-author, longtime aide Mark Salter. Their best collaboration is *Faith of My Fathers: A Family Memoir* (Random House, New York, 1999), which covers not only his father's and grandfather's military career, but also his own through his release from captivity in 1973. The McCain who once rode the "Straight Talk Express" is especially evident in *Worth the Fighting For: A Memoir* (Random House, New York, 2002). Two studies of McCain worth reading are Elizabeth Drew, *Citizen McCain* (Simon and Schuster, New York, 2002), and Robert Timberg, *John McCain: An American Odyssey* (Simon and Schuster, New York, 1999). Both are laudatory portraits. Drew has long been one of the most respected political reporters in Washington, but in this book she incorrectly predicts that McCain has forever abandoned conservative dogma and become a true centrist. Perhaps he will, but 2010 and 2011 have scuttled that prediction for now. Timberg is a U.S. Naval Academy graduate who wrote another fine book that follows a group of academy graduates, including McCain, through their careers in Vietnam: *The Nightingale's Song* (Touchstone, New York, 1995). Mark Silva, *McCain: The Essential Guide to the Republican Nominee* (Triumph Books, Chicago, 2008), is a quick knockoff from previous profiles of McCain by the *Chicago Tribune* that provides no real insight but updates us on McCain's career through the early stages of the 2008 election. Two full accounts of the 2008 election consulted were Dan Balz and Haynes Johnson, *The Battle for America 2008: The Story of an Extraordinary Election* (Viking, New York, 2009), and John Heilemann and Mark Halperin, *Game Change: Obama and the Clintons, McCain and Palin, and the Race of a Lifetime* (Harper, New York, 2010).

INDEX

ABOUT THE AUTHOR

Scott Farris is a former bureau chief for United Press International and a political columnist, who has interviewed many of the men and women who have sought the presidency over the past thirty years. He has managed several political campaigns and was the Democratic Party's 1998 congressional nominee for Wyoming's at-large district, the seat once held by former vice president Dick Cheney. His loss in that race led to his ruminations on the role losers play in democracy. Farris worked as a senior policy and communications advisor to a U.S. senator, the governors of Wyoming and California, the mayor of Portland, Oregon, two university presidents, and the bishop of the Roman Catholic Diocese of Cheyenne. The first American journalist selected to participate in the Georgetown University School of Foreign Service's prestigious International Leadership Seminar, Farris now lives in Portland, Oregon, with his wife and two children.